James Drummond

The Jewish Messiah

A Critical History of the Messianic Idea Among the Jews from the....

James Drummond

The Jewish Messiah
A Critical History of the Messianic Idea Among the Jews from the....

ISBN/EAN: 9783337033026

Printed in Europe, USA, Canada, Australia, Japan

Cover: Foto ©Lupo / pixelio.de

More available books at **www.hansebooks.com**

THE
JEWISH MESSIAH

A CRITICAL HISTORY OF THE MESSIANIC IDEA AMONG
THE JEWS FROM THE RISE OF THE MACCABEES
TO THE CLOSING OF THE TALMUD

BY

JAMES DRUMMOND, B.A.

PROFESSOR OF THEOLOGY IN MANCHESTER NEW COLLEGE, LONDON

Ὦ μακαριστὸς ἐκεῖνον ὃς ἐς χρόνον ἔσσεται ἀνήρ
Sib. Orac. iv. 190

LONDON
LONGMANS, GREEN, AND CO.
1877

PREFACE.

THE OBJECT of the present work is twofold. It endeavours to exhibit, in a properly classified form, the doctrine concerning the Messiah, as it was held among the Jews in the centuries during which Christianity appeared; and, as subsidiary to this main purpose, it seeks to introduce the English reader, more fully than has hitherto been done, to the Apocalyptic and kindred literature.

In accepting this literature as in any way a trustworthy expression of Jewish belief, we run counter to the judgment of so high an authority as Jost, who pronounces it to be destitute of value in the history of Jewish religion.[1] It cannot, I think, be denied that Christian scholars have been inclined to attach too much importance to works of this kind. Such writings do not possess even the authority of distinguished names, for the real authors are unknown; and, when we except the Book of

---

[1] 'Jedenfalls sind alle diese Erscheinungen ohne Bedeutung für die jüdische Religionsgeschichte.' Gesch. des Judenth. und seiner Sekten, ii. S. 218, Anm.

Daniel, there is no evidence that they exercised any appreciable influence upon the course of Jewish thought. But in the study of religious belief we do not confine ourselves to the decrees of councils or other authoritative documents, but have recourse to the sermon, the pamphlet, or even the lampoon. The former present us with the finished product, and mark the completed stages of advance; the latter admit us into the process by which dogmas are formed, and give us a vivid picture of the turmoil and passion, the vicissitudes of happiness and misery, of hopes and fears, by which the shapes of human thought are so largely influenced. So the Apocalyptic literature, if it does not possess the authority which attaches to the discussions and decisions of the Rabbinical schools, yet brings us nearer to the popular heart, and speaks to us in the very tones of hope and despair, of aspiration after an ideal kingdom and hatred of heathen domination, which so deeply coloured the Messianic belief. It possesses also for the Christian student the advantage of proximity to the Christian era. It thus furnishes a sample of the soil in which Christianity was first planted, and may assist those who have the courage for the task, to strip off the ephemeral popular conception from the permanent nucleus of spiritual truth. And, lastly, it will be found that the Messianic views presented by this literature are to a large extent confirmed by the Rabbinical authorities, so that it has at least the merit of proving that these views are much earlier than the writings in which they find their first authoritative expression. For these reasons the Apocalyptic works appear deserving of more respectful consideration than is allowed to them by Jost.

It was, however, necessary to have recourse to the Targums and the Talmud, and kindred works, as the authentic exponents of Jewish faith. Of these I cannot pretend to have made any special study, and though I have read portions for myself, either in the original or in translations, I am chiefly indebted to secondary authorities for the passages which are cited. If these, however, are not exhaustive, their accuracy at least may be relied on; for Dr. Schiller-Szinessy, of Cambridge, has most kindly verified and corrected the numerous extracts in our Second Book. I need scarcely say that in rendering this service, for which I am so greatly indebted to him, he has in no way made himself responsible for any of the criticisms or opinions which are expressed in the course of the volume, as he was not even acquainted with them at the time of verification.

In regard to the citation of Rabbinical passages I ought to explain that where I have simply borrowed the words from some modern writer (as is occasionally the case in the First Book), they are referred to in the footnote as 'quoted by' that writer. Where I am indebted for a reference, but the passage is translated freshly from the original, this fact is indicated by the words 'referred to by' so and so. Where the passage either belongs to the common stock of all works on this subject, or has been met with in my own reading of the original sources, only the Rabbinical reference is given. In this way I hope sufficient acknowledgment is made to the authors of whose labours I have availed myself.

In the transliteration of Jewish names a twofold rule has been followed, giving rise to some apparent inconsistency. Most of the Rabbinical names have been so transliterated as to preserve as far as possible the original pronunciation, and to retain the same symbols for the same Hebrew characters; but in the case of Biblical and a few other familiar names (such as Akiba and Onkelos) I thought this practice would seem pedantic, and have therefore conformed to the usual spelling.

In quoting Biblical passages I have generally followed the Authorised Version, unless some critical reason connected with the subject under discussion required a departure from it. In translating the numerous extracts from non-Biblical works, I have studied accuracy rather than elegance. These extracts are so copious, because the manner in which the thought is expressed is quite as important as the thought itself, and by reading the very words of these ancient writings we are brought into closer contact with the mental condition to which the Messianic doctrine appealed, and in which it found its nutriment and strength.

It is to be feared that a volume containing so many references, and dealing with a subject which has received comparatively little attention in England, must not only be marked with imperfection, but cannot be altogether free from errors both of oversight and of judgment. Such as it is, it is offered to the public in the hope that it may not only be of service to the student of theology, but prove interesting to those who love to wander in the by-paths of literature, or who care to trace sympathetically the movements of human faith, and feel the pathos even of men's errors and dreams.

HAMPSTEAD: *September* 19, 1877.

ANALYTICAL CONTENTS.

BOOK I.
SOURCES.

GENERAL REMARKS . . . . PAGE 1-2

CHAPTER I.
THE APOCALYPTIC LITERATURE.

SECTION I.—INTRODUCTORY.

Source of the name, 3. Sketch of the study, 3. Origin and characteristics, 4. Value in present inquiry, 5 3-6

SECTION II.—THE BOOK OF DANIEL.

Question of its genuineness, 6. Probable date, 8. Not 'the work of an impostor,' 8. General nature of the evidence, 9 6-10

SECTION III.—THE SIBYLLINE ORACLES.

Nature of their contents, 10. Views of Lardner, and of Bleek, as to their origin, 11; view of Friedlieb, 12. Lines to be deducted from Book III., 12. Fragments to be added, 13. Date, 14; Volkmar's view, 15. Place of composition, 16 10-17

SECTION IV.—THE BOOK OF ENOCH.

Uncertainty of critical opinion, 17. Recent literary history, 18. Contents, 19. Different views as to unity of authorship, 28; Philippi's view, 29; Dillmann's, 29; Ewald's, 31; Tideman's, 34. Date of original book, 37: The historical vision, 37; view of Laurence, Hofmann, and Gfrörer, 39; view of Ewald and Dillmann, 39; Schürer's view of the seventy shepherds, 40: The ten weeks, 41: General conclusion, 43: Volkmar's view of its late date, 43; general arguments, 43; explanation of the seventy shepherds, 44; criticism of his view, 46. The Similitudes, 48: Views of Lücke and Köstlin, 48: Indications of different authorship, 48; account of the Messianic doctrine, 49: Evidence of post-Christian date, 55; from the allusion to the Parthians, 55; from the description of the neighbourhood of Vesuvius, 57; evidence of Christian authorship from the Messianic doctrine, 59: Objection to the view that the Similitudes proceeded from a Christian author, 60: Suggestion that the Messianic passages are an interpolation, 61; evidence from the first Similitude, 61; from the title of the second, 63; from the Messianic passages in the second, 63; from the consistency of the text without these passages, 65; from the third Similitude, 68; from the closing chapter of the whole section, 69; from the literary history of the work, 71. General conclusion, 73 . . . . PAGE 17–73

SECTION V.—THE ASSUMPTION OF MOSES.

Recent literary history, 74. Latin translation from a Greek original, 75. Contents, 75. Date, 77: Its fixed limits, 77: Ewald's view, 78; evidence that it was written soon after Herod the Great, 78: Hilgenfeld's view, 79; criticism of it, 80: Volkmar's view, 81; criticism of it, 81: Argument that it is later than 4th Ezra, 82: Philippi's view, 84 . 74–84

SECTION VI.—FOURTH EZRA.

Uncertainty about its date, 84. Versions, 84: Latin, 85; editions, 85; consists of three works, 85; lacuna, 86; Hilgenfeld's supposition of interpolation, 87: Arabic, 88: Æthiopic, 89: Armenian, 89: Syriac, 89: Importance of the Versions for the criticism of the text, 90. Contents, 91. Date, 93: Its fixed limits, 93: Argument from 'the thirtieth year,' 94; from 'Esau the end of this age,' 95: The vision of the eagle, 95, and its interpretation, 97; various explanations of it, 98; Hilgenfeld's, 99; Laurence's, 101; Gfrörer's, 101; Wieseler's, 102; Volkmar's, 104; Ewald's, 107; considerations in support of Ewald's, 108; Gutschmid's view, 110; objections to it, 112: Gutschmid's opinion as to the date of the rest of the book, 114: General conclusion, 117. Place of composition, 117 84–117

SECTION VII.—THE APOCALYPSE OF BARUCH.

Literary history, 117. Contents, 118. Translated from Greek, 124. Of purely Jewish origin, 125. Resemblances between it and 4th Ezra, 126; differences, 128. Date, 129: After the destruction of Jerusalem, 129; not very long after, 130: Argument from 'two parts, weeks, of the seven weeks,' 130: Conclusion, 132 117–132

CHAPTER II.

LYRICAL LITERATURE. THE PSALMS OF SOLOMON.

Literary history, 133. Unity of authorship, 133. Original language, 133. Perhaps by a native of Palestine residing in Egypt, 134. Date; different views, 135: Ascription of the Psalms to Solomon, 135: Circumstances referred to, 136: Conclusion, 141. Grätz's statement, that the Psalms have a 'Christian character,' untenable, 141 . PAGE 133-142

CHAPTER III.

HAGGADISTIC LITERATURE. THE BOOK OF JUBILEES, OR LITTLE GENESIS.

Recent literary history, 143. Nature of contents, 144. Origin of names, 144. Purpose of the writer, 144. Original language, 145. The author a Palestinian, 145; nearest to the Pharisees, 146. Date, 146: Before the destruction of Jerusalem, 146: How long before, uncertain, 146; views of Rönsch, Dillmann, and Hilgenfeld, 147 . . . 143-147

CHAPTER IV.

THE TARGUMS.

Their origin, 148. THE TARGUM OF ONKELOS, 150: Its language and character, 150: Traditional account of Onkelos, 151: Nature of the evidence that he was author of the Targum, 151: Evidence that the work belongs to Babylonia, 152: Its date, 153: Gfrörer's argument in favour of its earlier origin, 154: Reason for ascribing it to Onkelos, 155. THE TARGUM OF JONATHAN BEN UZZIEL, 155: Its contents and character, 155: Traditional account of Jonathan, 155: Nature of the evidence that he was author of the Targum, 156: Its real author and date, 157: Reason for ascribing it to Jonathan, 157. PALESTINIAN TARGUMS, 158: Their contents and titles, 158: Their mutual relation, 158: Their date, 159: Their character, 159. Later Targums, 159. Value of the Targums as evidence of Jewish belief, 159 . . 148-160

CHAPTER V.

THE TALMUD, AND OTHER RABBINICAL WORKS.

Remote origin of the Talmud, 161; legendary account, 162. The Great Synagogue, 162, *note* 4. Hillel, 164. Gamaliel, and his successors, 165. R. Yehudah, 166. Meaning of Mishnah, 167. Modes of instruction in the oral law; Halakhah, Midrash, Talmud, Haggadah, 167. Contents and divisions of the Mishnah, 169. The Mishnah perhaps continued to be transmitted orally, 170. Value of the Mishnah for the study of Jewish opinion, 170. Origin and meaning of Gemara, 171. The Jerusalem Talmud, 172. The Babylonian Talmud, 172: Its compilation, 173: Rab Ashi's work perhaps not at first written, 173: Closing of the Talmud, 174. Language of the Gemaras, 174. Their extent in relation to the Mishnah, 174. Their value, 175. Baraitha and Tosiphta, 175. Midrashim, 176. Seder 'Olam Rabbah, 176. Yalqut Shim'eoni, 177 . . . . PAGE 161–177

BOOK II.

HISTORY.

CHAPTER I.

INTRODUCTORY.

Different methods of treatment, 179. Origin of the Messianic Idea, 180. Source of its baser elements, 181. Examples of the influence of disaster on belief, 181 179–184

CHAPTER II.

SKETCH OF THE MESSIANIC IDEA AS EXHIBITED IN THE PROPHETS.

Subsidiary character of this sketch, 185. Joel, Amos, and Hosea, 185. Isaiah, the elder Zechariah, and Micah, 188. Zephaniah, 190. Jeremiah 190. Obadiah, 191. Isaiah xxiv.–xxvii., 191. Ezekiel, 192. The later Isaiah, 193. Haggai and Zechariah, 194. Malachi, 195 . 185–195

CHAPTER III.

THE SON OF SIRACH, TOBIT, AND BARUCH.

Different views about the dates of these works, 196. The Wisdom of the Son of Sirach, 196. Tobit, 197. Baruch, 197. Absence of belief in the Messiah, 198 196–199

CHAPTER IV.

DIVISIONS OF TIME.

Gloomy character of the period under treatment, 200. Division into two ages, 200; in Daniel, 200; in Enoch, Psalms of Solomon, and Assumption of Moses, 201; in 4th Ezra, 201; in the Talmud, 202. Divisions of the first age, 202; the four kingdoms in Daniel, 202; the seventy weeks in Daniel, 204; the seventy shepherds and seventy generations in Enoch, 204; the 250 times in the Assumption of Moses, 205; the eleven generations of Sib. Oracles IV., 206; the twelve parts in 4th Ezra and the Apocalypse of Baruch, 206; Rabbinical views, 207 . . . . PAGE 200–208

CHAPTER V.

SIGNS OF THE LAST TIMES.

Signs in Daniel, 209. In the Sibylline Oracles, 210. In Enoch, 211. In the Book of Jubilees, 213. In the Apocalypse of Baruch, 214. In 4th Ezra, 217. In the Mishnah, 218. In the Babylonian Talmud, 219. The birth-pains of the Messiah, 221 209–221

CHAPTER VI.

FORERUNNERS OF THE MESSIAH.

Elijah, 222: References in Justin Martyr, 222; in Seder 'Olam Rabbah, 223; in the Mishnah, 223. Other forerunners, 224: Reference in the New Testament, 224: Jeremiah in 2nd Maccabees, 225: Possible allusion in 4th Ezra, 225: Moses with Elijah in Debarim Rabbah, 225 222–225

CHAPTER VII.

CONCEPTION OF THE IDEAL KINGDOM WITHOUT A MESSIAH.

The Book of Daniel, 226. Principles of investigation, 226. The vision of 'one like a son of man,' 228: The explanation suggested by the rest of the vision, 228; and by the interpretation of the vision, 229: Adverse argument from Daniel's connection with the Prophets, 231; reply, 232; confirmation from the two parallel passages, 232: Hengstenberg's arguments in favour of the Messianic explanation, 233; from the history of Biblical interpretation, 233; from the mode in which the readers would naturally understand the passage, 234; from the meaning of the clouds, 235; from the impropriety of comparing Israel to a son of man, 239; from the analogy of other passages, 240: Conclusion, 241. The 'saint' in the vision of the ram and the goat, 241. The vision by the river Hiddekel, 241. The prophecy of the seventy weeks, 243: Hengstenberg's translation, 243: The Messianic interpretation, 244; the non-Messianic, 245: Method of inquiry, 246: Argument from particular phrases, 247; 'to anoint a holy of holies,' 247; 'an anointed, a prince,' and 'an anointed,' 248: Messianic character of the opening verse admitted, 249: Considerations which connect the prophecy with Antiochus Epiphanes, 249; the description in xi. and xii., 249; correspondences with passages confessedly relating to Antiochus, 250: Hengstenberg's arguments against the Maccabean interpretation, 251; the writer could not regard the prophecies of Jeremiah as unfulfilled, 251; he would not 'make fun of Jeremiah,' 252; no divine command to rebuild Jerusalem was given at the time of Jeremiah's prophecy, 252; the antithesis of verse 24 to verse 2, 253; הָבָר without the article cannot refer to the announcement of Jeremiah, 253; the blessings are not mentioned by Jeremiah, 254; the chronology does not suit, 254; the restoration of the Temple is not alluded to, 257; difficulty of explaining 'an anointed one shall be cut off,' 258; Jewish tradition, 258; 'the word of Christ,' 259: Argument against the Messianic interpretation from the position of the passage, 260: Apparent advantages of that interpretation, in chronology, and in regard to the destruction of the city, 261: Arguments against it from the statements of the passage itself, 264; Christ was not anointed at the end of the seventy weeks, 264; there is nothing to account for the division of the sixty-nine weeks, 264; Christ was not cut off, nor was Jerusalem destroyed, at the end of the sixty-two weeks, 265; the sacrifices did not cease at Christ's death, 265; the second half of the last week cannot be accounted for, 266; the blessings were to be enjoyed by the holy city, 266: Conclusion, 267. The Book of Wisdom, 267. First Book of Maccabees, 268: Second Book, 269. The Assumption of Moses, 269. The Book of Jubilees, 270. Philo, 271: De Exsecrationibus, 271; De Præmiis et Pœnis, 272. Rabbinical opposition to the Messianic hope, 273. Conclusion, 273 . . . . . PAGE 226–273

CHAPTER VIII.

THE TIME OF THE MESSIAH'S APPEARANCE.

View of the third Book of Sib. Oracles, 274; Holtzmann's opinion that the Messiah is not referred to, 274. The Book of Enoch, 275. Psalms of Solomon. Sibyl of time of triumvirs. Fourth Ezra, 276. Apoc. of Baruch. Rabbinical views, 277 274–278

CHAPTER IX.

THE BIRTH-PLACE, CONCEALMENT, AND DESCENT OF THE MESSIAH.

Birth-place: Jerusalem; Bethlehem, 279. Concealment, 280. Appearance, 281. Descent, 282 279–282

CHAPTER X.

TITLES AND NAMES OF THE MESSIAH.

Messiah, 283: χριστὸς κύριος in Psalms of Solomon, 283. Son of David, 284. Son of Man, 284. Son of God, 284; in the Book of Enoch, 284; in Fourth Ezra, 285: Origen's statement, 288. Personal names, 288. Exalted titles applied to the Israelites, 288 . . PAGE 283–289

CHAPTER XI.

THE NATURE OF THE MESSIAH.

Statement of Justin Martyr, 290. Gfrörer's appeal to the LXX. as teaching the pre-existence of the Messiah, 290. The king 'from the sun,' in Sib. Or. III. 652, 291. View of the Book of Enoch, 291. Psalms of Solomon, 292. Later Sibyl, 292. Fourth Ezra supposed to teach the Messiah's pre-existence, 292. The Targums: Micah v. 1; Isai. ix. 5, 294. The Talmud, 295 290–295

CHAPTER XII.

THE LAST ENEMIES.

Ideas drawn from Ezekiel and Daniel, 296. The attack, 296: Picture in the Apocalyptic books, 296; the Targums, 297. Antichrist, 298: Beliar in the Sib. Oracles, 298: The 'last leader' in the Apocalypse of Baruch, 299: Gog and Magog, 299: Armilûs, 299. The destruction of the enemies, 299): Sib. Oracles, 300: Enoch, 301: Psalms of Solomon, 302: Philo, 302: Book of Jubilees, 303: Post-Christian Sibyl, 303: Fourth Ezra, 304: Apocalypse of Baruch, 305: The Targums, 307 296–308

CHAPTER XIII.

GENERAL CHARACTER OF THE MESSIANIC REIGN.

Sibylline Oracles, and Psalms of Solomon, 309. Fourth Ezra, and Apocalypse of Baruch, 310. Targums, 310: Gfrörer's argument from the Targum of Zech. vi. 12, 13 that the Messiah was to have priestly functions, with criticism on it, 310 309–311

CHAPTER XIV.

PLACE, EXTENT, AND DURATION OF THE MESSIAH'S KINGDOM.

Jerusalem the centre of the future kingdom, 312. Universal extent and indefinite duration of the kingdom in Daniel and other books, 313. The limitation to four hundred years in Fourth Ezra, 314; indefinite duration, up to the close of the present age, in the Apocalypse of Baruch, 315; universal extent in these books, 315. Extent in the Targums, 315. Various Rabbinical views as to the duration of the kingdom, 315 . . . . PAGE 312–318

CHAPTER XV.

HAD THE KINGDOM A DISTINCTIVE NAME?

'The kingdom of God' not synonymous with the kingdom of the Messiah, 319 : Use of the expression in the Psalms of Solomon, the Sibylline Oracles, and the Assumption of Moses, 319; in the Wisdom of Solomon, 320. 'The kingdom of heaven,' 320; probably derived from Dan. vii. 13, 14, 320; not used to denote the Messianic reign, 321: Lightfoot's account of its Rabbinical use, 321; Wetstein's, 321; Schoettgen's, 322 319–322

CHAPTER XVI.

MORAL NATURE OF THE KINGDOM.

View of the Sibylline Oracles, 323; observance of sacrificial rites, 323. Book of Enoch, 324. Psalms of Solomon, 324. Assumption of Moses, 325. Book of Jubilees, 325; ceremonial law eternally binding, 325. Fourth Ezra, 325. Observance of the Law in the Messianic time according to the Targums, 326. Criticism of Gfrörer's opinion that according to one view the ceremonial law would be abolished, 326 . . 323–327

CHAPTER XVII.

THE CONVERSION OF THE GENTILES.

Merciful view of the Sib. Oracles, 328; and of the Book of Enoch, 329. Apparently adverse view of the Psalms of Solomon, 330. Philo's idea of the influence of a virtuous nation, 330. Hostile view of Fourth Ezra and Apocalypse of Baruch, 331; compared with story in the Yalqut, 331. Rabbinical views, 331 328–332

CHAPTER XVIII.

THE RETURN OF THE SCATTERED ISRAELITES.

References in the Psalms of Solomon, Philo, and the Book of Jubilees, 333. Account of the ten tribes in Fourth Ezra, 334; Arzareth, 334, *note* 5. The letter of Baruch, 335. The Targum of Jonathan, 335. The Talmudists divided in opinion, 335 333–336

CHAPTER XIX.

DESTRUCTION OF THE OLD JERUSALEM, AND APPEARANCE OF THE NEW.

Daniel the source of the expectation that Jerusalem would be destroyed, 337. The evidence in Josephus, 337; criticism of Gfrörer's view that Josephus referred to Daniel, 338. Passage in Revelation, 339. Legend in the Jerusalem Gemara, 340. Connection between the destruction of Jerusalem and the appearance of the Messiah, 340. The view of the Apocalyptic Books, 340. The new Jerusalem, 341: Book of Enoch, 341: Fourth Ezra, 342: Apocalypse of Baruch, 342: Rabbinical fancies, 343 . . . . PAGE 337–344

CHAPTER XX.

EARTHLY BLESSEDNESS.

Description in the Sib. Oracles, 345. Book of Enoch, 346. Philo, 347. Book of Jubilees, 349. Apocalypse of Baruch, 349. Talmud, 350 345–351

CHAPTER XXI.

BEHEMOTH AND LEVIATHAN.

Source of the fancy about these monsters, 352. Account in the Book of Enoch, 353. Fourth Ezra, 354. Apocalypse of Baruch, 355. Rabbinical views, 355 352–355

CHAPTER XXII.

MESSIAH BEN-JOSEPH, AND THE SUFFERINGS OF THE MESSIAH.

Messiah the son of Joseph first mentioned in the Babylonian Gemara, 356: Altered view of the later Targums, 357: Source of the belief in a second Messiah, 357. The Messiah was not expected to suffer, 357: Faint traces of a different view in Justin Martyr, 358; and in the Talmud, 359 356–359

CHAPTER XXIII.

RESURRECTION AND JUDGMENT.

Doctrine of the Book of Daniel, 360. The Book of Enoch, 362: Names for the final judgment, 362: Connected description of the judgment, 362: Fate of the fallen angels, 363: Dwelling-place of departed spirits, 363:

Mode in which the judgment was to be conducted, 365: Reward of the righteous, 365: Place of punishment, 366: The condition of things after the judgment unalterable, 367: The doctrine of resurrection, 368. The Wisdom of Solomon teaches the doctrine of immortality, and of the pre-existence of souls, 369. Doctrine of 2nd Maccabees, 369. The Psalms of Solomon, 369. The Sib. Oracles of the time of the Triumvirs, 371. Description of the judgment in the Assumption of Moses, 371. Doctrine of 4th Maccabees, 372. The Book of Jubilees agrees closely with Enoch, 373. The post-Christian Sibyl, 374. Fourth Ezra, 374: The writer's views principally in the omitted portion of the Latin Version, 374: Condition of souls between death and the judgment, 374: The time of judgment, 377: Few shall be saved, 378: Intercession will not be allowed, 379: The blessings of the righteous, 379: Men perish through the abuse of their liberty, 380. The Apocalypse of Baruch, 380: Criticism of the passage which places the resurrection in the time of the Messiah, 380: Bodily identity, and change, after the resurrection, 381. General Rabbinical view, 382: Persons excluded from the world to come according to the Mishnah, 383; according to the Gemaras, 384: Different views as to the agent by whom the resurrection would be effected, 385: The manner of the resurrection, 385: Description of the judgment in 'Abodah Zarah, 386: Place of judgment, punishments, and rewards, 387 . . . . PAGE 360–387

CHAPTER XXIV.

GENERAL VIEW OF THE MESSIANIC IDEA BEFORE THE TIME OF CHRIST 388

APPENDIX 391

INDEX OF MODERN WORKS 393

Errata.

On p. 171, line 22, *for* גְּמָרָה *read* גְּמָרָא.

On the same page and elsewhere in Book I. Ch. v. and on p. 219, line 14 and p. 224, line 17, *for* Gemarah *read* Gemara.

THE JEWISH MESSIAH.

BOOK I.

SOURCES.

GENERAL REMARKS.

As the sources from which our information respecting Jewish belief is drawn are not very familiar to the English reader, and as some of them are still the subjects of critical discussion, it is necessary to prefix to our account of the Messianic idea a sketch of the literature on which we must rely as we unfold its successive phases. We need not, indeed, pause upon those writings of which an adequate knowledge may readily be obtained from English works, but content ourselves with referring, when occasion requires, to some of the leading authorities respecting them. This remark applies chiefly to the apocryphal books of the Old Testament, with the exception of II. Esdras. These, though not wholly devoid of interest in the present connection, yet throw so little light upon our inquiry, that a discussion of their probable origin and date would be out of place. In the case of some other compositions, in regard to which the results of criticism are sufficiently established for our purpose, the most essential points will be laid briefly before the reader, while a more complete investigation will be reserved for those productions about which a wide difference of opinion prevails. With these preliminary observations, we may proceed at once to the consideration of an important class of literature—the apocalyptic.

CHAPTER I.

THE APOCALYPTIC LITERATURE.

SECTION I.—*Introductory.*

THE name of Apocalyptic Literature has been applied in recent times to a series of writings connected together by the possession of common characteristics, which find their earliest type in the Book of Daniel, and most of which reappear in the Apocalypse of John. This last circumstance has suggested a designation for the entire group; and the term apocalyptic may be fitly used to distinguish compositions of this class from the prophetical writings, to which, in some of their aspects, they are closely akin. It was impossible to treat all these works together as forming one literary species, so long as canonical and extra-canonical books were separated by an impassable line; and it was, therefore, reserved for the freer thought of modern days, and indeed for the researches of the present century, to draw forth to light the curious treasures which they contain. Fabricius made the earliest, and necessarily a very imperfect, collection of the apocalyptic writings in his 'Codex Pseudepigraphus Veteris Testamenti,' published at Hamburg in 1713. Semler, Corrodi, Eichhorn, and others, made valuable advances towards a more thorough study of the subject; but the honour of giving the most marked impulse to the investigation of this class of literature belongs to an English scholar. In 1819, Richard Laurence (afterwards Archbishop of Cashel) published the Anabaticon or Ascension of Isaiah, in Æthiopic, along with an English and a Latin translation. In the following year he issued the Æthiopic text of 4th Ezra, accompanied also by translations into English and Latin. But the most important work appeared in 1821 in the form of an English translation of the Book of Enoch from an Æthiopic manuscript. In the earliest of these years, 1819, the investigations of Bleek (to be more fully referred to further on) threw an unexpected light upon the Sibylline Oracles. From this time several German theologians, enriched by these new materials, have directed especial attention to the apocalyptic literature. Their most important works will be mentioned as we proceed.

We must now glance at the historical origin and leading characteristics of this literature. After the destruction of Jewish independence the creative prophetic impulse gradually died away, and was superseded by study and interpretation. While the exposition of the Law strengthened the people's attachment to their monotheistic faith, and deepened their aversion to heathenism, the triumph of the great pagan empires over the afflicted Israelites must have appeared a strange reversal of the old ideal of the prophets. The disposition of a number of the people to submit quietly to hellenizing influences, stirred the grief and zeal of those who valued the principles of the ancient religion; and at last the violence of Antiochus Epiphanes, who desecrated the Temple with a heathen altar, in 168 B.C., drove the patriotic party into armed revolt under the leadership of the Maccabees. The forces of heathenism recoiled before the shock; and when, in the year 165 B.C., Judas purified the Temple, it might well seem that the long-promised reign of the chosen people could not be far off. Out of this conflict sprang the apocalyptic literature, the strange product of blended political and religious enthusiasm. It attached itself to ancient prophecy, on which its hopes depended, and from the interpretation of which it sought to anticipate the fulfilment of times and seasons. Its process of interpretation is, however, for the most part concealed, and it speaks not in the style of an expositor, but of a prophet, and accordingly couches its language, not in the past, but in the future. This may explain the fact that it generally chooses as its mouthpiece some ancient worthy, who lived before the period which it undertakes to survey. Enoch, Moses, Ezra, Baruch, and even the heathen Sibyl are pressed into the service. The Apocalypse of John can hardly be treated as an exception to this rule, because it does not deal with old-world history, and the author might therefore speak in his own person. In some cases the retrospect extends over the whole course of mundane events, and a sort of divine plan of human affairs (perhaps the first vague anticipation of a philosophy of history) is sketched out. The object of this retrospect was to prepare the way for what to the real writer was still predictive. God's righteous judgments were to come speedily upon the world, and the most glorious hopes of Israel to be fulfilled. This kind of composition proceeds, not so much from the matter-of-fact intellect, as from a dreamy and imaginative enthusiasm, from that mystic frame of mind which sees a permanent conflict of principles amid the unsubstantial forms of a transient world ; and it is, therefore, quite in keeping with their whole purpose that the writers so often clothe their thoughts in the drapery of curious symbols, such as present themselves in dreams and visions.

The eschatological portion of these books is what

chiefly concerns us in our present investigation; but a general introduction to those which are less familiarly known will not be devoid of interest. As some of the apocalyptic works have confessedly proceeded from Christian authors, it may be as well to observe that only those which appear to be of purely Jewish origin will come under review. Although in regard to the date of a few of the more important of these a serious difference of opinion exists, it will be seen that we may safely use them as representing one phase of Jewish opinion at the opening of the Christian era; but perhaps it is not always easy to decide how far the sentiments expressed in them belong to the nation, to a school, or only to the individual author.

We may now proceed to notice the several works a little more in detail.[1]

Section II.—*The Book of Daniel.*

Delitzsch[2] describes the Book of Daniel as 'a book whose genuineness had for nearly two thousand years no other opponent than the heathen scoffer, Porphyry, in his Λόγοι κατὰ χριστιανῶν, but whose spuriousness has, since Semler and Eichhorn, become step by step a constantly less dubious fact to the biblical criticism in Germany which proceeds from rationalistic suppositions.' A wide and difficult discussion is suggested by this quotation; but as good summaries of the arguments on each side are readily accessible,[3] we may here confine ourselves to a

[1] On the subject of the above section, see especially Lücke's *Versuch einer vollständigen Einleitung in die Offenbarung des Johannes*, &c., 2te Aufl. 1852, i. S. 9 sq., and Hilgenfeld's *Die jüdische Apokalyptik in ihrer geschichtlichen Entwickelung*, &c. (Jena, 1857), Einleitung, S. 1 sq.

[2] In his article on the subject in Herzog's *Encyklopädie*.

[3] It may be sufficient to refer here to the article in Smith's *Dictionary of the Bible*, by Dr. Westcott, where the literature of the subject is given,

broad outline of the considerations by which the date of the work must be determined.

The supposed acquiescence of two thousand years cannot be accepted as evidence of a questionable fact, but it may readily explain the existence of prepossessions other than rationalistic. Yet this is practically the main evidence on which the Danielic authorship is made to rest. As in so many inquiries, it is unconsciously assumed that a large body of conclusive evidence is ready for use, and that, if only objections can be repelled and difficulties solved, the case is complete. But those who are not under its spell cannot take for granted that the Church is always right except when it can be proved to be wrong; nor can they quietly remove every literary difficulty by the admission of the most stupendous miracles, simply because a work is found within the canon. Now, if we apply to Daniel the same kind of criticism which we should deem conclusive in the case of any extra-canonical book, and by which we actually determine the dates of other apocalyptic works, I think we must accept the judg-

---

to the *Introduction to the Book of Daniel*, by Mr. Rose and Mr. Fuller, in the *Speaker's Commentary*, and to the article in Herzog's *Encyk.*, which support the conservative side; and to Dr. Davidson's *Introduction to the Old Testament*, 1863, and Graf's article in Schenkel's *Bibel-Lexikon*, which advocate the later date. Some of the more important points affecting the interpretation, and bearing indirectly on the date of the work, will be fully discussed in our second book. For a general view of the book, its merits and its influence, the reader may be referred, among more recent works, to Kuenen's *Religion of Israel to the Fall of the Jewish State*: translated from the Dutch by Alfred Heath May, 1875, vol. iii. pp. 106-114.

Those who wish to see a full and elaborate defence of the traditional view should read *Daniel the Prophet: Nine Lectures, delivered in the Divinity School of the University of Oxford*. With copious notes. By the Rev. E. B. Pusey, D.D., &c. 1864. My references will be to the third edition, 1869. This work, written to defend what the author holds as an article of faith, destroys by its fundamental assumption our confidence in its critical impartiality, and repels by its scornful and insulting tone those whom it is meant to convince.

ment of those who believe that it was written in the time of Antiochus Epiphanes, about the year 165 or 164 B.C.

Dr. Westcott asserts that by this view the whole book is 'rejected as the work of an impostor.'[1] This is hardly a correct description of the case. If the author deliberately intended to pass off his own production as a genuine composition of an ancient prophet, he no doubt lies open to a charge of imposture; but if, without any such intention, he simply adopted the history and visions of Daniel as a literary vehicle in which to convey his own thoughts, he is not obnoxious to so serious an accusation. If in the present day anyone, with some political purpose, were to write a book entitled 'The visions of William the Conqueror,' in which the fortunes of the English people were symbolically portrayed, it would be ridiculous to brand him as an impostor. So the authors of the various apocalyptic works, although an uncritical age was sometimes misled by their effusions, are not justly open to a suspicion of wilful deceit. Our modern taste accords little welcome to this kind of literary inventiveness, and our modern strictness may regard it as not altogether permissible; but I can see no reason why it may not have been practised by high-minded and honourable men.

How, then, stand the facts in regard to the Book of Daniel? The work itself, taken as a whole, does not pretend to be written by Daniel. Throughout the first six chapters Daniel is spoken of, like all the other persons who figure in the narrative, in the third person; and the conclusion especially of this section—'So this Daniel prospered in the reign of Darius, and in the reign of Cyrus the Persian'—has all the appearance of an historical statement made by some later writer. If the book ended here, it would be more reasonably ascribed to

[1] Article in Smith's *Dictionary of the Bible*, i. 393.

Nebuchadnezzar than to Daniel, for in iv. 34-37 the story of that monarch is related, without any sign of quotation, in the first person. The second part of the work, containing Daniel's dreams and visions, also begins by referring to the prophet in the third person, and the same style recurs in x. 1. Nearly the whole of this section, however, professes to quote the words of Daniel; for in vii. 1 it is stated that he wrote his dream, and then it is added, 'Daniel spake and said, "I saw in my vision."' But it is not alleged that what follows is a genuine quotation from an ancient writing, nor is there anything to indicate that it is not the composition of the author of the whole book. We must further observe that it is intimated with sufficient distinctness in the last chapter that the writing had never been heard of before the stirring events which seemed to mark the final crisis in Jewish affairs; for Daniel is desired to 'shut up the words, and seal the book, even to the time of the end.'[1] This might, however, appear like an endeavour to pass off the portion of the book containing Daniel's visions as a genuine copy of an ancient document which had not hitherto been published. But as it is not asserted that this document was anywhere discovered, or that it had been in anyone's keeping, the statement hardly goes beyond what is allowable to give verisimilitude to the narrative. The work, therefore, even if it belongs to the time of the Maccabees, cannot justly be regarded as a forgery. It unmistakeably suggests the supposition that some later author makes Daniel the spokesman of his own ideas; and we are accordingly at liberty to ascertain his date by reference to the events with which he deals.

Now Daniel's four visions, with the accompanying interpretations, lead invariably to Antiochus Epiphanes,

---

[1] See xii. 4 and 9.

by whom 'the daily sacrifice was taken away, and the place of his sanctuary was cast down.'[1] Up to this point the historical details are clearly traced; but beyond it lies only the obscure though glorious future. The dream of Nebuchadnezzar[2] readily yields the same result; and the seventy weeks,[3] though not without difficulties, bring us sufficiently near to the same date, when they are understood as weeks of years. In the case of any other book, if all its correct historical accounts terminated in one point, while everything assigned to a later date was the nebulous creation of religious hope, we should have no hesitation in concluding that this point fixed the precise date of its composition; and till very cogent reasons are shown for departing from this rule, we must accept it as valid in the instance before us. And surely it is not all loss if the work, from being the plaything of pseudo-prophets and quasi-interpreters, has found its true place in literature—has rewarded the critic's search with the key to its mysterious imagery, and been made to shed a valuable light upon the feelings, convictions, and hopes which animated the patriotic party in one of the most momentous struggles of the Jewish people.

Section III.—*The Sibylline Oracles.*

The Sibylline Oracles, as we at present possess them, consist of twelve books of Greek hexameters, besides a few fragments. The contents of these books are very various, but consist for the most part of a description of historical events dressed in the guise of prophecy. There are also predictions of the fate of peoples, cities, and temples, and of an ideal future; and moral precepts and

---
[1] viii. 11.   [2] ii.
[3] ix. 24 *sq*. The interpretation of this passage will be fully discussed further on, Book ii. ch. vii.

religious admonitions are not wanting. The last book was printed for the first time in 1817 by Angelo Mai, and the last four collectively by the same editor in 1828;[1] so that before this time only eight books came under investigation. In the time of Lardner and earlier, although transpositions and interpolations were suspected, these eight books were treated as substantially one work, and were therefore declared without hesitation to be a Christian forgery of the second century, the evidence appearing amply sufficient for this conclusion in regard to certain portions.[2] But the searching investigations of Bleek into the indications of time and of authorship presented by the first eight books completely established their composite character;[3] and it is now an accepted result of criticism that the date and origin of the various parts can be determined only by the contents of those parts themselves, and that the several oracles in their present form have proceeded partly from Jewish, partly from Christian authors, while here and there earlier materials of heathen origin have most probably been worked into the later monotheistic texture. A more thorough examination, following the track indicated by Bleek, seems to require some modification of his particular conclusions. As the great majority of the Books have no bearing on our present subject, it is unnecessary to bring them under discussion ; but it may be useful to subjoin a summary of the results arrived at by Professor

[1] In his *Scriptorum Veterum Nova Collectio*, vol. iii. part 3, p. 202 *sq.* Rome, 1828. These four books were published from manuscripts in the Vatican.

[2] See Lardner's collected works, 1838, ii. 333 *sq.*

[3] ' Ueber die Entstehung und Zusammensetzung der uns in acht Büchern erhaltenen Sammlung sibyllinischer Orakel,' in the *Theologische Zeitschrift* of Schleiermacher, De Wette, and Lücke, Heft 1, 1819, S. 120-246, Heft 2, 1820; S. 172-239. I have failed to obtain these articles, and am therefore obliged to refer to them at second hand. The above title is taken from Hilgenfeld's *Jüd. Apok.* S. 55, Anm. 5.

Friedlieb, who in 1852 published a very careful and complete edition of the Greek text, preceded by a critical introduction, and accompanied by a metrical German translation.[1] In his view the Books of Jewish origin are the following: III., in the main by an Egyptian Jew, about 160 B.C.; IV., 79 or 80 A.D.; V. by an Egyptian Jew, in the earlier part of the reign of Hadrian (ascribed by Bleek to a Christian, on account of the appearance of Nero as Antichrist, and the favourable view of Hadrian; but the opinion that Nero was Beliar might have been held by a Jew, and at the time when the book was composed Hadrian may not have begun to display his hostility towards the Jews); IX., by an Egyptian Jew, between 115 and 118 A.D.; XII., probably by an Egyptian Jew of the third century. The remaining books proceed, in Friedlieb's opinion, from Christian writers of the second and third centuries, though Bleek, chiefly on account of the silence of the Fathers, would place I. and II. as late as the middle of the fifth century.[2]

From the above summary it is evident that the third Book is the one which, on account of its date and authorship, most nearly concerns us; and it fortunately contains a long description of what, though it is not mentioned under that name, we may call the Messianic period. From this book, however, we must detach lines 1-45, which, though they may contain an altered extract from the original prooemium, have probably come from the author of the first two Books. Lines 46-96, though of Jewish and pre-Christian origin, also belong to a later date than that which we have assigned to the rest of the Book, for

---

[1] *Oracula Sibyllina, ad fidem codd. mscr. quotquot extant recensuit, prætextis prolegominis illustravit, versione Germanica instruxit, annotationes criticas et rerum indicem adjecit Josephus Henricus Friedlieb*; Lipsiæ, MDCCCLII. There is also a German title.

[2] See Friedlieb's edition, Einleitung.

there is a clear allusion to the triumvirs, Antonius, Octavius, and Lepidus, and also to Cleopatra.[1] As in their time, according to the Pseudo-Sibyl, God was to come to judge the world, we may assign this section to the period immediately preceding the battle of Actium, 31 B.C. Friedlieb apparently sees no difficulty in line 63, Ἐκ δὲ Σεβαστηνῶν ἥξει Βελίαρ μετόπισθεν, but is content to refer the expression Σεβαστηνῶν to the Roman rulers generally, and thinks the author may have regarded Antonius himself as the future Beliar. But it is difficult to understand how such a title could have been used to describe Roman rulers at that time; and surely those critics must be right who see here a later interpolation, and an allusion to the derivation of Antichrist from the line of the Roman emperors in the person of Nero.[2] It is probable also that lines 818–828 are from a later hand, as they contain an account of the origin of the Sibyl at variance with that which has immediately preceded, and the Book naturally closes with line 817. On the other hand, there is sufficient evidence to show that two fragments (comprising together 84 lines), preserved by Theophilus of Antioch,[3] and now prefixed to the whole collection, formed parts of the prooemium of this Book. It thus appears that we possess by far the larger part of the verses (amounting according to Lactantius[4] to about a thousand) of the old Hebrew or Erythræan Sibyl.[5]

---

[1] v. 51 *sq.* and 75 *sq.*

[2] The connection may be restored by omitting from Ἀτὰρ in line 61 to ἥξει in 63, both words inclusive, and then supplying κατὰ γῆν to complete the metre. The lines will then read thus:—

Ἥξει γάρ, ὁπ᾽ ταν θείου διαβήσεται ὀδμή
Πᾶσιν ἐν ἀνθρώποις κατὰ γῆν, Βελίαρ μετ.᾽πισθεν.

B'eck is followed in this supposition by Gfrörer (*Philo und die alexandrinische Theosophie*, 1831, ii. S. 134) and Lücke (*Einl. in die Offenb.* i. S. 79–80).

[3] *Ad Autol.* lib. ii. c. 36.   [4] *Divin. Instit.* lib. i. c. 6.

[5] Friedlieb says we have 995. My arithmetic produces only 808. The

With the exclusion of the passages just pointed out, the date of the third Book is shown by express statements to fall within the reign of Ptolemy VII. Physkon, of Egypt; for immediately after the miseries of that time the glorious future of the 'sons of the great God,'[1] was expected to come in. There are three distinct references to the seventh king of Egypt, who is twice said to be of Grecian lineage.[2] In the first of the passages where these references occur, the 'nation of the great God' is promised renewed strength and leadership at this time; and in the second it is said that the miseries of Egypt should then cease. The most important passage, however, is the last. In this the invasion of Egypt by Antiochus Epiphanes, 'a great king from Asia,' immediately after the accession of Physken, is indicated with sufficient clearness. If, therefore, the author represents the Messianic period as following closely upon this event, we must agree with Bleek and Friedlieb in assigning to the work a date not long after 170 B.C., the year in which the invasion occurred. Hilgenfeld, however, thinks, with good reason, that this long and troubled reign allows us a greater latitude of choice; and he fixes the date between 142 and 137 B.C.[3] The chief indication of a later period in the passage before us he finds in the predicted desolation of 'all Greece' by a 'barbarous empire,'[4] which, in his opinion, must refer

---

fragments of Theophilus comprise 84 verses; but Friedlieb adds to the first fragment three verses found in Lactantius (*Div. Inst.* ii. 11), bringing the number up to 87. The case accordingly stands thus: $828 - (96 + 11) + 87 = 808$.

[1] v. 702.

[2] v. 192-3, 318, 608 *sq*. In 318 the Greek descent is not specified. These notices, occurring in different parts of the poem, and all pointing to the same date, help to prove the identity of authorship of the successive sections.

[3] *Jüd. Apok.* S. 75.

[4] Βάρβαρος ἀρχή, v. 638-40.

to the conquest of Greece by the Romans in 146 B.C. The decisive evidence he detects in an earlier passage,[1] in which the fortunes of the Seleucids are enigmatically described. By carefully comparing with historical events the allusions which here occur, he arrives at the reign of the usurper Tryphon, who seized the throne in 142 B.C. Tryphon was overthrown by Antiochus Sidetes, who succeeded him in 137 B.C.; and thus are determined the limits within which the work must have been written.[2] Other indications are found in the prophecy of the desolation of Libya by barbarous-minded enemies,[3] which it is most natural to refer to the destruction of Carthage by the Romans in 146 B.C., and in the predicted ruin of Greece by a 'very barbarous nation,'[4] which, though generally referred to the conquest of Perseus of Macedonia in 168 B.C., seems to suit best the overthrow of Achæa in 146 B.C., as it is expressly said that 'a servile yoke shall be upon *all* Greece.'[5]

There appears, therefore, to be satisfactory evidence for placing the third Book of the Sibylline Oracles in the second century before Christ. Volkmar, however, while admitting that it is in the main pre-Christian, places it as late as 63 B.C. He does so on the alleged ground that the entrance of Pompeius into Jerusalem is clearly indicated. He appeals to the passage[6] where the Sibyl, having spoken of the prosperity of Judæa, declares that kings will begin to be angry with one another, and that again kings of the nations will come and threaten the Temple. The first allusion he refers to the disputes between Hyrcanus and Aristobulus for the sovereignty of Judæa, and the second to the interference of Aretas, an

---

[1] v. 388–400. [2] *Jüd. Apok.* S. 68–71. [3] v. 323 *sq.*
[4] v. 520 *sq.* [5] Ἑλλάδι πάσῃ, v. 537. [6] v. 660 *sq.*

Arabian prince, and subsequently of Pompeius.¹ But we may surely object that Pompeius was not a king; that the exaggeration would be too gross to describe Aretas and Pompeius, who came to Jerusalem in succession, as kings of the Gentiles coming 'in crowds' ("Αθρooι) against the land; and that Pompeius at all events, instead of 'bringing fate' upon himself by his invasion of Palestine, withdrew in triumph. This last objection might be obviated if we supposed the book to have been written during the three months of the siege; but the whole passage appears to me to be an apocalyptic picture of the destruction of the Gentile powers; and the coincidence between the quarrel of the kings and the inroad of the Gentiles does not seem sufficient to disturb our former conclusion.

In the Jewish Sibylline Oracles we meet with that tendency to clothe Hebrew ideas in an Hellenic dress, which is so marked a feature in the Jewish Alexandrine philosophy; and this circumstance points to Egypt as the place of their composition. The name of Sibyl was given generally among the Greeks to supposed prophetesses of the olden time. According to Lactantius,² Varro enumerates as many as ten of these. Attached to no historical figures, the title may represent, under a mythological form, a kind of impersonal spirit of prophecy. Sibylline vaticinations may at first have circulated orally, and only gradually have been committed to writing and formed into collections.³ None of the original collections have come down to us; but parts of them may have been

---

¹ See Volkmar's *Handbuch der Einleitung in die Apokryphen.* Zweite Abtheilung. *Das vierte Buch Esra. Zum erstenmale vollständig herausgegeben, als ältester Commentar zum Neuen Testament.* Tübingen, 1863, S. 396, Anm. 2. Also the same work, Dritter Band. *Mose Prophetie und Himmelfahrt, eine Quelle für das Neue Testament, zum ersten Male deutsch herausgegeben, im Zusammenhang der Apokrypha und der Christologie überhaupt.* Leipzig, 1867. S. 58.

² *Div. Inst.* i. 6.

³ See Lücke, *Einl. in die Offenb.* i. S. 84.

adopted by the Jewish and Christian authors of those which we now possess. At a time when rationalistic explanations were given of the old mythology, and monotheistic belief was making way among the educated classes, it was not unnatural that a Jew who believed that God was accessible to all, and indeed dwelt 'in all mortals,'[1] should seek to address the Grecian world in the name of its own mysterious prophetess, and, making her a prophetess of the true God, appeal through this accepted medium to the common conscience of mankind.

Section IV.—*The Book of Enoch.*

On the Book of Enoch we must bestow a more lengthened consideration, both on account of the interesting nature of its contents and on account of the great diversity of opinion which prevails as to its origin and date. If it could be proved to be in its entirety a Jewish work proceeding from the time of the Maccabees, its Messianic doctrine would be of the highest value as indicating the belief of at least a section of the Jews in the pre-Christian period. But when we find that not only does such an orthodox writer as Philippi regard it as wholly Christian, but such an able critic as Hilgenfeld, followed by Colani and others, considers the most Messianic portion to be from a Christian hand, while Volkmar, though accepting in part its Jewish origin, places it as late as 132 A.D., and supposes that it has been involuntarily coloured by Christian teaching, and those who contend for the earliest date admit that it has been interpolated with Christian phrases, we cannot but feel that it is impossible to accept it on the mere

---

[1] See Fragment I. of the Procemium, v. 18. Πᾶσι βροτοῖσιν ἐνὼν τὸ κριτήριον ἐν φαῖ κοινῷ. Otto adopts the emendation of Maranus, νέμων for ἐνών. See his edition of *Theophilus of Antioch*, ii. 36, n. 16.

authority of critics as a trustworthy evidence of Jewish belief before the time of Christ.

It is only in recent times that these questions have come under discussion; for no Greek copy of the Book of Enoch has survived, and it was long supposed that the work had been irrecoverably lost. A few Greek fragments, indeed, had been discovered in the Chronographia of Georgius Syncellus, a Byzantine monk about the end of the eighth century.[1] But in 1773, Bruce, the celebrated traveller, brought three Æthiopic copies from Abyssinia. One of these, a magnificent copy, in quarto, he consigned to the library at Paris. A second, which he took home, was in a collection of the books of Scripture, 'standing,' he says, 'immediately before the book of Job, which is its proper place in the Abyssinian canon.'[2] The third he presented to the Bodleian Library. Several other manuscripts have since that time been found in Abyssinia. For many years this literary treasure was allowed to rest undisturbed in the libraries. At length, in 1800, Silvestre de Sacy published in the Magasin Encyclopédique[3] a notice of the book, together with a Latin translation of the first three chapters, of the 6th to the 16th inclusive, and of the 22nd and 32nd, from the Paris manuscript. The first complete edition appeared in the form of an English translation by Laurence in 1821.[4] Dr. Hoffmann, of Jena, was the first to bring the labours of Laurence before the attention of

---

[1] These, with one exception, have their counterparts in the Æthiopic translation.

[2] Quoted by Laurence, 3rd edition, Preliminary Dissertation, p. xiv.

[3] *An.* vi. tom. i. p. 382 *sq.*, referred to by Laurence.

[4] Second edition, 1833, third 1838. 'The Book of Enoch the Prophet: an apocryphal production, supposed for ages to have been lost; but discovered at the close of the last century in Abyssinia; now first translated from an Ethiopic MS. in the Bodleian Library. By Richard Laurence, LL.D. Oxford.' My references are to the third edition.

German scholars.[1] He translated the English version of the first fifty-five chapters into German,[1] and enriched it with an introduction and commentary. The first part, embracing these fifty-five chapters, was published in 1833; the second, in which the editor made use of a newly-acquired manuscript, and translated from the original Æthiopic,[3] appeared in 1838. Gförer translated the English into Latin for his Prophetæ Veteres Pseudepigraphi, 1840. Dillmann published the Æthiopic text in 1851,[4] and a German translation, with introduction and commentary, in 1853. This last edition still holds its place as the best representative of the Æthiopic version.

As the value which we attach to this work depends largely on the answer which we give to the question whether it is the production of one or of several authors, it is necessary to take a survey of its contents. It will be best to do this in the first instance without inserting any explanations or inferences of our own. The division into chapters is rather differently given in different manuscripts; but we shall follow that which Dillmann has preferred. According to his arrangement there are one hundred and eight chapters, occupying eighty octavo pages; and as the chapters are of very unequal length, from a few lines to several pages, I will refer not only to them, but to the pages of Dillmann's edition.

The first five chapters (pp. 1–2) form a general introduction to the work. The first three lines seem like a

---

[1] *Das Buch Henoch in vollständiger Uebersetzung mit fortlaufendem Commentar, ausführlicher Einleitung und erläuternden Excursen,* von Andreas Gottlieb Hoffmann. Erste Abth. Kap. 1-55, Jena 1833. Zweite Abth. 1838. This was intended as a first volume of a work on *Die Apokalyptiker der ältern Zeit unter Juden und Christen*; but a second volume never appeared.

[2] Erste Abth. Vorrede, S. xiii.

[3] Zweite Abth. Vorrede, S. iv–v.

[4] See the Vorwort to his *Das Buch Henoch, übersetzt und erklärt,* 1853.

title or superscription:—'The words of blessing of Enoch, wherewith he blessed the elect and righteous, who shall exist in the day of trouble, when all wicked and godless men shall be removed.' In the next verse the writer passes without any mark of transition from his own words to those of Enoch, and the narrative then proceeds in the first person. We should observe, however, that this changes to the third in different places throughout the book, so that there is no consistent attempt to conceal the later hand of an editor. Enoch declares that he saw a vision in the heavens, shown to him by the angels; but what he saw was not for the present, but for distant generations. He spoke with God about the elect, and learned that he would come down upon Mount Sinai, and execute judgment; and then the elect should be blessed, but the godless destroyed. He observed everything in heaven and on earth, and perceived that every work of God went on regularly, without transgressing its laws. He specifies the lights in heaven, summer and winter, water, clouds, dew, rain, trees (of which fourteen are evergreen), and again the days of the summer with the heat of the sun, seas and rivers. 'But you,' he says, 'have not persevered, and have not fulfilled, but transgressed, the law of the Lord.' Therefore the sinners should receive everlasting condemnation, and find no favour. But the righteous should not be punished their life long, but should complete the number of the days of their life, and become old in peace; and of the years of their happiness there should be many ' in everlasting delight and peace, their whole life long.'

After this general introduction, the first main division of the book embraces chapters vi.–xxxvi.; for the thirty-seventh chapter begins—'The second vision of wisdom which Enoch saw.' This larger section, however, easily falls into three subdivisions.

The first section (vi.–xi., pp. 3–6) contains the history of the fall of the angels, with its immediate consequences. Two hundred angels resolved to take wives from among the daughters of men; and as a consequence of this purpose, they became the parents of giants, whose height was 3,000 yards.[1] These giants having consumed all the substance of mankind, proceeded to devour men themselves. Several of the bad angels taught men the arts of war, luxury, and magic, and it was a time of great corruption. The cry of perishing men, however, attracted the attention of Michael, Gabriel, Surjân, and Urjân, and they laid the case before God. An angel was accordingly despatched to the son of Lamech to warn him of the flood. Another was sent to bind Azâzel in a dark opening in the desert till the day of judgment. Gabriel was to set the giants to destroy one another. Michael was to bury the fallen angels under the hills of the earth for seventy generations, till the day of judgment, when they should be sent into the fiery abyss for ever. This should take place 'at the end of all generations.' Every evil work should come to an end, and 'the plant of righteousness' should appear. Then all the righteous should live till they begat a thousand children, and should 'complete all the days of their youth and their sabbath in peace.' The earth should be very fruitful, so that of every seed one measure should yield ten thousand; and one measure of olives should produce ten presses of oil. And all the children of men should become righteous, and all peoples give honour and praise to God. The account in this section, we should observe, appears

---

[1] One MS. has 300. In the Greek fragment the measure is omitted, so that this extravagance may be an interpo'ation. See Dillmann *in loco*.

throughout to be related by the editor, and is not put into the mouth of Enoch.

In the next section (xii.–xvi., 6–10) Enoch is again introduced. 'Before all this happened Enoch was concealed, and none of the children of men knew where he was concealed and where he dwelt, and what had become of him. And all his doing was with the holy ones, and with the watchers during his life.' After this prefatory notice, Enoch proceeds to tell how the good angels sent him to those that had fallen, to announce to them the impending judgment. Terrified, they asked him to prepare for them a petition. He did so; but as he read it, he fell asleep, and had a vision of judgment. He informed the sinning angels that their petition was refused. He then relates how he had seen a vision of God Himself, and had heard from Him the answer which he was to bear to the watchers.

The next section (xvii.–xxxvi., 10–18) describes the journeys of Enoch under the guidance of angels, and his initiation into various wonders of nature. These stand in relation to the moral government of the universe, and the future judgment is not forgotten. The stars are regarded as living beings; and in a desolate place he saw seven stars bound on account of their sin. Uriel informed him that they had transgressed the command of God, and should be bound there for 10,000 worlds, the number of the days of their guilt (xxi.). In the course of his wanderings, he 'went to the middle of the earth, and saw a blessed and fruitful place, where there were branches which struck root and sprouted out of a tree that had been hewn down.'[1] A geographical description

---

[1] The fallen tree must denote the Israelites. Another reading, however, gives the sense of 'planted trees,' so that the description would refer merely to the fruitfulness of the place. See Dillmann *in loco*.

follows, by which Jerusalem is unmistakeably identified; and he is told by Uriel, in answer to his inquiry about one of the valleys, that 'this accursed valley' is destined for those who shall be cursed for ever, and that for the punishment of the wicked those who find pity shall praise the Lord, the eternal king (xxvi.–xxvii.). Towards the end of this section, he relates how he saw in the east the ends of the earth, whereon the heaven rests, and the gates of heaven; and he then proceeds in these words (which are important for the criticism of the book): 'I saw how the stars of heaven come forth, and counted the gates out of which they come, and wrote down all their exits, of each one separately, according to their number, their names, their connection, their position, their time and their months, as the angel Uriel who was with me showed me. He showed me everything, and wrote it down for me; also he wrote down their names for me, and their laws, and their functions' (xxxiii.). In the three short chapters that remain, he tells how he saw in the north the three gates of the north wind, in the west three gates answering to those in the east, in the south the three gates of the south wind; and returning to the east, he praised the Lord of glory.

The second part, formally introduced as above stated, includes chapters xxxvii.–lxxi. (pp. 18–41). The characteristic contents of this part may be described generally, as relating to the ideal future. The writer himself divides it into three 'similitudes,' or figurative addresses. The first extends from xxxviii. to xliv. inclusive (18–22). In this Enoch describes the heavenly abodes of the righteous, speaks of the four angels of the highest God, and refers to 'all the secrets of heaven,' thunder and lightning, winds, clouds and dew, hail and mist, sun and moon. With his notice of these things he interweaves moral reflections; and he finds in the stars, so faithful in their relations to one another, an image of the righteous who dwell on earth, and believe on the name of the Lord of the spirits to all eternity.

The second figurative address (xlv.–lvii. 22–28) relates to the future judgment, with its consequences to righteous and unrighteous, and treats particularly of the person and office of the 'Son of man.' The details of this portion, as they will be the subject of special criticism, may be reserved for future consideration. It should be noticed, however, that chapters liv. and lv. refer to the flood as 'the penal judgment of the Lord of the spirits,' and as destined to take place 'in those days.'

The third address (lviii.–lxix. 28–40) professes to be about the righteous and the elect; but various matters are spoken of, and the connection is not very carefully observed. We must notice particularly that in ch. lxv. Noah is introduced and becomes the narrator; and this Noachic section extends into ch. lxix. (35–40). In ch. lx. also, Noah is evidently the speaker (*see* v. 8), though his name does not occur.

The two following chapters (lxx., lxxi. 40, 41) form a conclusion for the whole Book of Similitudes. Enoch is declared to be 'the son of man who has been born to righteousness,' on whom 'righteousness dwells,' and whom 'the righteousness of the Head of days does not forsake;' and he is assured that in the future world the righteous shall dwell with him for ever and ever.

With lxxii. (p. 42) another division of the work clearly begins, for it is marked by its own separate title, which runs thus:—'The book about the revolution of the lights of heaven, how each is circumstanced, according to their classes, according to their dominion and their time, according to their names and places of nativity, and according to their months, which their leader, the holy angel Uriel who was with me, showed me; and their whole description, how they are circumstanced, he showed me, and how all the years of the world are circumstanced for ever, until the new creation which endures for ever is created.' The range of this title seems to me to extend to the close of xci., for the latter part of it may fairly be applied to the historical visions, and there is nothing like a fresh title till we reach xcii. We may, however, conveniently follow Dillmann's arrangement, according to which lxxii.-lxxxii. (42-53) constitute a third division, which again distributes itself into three sections.

The first of these, lxxii.-lxxv. (42-47) treats of the sun and moon. We need not dwell on the details of this portion, which are to a great extent founded on observation. Some of the inferences, however, are not very sound. The author clearly regards the earth as a disk, over which rises the solid hemisphere of the sky, with its gates and windows. The wind drives the chariots of the sun, which at night returns by the north from west to east. We should observe that the longest day is represented as being exactly twice the length of the night (lxxii. 14).

The mention of the apertures 'for the winds and the spirit of the dew,' prepares us for the second section (lxxvi., lxxvii. 47, 48), which relates to the winds, and brings in an allusion to seven mountains, rivers, and islands.

The third section (lxxviii.-lxxxii., 49-53) returns to the sun and moon, and gives their names and their relation to one another. After Uriel had shown all the heavenly secrets to Enoch, he told him that 'in the days of the sinners' everything on earth should be changed, and the moon no longer appear at its proper times; and having done so, he desired him to 'observe the writing of the heavenly tablets, and mark every particular.' Enoch states that he did so, and 'read the book and all its contents, all the deeds of men, and all born of the flesh who shall be upon the earth until the remotest generations.' When he had praised the Lord, 'those three holy ones' brought him and set him on the earth before the door of his house, and told him that he should be left for a year, during which time he was to teach Methuselah and all his children. In lxxxii., which might, I think, be as appropriately reckoned in the next division, Enoch begins an address to Methuselah, which he opens by desiring him to keep the writings which he gives him, and hand them down to coming generations; and then, in connection with the writings, he returns once more to the heavenly bodies. This last circumstance furnishes a plausible reason for connecting this chapter with those which have preceded; but its ambiguous position confirms our remark that there is no real pause in the narrative at this place.

The fourth division (lxxxiii.–xci. 53–67) describes two visions which Enoch saw before he 'took a wife,' and which he relates in continuation of his address to Methuselah. This part also may be divided into three sections. The first two chapters (lxxxiii., lxxxiv. 53–55) contain the first vision, in which he saw the earth swallowed up in a great deep, and Enoch's prayer that some of his posterity might be spared. Chapters lxxxv–xc. (55–65) contain the second vision, in which the world's history is symbolically described down to its great consummation. As the question of date depends largely on the interpretation of this vision, we need not dwell further upon it at present. A third section is formed by xci. 1–11, and contains a hortatory address of Enoch to his children, founded on the previous visions. The rest of this chapter, unless we except the last two verses, which may belong to the previous passage, refers to the eighth and succeeding weeks of the world's history, and seems evidently to have been misplaced,—unless, indeed, this remark should be applied rather to its preceding context, which is found in xciii.

The fifth division (xcii.–cv. 67–77) is said to be 'written by Enoch the writer,' and to contain the doctrine of wisdom, and is mainly hortatory in its character. He predicts the resurrection of the just and the disappearance of sin; but after a very short chapter, xciii. states that 'Enoch began to give an account out of the books,' and to relate what had appeared to him in the heavenly vision, and what he had learned out of the tablets of heaven. Then follows the description of the world's weeks, to which the fragment in xci. obviously belongs. Next come the admonitions, in which at first he alternately exhorts the righteous and denounces woe upon the wicked (xciv.–xcvii. 68–71). He then addresses himself to the sinful (xcviii.–cii. 71–75), and finally in words of advice and consolation to the righteous (cii. 4–cv. pp. 75–77). In the last-mentioned section he swears in the most solemn manner that he knows the secret of which he speaks, and has seen the book of the holy ones, and thereon it was written that all good and joy and honour were prepared for the spirits of those who have died in righteousness, and therefore the righteous were to have no fear. For a moment near the end he turns to warn the sinners that light and darkness, day and night, see all their sins. His last secret is that 'to the righteous and wise will the books be given for joy and righteousness and much wisdom; to them will the books be given, and they will believe on them and rejoice in them, and all the righteous who have learned therefrom all the ways of righteousness shall receive the reward.' A few lines put into the mouth of the Lord close the section. In these are the words, 'for I and my Son will join ourselves with them for ever and ever.'

The book might seem now to have reached its close; but unexpectedly Enoch proceeds to relate the circumstances attending the birth of Noah, and to describe the supernatural appearance of the infant and his own prediction of the deluge (cvi., cvii. 78, 79). Lastly comes 'another writing which Enoch wrote for his son Methuselah, and for those who shall come after him, and observe the law in the last days.' Here he seems to be again on his journey with the angels, and he sees a place of burning fire destined for the spirits of the sinful, of those 'who do evil and alter all that God spoke through the mouth of the prophets about future things.' He is also told of the blessings of the righteous; and with a brief contrast between the shining of the righteous and the darkness into which the wicked shall be thrown the book closes.

From the above survey of the contents it is apparent that, while our opinion about the date of the work depends mainly on our interpretation of the fourth division (including the fragment about the world's weeks in the fifth), the most important Messianic passages are contained in the second; and therefore our first question is whether the second and fourth parts proceed from the same author, and if not, whether there is anything to prove that the second is earlier than the fourth. Now, in regard to the authorship of the whole work, three distinct views may be entertained. It may be supposed that the book is the production of a single author, and has been preserved in its integrity down to our own time; or, secondly, that it is substantially from one author, but has been more or less corrupted by later interpolations; or thirdly, that it consists of a series of tracts from different hands, pieced together into one work by a compiler.

The first view is maintained by Philippi.[1] This writer bases his conclusion upon the unity of plan which pervades the several parts of the work; but I cannot think that he contributes much to the criticism of the subject, or adequately meets the difficulties which stand in the way of his theory; and as his volume has left no permanent impression upon the literature of the question, we need not further consider it.[2]

Of the second view we may take Dillmann as the representative. He also infers the substantial unity of authorship from the unity of plan, and from the fact that there is throughout a natural progress and an inartificial transition from one part to another; and he endeavours to establish this view by a careful analysis of the contents, and by tracing the relation of each part to the general aim of the writer.[3] He seeks, however, to distinguish from the original work some considerable interpolations. First, he classes together as 'historical additions,' which he ascribes collectively to the same later author, the following passages:—vi.-xvi. relating to the fall of the angels and subsequent events, which he thinks have taken the place of a rejected section of the original work; xciii. and xci. 12-17, describing the weeks of the world's history;

---

[1] *Das Buch Henoch, sein Zeitalter und sein Verhältniss zum Judasbriefe.* 1868.

[2] Philippi was preceded by Hofmann in the ascription of the book to a Christian author. See Schürer's *Lehrbuch der neutestamentlichen Zeitgeschichte,* 1874, S. 525. Hofmann's views are expressed in an article in the *Zeitschr. der deutschen morgenländ. Gesellsch.* Bd. vi. 1852, S. 87-91 (Schürer, S. 521).

[3] *Das Buch Henoch,* Einleitung, S. i.-xxxiv. For a summary of his arguments, see S. v. vi. xxxiii. xxxiv.

and cvi., cvii., about the birth of Noah.[1] He believes that a still later interpolator inserted the 'Noachic additions,' liv. 7–lv. 2, lx., and lxv.–lxix. 25, relating to the flood. To the same author he attributes lxx., and either to the same author, or at least to the same circle of thought, xx., upon the names of the angels; lxxxii. 9–20, relating to the regulation of the stars and the seasons; and lxxv. 5, about the winds and dew. Finally, he ascribes cviii. to yet another hand.[2] It is not necessary for us to follow him through the details of his argument. We may admit at once that a general survey of the work brings before us a sufficient unity of plan to suggest a prevailing identity of authorship. But, on the other hand, the concatenation of thought is not so close that it is impossible to leave out any considerable section without rendering the remainder of the book unintelligible. Dillmann himself admits that the work has been subject to serious tampering in the way both of interpolation and of omission. We may remark also that compositions of this kind, which are really anonymous, though flung upon the world in the name of some ancient worthy, and which are designed, not to win a literary reputation, but to accomplish some political or religious purpose, are much more likely than literature of a higher class, and published with the author's name, to be dealt with freely, and altered to suit the wants of successive times. The fact, moreover, that Georgius Syncellus quotes 'from the first book of Enoch,' a passage which is not contained in the Æthiopic translation, is an external evidence that the work was not secure against serious variations in its transmission. We must, therefore, judge each section upon its own merits; and if we find traces of different dates or conflicting opinions, we shall hardly feel that the general

---

[1] S. vii., viii. and xxxiv.–xxxviii.   [2] S. viii. ix. and xxxviii–xl.

thread of connection is such as to justify us in driving these into forced reconciliation.[1]

Ewald is the most celebrated supporter of the third view.[2] According to him the Similitudes (xxxvii.–lxxi.) are the earliest portion of the complex work. They, however, comprise only part of the original treatise, and have been interpolated by the compiler with sections from later writings. The interpolated passages are the following:—xxxix. 1–2a, liv. 7–lv. 2, lx. 1–10, 24, 25, lxiv.–lxix. 14.[3] The second of the three parts he believes to have been more fully preserved than the other two, which have suffered from abbreviations. Some passages are shown by their present want of connection to have been transposed.[4] He confidently assigns the priority to this book, not on account of any marks of date which it contains, but purely on grounds of literary estimate, on account of the freshness of its inspiration, and the creative power manifested in its thought and language. He observes also that the writer's threats are directed against the outward enemies of the people; and these naturally belong to an earlier period than warnings against internal dissentions and corruption. The second author directed his composition against the inward foes, and, for an example suitable to his purpose, turned to the story of the

---

[1] Dillmann himself retracted this view at a later time, and admitted that after the withdrawal of the Noachic portions, the remainder of the book must have been made up out of at least two, if not three writings. In doing so he accepted Ewald's opinion that the Similitudes are the earliest work, and proceeded from the first decade of the Asmonæans. The whole work in its present form he believes to be pre-Christian, as there is no reference to the power of the Romans. See his article, 'Pseudepigraphen des A.T.' in Herzog's *Encyklopädie*, vol. xii., 1860, S. 309; and his article 'Henoch,' in Schenkel's *Bibel-Lexikon*, vol. iii. 1871, S. 12, 13.

[2] See his *Abhandlung über des äthiopischen Buches Henokh Entstehung, Sinn, und Zusammensetzung*, 1854. *Geschichte des Volkes Israel*, iv. S. 451 sq., dritte Ausgabe, 1864.

[3] *Abh.* S. 14, Anm.   [4] *Abh.* S. 18.

giants. The work, as far as can be gathered from its present mutilated and interpolated condition, comprised an introduction, i –v. ; an account of the fall of the angels, vi. 1, 2, vii. 1–6, viii. 4, ix. 1–6, 8–11, x. 4–10, 12–xi. 2, xii.–xvi. ; a transition section, the fragment of Georgius Syncellus not found in the Æthiopic text, lxxxi. 1–4, and lxxxiv; and lastly, what Ewald calls the second half, xci. 3–cv., which, though nearly in their original connection, are not without a few transpositions. Ewald believes that this writer betrays an intimate acquaintance with the previous one ; but he gives hardly any evidence in support of his view, and adduces much more striking instances of independence than of imitation.[1] A third author undertook to explain the secrets of creation ; but we possess only the remnants of his great work, entitled, 'Book of discourses of Enoch to his son Methuselah.' These remnants are xx.–xxxvi. ; lxxiii.–lxxxii. (with the exception of lxxxi. 1–4 ; by no means without mutilations and transpositions, and wanting the whole second half of the book on the 'lights of heaven'); lxxxiii.–xc. (in which lxxxiv. is borrowed from the second author); and cvi., cvii. This third work received from a later hand cviii. The partial dependence of this book on the two previous ones is affirmed rather than proved.[2] The circle of Enoch-books is now fully described ; but in imitation of these a later author composed a Noah-book, for the purpose of drawing a comparison between the primitive judgment by the deluge and the final judgment of the world. Fragments of this work are found scattered through our present Book of Enoch. They are vi. 3–8, ix. 1, 7, x. 1–3, 11. 22b, (in ix. 1 only the names of the angels), liv. 7–lv. 2, xvii.–xix., lx. 1–10, 24, 25, lxiv. lxv.–lxix. 1, and lxix. 2–16a, (which was originally nearer the beginning). The author made use

[1] *Abh.*, S. 40.   [2] *Abh.*, S. 55, 56.

of the three Enoch-books, but principally the first, which he diligently endeavours to imitate in his diction.¹ Lastly, our present work was compiled by an author who was anxious to preserve what was most important in the books just enumerated, and to add some little of his own. Ewald ingeniously traces the mode of his compilation, and the grounds for his selection of the various parts.² This work obtained the public favour, and the originals sank into disuse and disappeared.

The above criticism of Ewald's does not appear to me calculated to carry conviction to the mind. The evidences of the separate authorship of the several fragments are not very cogent. It seems extremely unsafe to determine the relative dates of a series of writings merely by their literary characteristics. One cannot see why the most original in style and thought should be necessarily the most original in time; and it is not alleged that there are such plain references from one to another as to place the question of priority beyond reasonable doubt. The one result that appears to be established with some degree of certainty is this: that the present Æthiopic text does not correctly represent the earliest Book of Enoch; but that this book, whatever may have been its compass, has been subjected to both omissions and interpolations. If this be so, we can feel but little confidence in the genuineness of casual expressions; and I think it is quite arbitrary to assume that the work of the pre-Christian compiler has remained untouched, and to maintain the integrity, for instance, of the clause in which the Messiah is styled 'the Word.'³ As the book was principally used by the Christians of the earlier centuries, and as we owe its preservation to a Christian Church, it surely may have borrowed something from the medium of its transmission,

---

[1] *Abh.*, S. 58.   [2] *Abh.*, S. 65, *sq.*   [3] *Abh.*, S. 55, Anm. 1.

even if we do not suppose the original documents to have been exposed to such violent treatment as Ewald's theory suggests.

In this connection the views of one of the most recent writers on the subject, B. Tideman,[1] deserve to be noticed. His chief contribution[2] to the criticism of the work consists in his suggestion that chapters lxxxiii.–xci., in which is included the historical vision, do not belong to the original book, but were added not many years after its first publication by an Essenic writer. His argument turns chiefly on the fact that Enoch is said to have had the dreams which he relates in these chapters before he was taken up into heaven, and thus the natural order is disturbed by a new and unexpected narrative. Enoch had just seen 'all the deeds of men' described upon the 'heavenly tablets,' and we expect his predictions of the future destinies of mankind to be based on what he had there read. Now this expectation is fulfilled in xciii., where he begins to forecast the events of the successive weeks of the world's history in accordance with what he had learned 'from the tablets of heaven.' If, therefore, we simply omit the dream-visions, the connection is restored. These chapters are also said to be in some respects inconsistent with other portions of the work. In the earlier part of the book Enoch first obtains his supernatural knowledge when he is taken up to heaven; whereas here he speaks of dreams that he had before he

[1] See his article, 'De Apocalypse van Henoch en het Essenisme,' in the *Theologisch Tijdschrift*, Mei 1875.

[2] I learn, however, from Schürer (*Lehrb. der neut. Zeitg.* S. 528) that Sieffert, whose treatise I have not seen, regarded lxxxii.–xc. as an interpolation, composed in 108 B.C. Sieffert's treatise is entitled, *Nonnulla ad apocryphi libri Henochi originem et compositionem necnon ad opiniones de regno Messiano eo prolatas pertinentia*. Regimonti Pr. 1867. It will be remembered also that Ewald regards the dream-vision as later than the revelation of the weeks.

was married, and apparently in his childhood. According to the first chapter [1] the judgment was to be held on Mount Sinai; but here the spot selected is 'the lovely land,' Palestine.[2] And again, the rejection of the second temple at the time of the judgment [3] is hardly consistent with the description in xci. 13, where it is said that in the eighth week 'a house shall be built to the great king for ever and ever.' This last difficulty, however, is not very serious, for in both passages the ideal temple suited to the Messianic period is spoken of, and its erection implies the previous disappearance of the old one. In regard to the judgment, too, it should be observed that in the account of the weeks several judgments are mentioned. In the eighth week a sword shall be given to the righteous to execute judgment upon the wicked. In the ninth 'the righteous judgment' shall be manifested to the whole world. And towards the end of the tenth week the judgment for ever, which shall be held upon the watchers, shall take place.[4] Now only a single judgment, preparatory to the Messianic time, is mentioned in the dream-vision; and as this was intended specially for the benefit of the Israelites, it is naturally represented as taking place in Palestine.[5] The other difficulties are more serious, and may at least induce us to hesitate before we accept the dream-vision as part of the original treatise. The decision of this question is not important; for if the historical vision does not belong to the context in which it is found, it is certainly a later interpolation, and there-

---

[1] i. 4. [2] xc. 20. [3] xc. 28. [4] xci. 12–15.

[5] Köstlin escapes the difficulty by supposing that the mountain in the south was only the place where God would descend to the earth, but not the spot where the judgment would be held. See his articles, 'Ueber die Entstehung des Buchs Henoch,' in the *Theologische Jahrbücher*, Tübingen, 1856; S. 257. It must be confessed, however, that it requires some forcing to harmonize the picture of a single judgment with that of three widely separated from one another. See Köstlin, S. 257 *sq.*

fore its date fixes a chronological limit for the earliest work.

We need not criticise the other parts of Tideman's view, but simply present a summary of his conclusions. The oldest book contains i.–xvi.; xx.–xxxvi.; lxxii.–lxxxii.; xciii.; xci. 12–19; xcii.; xciv.–cv., and is from the hand of a Pharisee, between 153 and 135 B.C. The second book comprises lxxxiii.–xci., and is the work of an Essene between 134 and 106 B.C.[1] Thirdly comes an Apocalypse of Noah, xvii.–xix.; xli. 3–9; xliii. 1, 2; xliv.; liv. 7–lv. 2;[2] lix.; lx.; lxv.–lxix. 25; lxx.; cvi.; cvii. This was written after 80 A.D. by a person versed in the Jewish Gnosticism and the Cabbala.[3] The Similitudes, including xxxvii.–lxxi. with the exception of the parts belonging to the Apocalypse of Noah, are from a Christian of the days of Domitian or Trajan, 90–100 A.D. Lastly comes the final redactor, the author of cviii., a Christian Gnostic of the tendency of Saturninus, after 125 A.D.

In regard to a book which is all but universally admitted to have been seriously tampered with, it is impossible to feel great confidence in the detailed distribution of its parts among several authors. I think, how-

---

[1] The supposition that the writer was an Essene is founded on the contempt which he displays for the second temple (p. 279-280). But this contempt may have been felt by others besides Essenes, and certainly the language of Enoch is not stronger than that of the prophet Malachi, i. 7 sq. Tideman might also have referred to the fact that Enoch is said to have had the dreams before his marriage (lxxxiii. 2), as though there were some connection between celibacy and the power of prediction. If in these indications we may detect an Essenic tendency, yet far stronger evidence would be required to justify us in regarding these chapters as an emanation from one of the separatist communities, and as a trustworthy expression of the hopes and fancies of the Essenes.

[2] I give what seems to be intended: but there are a few misprints in the numbers.

[3] To which he ascribes the statements about Leviathan and Behemoth in lx. See p. 288.

ever, that we may fairly accept Tideman's arrangement of the original book as substantially correct.[1] For practical purposes we may include with this the dream-visions, which, at all events, belong very nearly to the same period; and in proceeding to discuss the date of the earliest work we must attend first and chiefly to the long historical vision, which contains the clearest intimations on the subject. The origin and date of the Similitudes will be reserved for separate consideration.

The vision[2] traces the history of mankind, so far as it is connected with that of the Israelites, from the time of Adam down to the great consummation of human affairs. The chosen people are represented symbolically in the form of sheep, and their enemies appear as various wild animals. Down to the time of the Captivity the allusions are easily understood; but from this point the description is much more obscure. Shortly before the destruction of Jerusalem the Lord of the sheep called seventy shepherds, and committed to them the sheep, with instructions to destroy as many as they were ordered. It was, however, foreseen that they would exceed their instructions; and the Lord, accordingly, 'called another,' and desired him to keep a book, and to enter how many sheep every shepherd killed by order, and how many for his own pleasure. This account was to be kept secret from the shepherds, but to be laid before the Lord. Then follows a plain allusion to the destruction of Jerusalem, and the sufferings of the Captivity; and afterwards 'the book was read before the Lord of the sheep,

---

[1] His results, with the exception of the removal of the dream-visions, agree closely with those obtained by the careful examination of Köstlin, who supposes the original book to have contained i.-xvi., xxi.-xxxvi., lxxii.-cv., l. c. S. 249-264. Hi'genfeld, in his *Jüd. Apok.*, accepts this arrangement, except that he includes chapter xx.

[2] lxxxv.-xc.

and he took the book in his hand, and read it, and sealed it, and laid it down.'[1] At that time the shepherds had tended for twelve hours; and immediately follows a reference to the return from the Captivity and the rebuilding of Jerusalem and the Temple, or 'high tower,' as the latter is called. But this was a mere nominal 'high tower,' and all the bread on the table before it was defiled. The eyes of the sheep were blinded, and many were given up to be destroyed by the shepherds, and they all scattered themselves on the field, and mixed themselves with the wild animals. Then the writer again brought the book to the Lord, who took it and laid it down. In this way thirty-six (or thirty-five)[2] shepherds tended the sheep; and afterwards 'others received them into their power.' The animals that tormented them are now represented as birds of prey led by the eagles. These birds devoured the sheep until twenty-three shepherds had fulfilled their commission, and so completed 'fifty-eight times.' From this point commences the work of recovery. 'Little lambs were born from those white sheep, and they began to open their eyes.'[3] At first they cried in vain to the sheep, and the ravens flew upon them, and took one of them. Horns grew upon them, which the ravens threw down, until a great horn grew, and at last the eyes of the sheep were opened. Then began a terrible conflict; but the ravens could effect nothing against that horn. In answer to a cry for help 'that man who wrote down the names of the shepherds' came to the assistance of the young ram; and finally the Lord of the sheep himself came in anger, while the birds

---

[1] lxxxix. 71.

[2] The number here, which in the Æthiopic is either 36 or 37, is probably corrupt, as the addition of 23 is said to raise the total to 58; xc. 5. The division of the seventy apparently is meant to be 12 + 23 + 23 + 12.

[3] xc. 6.

of prey were aided in their war by 'all the sheep of the field.' We have now clearly entered on the apocalyptic portion of the dream; and it is generally agreed that the interpretation of the great horn must decide the date of the author.

In the explanation of this dream, we may regard it as certain that the seventy shepherds cannot include the native rulers of the Israelites, but refer exclusively to the period of heathen domination. The former view was, indeed, maintained by Laurence,[1] who was followed by Hoffmann[2] and Gfrörer;[3] but the time at which the shepherds are introduced is inconsistent with this supposition, and one cannot readily believe that the most theocratic of Jewish writers would consign all the kings after Solomon indiscriminately to the fiery abyss.[4] With the rejection of this interpretation, we abandon also the ascription of the book to the time of Herod the Great. Far more probable is the view supported by Ewald[5] and Dillmann,[6] that the author belongs to the time of John Hyrcanus, 135–106 B.C.[7] The seventy shepherds are divided by the writer himself into three groups, by his references to the books in which their names were kept. The first group lasts for twelve hours; and as each shepherd has his fixed time, twelve shepherds must be included in the group. These may be found in five Assyrian, three Chaldæan, and four Egyptian kings. The next group brings us to the end of thirty-six, or, as it probably ought to be, thirty-five shepherds, who completed each his time. The second group, therefore, consists of twenty-three, re-

---

[1] Prelim. Dissertation, p. xxxii. sq.
[2] *Das Buch Henoch*, Einleit. S. 24–5.
[3] *Das Jahrhundert des Heils*, 1838; Erste Abth. S. 96 sq.
[4] See xc. 25.   [5] *Abhandlung*, S. 41 sq., esp. S. 54. See also S. 76.
[6] Comment. *in loco*.
[7] In the synopsis of their views I omit minor differences.

presenting twenty-three kings of the Persian period. The remaining thirty-five, who are so expressly marked as different from the others, must stand for the Græco-Macedonian dominion. These again are subdivided into twenty-three—the Ptolemies, the Seleucids, and the Macedonian kings, down to the time of Antiochus Epiphanes—and twelve, the Syrian line from the last-named king, to the second reign of Demetrius II. The lambs, then, are the Chasidim, or pious men, who rose against this tyrannical power. The horned lambs are the Maccabæan leaders. The lamb that was taken away by the ravens is Jonathan, who in 143 B.C. was treacherously seized by Tryphon, and afterwards put to death. The horns that were thrown down refer not only to the event just mentioned, but to the defeat and death of Judas, and the murder of Simon, which was perpetrated in the Syrian interest. The great horn is John Hyrcanus; and in Dillmann's opinion, various indications, on which we need not pause, prove that the writer had lived through the greater part of his reign.

The above explanation, taken in its broad outlines, appears to give a suitable account of the author's meaning. I think, however, that Schürer (following Hofmann)[1] is right in regarding the shepherds not as heathen kings, but as angels appointed to superintend the punishment of the Israelites by their enemies. Throughout the rest of the vision, human beings are represented under the forms of lower animals, and only angels are dignified with the appearance of men.[2] Accordingly here the heathen powers are presented under the figure of beasts and birds. The shepherds cannot be their successive kings, for they are all summoned contemporaneously before God to receive their commission.[3] The

---

[1] *Lehrb. d. n. Zeitg.* S. 531 *sq.*   [2] See lxxxvii. 2.   [3] lxxxix. 59.

angel, moreover, who was to keep account of the number of sheep that were destroyed, is called simply 'another,' as though he belonged to the same class as the shepherds. The latter, having failed in their duty, are, like the fallen angels, condemned to the fiery depth. It is needless, therefore, to find out seventy historical kings (and no seventy can be found reigning in succession for equal periods); but we may rest satisfied with the more general features of the historical portraiture.[1]

The description of the ten weeks of the world's history may also be so explained as to lead us to the Maccabæan period. The limits of the first six weeks are marked with unmistakable clearness. Enoch was 'born as the seventh in the first week.' In the second week should take place 'the first end' (the flood), and 'a man' (Noah) should be rescued. There is nothing here to mark the close of the week. At the end of the third a man (Abraham) should be chosen, and after him should come

[1] Hilgenfeld accepts in the main the view of Ewald and Dillmann. He believes, however, that John Hyrcanus is referred to in xc. 13, as already belonging to the past, and therefore places the composition of this portion of the book in the early part of the reign of Jannæus Alexander, 105-79 B.C. (*Jüd. Apok.* S. 145, Anm. 2). I fail to see how his inference is supported by the verse to which he appeals.

The view that the historical vision was composed in the time of John Hyrcanus is accepted by Anger, *Vorlesungen über die Geschichte der messianischen Idee*, 1873, S. 83; Hausrath, *Neutestamentliche Zeitgeschichte*, erster Theil, 2te Auflage, 1873, S. 166; Holtzmann, *Judenthum und Christenthum im Zeitalter der apokryphischen und neutestamentlichen Literatur*, 1867, S. 202; Keim, *Geschichte Jesu von Nazara*, i. 1867, S. 241; Köstlin, *l. c.* S. 264; Lücke (in his latest view) *Einl. in die Offenb.* S. 1072; Oehler, 'Messias,' in Herzog's *Encyk.* ix., 1858, S. 427; Schenkel ('towards the end of the second century before Christ'), *Bibel-Lexikon*, iv., 1872, S. 205; Schürer, *Lehrb. der neut. Zeity.*, S. 533; Kuenen, *Religion of Israel*, iii. p. 265; Tideman, *l. c.* p. 277; Colani, *Jésus-Christ et les Croyances Messianiques de son Temps*, deuxième édition, 1864, p. 26.

Wittichen, *Die Idee des Reiches Gottes*, 1872, thinks that Judas Maccabæus is signified by the great horn (S. 126), and places this, which he considers the oldest part of the book, between 166 and 161 B C. (S. 120, in the note).

'the plant of righteousness,' (the chosen race in the person of Isaac). At the end of the fourth 'a law' (the Mosaic) should be given. At the end of the fifth 'the house of glory' (the temple of Solomon) should be built for ever. At the end of the sixth the house should be burned, and 'the whole race of the chosen root' be scattered (the Babylonian captivity). At the end of the seventh the elect should be rewarded. Here we pass from history into apocalyptic vision; and our problem, therefore, is to determine the duration of the seventh week. Now the great inequality in the length of the weeks shows that we must not reckon them by any fixed number of years. Our alternative course, suggested by the mention of Enoch as 'the seventh,' is to calculate by generations, counting seven to a week in the earlier times, and in the later, when the generations succeeded one another more rapidly, fourteen. The generations of the successive weeks may be exhibited thus:—First week, Adam to Enoch. Second, Methuselah to Eber. Third, Peleg to Isaac. Fourth, Jacob to Nahshon (one of the heads of the tribe of Judah in the time of Moses). Fifth, Salmon to Rehoboam. (Thus far seven generations to each week). Sixth, (by omitting, as is done in the genealogy in Matthew, Ahaziah, Joash, and Amaziah) fourteen generations from Abijam to Salathiel. Seventh, Joshua to Alcimus (160 B.C.). It will be observed that the terminations of the weeks correspond sufficiently with the genealogical arrangement to procure for this method of interpretation a high degree of probability. Dillmann, however, is not willing to accept Alcimus as the close of the series. He supposes that, on account of their friendship for the Greeks, the author would not include Jason, Menelaus, and Alcimus in the line of high-priests, and therefore substituted for them Jonathan, Simon, and John

Hyrcanus. We are thus conducted to the same reign as by the dream-vision.[1] The omission of three members of the line, however, throws some doubt upon the precise termination of the series, and Tideman[2] believes that the chronological limits must be found under Jonathan or Simon, 153–135 B.C. These slight differences of opinion are of very subordinate importance; and it is sufficient for our present purpose if we are able to conclude, as I think we may with some degree of confidence, that the original Book of Enoch was written in the latter half of the second century before Christ.

Notwithstanding the above exposition, which depends solely on the contents of the work itself, so eminent a critic as Volkmar has the hardihood to assert that the desire to retain the canonicity of the Epistle of Jude is 'the inner' and indeed 'the only ground for considering the Jewish book pre-Christian.'[3] One might with equal justice say that the inner ground of Volkmar's view was his violent prejudice against everything canonical, and his anxiety to make the writings of the New Testament as late as possible. He places the publication of the Book of Enoch in the first year of the revolt of Bar-Cochba, 132 A.D., immediately after R. Akiba had given in his adhesion to the movement.[4] He briefly suggests the following general indications of this late period: the fanaticism pervading the book, seen especially in xc. 20 *sq.*, relating to the punishment of the stars and the shepherds; the rejection of the offerings of the second temple as im-

---

[1] See Dillmann, S. 208 *sq.*   [2] *L. c.* p. 266.
[3] See his article entitled, 'Beiträge zur Erklärung des Buches Henoch nach dem äthiopischen Text,' in the *Zeitschrift der deutschen morgenländischen Gesellschaft*, Bd. xiv. 1860, S. 87–134. The quotation in the text is from S. 99. See also his *Eine neutestamentliche Entdeckung und deren Bestreitung, oder die Geschichts-Vision des Buches Henoch im Zusammenhang*, 1862.
[4] *Beitr.* S. 100.

pure, which is intelligible only after the destruction of the temple by the heathen; the connection of the mysteries of stars and spirits with the beginning of the Cabbala in the book Jezirah, which points in its foundation to Akiba's Halachah; the doctrine of angels and demons, which cannot be proved to be earlier than the second century; and many approximations to Christian views of that time.[1] In regard to these considerations we may observe that the fanaticism is quite as suitable to the Maccabæan period; that in regard to the state of opinion the question is not whether the views in the book cannot be shown to be earlier than the second century, but whether they can be shown not to be earlier; and in reference to the second temple, its destruction by the heathen was no more complete than that of the first, and consequently afforded no reason for making a distinction between the two.

Volkmar's chief argument, however, rests on his interpretation of the seventy shepherds. He lays emphasis on the fact that the shepherds were each to have a fixed time,[2] and concludes that they must therefore represent seventy periods of heathen power. The mode in which he determines the length of these periods must be presented in his own words:—'It follows from 10 into 70, as from the nature of the thing in reign-periods in a longer succession, that these are to be thought of on the whole as ten years.'[3] He has another proof farther on. The seventy periods must have been seventy Epiphanes-periods, and Epiphanes reigned ten years and a little over.[4]

[1] S. 99, 100. [2] lxxxix. 65, 68, 72; xc. 1, 5.
[3] S. 102. Perhaps the argument will be more convincing in German:—
'Führt aber das Orakel des Jeremia näher gefasst auf "70 Hirten" Zeiten, so ergiebt sich aus der 10 in 70 selbst, wie aus der Natur der Sache bei Regierungs-Zeiten in einer längern Aufeinanderfolge, dass diese (über die Danielsche 7 Zahl hin) im Ganzen zu 10 Jahren zu denken sind.'
[4] S. 110.

The period, then, is not exactly ten years, but ten years and a little over. Starting with the year 588 B.C., as the date of the destruction of Jerusalem, he makes the first 'twelve hours' represent 130 years, and we thus reach the time of Ezra's return, 458 B.C. To this period answers the last, from 6 to 132 A.D., in which the Jews were under the immediate government of Rome. Retaining the reading 'thirty-seven' in xc. 1., and dispensing with the 'little over,' he obtains 370 years, and so reaches the time when Antiochus the Great first conquered Palestine, 218 B.C. The second division has thirty-five shepherds, making in all seventy-two, and therefore we must take seventy as a round number. Three hundred and fifty years from 218 B.C. conduct us to 132 A.D. This division falls into three smaller periods. In the first the birds were led by the eagles, that is the Romans, who defeated Antiochus the Great at Magnesia in 190 B.C.; on whom Epiphanes was really dependent; and to whom Egypt was practically subject from the year 201 B.C. The second period includes the government of the sheep by the dogs of the eagle-shepherds [1]; and these dogs were the Maccabees, who made a treaty with Rome, and the Herods. Lastly comes the direct eagle government, which began in 6 A.D. Unfortunately this is placed in the dream at the end of fifty-eight shepherd-periods, which bring us only to the year 8 B.C. But Volkmar is at no loss. We have already seen that the thirty-seven periods of xc. 1. conduct us to 218 B.C. Add to these the twenty-three succeeding periods of verse 5, and we obtain 230 years, and arrive at 12 A.D. This year is too late; but combine the two methods of calculation, and we drop upon the required time, 6 A.D. The last twelve shepherds, who destroyed

---

[1] The language of the original, xc. 4, is,—'Those sheep were devoured by the dogs and eagles and kites.'

more of the sheep than their predecessors, he takes to denote not only periods but twelve Roman Emperors from Augustus to Hadrian—Galba, Otho, and Vitellius being counted as 'one interregnum of three usurpers.' By the man who wrote down the names of the shepherds, and came to help the young ram, generally supposed to be Michael, the guardian-angel of the Jews, he understands R. Akiba. This great Rabbi, in whom all earlier learning was united in an ideal form, came as one of the angels of God, and recognised Bar-Cochba as the Messianic King. We need not dwell upon Volkmar's exposition of minor circumstances, which may be equally suitable to either the earlier or the later revolt.

All this seems to me far more ingenious than convincing, and could be accepted only if we had clear independent evidence of the later date. It is inconsistent to assume that the shepherds represent equal periods, and then to make the last twelve stand for twelve emperors with reigns of most unequal duration. The mode in which he squeezes fourteen emperors into twelve, simply converts hypothesis into the arbiter of facts. The marvellous process of combination by which he extracts the year 6 of our æra, yields in reality the year 2. His periods also are stretched or shortened to suit his convenience. The period of ten years breaks down in its very first application, and has to be altered into ten years and a little over, in order, when multiplied by twelve, to produce 130; and in the last group of twelve periods the 'little over' has to be somewhat diminished, for we have only 126 years to account for. If we took the first measure as our standard, and reckoned 130 years to each group of twelve shepherds, Volkmar's dates would be quite astray, and for the whole time of seventy-two shepherds, instead of having 720 years we should have 780, and so reach 192 A.D. as the date of composition. Again, his statement that the direct eagle government is depicted in xc. 6 *sq.* is founded upon nothing in the text; for although the eagles are mentioned again in conjunction with the other birds, it is the ravens who are foremost in the attack, so much so that they are referred to separately as flying upon the lambs,[1] again as throwing down their horns,[2] and once more as fighting with the great horn while the eagles and other birds only come to help the ravens.[3] The notion that the Maccabees and the Herods are classed together as devouring dogs is not very easily entertained,[4] especially as even apostate Israelites are still represented as sheep. It seems also extremely improbable that the whole of the Greek period should be confounded with the Roman, and that the Roman eagles, though introduced as *leading* the birds, should afterwards leave the attack principally to the ravens; whereas, in the other explanation, in which the eagles are the Macedonian power,[5] and they, along with the vultures, the kites, and the ravens, are the four kingdoms into which, according to the Book of Daniel, the empire of Alexander was divided, the real historical order is substantially preserved. And lastly, it is in the highest degree unlikely that the great events of the Roman period should not be more distinctly and fully alluded to, and that while the early destruction of Jerusalem and the temple is expressly

---

[1] xc. 8.   [2] xc. 9.   [3] xc. 12, 13.

[4] See, however, the contemptuous allusion to the Maccabees as the offspring of slaves in the Assumption of Moses (v. 15 in Hilgenfeld's restoration of the Greek).

[5] As an evidence that the eagle is not necessarily a symbol of the Roman power we may refer to Sib. Or. iii. 611, where it is used to describe Antiochus Epiphanes:—"Ἔλθῃ δ' ἐξ 'Ασίης βασιλεὺς μέγας, αἰετὸς αἴθων. This image may, as Gfrörer (*Philo*, &c. ii. S. 150) suggests, be borrowed from Deut. xxviii. 49, 'The Lord shall bring a nation against thee from far, from the end of the earth, as swift as the eagle flieth.' See also Hosea viii. 1, and Habak. i. 8. Compare Dan. vii. 4.

recorded,[1] the still recent and more appalling one under Titus should be passed over in total silence, and the reader be allowed to suppose that the second temple was to be removed by supernatural agency after the judgment had taken place. This latter circumstance alone may well be deemed conclusive.

I have no hesitation, therefore, in rejecting Volkmar's opinion; and I think we are within the bounds of reasonable probability in using the original Book of Enoch as a pre-Christian testimony to Jewish belief and expectations,—if at least we make this reservation, that we cannot place much dependence upon single and casual expressions.

We must now turn to the portion which contains the fullest Messianic doctrine, xxxvii.-lxxi. If this could be proved to be earlier than the part we have just examined, we should then, in accordance with the conclusion we have arrived at, be bound to accept it as a Jewish work from the second century before Christ. But against the literary judgment of Ewald we may set that of Lücke[2] and Köstlin,[3] that this section is among the later additions, though they still regard it as pre-Christian, the former placing it in the time of Herod the Great, the latter between 100 and 64 B.C.[4] If its later origin be conceded, the whole question of its date is open, and the solution must be sought solely in the indications presented by the section itself.

Now diversity of authorship seems to be indicated by several contrasts with other portions of the work. God

---

[1] lxxxix. 66.   [2] *Einl. in die Offenb.* i. S. 141 *sq.*
[3] *L. c.* S. 269, *sq.*
[4] *L. c.,* S. 275. His argument is founded on the reference to the Parthians and Medes in lvi. 5 *sq.*, as the representatives of heathen power in the final conflict with evil. He thinks the Parthians could not be referred to in this way except at a time when they were the only formidable power in the heathen world, a time therefore when the Syrian rule was in its decline and the might of Rome had not yet appeared upon the scene.

is distinguished by peculiar names. He is usually called 'the Lord of the spirits,' a designation which occurs here no less than 103 times, and not once in the rest of the book. Dillmann is indeed correct in saying that the name of God is varied according to the subject; and he believes that the writer selected this name in the Similitudes because they deal with the realm of spirits.[1] But there are several other places where so general a term would be equally appropriate; and it is difficult to believe that the same writer would have used it to satiety in about a quarter of his work and nowhere else. So far as this argument is valid, it tends to prove also the later origin of this section; for an imitator would hardly have avoided the title with such scrupulous care. The name 'the Head of days,' borrowed from the Book of Daniel, also occurs several times; but this might be sufficiently explained by the Messianic connection. The doctrine about angels is peculiar, chiefly in the appearance of Satan, who is apparently conceived as a spirit presiding over the world of evil prior to the fall of the angels.[2]

The Messianic doctrine is unfolded in a way which not only distinguishes this section from all the others, but very forcibly suggests the question whether it must not be, as Hilgenfeld supposes, of Christian origin. As we shall not recur to the descriptions which are here given, I will at once present them in the words of the book itself, taking the passages in the order in which they are there found. They begin almost at the opening of the second Similitude, which relates to 'those who deny the name of the dwellings of the holy ones, and of the Lord of the

---

[1] S. xxxiii. and 140.
[2] See especially liv. 6; xl. 7, and lxix. The peculiarities of this section are fully stated by Köstlin, *l. c.* S. 265 *sq.*

spirits.' 'On that day,' it is said, 'will the elect one sit on the throne of glory, and will hold a selection among their deeds and places without number; and their spirit will become strong within them when they see my elect one and those who have implored my holy and glorious name. And on that day will I cause mine elect one to dwell among them, and will transform the heaven, and make it an eternal blessing and light. And I will change the earth and make it a blessing, and cause mine elect ones to dwell on it; but those who commit sin and misdoing shall not set foot on it. For I have seen and satisfied with peace my righteous ones, and set them before me; but for sinners there is reserved with me a judgment, that I may destroy them from the surface of the earth. And there I saw one who had a head of days, and his head was white as wool; and beside him was another, whose countenance was as the appearance of a man, and his countenance was full of grace like one of the holy angels. And I asked one of the angels who went with me, and showed me all the hidden things, concerning that Son of man, who he was, and whence he was, why he went with the Head of days. And he answered me and spake to me: This is the Son of man, who has righteousness, with whom righteousness dwells, and who reveals all the treasures of that which is concealed, because the Lord of the spirits has chosen him, and his lot before the Lord of the spirits has surpassed everything through righteousness for ever. And this Son of man whom thou hast seen will stir up the kings and the mighty from their resting-places, and the violent from their thrones, and will loose the bridles of the violent and break the teeth of sinners. And he will thrust the kings from their thrones and out of their empires, because they exalt him not and praise him not, nor thankfully acknowledge whence the empire is lent to them.'¹ 'And in that place I saw a fountain of righteousness which was inexhaustible; and round about, many fountains of wisdom encircled it, and all who were thirsty drank out of them, and became full of wisdom, and had their dwellings with the righteous and holy and elect ones. And at that hour was that Son of man named in presence of the Lord of the spirits, and his name before the Head of days. And before the sun and the constellations were created, before the stars of heaven were made, was his name named before the Lord of the spirits. He will be a staff to the righteous and holy, that they may support themselves thereon and not fall, and he will be the light of the peoples, and the hope of those who are troubled in their heart. All who dwell upon earth shall fall down and pray before him, and shall celebrate and extol and sing praise to the name of the Lord of the spirits. And therefore was he elected and concealed before him ere the world was created, and unto eternity will he be before him. And the wisdom of the Lord of the spirits has revealed him to the holy and righteous, for he preserves the lot of the righteous, because they have hated and despised this world of unrighteousness, and have hated all its works and ways in the name of the Lord of the spirits; for in his name are they saved, and he becomes the avenger of their life.'² 'For wisdom is poured out as water, and glory ceases not before him from eternity to eternity. For he is mighty in all the secrets of righteousness, and unrighteousness shall pass away as a shadow, and have no continuance, because the elect one is risen up before the Lord of the spirits, and his glory is from eternity to eternity, and his might from generation to generation. In him dwells the spirit of wisdom, and the spirit of him

---

¹ xlv. 3-xlvi. 5.   ² xlviii. 1-7.

who gives insight, and the spirit of doctrine and of power, and the spirit of those who have fallen asleep in righteousness. And he will judge the concealed things, and no one will be able to deliver an idle speech before him, for he is elect before the Lord of the spirits according to his good pleasure.'[1] 'And in those days will the earth give back its trust, and the empire of the dead will give back its trust which it has received, and hell will give again what it owes. And he will choose the righteous and holy ones among them, for the day is come that they shall be saved. And the elect one will in those days sit upon his throne, and all the secrets of wisdom will stream from the thoughts of his mouth; for the Lord of the spirits has granted it to him, and glorified him. And in those days shall the mountains spring as rams, and the hills skip as lambs that are satisfied with milk; and they shall all become angels in heaven. Their face shall shine for joy, because in those days the elect one has risen up, and the earth shall rejoice, and the righteous shall dwell on it, and the elect go and walk on it.'[2] 'And after this [that is, according to the present connection, after the destruction of the kings and mighty of the earth] will the righteous and elect one cause the house of the assembly of his community to appear, which henceforth shall no more be hindered, in the name of the Lord of the spirits. And these mountains shall be before his face as the earth, and the hills shall be as a spring of water, and the righteous ones shall have rest from the oppression of sinners.'[3] 'God, the Lord of the spirits, says, Ye mighty kings who shall dwell upon earth, ye shall see mine elect one, how he sits on the throne of my glory, and judges Azâzêl and his whole company and all his hosts, in the name of the Lord of the spirits.'[4] 'These measures

[1] xlix.   [2] li.   [3] liii. 6, 7.   lv. 4.

[which had just been given to angels, and into the meaning of which Enoch had inquired] will reveal every thing that is concealed in the depth of the earth, and those who have perished through the wilderness, and who have been devoured by the fishes of the sea and by beasts, in order that they may return and support themselves upon the day of the elect one, for no one shall perish before the Lord of the spirits, and it will not be possible for any to perish.'[1] 'And the Lord of the spirits will set the elect one on the throne of his glory, and he will judge all the works of the holy ones in heaven,[2] and weigh their deeds with the balance.'[3] 'And one part of them [that is, of the kings and mighty men] will look at the other, and they shall be terrified and cast down their countenance, and pain shall seize them, when they see that Son of the woman sitting on the throne of his glory. And the kings, the mighty men, and all who possess the earth, shall celebrate and praise and extol him who rules over all, who was concealed. For formerly was the Son of man concealed, and the Highest has preserved him before his might, and has revealed him to the elect ones; and there shall be sown the community of the holy and elect ones, and all the elect ones shall stand before him on that day. And all the mighty kings, and the high, and those who rule over the solid earth, shall fall on their face before him, and pray, and set their hope on that Son of man, and supplicate him, and entreat compassion from him.'[4] 'And the Lord of the spirits shall dwell over them [the righteous] and with that Son of man shall they dwell together, and eat, and lay themselves down and rise up from eternity to eternity.'[5] At the end of a chapter in which the evil

---

[1] lxi. 5.
[2] This expression must, in conformity with its use elsewhere, denote the good angels.
[3] lxi. 8. [4] lxii. 5-9. [5] lxii. 14.

angels and the secrets of the oath through which the universe was created are spoken of at some length, occurs, obviously out of its connection,[1] the closing Messianic passage :—' And it became to them a great joy, and they praised and celebrated and extolled because to them was revealed the name of that Son of man. And he set himself on the throne of his glory, and the sum of the judgment was given over to him, the Son of man; and he causes the sinners and those who have led the world astray to pass off and be destroyed from the face of the earth. With chains are they bound, and at their assembling-place of destruction are they shut up, and all their works vanish from the face of the earth. And henceforth there will no more be anything transitory; for he, the Son of the man,[2] has appeared, and sits on the throne of his glory, and all evil shall vanish and pass away before his face; but the word of that Son of the man[2] shall prevail before the Lord of the spirits.'[3]

A few other verses may be more briefly noticed. 'The elect one' is spoken of also in xl. 5, where, in speaking of the four angels that he saw on the four sides of the Lord of the spirits, Enoch says that he heard the voice of the second 'praising the elect one and the elect ones;' in lii. 6 and 9, where it is said that certain mountains shall melt and vanish before him; and in lxii. 1, where the kings and mighty are desired to recognise him. The 'Son of man' is mentioned in lxiii. 11, where it is said that the face of the mighty kings shall be filled with darkness and shame before him; in lxx. 1, where the meaning of the text is doubtful, but which probably refers to the translation of Enoch ' to that Son of man,

---

[1] This is admitted by Dillmann, who would transfer the passage to the end of lxi.

[2] Der Sohn des Mannes, instead of the usual Menschensohn.

[3] lxix. 26-29.

to the Lord of the spirits,' thus implying the existence of the Son of man in the time of the Patriarch; and lastly, in lxxi. 17 (if the reference be certain), where it is promised that for the righteous there will be long life with that Son of man. The designation, 'the righteous one,' is found at the beginning of the first Similitude, xxxviii. 2,—'When the righteous one shall appear before the eyes of the elect righteous,' where, however, God might be referred to. The name 'his anointed' occurs in xlviii. 10, where it is said that the kings and violent men 'have denied the Lord of the spirits and his anointed;' and again in lii. 4, where the secret things of heaven and the mountains that Enoch had seen are said to serve the dominion of his anointed, that he may be powerful and mighty on the earth.

It cannot be denied that there is much in the above passages which reminds one of Christian ideas and expressions; but before considering on which side the dependence lies we may refer to two evidences of post-Christian date, which are insisted upon by Hilgenfeld.

In lvi. 5 *sq.* it is said that 'in those days will the angels assemble themselves, and direct their heads towards the east, towards the Parthians and Medes,' and that these 'shall march up and tread the land of their elect ones, and the land of his elect ones shall be before them a threshing-floor and a path;' that they shall wage war amongst one another, and no one shall know his brother, or father, or mother; and that finally the empire of the dead shall swallow up the sinners. Lücke,[1] following Laurence[2] and Hoffmann,[3] believes that this description must refer to the political events of the author's time, and that these can be found only in the Parthian invasion of Palestine about the year 40 B.C. He would therefore place

---

[1] *Einl. in die Offenb.* i. S. 125, *sq.*   [2] P. xxxvii. *sq.*
[3] *Das Buch Henoch*, Einleit. S. 26.

the composition of this portion of the book between 38 and 34 B.C., as after the latter year the expectation of the immediate end of the world would no longer have been entertained. But I think Dillmann [1] and Hilgenfeld [2] are right in supposing that the whole passage refers to the ideal future and to the last great conflict with the heathen powers. But why should these powers be represented by the Parthians and Medes? Dillmann can only suggest that they already formed the mightiest empire in the East and were well known in Palestine. But a Jewish writer was not likely to select the Parthians as the symbol of heathen wickedness and despotism at a time when they had not yet come into hostile contact with Palestine, and when his fellow-countrymen still looked upon the successors of Alexander the Great as the most formidable foes of their liberty and their religion. Hilgenfeld finds the explanation in the later belief that Nero, supposed to be dead, would return with the kings of the east against Rome, and then turn his arms against Jerusalem. The Roman Empire is indicated by the expression 'their elect ones,' that is, the elect of the angels of punishment mentioned at the beginning of the chapter. This certainly appears to afford a satisfactory explanation. But whatever doubts may attach to it, the passage seems to point decidedly to a later date than that which we have assigned to the historical dream. Although the Parthian empire originated in the middle of the third century before Christ, it is, as we have already remarked, most unlikely that the Jews would refer to it as the representative of oppressive heathen power before they had ever suffered from its attacks; and the mere occurrence of the word 'Parthians' is itself suggestive of a later time, for in the first Book of Maccabees their country still bears the name of Persia.[3]

---

[1] Com. *in loco*.   [2] *Jüd. Apok.* S. 169.
[3] xiv. 2. 'Ἀρσάκης ὁ βασιλεὺς τῆς Περσίδος καὶ Μηδείας.

A remarkable passage occurs in the Noachic section,[1] which, in the opinion of Hilgenfeld, points to a later date than 79 A.D.; and, if his argument be correct, the *compilation* at least of the Similitudes must fall within the Christian era. The Lord, according to the narrative, has just told Noah that the angels are preparing an ark for him, to preserve his family; and then Noah proceeds thus with his discourse: 'And they will enclose those angels who have shown unrighteousness in that burning valley which my grandfather, Enoch, had previously shown me in the west, beside the mountains of gold, and silver, and iron, and dropping-metal [probably lead], and tin. And I saw that valley, wherein was a great movement and the surging of waters. And when all this happened, a smell of sulphur was produced in that place out of that fiery molten metal and the movement which moved them [the waters]; and it united itself with those waters, and that valley of the angels who had led astray burns on under that earth. And through its valleys come forth streams of fire, at the place where those angels are punished who have seduced those that dwell upon the solid earth. But for the kings, and the mighty, and the high, and those who dwell on the solid earth, shall those waters serve in those days for the healing of the soul and the body, but for the punishment of the spirit, since their spirit is full of voluptuousness, in order that they may be punished in their body, because they have denied the Lord of the spirits, and daily see their punishment, and nevertheless do not believe on his name.' Now this passage expressly refers back to ch. lii., where the mountains of metals in the west are mentioned. In that chapter there is no reason to suppose that real mountains are intended, though Dillmann thinks that the notion may have been derived from

[1] lxvii. 4 *sq.*

the mining operations of the Phœnicians in Spain. In the present passage, however, an actual locality seems to be described; and Dillmann, followed by Köstlin,[1] believes that the region extending from the valley of Hinnom to the Dead Sea is the one referred to. That region was not without its medicinal springs; for Herod the Great, shortly before his death, made use of the warm baths at Kallirrhoe, the waters of which fell into the Dead Sea on its eastern side.[2] To this interpretation there are serious objections. The region in question was, as is expressly repeated, 'in the west;' but the Dead Sea lay to the east of Jerusalem, and could not be spoken of as in the west by any inhabitant of Palestine. A volcano seems to be referred to by the streams of fire. The kings and mighty of the earth were not in the habit of resorting to the baths of Palestine, and daily witnessing there any fearful phenomena; and the example which is appealed to is too late for the time assigned to the composition of the book by either of the above-named critics. And we may add that the baths at Kallirrhoe, instead of being impregnated with the sulphur with which the district abounds, are stated by Josephus to have been sweet enough for drinking purposes.[3] On the other hand, everything suits the country at the foot of Mount Vesuvius after the first eruption in 79 A.D. The scene is in the west; the kings, the mighty, and the high, planted their villas there, and abandoned themselves to voluptuous enjoyment; Baiæ was famed for its hot sulphur baths; and the adjoining mountain gave daily premonitions of a fiery judgment.[4]

Having thus traced this section of the work to the

[1] *L. c.* S. 383. He merely refers, with assent, to Ewald and Dillmann.
[2] Josephus, *Antiq.* xvii. 6, 5. *Bell. Jud.* i. 33, 5.
[3] *Bell. Jud. l. c.* ὑπὸ γλυκύτητος δ' ἐστὶ καὶ πότιμα.
[4] This interpretation is accepted by Tideman, *l. c.* 290.

latter part of the first century, Hilgenfeld naturally attributes the Christian expressions to a Christian reviser. This reviser he regards as the author of xvii.–xix, xxxvii.–lxxi., (in which he may have made use of older materials), and cvi.–cviii. The Gnostic dualism which he thinks is apparent in the doctrine about evil spirits, leads him to place the revision in the time between Saturninus and Marcion.[1]

Now if we are content to accept a post-Christian date for the Similitudes, the probability that much is due to a Christian hand certainly becomes very great. But setting this aside, what evidence is presented by the Messianic picture itself? The special titles which are applied to the Messiah might find a sufficient explanation in different passages of the Old Testament; and his supernatural character might be borrowed from Daniel vii. 13, 14, even if a just interpretation cannot admit here a Messianic reference. But nevertheless the whole conception of a mysterious pre-existent being, who even in his concealment stands in intimate relation with the world's history, and who is some time to appear as judge not only of the world, but of the fallen angels, and with whom the righteous shall dwell for ever, is far more agreeable to Christian than to what we know of Jewish thought.[2] In addition to this more general consideration there are a few special statements which afford, in Hilgenfeld's opinion, strong evidence of Christian origin. In xlviii. 7 it is said that 'the wisdom of the Lord of the spirits has revealed him [the Son of man] to the holy and righteous . . . because they have hated and despised this world of

[1] *Jüd. Apok.* S. 181.
[2] The force of this argument will be much more apparent when we have unfolded the details of the Jewish doctrine. It will then be seen that if this part of the Book of Enoch be Jewish, it stands quite alone in Jewish literature of the period within which our inquiries are confined.

unrighteousness.' Dillmann[1] explains this as referring simply to prophetic revelation, remarking that it is ascribed to 'the wisdom of the Lord.' It may, perhaps, refer to Christ's actual appearance, while the subsequent clause accords with that revolt against the world which distinguished the first Christians. The latter view may seem to be supported by verse 10, in which 'the kings of the earth' are said to have 'denied the Lord of the spirits and his anointed;' for how could the kings be thus reproached if the 'anointed' had never come to demand their allegiance? Yet I cannot help thinking that this statement might be taken from Psalm ii. 2. Hilgenfeld further appeals to lxii., in which the kings are ordered to open their eyes and recognise the elect one, as though there had been a time when, having the opportunity of recognising him, they had failed to do so;[2] but this seems to me too obscure to be relied on. Much more convincing is his appeal[3] to the expression 'son of the woman,' which could hardly have been applied by a pre-Christian Jew to a supernatural Messiah. It was possible to believe either that the Messiah would come in celestial glory on the clouds of heaven, or that he would be a chosen man born in the usual way; but it was not possible to hold both these views at the same time till Christianity reconciled them by its doctrine of a first coming in humiliation, and a second coming with angelic pomp. These considerations taken together are certainly sufficient to excite serious doubts whether the Book of Enoch may not have passed through the transforming hands of a Christian reviser.

There is, however, one grave objection to Hilgenfeld's view. How came a Christian to be so singularly reticent about everything connected with Christ's history? If a

---

[1] S. 161.   [2] *Jüd. Apok.* S. 174, *sq.*   [3] S. 157 *sq.*

Christian really undertook to make Enoch the vehicle of his apocalyptic thoughts, how is it that he did not point, as clearly as is done for instance in the Testaments of the Twelve Patriarchs,[1] to the rejected and crucified and risen Jesus?[2] This appears to be a formidable difficulty, if we are asked to believe that the whole tract containing the Similitudes is the work of a Christian author; but it is very much diminished if we suppose that the Christian writer acted only as an interpolator, for an interpolator would be careful not to depart too widely from the character of the book in which he made his insertions. Now there is no part of the Book of Enoch which exhibits clearer indications of corruption than the Similitudes. Both Ewald and Dillmann admit that the Noachic portions, which occur in three different places, have been interpolated. But if so, may there not be further interpolation, even if it be no longer possible to determine its precise limits? A somewhat careful examination of the Messianic passages has excited in my own mind very strong suspicions that they form no part of the original book of Similitudes. In order to justify these suspicions it will be most convenient to review the contents of the Similitudes in their order.

The name given in xxxvii. to the whole section, 'the discourse of wisdom,' is too indefinite to enable us to form any opinion as to the writer's intentions. We must pass, then, to the Similitudes themselves.

The first contains no reference to the Messiah, with the exception of two expressions, 'the righteous one' in

---

[1] See, *e.g.*, Levi, § 4.
[2] A reference to Christ's death might be found in xlvii. 1, 'in those days the prayer of the righteous ones and the blood of the righteous one ascend from the earth before the Lord of the spirits;' but as the next verse speaks of the blood of 'the righteous ones,' Dillmann is probably right in assigning to the singular here a collective sense.

the opening sentence,[1] and the 'elect one.'[2] Such expressions might easily be inserted, if it were only by a translator, or a copyist. They contain indeed nothing that startles us as coming from a Jew; but they are open to suspicion, because there is nothing whatever to explain who is meant by them. 'The righteous one,' if interpreted by the previous part of the book,[3] might be presumed to refer to God himself; but 'the elect one' cannot be so understood, and does not become intelligible till we enter on the next Similitude. Another important point is this, that in the rapturous description of the dwellings of the righteous,[4] though they are said to be with the angels and the holy ones, and under the wings of the Lord of the spirits, there is not the faintest allusion to the mysterious being of the second Similitude. In the first verse of the same chapter, also, it is said that in those days 'the elect and holy children will come down from the high heavens, and their seed unite itself with the children of men.' It is strange that the writer should speak of the descent of the angels, the usual retinue of a supernatural Messiah, but take no notice of their great leader, if he really anticipated his coming. As general indications that we do not possess the text in its original form we may observe that the short chapter[5] which tells how wisdom came to dwell among the children of men, and, finding no dwelling-place, returned to heaven and took its seat among the angels, has all the appearance of a detached fragment, for it merely disturbs the context in its present position; and that chapter xliv. forms no

[1] xxxviii. 2.   [2] xl. 5.
[3] See especially xxv. 3, where Enoch sees the 'throne where the holy and great one, the Lord of glory, the eternal king, will sit when he comes down to visit the earth with good.'
[4] xxxix. 4 sq., extending through nearly a page.
[5] xlii.

suitable ending to the Similitude, and excites the conjecture that the original conclusion has been lost.

The second Similitude is that which contains far the most important Messianic passages; and fortunately the writer expressly states the subject of it in the first verse.[1] It is 'concerning those who deny the name of the dwelling of the holy ones, and of the Lord of the spirits.' Is this a title which could have been chosen by the author of the exalted descriptions of the Messiah which follow? Dillmann is constrained to observe that this is no exact and complete description of the contents, and he seeks to supplement its deficiencies by extending the title through the whole introductory address. But he himself admits that the words have the appearance of being a statement of the contents, and that the truth of this appearance is rendered more plausible by the opening of the third Similitude, which is simply declared to be 'concerning the righteous and the elect ones.'[2] It is instructive to compare the author's account of his subject with that given, in perfect correspondence with the present state of the text, by Dillmann. He says, 'The principal object of the exposition is *the Messianic judgment in its course and in its consequences for righteous and unrighteous, and the person of the Messianic judge himself.*'[3] The very title, then, appears to me to excite a just preliminary doubt against the Messianic passages, and to offer us a key by which to discover the original contents.

Turning now to these passages themselves, we notice in the very first certain features which, if not absolutely inconsistent with other parts of the Similitudes, at least exhibit a very different picture. Here it is the Messiah who sits upon the throne of glory and is the judge of the world. In another place he appears as the judge of

---

[1] xlv. 1.   [2] lviii. 1.   [3] S. 154.

Azâzêl and all his hosts,[1] and in the next Similitude it is said that he will judge all the works of the holy ones in heaven,[2] and at the end he is represented as the universal judge, though by commission from God.[3] Now what is done by his deputy may be said to be done by God himself; but nevertheless one cannot help suspecting a different hand when the Messiah vanishes, and his functions are ascribed to God alone. In xlvii. 3 it is the Head of days that sits on the throne of his glory, and while the whole host of angels is present, the Messiah does not appear; and in l. 4, it is he that exercises judgment, quite agreeably to the doctrine of the other parts of the Book of Enoch.[4] Again, in xlvi. 5, if we retain the present context, the great offence of the kings consists in their not extolling the Son of man, and it is certainly implied that he was the source of their imperial power. With this may be compared the statement in xlviii. 10, that 'they have denied the Lord of the spirits and his anointed.' Not only is it very improbable that a Jew could have penned the sentiment of the former passage, but in several parts of the Similitudes the denial of the Lord of the spirits is represented as the great sin, without any allusion to a Messiah.[5] The thought readily suggests itself, that the one style of representation proceeds from a Jew, the other from a Christian.

Passing on to the next Messianic sections, I think that xlviii. 1–7, xlix., and li., relating to the fountains of

---

[1] lv. 4.   [2] lxi. 8.

[3] lxix. 26, *sq*. Compare verse 27,—'the sum of the judgment was given over to him, the Son of man,'—with John v. 22 and 27,—'the Father . . . hath committed all judgment unto the Son . . . . because he is the Son of man.'

[4] See especially i. 4 *sq*., and c. *sq*.

[5] See xxxviii. 2; xli. 2; xlv. 1, 2; xlvi. 6, 7; lxvii. 8, 9, (Noachic); and compare xliii. 4, where believing on the name of the Lord of the spirits is the characteristic of the righteous.

wisdom and righteousness, and the blessedness which there will be when the Messiah appears, form naturally a continuous piece. This piece, again, easily attaches itself to the previous one in xlv. xlvi., if we close the latter with the words, 'his lot before the Lord of the spirits has surpassed everything through righteousness for ever,' and omit the clause about the kings and mighty. This clause is unlike all the rest, and mars the otherwise beautiful description of the Son of man. Is it not possible that a Christian apocalypse has been worked into the tissue of an earlier Jewish production, and that the reviser who inserted the Messianic and Noachic passages, and perhaps some others, added the connecting clause about the kings, and a few other minor interpolations, out of his own resources? The rest of the second Similitude contains nothing Messianic except five casual allusions,[1] which, to say the least, either are not essential to the context, or are (in two instances) ambiguous, as the singular 'the elect one' might be understood in a collective sense.

One other test must be applied. Have we a more consistent text if we omit the Messianic passages, or would such omission render the remainder unintelligible? The following summary of the contents, apart from these passages, will enable us to judge:—

Sad will be the lot of the sinners, who have denied the name of the Lord of the spirits. On that day he will sit on the throne of his glory, and judge mankind.[2] [Messianic passage.] He will thrust from their thrones the kings who have not acknowledged him as the source of their power, but have raised their hands against the Highest and trodden down the earth, who have wor-

[1] lii. 4, 6, 9; liii. 6; lv. 4.
[2] This includes part of xlv. 3, simply changing the expression, 'the elect one.' The very hypothesis of interpolation presupposes such minor changes, so as to obtain a plausible connection.

F

shipped idols and denied the name of the Lord of the
spirits. The holy ones who dwell in heaven will praise
the name of the Lord of the spirits, on account of the
blood of the righteous ones that was shed, and on account
of the prayer of the righteous, entreating him that the
prayer may not be in vain, but that judgment may be
executed for them, and they may not have to suffer for
ever. Then Enoch saw the Head of days seating himself on the throne of his glory, and the books of the
living were opened in his presence, and his whole host
stood before him. And the hearts of the holy ones were
full of joy that the prayer of the righteous was heard,
and the blood of the righteous atoned for before the
Lord of the spirits.[1] [Messianic passage.] And in those
days the kings of the earth will be of fallen countenance,
for in the day of their need they shall not rescue their
souls. And they shall be given into the hands of the
elect ones, and burn before the face of the righteous, and
sink before the face of the holy ones. And in the day of
their need there will be rest on the earth; and they shall
fall before him, and not rise again, for they have denied
the Lord of the spirits [omitting here, ' and his anointed ']
The name of the Lord of the spirits be praised.[2] [Messi-
anic passage.] And in those days a turn of affairs will
take place for the holy and elect ones; the light of days
will dwell upon them, and glory and honour will turn
themselves to the holy ones. And in the day of need
the sinners shall suffer harm, but the righteous shall
conquer in the name of the Lord of the spirits; and he
will cause the others to see it, that they may repent and
leave the works of their hands. They shall have no
honour before the Lord of the spirits; but in his name
shall they be saved, because he will have pity on them.

[1] xlvi. 5-xlvii. 4.   [2] xlviii. 8-10.

Righteous is he in his judgment, and the impenitent shall perish, and 'I will no more pity them, says the Lord of the spirits.'[1] [Messianic passage.] After those days Enoch was carried towards the west, and there he saw the hidden things of heaven, all that should happen on earth, mountains of iron, copper, and other metals. He asked the angel who was with him, what these things were.[2] [Messianic verse.[3]] The angel tells him that these shall melt before the elect,[4] and none shall be able to save himself with gold or silver; for all these shall vanish when the elect[4] shall appear before the face of the Lord of the spirits. The sinners shall perish before the face of the Lord of the spirits, and be hunted from the surface of his earth. For Enoch saw the angels of punishment, how they went and prepared all instruments for Satan. The angel told him that these instruments were for the kings and mighty, that they might be destroyed with them.[5] [Messianic verse.] And the righteous shall have rest from the oppression of sinners. And he turned to another part of the earth, and saw a deep valley with burning fire; and they laid the kings and mighty men in it. And he saw them preparing iron chains for the hosts of Azâzêl, that they might be laid in the nethermost hell, as the Lord of the spirits has commanded.[6] [Noachic passage.[7]] 'And then it is done according to my order ... my wrath and my penal judgment shall remain upon them, says God, the Lord of the

---

[1] l.   [2] lii. 1–3.

[3] This verse—'And he said to me, all these things which thou hast seen serve the dominion of his anointed, that he may be powerful and mighty on the earth,'—has all the appearance of an interpolation, for the next verse goes on,—'And that angel of peace answered me.'

[4] The singular is here used, but it may have been employed in a collective sense, or the text may have been slightly altered. There would, however, be no difficulty in accepting this doctrine as Jewish.

[5] lii. 5–liii. 5.   [6] liii. 7–liv. 6.   [7] liv. 7–lv. 2.

spirits.'[1] [Messianic verse.[2]] And he saw there the hosts of the angels of punishment, and was told that they would go each to his chosen and beloved, with whom that valley should be filled. The Similitude concludes with a description of the final conflict and mutual destruction of the kings in the land of the elect ones, and of the coming of a host of chariots, conveying men on the wings of the wind from east and west. 'And the holy ones observed it from heaven; and the pillars of the earth were moved from their place, and it was heard from the ends of the earth to the ends of the heaven, on one day. And they shall all fall down, and pray to the Lord of the spirits. And this is the end of the second figurative address.'[3]

Now we have here a sufficiently continuous text, which answers to the title that is placed at its head; and instead of missing passages which ought to impress their character on the whole piece, we obtain, I think, a better connection and more consistent representation without them. And lastly, it is very remarkable, if the Messianic passages are genuine, that there is not the faintest allusion to a Messiah in the description of the final war with heathenism, and the gathering together of the chosen people.

The third Similitude more easily admits the suspicion of being interpolated on account of the appearance of long Noachic sections. Chapter lxiv., moreover, is like a misplaced fragment. The Similitude professes to treat of the righteous and the elect ones, and we might therefore expect to hear a good deal about the Messiah. There are, however, only two important passages which speak of

---

[1] lv. 3.
[2] This verse, lv. 4, is an unexpected addition, telling the kings that they shall see the elect one judging Azâzêl.
[3] lvi.; lvii.

him, and we need not pause on the brief allusions in lxi. 5, 8, 9, lxii. 1, 14, lxiii. 11. The passage[1] in which the kings and the mighty see the 'son of the woman,' may be simply omitted without the slightest detriment to the context; and there is one circumstance which lays it open to suspicion. In the following chapter these same kings speak at some length, acknowledging God as the Lord of kings, confessing their past unbelief and misplaced trust, and longing for rest; but they say not a word about the Messiah; and instead of setting 'their hope on that Son of man,' and entreating compassion from him, they implore the angels of punishment to grant them a little rest, that they may pray before the Lord of the spirits. The passage at the end[2] may be simply omitted. As Dillmann observes,[3] it is entirely out of its connection. He thinks it has been transposed from the end of lxi.; but if so, what sort of reliance can be placed on a work which has been so recklessly tampered with by an unknown hand? We must further notice the total omission of the Messiah from the picture given in the opening chapter[4] of the blessedness of the righteous.

The conclusion to which this examination has led us is confirmed in a very striking way by the closing chapter of the whole section.[5] There Enoch has a vision of 'the sons of the angels,' and, caught up into the heaven of heavens, he sees the very house of God in the midst of its streams of living fire. Round it are innumerable angels, who go in and out; and with them is the Head of days, his head white and pure as wool and his dress indescribable. Enoch offers praise, which is accepted, before that Head of days. And the Head of days himself comes with thousands of angels; and then the account proceeds,

---

[1] lxii. 4-9.   [2] lxix. 26-29.
[3] *Das B. Hen.*, S. 214.   [4] lviii.   [5] lxxi.

'that angel came to me, and with his voice greeted me and said, "Thou art the Son of man[1] who is born to righteousness, and righteousness dwells over thee, and the righteousness of the Head of days leaves thee not." And he said to me, "He pronounces peace upon thee in the name of the future world, for thence peace goes forth since the creation of the world; and so shalt thou have it to eternity, and from eternity to eternity. And all who in the future walk in thy way, thou whom righteousness leaves not to eternity, their dwelling shall be with thee, and their inheritance with thee, and from thee shall they not be separated unto eternity, and from eternity to eternity."' Thus far there is no reference to the Messiah. He has vanished from the vision of glory, and Enoch himself has stepped into his place. Can this be from the same hand as the Messianic passages? A verse, however, is added as though to save the Messianic character of this conclusion: 'And so will there be long life with that Son of man, and peace will be to the righteous, and his straight way to the righteous, in the name of the Lord of the spirits from eternity to eternity.' If we judged from the context, 'that Son of man' ought to refer to Enoch; and it might do so, with a slight change of text, if we regarded this verse as part of the address of the angel, or without any change, if we considered it to be a closing reflection of the writer's, who had for the moment forgotten to identify himself with Enoch. The verse, however, is weak and tame after what has preceded, and I am inclined to think that it is a later Messianic addition.

The general conclusion to which we are thus led is that the Messianic, like the Noachic, passages have been interpolated into an earlier Book of Similitudes; and our

---

[1] Here der Menschensohn.

suspicion of their Christian origin receives thereby an additional justification.

This conclusion derives support from some facts in the literary history of the work. The earliest traces of the Book of Enoch are found in the Book of Jubilees, a composition which is supposed by Rönsch to have proceeded from a Palestinian Jew between 50 and 60 A.D.[1] In this work Rönsch finds nineteen references to the Book of Enoch.[2] Of these only two appear to concern the Similitudes. The first is merely an allusion to Enoch as 'the seventh in his generation.' But even if this were not far too commonplace to prove borrowing, it might be taken from Enoch xciii. 3. The second supposed reference is found in the ascription of a spirit to fire, wind, clouds, and other natural objects, which agrees with the doctrine in Enoch lx. 11 *sq*. A doctrine of this kind is hardly sufficient to prove the dependence of one writer on another; and even if it were, there is nothing to indicate which author is the dependent one. In any case there is not a vestige of the writer's acquaintance with the Messianic passages. More important is the silence of the Testaments of the twelve Patriarchs, a Christian book of uncertain date, but later than the destruction of Jerusalem. In this there are several references to books or writings of Enoch.[3] These, indeed, are made responsible for various statements which are not contained in the work that has come down to us; but still the evidence seems sufficient to prove that the writer of the Testaments was more or less acquainted with an actual book passing under the name of Enoch, and that this corresponded more or less with the surviving work. Now the Testa-

---

[1] *Das Buch der Jubiläen oder die kleine Genesis*, &c. 1874, S. 523 *sq*. An account of the Book of Jubilees will be given farther on.

[2] Ibid., S. 403 *sq*.

[3] See them collected in Fabricius, *Codex Pseudep. V. T.* p. 161 *sq*.

ments, in treating of the Messiah, contain no trace of the Messianic passages in the Book of Enoch; and this is the more curious because an appeal is expressly made to it as containing a prediction of the rejection, death, and resurrection of 'the man renewing the law in the power of the Highest.'[1] There is, as we have seen, no such prediction in the Similitudes; but do we not here perceive some evidence of an unsettled text, and of a tendency to Christian interpolation? Tertullian's defence of the book is well known.[2] He says that Enoch in it prophesies about the Lord. He does not, however, tell us the contents of the prophecy; so that although we may be satisfied that his copy of the book contained Messianic passages, we cannot be equally certain that they were the same as those which we now possess. Very likely they may have been so; but there is a point of greater interest in Tertullian's testimony. He expressly informs us that the book was not admitted into the Jewish chest (armarium), by which he must mean the canon; and he thinks that it may have been 'rejected by the Jews, as well as everything else nearly which speaks of Christ,'[3] on account of its prophecies about the Lord. This language points most naturally to prophecies referring to the personal history of Christ, such as those alluded to in the Testaments of the Twelve Patriarchs, and at least awakens a suspicion that the Jews declined to regard the work as an unadulterated product of Judaism. Origen also says that the 'books' of Enoch 'do not seem to be held in authority among the Hebrews.'[4] Augustin, too, attests that the writings of Noah and Enoch are not held in

---

[1] Levi § 10.   [2] *De Cultu Feminarum*, lib. i., c. 3.
[3] Cetera fere quæ Christum sonant.
[4] *Hom. in Numeros* xxviii. § 2, in Rufinus's translation; p. 366 in Lommatzsch's edition.

authority among either Jews or Christians.[1] These testimonies, indeed, affect only the canonical character of the book; but there is no evidence to show that it was ever held in high estimation among the Jews,[2] nor do the Christians venture to appeal to it as a work which, if not authoritative, at least incorporated the prevalent Jewish belief. In fine, we must notice the significant fact that the Messianic passages are nowhere cited by the very authors who condescend to avail themselves of the questionable support which the book lends to their tenets.

In the above discussion we cannot profess to have arrived at more than a certain degree of probability; but I fear we must rest in the following conclusion: that we cannot rely upon the integrity of the present Book of Enoch; that the Messianic passages in the Similitudes are of unknown, but probably Christian origin; and that therefore we cannot safely appeal to them as evidence of pre-Christian Jewish belief.[3]

---

[1] *De Civitate Dei*, xviii. 38.

[2] The allusions to the book in the later Jewish literature do not invalidate this statement. See these, five in all, collected by Jellinek in the *Zeitsch. der d. m. Gesell.* Bd. vii., 1853, S. 249.

[3] This conclusion is accepted, in addition to Hilgenfeld, by Holtzmann, *l. c.* S. 203 (with hesitation, and chiefly on account of the position of judge assigned to the Messiah, a feature which is not found elsewhere except in connection with Christianity); Keim, *Gesch. Jesu*, i. S. 242, Anm. 1; Oehler, *l. c.* S. 429; Volkmar, *Zeitsch. d. deut. morg. Gesell.* S. 133; Kuenen, *Rel. of Isr.* iii. 265; Tideman, *l. c.* 290; Colani, *Jésus-Christ et les cr. mess.* 30–32.

On the other hand Anger, *Vorl. üb. d. Gesch. d. mess. Idee*, S. 83, thinks Hilgenfeld's reasons inconclusive; Schenkel, *Bib. Lex. Messianische Weissagungen*, S. 201, apparently accepts the whole book as pre-Christian; Schürer, *N. Zeitgesch.* S. 534–5, thinks that a Christian would have spoken more clearly, and referred to Christ's history.

Wittichen, *Die Id. d. Reich. Gott.* S. 119, regards the Similitudes, after the removal of the Noachic passages, as part of the original book, and thinks that we may not even doubt his verdict.

Section V.—*The Assumption of Moses.*

For the possession of an important fragment of the Apocalypse known as the Assumption of Moses we are indebted to the labours of Ceriani. This fragment was discovered in a parchment palimpsest which had found its way from the monastery of Bobbio to the Ambrosian Library at Milan. The ancient writing had been as far as possible erased, and the volume broken up into separate leaves. The manuscript was known to Peyron, who deciphered p. 79 of Little Genesis and p. 86 of the Assumption of Moses, and to Angelo Mai, who seems to have tried some chemical experiments upon it in order to obliterate the more recent characters; but it was left for Ceriani finally to arrange and decipher it. Thus were brought to light valuable fragments of an old Latin translation of the Book of Jubilees or Little Genesis and the first part of the Assumption of Moses. Of the latter, indeed, the title is wanting; but it is identified through a citation from the ᾽Ανάληψις Μωυσέως which occurs in the Acta Synodi Nicenæ.[1] The nature of the writing, in uncial letters, without division of words, with few abbreviations and a rare use of interpunction, proves that the manuscript belongs to the sixth century.[2] The text was given to the public in the Monumenta Sacra et Profana, Tom. I. Fasc. i. 1861.

From the Stichometry of Nicephorus we learn that the ᾽Ανάληψις Μωυσέως contained fourteen hundred στίχοι, the number which is assigned in the same list to the

---

[1] ii. 18, quoted in Fabricius, *Cod. Pseud. V. T.* i. 845.

[2] See Ceriani, *Monumenta Sacra et Profana ex codicibus præsertim Bibliothecæ Ambrosianæ*, &c. Tom. I. fasc. i. Mediolani, 1861, preface to the fragments of the Gospel of Luke, and preface to the fragments of the *Parva Genesis* and *Ass. Mosis*.

Apocalypse of John;[1] and hence we infer that only about one third of the work has been recovered. Unfortunately even this third is not in a very satisfactory condition. Several words have been wholly or partly obliterated, so that the sense must be completed by conjectures more or less trustworthy; and the passage which is of most importance for determining the date of composition is precisely the one which has suffered most severely. Hilgenfeld was the first to publish a critical edition, with an attempted restoration of the text.[2] In his Messias Judæorum[3] he gives a translation of his own into Greek, unaccompanied by the Latin text. Volkmar devoted to this fragment the third volume of his 'Handbuch zu den Apocryphen,' which appeared in 1867;[4] and other editions have been published by Schmidt and Merx,[5] and by Fritzsche.[6]

That the Latin translation has been made from Greek is evident from the retention of Greek words and constructions;[7] and as there is no sufficient reason for supposing a Hebrew or Aramæan original, we may assume that the book, notwithstanding its Hebraic colouring, was composed in the language in which it was known to the early Christian writers.

We need not dwell long upon its contents. The part

---

[1] Credner's *Geschichte des neutestamentlichen Kanon*; herausg. von Dr. G. Volkmar, 1860, S. 243.
[2] *Novum Testamentum extra Canonem receptum*: Fasc. i. 1866.
[3] *Messias Judæorum, libris eorum paulo ante et paulo post Christum natum conscriptis illustratus*; Lipsiæ, 1869.
[4] *Mose Prophetie und Himmelfahrt.*
[5] 'Die *Assumptio Mosis* mit Einleitung und erklärenden Anmerkungen herausgegeben; in Merx' *Archiv für wissenschaftliche Erforschung des A. T.* Bd. i., Hft. 2, 1868, S. 111-152. This I have been unable to see. Referred to by Schürer, *Lehrb.* S. 536.
[6] *Libri apocryphi Vet. Test. Græce. Accedunt libri Vet. Test. pseudepigraphi selecti*, 1871. This also I have failed to see.
[7] Hilgenfeld, *Mess. Jud.* p. lxxiii. Volkmar, *Mose Proph.* S. 56.

preserved for us consists of a conversation between Moses and Joshua immediately before the death of the former. The great legislator, in handing over to his successor the leadership of the people, warns him to be faithful to his trust, and to keep with all care the writings which are committed to him. He then sketches prophetically the general course of Israelitish history, in lines sufficiently distinct down to the successors of Herod the Great. How far events are indicated beyond this period is a question upon which critics are divided. The writer describes the domination of wicked and arrogant men who shall live in those times, and who shall be punished by a terrible persecution, such as was not experienced 'until that time in which [God] stirred up against them the king of the kings of the earth.'[1] 'Then a man of the tribe of Levi, whose name shall be Taxo,' will desire his seven sons to fast with him for three days, and to retire on the fourth into a cave, because it will be better for them to die than to transgress the commands of the Lord of lords. 'Then will appear his kingdom in all his creation,' and God ' will come forth from his holy dwelling, with indignation and anger on account of his sons.' Israel will then be in bliss, and will ' mount up above the necks and wings of the eagle,' and dwell among the stars. This address closes with a few further words of advice, and with the statement that there will be ' 250 times ' till the final consummation. Joshua, in reply, expresses his grief at the approaching departure of Moses, and his sense of his own incompetence for the great task which lies before him. Moses strengthens him with the thought that God has foreseen everything from the beginning, and that he himself had been chosen, not on account of his fortitude

---

[1] Usque ad illum tempus in quo suscitauit. For the present we need not adopt the editorial emendation, suscitabit.

or his weakness, but through the compassion of God. If the people kept the divine commandments, they would prosper; but if not, they would be punished by the heathen. 'For God will go forth, who has foreseen everything to the end; and his covenant is established; and with the oath which . . .'—at this point the fragment comes to a close.

A few references in ancient writers enable us to form some idea of the further progress of the work. When Moses died on the mountain, the archangel Michael was sent to remove the body. The devil also appeared upon the scene, and claimed the body as being the lord of matter, and charging Moses with the murder of the Egyptian. Hereupon ensued an altercation between Michael and the devil, in the course of which the former said: 'God rebuke thee.' We can have little doubt that it was this book also which recorded the vision seen by Joshua, and less perfectly by Caleb. A double Moses was seen. One was deposited in the valley of the mountain, but the other was with the angels.[1]

The limits of the possible range which can be allowed to the date of this book may be easily determined. Its contents, as we have seen, prove that it cannot be earlier than the close of the reign of Herod the Great, whose tyranny is decribed in chapter vi.[2] Again, it cannot be later than Origen, who refers to it by name.[3] But Origen says in the same passage that 'the apostle Jude in his epistle,' borrowed from it the allusion to the dispute between Michael and the devil about the body of Moses.

---

[1] See this last story in Clemens Al. *Strom.* vi. 15, p. 806 *sq.*; referred to by Origen, *Hom. in Jos.* ii. 1, and by Euodius, *Ep. ad Augustinum* (258 among those of Augustine). Other authorities and quotations may be found in Hilgenfeld, *Mess. Jud.* 458–461.

[2] I follow, according to general usage, Hilgenfeld's division.

[3] *De Principiis*, iii. 2, 1.

Now we can hardly, upon any theory of its origin, place the epistle later than the middle of the second century; and therefore the Assumption of Moses must have been written at least some little time before that date. It is accordingly between the limits thus determined that the opinions of critics oscillate.

Ewald believes that the work was written immediately after the rebellion of Judas the Gaulonite, who called the people to arms against the taxation under Quirinus, A.D. 6.[1] He thinks that the Gaulonite himself is indicated by the mysterious name of Taxo, though he is unable to offer any solution of the riddle.[2] The most weighty argument, as it appears to me, in favour of this early date is furnished by the absence of all clear reference to later events. The expedition of Quintilius Varus to quell the sedition in Jerusalem, in the year 4 B.C., is unmistakably alluded to in the words,—'he will burn a part of their temple, and crucify some around their colony.'[3] At this point the historical recital either comes to a close, or passes into statements of bewildering vagueness. It is, moreover, expressly affirmed that from the coming of the 'powerful king of the west' (that is Augustus as represented by Varus) 'the times shall be ended.'[4] This might seem to be conclusive; but it must be admitted that the writer dwells rather on the characteristics of periods than on the succession of events which marked their course, and having introduced his readers to the Roman domination, he might have regarded that as sufficiently descriptive of the final period in mundane affairs. The succeeding passage, too, may seem to imply the lapse of some time after the appearance of the Romans on the scene, even if we cannot

---

[1] *Gesch. d. V. I.* v. S. 73 *sq.*   [2] Ibid., S. 81.
[3] End of vi. For these events see Josephus, *Antiq.* xvii. 10, § 2 and 10.
[4] vii., ex quo facto finientur tempora.

follow the confident attempts which have been made, on the authority of conjectural restorations of a mutilated text, to compute the precise number of years which the writer was able to review. Another argument of considerable force in favour of the early date is found in the statement [1] that the sons of Herod should reign for a shorter time (breviora tempora), whereas Philip and Antipas really reigned longer than their father. The natural inference is that the book was composed when the anticipation of a short period for their power had not yet been falsified by the event. Hilgenfeld endeavours to evade this argument by his rendering of the corrupt Latin, (οἳ) παράλληλοι βραχυτέρους χρόνους ἄρξουσιν.[2] In conformity with this rendering he makes the statement refer only to the duration of their 'parallel dominion,'[3] that is, in other words, of the short reign of Archelaus. Volkmar boldly removes the difficulty by reading, instead of βραχυτέρους τοὺς καιρούς breviora tempora, τραχυτέρους duriora.[4] But we are hardly justified in resorting to such expedients, unless they are required for the explanation of a palpable contradiction.

Hilgenfeld, with great confidence, assigns the book to the reign of Claudius, about 44 A.D.[5] His main argument is based on a conjectural restoration of the faulty passage in chapter vii., and a suitable interpretation, in which he follows substantially the leadership of Gutschmid.[6] The latter, however, places the work rather later, in the beginning of the reign of Nero. The only

[1] vi.
[2] This παράλληλοι, so far as I can discover, is a pure invention of Hilgenfeld's. His own emendation of the Latin text, in his *Nov. Test. ex. Can. Recept.*, is as follows:—et producet natos succedentes sibi breviora tempora, donec in partes eorum hostes venient. The best answer to the argument is simply to plead the uncertainty of the text.
[3] *Mess. Jud.* pp. lxxiv. and 463.
[4] *Mose Pr.* S. 34 and 144.
[5] *Mess. Jud.* p. lxxiv.
[6] Ibid.

thing certain in the text is an allusion to 'four hours.' By these Hilgenfeld understands four emperors. Ewald, if I rightly apprehend his meaning, regards the passage as descriptive of the past, and refers the hours to the native line of Hebrew kings and the succeeding foreign dynasties, Persian, Greek, and Roman.[1] Volkmar, as we shall see, discovers in them four groups of Roman emperors. I cannot but think that we have here rather a riddle for the exercise of a fruitless ingenuity than any ground for reasonable confidence.[2] As regards more general indications, I think that, although Claudius was unfriendly to the Jews, the language of this apocalypse, describing a persecution conducted with fire, sword, and cross, cannot be explained by anything that took place in his time; and Hilgenfeld himself has to admit that the description is founded not on fact, but on anticipation.[3] The man of the tribe of Levi named Taxo represents, in this view, not any historical person, but the Messiah; though how a man who despairingly proposes to retire and die in a cave rather than be unfaithful can stand for the Messiah it is difficult to see. Hilgenfeld, however, has his proof. Taxo was corrupted from the Greek τξγ' = 363, a number which corresponds to the word הַמָשִׁיחַ the Messiah, the letters being equivalent to 5, 40, 300, 10, 8, = 363! I agree with Colani that we might as well refer the name to the Emperor Barbarossa.[4]

[1] *Gesch. d. V. I.*, v. S. 77–8.
[2] The reader may wish to have the hopeful passage before him. 'Ex quo facto finientur tempora momento . . . . etur cursus a . . . . horae iiii. ueniant coguntur secun- . . . . ae . . . . pos . . . . . . initiis tribus ad exitus . viiii. propter initium tres septimae secunda tria in tertia duae h . . ra . . tae et regnarunt.' The italics indicate letters which Ceriani did not feel sure that he had correctly deciphered. See *Mon. Sac. et Prof.* I. i.
[3] *Mess. Jud.* p. 465 6.
[4] Quoted by Hilgenfeld *Mess. Jud.* p. 467. The hint is too good to be lost. Taxo is clearly a corruption of Taro, ταρο, 300, 1, 100, 70 = 471. Barbarossa

THE ASSUMPTION OF MOSES.

Volkmar, though apparently driven by his usual anxiety to prove the late origin of the Epistle of Jude, yet displays more than his usual skill in claiming a late date for the Assumption of Moses. He thinks it describes the persecution under Hadrian, and was written in the year 137, after the defeat and death of Bar-Cochba and the martyrdom of the Rabbi Akiba. The four hours become with him four Roman dynasties, the Julian, the three usurpers', the Flavian, and that of Nerva, Trajan, and Hadrian.[1] Taxo ($Ta\xi o$, 300, 1, 60, 70 = 431) is the Rabbi Akiba (עקבא רבון, 200, 2, 6, 50, 70, 100, 2, 1 = 431). Here a ו is wanting after the ק; but it may have been intentionally left out, or the author may have written $\tau a\xi\iota o$, and the translator have mistaken this for $\tau a\xi\omega$.[2] These subtleties are not very convincing. But the despairing tone of the writer, who expects no further help till God himself appears upon the scene, the relentless character of the persecution, especially the attempt to root out circumcision, and other minor circumstances which Volkmar carefully compares with the history of the times, are all in agreement with the violent measures by which Hadrian endeavoured finally to extinguish the Jewish polity.[3]

The strongest point in Volkmar's argument is found in the details of the persecution, which have no historical example except under Antiochus Epiphanes and Hadrian. But Schürer believes that Epiphanes is the monarch denoted by the expression 'king of the kings of the earth,' and that the final persecution is only indirectly described by a portrayal of the terrible events of that hated reign. This opinion is confirmed by a suggestion

may be written thus, ברברומא = 2, 200, 2, 200, 6, 60, 1 = 471! What may not be proved by the help of arbitrary conjectures? Our emendation at least retains a pronounceable word; Hilgenfeld's has not even this trifling merit.

[1] *Mose Pr.*, S. 37.   [2] Ibid., 59 *sq.*   [3] Ibid., 56 *sq.*

of the same writer that the story of Taxo and his seven sons is only a variation of that of the woman with seven sons who were barbarously put to death by Antiochus.[1] Even if this interpretation be not accepted in its entirety, there can be no doubt that the persecution under Antiochus Epiphanes might have been adopted as the type of the final calamities of the Jewish people long before his exterminating cruelty reappeared in the person of Hadrian. I doubt, therefore, whether Volkmar's arguments, which, though displaying great ingenuity, are quite open to question, are sufficient to set aside the plain inference from the historical notices in the book. It is especially difficult to understand why a writer in the second century should select the expedition of Varus for such explicit mention, when in the long perspective its horrors must have seemed quite insignificant in comparison with more recent events. If we rely upon the broad and plain evidence rather than upon subtleties, we must decide that the work was written not very many years after the death of Herod the Great. The tone of the writer, so despairing of his country, so hot against the leading party, apparently the Pharisees, may in that case be explained by his position among the Zealots of his time.

We must not, however, pass over a criticism which is equally relied upon by Hilgenfeld[2] and Volkmar.[3] They believe that the expression in x. 28—adscendes supra cervices et alas aquilæ et implebuntur—must refer to the vision of the three-headed eagle in 4th Ezra.[4] Hilgenfeld thinks the allusion proves the early origin of Ezra; Volkmar, that it establishes the late origin of the As-

---

[1] See the account in 2 Mac. vii. See Schürer's view in *Lehrb. d. n. Zeitg.* S. 539.
[2] *Mess. Jud.* 467.   [3] *Mose Pr.*, S. 67.
[4] See the next section, p. 95 *sq.*

sumption of Moses. The former contends that the words *et implebuntur,* καὶ πληρωθήσονται, are decisive; for what can they mean? As he does not himself tell us what they mean, I miss the force of the argument. To suit his purpose they ought to mean, 'the prophecies of Ezra shall be fulfilled;' but there is nothing whatever in the context to suggest such an explanation. The real meaning of the statement, 'the necks and wings of the eagle shall be filled (or fulfilled),' is certainly not very obvious; but if nothing has been omitted, it seems most natural to understand 'fulfilled' in the sense of having completed their course, come to an end. To speak of necks being fulfilled in the sense in which a prophecy is fulfilled, would be simply unintelligible. But Volkmar has another argument. Anyone might reach the idea of representing the plurality of Cæsars under the image of several wings or of several heads, but none but the author of 4th Ezra could possibly have combined the two.[1] It is strange that an author who has nothing to do but alter the text when it is opposed to his theories is here so confident that the reading cannot be wrong. If for *cervices* we read *cervicem,* his whole argument would fall to the ground. We need not, however, change the text. The word 'necks' alone is sufficient to disprove the supposed reference; for 4th Ezra speaks always of 'heads,' and not of necks. The comparison of Rome to an eagle is one that might occur to any writer. Getting upon the necks of enemies is an Old Testament figure for utterly subduing them;[2] and the writer, having a multitude of

---

[1] That at least a second person existed whose genius was equal to such a conception is evident from the leopard in Daniel vii. 6, with its four heads and four wings, representing the third kingdom.

[2] Gen. xlix. 8; Josh. x. 24; Psalm xviii. 40. See also Baruch iv. 25, κατεδίωξέ σε ὁ ἐχθρ's, καὶ ὄψει αὐτοῦ τὴν ἀπώλειαν ἐν τάχει, καὶ ἐπὶ τραχήλους

enemies in his mind, naturally uses the plural, without considering its appropriateness to the figure of an eagle. The wings are an emblem of exaltation. The glorified Israel shall not only 'mount up with wings as eagles,' but shall be exalted to the stars, far above the highest range of the Roman eagle's flight.

The three opinions noticed above may suffice to represent the prevailing diversity of view, and it is not necessary for us to discuss the modifications of them which have found favour with different critics. It is sufficient to mention and dismiss the unsupported assertion of Philippi that the book is of Christian origin, and dates from the end of the first third of the second century.[1]

Section VI.—*Fourth Ezra*.

EZRA or Esdras the Prophet, also called the Apocalypse of Ezra, and generally cited as Fourth Ezra (though appearing as II. Esdras in the Apocrypha of the English Bible), is a book of the highest interest, and although there is the same diversity of opinion respecting its date as in the case of the Book of Enoch, some writers regarding it as pre-Christian and others as post-Christian, the researches of criticism have happily placed its Jewish character beyond question.

The original work, which was most probably written in Greek,[2] has long been lost; but we are so fortunate

αὐτῶν ἐπιβήσῃ. Also Enoch xcviii. 12.—'They [the righteous] will cut off your [the sinners'] necks.'

[1] *Das Buch Henoch*, S. 105-6.

[2] See the evidence in Lücke, *Einl. in d. Off.* i. S. 152-4; Volkmar, *Handbuch der Einleitung in die Apokryphen*; zweite Abtheilung; *Das vierte Buch Esra*, 1863, S. 325 *sq.*; and Hilgenfeld, *Mess. Jud.* pp. xxxviii. *sq.* On the other hand Bretschneider (in an article entitled 'Das Messiasreich nach dem 4 Buch Esdra, &c.,' in Henke's *Museum für Religionswissenschaft*, Bd. iii.,

as to possess no fewer than five different versions. Of these the oldest is the Latin. This was certainly made as early as the time of Ambrose, as is proved by his numerous citations, and perhaps was not unknown to Cyprian and Tertullian.[1] Although the work was not included in the list of canonical books by the Council of Trent, it is printed in copies of the Vulgate. The editions of Fabricius[2] and Sabatier[3] in the last century deserve particular mention; and in our own day critical texts have been published by Volkmar,[4] Hilgenfeld,[5] and Fritzsche.[6] The work, as it appears in the printed Latin Bible, consists of sixteen chapters; but in the great majority of the manuscripts it is divided into three distinct books, consisting respectively of chapters i.–ii., iii.–xiv., and xv.–xvi. Of these the second is evidently an independent work; and as the first and third are not found in any of the other versions, there is no doubt whatever that they do not belong to the original Apocalypse of Ezra. It is generally admitted that they are both of Christian origin; but Ewald believes that the third book is a purely Jewish work, written about 116 A.D.[7] It does not concern us to pause upon this question, and it may be sufficient to state that according to Volkmar the first two chapters

1806; S. 478 *sq.*) and Ewald (*Gesch. d. V. I.* vii., S. 69-70) think the original language was Hebrew.

[1] See the references in Hilg. *Mes. Jud.* p. xxii. *sq.*

[2] *Cod. Pseud. V. T.* ii. 193 *sq.* This edition gives readings from the Arabic taken from Ockley's translation, and from the same source a Latin translation of the missing passage after vii. 35.

[3] *Bibliorum sacrorum Latinæ Versiones antiquæ seu Vetus Itala*, tom. iii. P. ii. Remis, 1743, p. 1069 *sq.* Fourth Ezra is placed at the end, after the New Testament. Readings are given from the Codex Sangermanensis.

[4] In the *Handbuch* referred to in note 2, p. 84.

[5] In his *Mess. Jud.* This is very complete in its apparatus, and has the great advantage of giving a separate Latin translation of each of the versions. It also attempts a restoration of the Greek text.

[6] *Libri apoc. V. T.* This I have been unable to see.

[7] *Gesch. d. V. I.* vii. S. 82 *sq.*

were written about 160, and the last two about 260 A.D.,[1] an opinion not differing materially from that of Gutschmid, who, in an elaborate article,[2] endeavours to prove that the former were the production of a Christian in Egypt, 201 A.D.,[3] and that the latter also proceeded from a Christian in the same country, in 263 A.D.[4]

The Latin version is distinguished not only by its accompaniments, but by an important lacuna. All the copies known up to a recent period omit a long section which is found in the other four versions. This forms the sixth chapter in the Æthiopic, and its place in the Latin is between verses 35 and 36 of the seventh chapter. Even before the recent discovery of the missing fragment there was no room for doubt that it once occupied its proper position in the Latin translation; for there is a total want of connection between verses 35 and 36, which is restored by its insertion, and a considerable section of it is quoted by Ambrose, and expressly ascribed to Ezra.[5] It was probably omitted owing to objections which were felt by Christians to some of the doctrines contained in it.[6] So violent a measure may, however, be plausibly traced to a single hand. The researches of Professor Gildemeister render it likely that the passage was cut out of the Codex Sangermanensis, which was written in the year 822, and that from this manuscript in its mutilated form all the later copies which exhibit the same lacuna have been derived.[7] The discovery of a manuscript containing

---

[1] *Das Vierte B. Esra*, S. 277.

[2] 'Die Apokalypse des Esra und ihre späteren Bearbeitungen,' in the *Zeitschrift für wiss. Theologie*, 1860.

[3] S. 24–33.   [4] S. 1–24.

[5] *De Bono Mortis*, cc. 10 and 11.

[6] See Lücke, *Einl. in d. Off.* S. 155–8.

[7] See *The Missing Fragment of the Latin Translation of the Fourth Book of Ezra, discovered, and edited with an Introduction and Notes*, by Robert L. Bensly, M.A. &c. Cambridge, 1875, pp. 5 and 19 *sq*. Mr. Bensly, while

this long-lost portion has lately rewarded the industry of Mr. Bensly, sub-librarian of the University Library, and Reader in Hebrew, at Cambridge. This manuscript was found in the Bibliothèque Communale of Amiens, where its comparative obscurity had previously prevented it from attracting the notice of scholars. It is proved by its readings to be independent of the Codex Sangermanensis,[1] so that it must henceforward rank as a co-ordinate authority. This is a matter of great importance to the criticism of the text, since the discovery of Gildemeister shows that many readings of the manuscripts, hitherto adopted by editors, are merely the conjectures of transcribers.[2] Mr. Bensly has published the text of the missing fragment, accompanied by much valuable matter bearing on the criticism of the text.[3]

The above facts diminish the probability of Hilgenfeld's supposition that a large interpolation has been made in this place, though he does not think that it precisely coincides with the passage which has been omitted from the Latin. In his opinion it comprises (vi).[4] 17–vii. 45.[5] Such an interpolation may have been made in the Greek prior to translation, and therefore have found its way into all the versions; but Hilgenfeld's reasons do not appear very conclusive. The repetition of similar ideas in a work of this kind can hardly be viewed as an evidence of corruption. There is certainly an apparent inconsistency, in

substantially accepting this view, thinks that some other MS. allied to Codex A (the newly discovered MS.) may have been occasionally consulted in difficult readings (p. 81).

[1] Bensly, p. 30.   [2] Bensly, p. 23.   [3] See the title in note 7, p. 86.

[4] That is the Æthiopic chapter vi. It has hitherto been customary to follow the divisions of the Latin editions, and to distinguish the missing portion from the Latin vi. by placing the number in brackets, as in the text. This is a clumsy practice, and has the further oddity of making the work begin with chapter iii. It is necessary, however, for convenience of reference to follow the custom.

[5] *Mess. Jud.* p. xlix. *sq.*

the representations of the state of the dead before the final judgment, between this and other parts of the book; but I think they are capable of being fairly reconciled, and may be used to supplement one another. I am unable to find in the passage an interest in the fate of mankind which is inconsistent with the special devotion to the Jewish people manifested elsewhere. And lastly, the supposed references to the Gospel of Matthew seem more than doubtful. I can see, therefore, no sufficient ground for suspecting an interpolation.

An Arabic version has been preserved in a manuscript in the Bodleian Library.[1] An English translation of this, by Ockley, was printed side by side with the common translation from the Latin in Whiston's Primitive Christianity Revived, in 1711 A.D.[2] The Arabic text itself was given to the world by Ewald in 1863.[3] Hilgenfeld's Messias Judæorum contains a Latin translation from Ockley's English, revised and corrected from the Arabic by Steiner of Heidelberg. Besides this fuller version an Arabic compendium of 4th Ezra is preserved in the Bodleian. The text of this has been published by Ewald in the treatise just referred to,[4] and a German translation of it by Steiner.[5] Mr. Bensly announces the discovery in the Vatican of a second manuscript of this version,[6]

---

[1] Two leaves are missing, which contained iv. 24–44 and most of 45, and viii. 50 ix. i. (with the exception of the last few words).

[2] At the end of vol. iv.

[3] *Das vierte Ezrabuch nach seinem Zeitalter, seinen arabischen Uebersezungen, und einer neuen Wiederherstellung.* Aus dem elften Bande der *Abhandlungen der Königlichen Gesellschaft der Wissenschaften zu Göttingen.* Göttingen, 1863. The 'restoration' is a German translation made after critical comparison of the various sources.

[4] Page 48 *sq.*

[5] 'Der arabische Auszug des "Propheten Esra," nebst Berichtigungen zu der arabischen Uebersetzung,' in the *Zeitschrift für wiss. Theol.* 1868, S. 396 *sq.*

[6] *The Missing Fragment*, p. 2, n. 4.

exhibiting an 'unabridged form of the text.'[1] An Arabic translation referred to by Ewald[2] as existing in the Vatican, but not yet examined, has since been collated by Dr. Guidi, and proved to be only a copy of the Oxford manuscript; but it will be of service in supplying what is defective in the latter.[3]

The Æthiopic version was first published, accompanied by a Latin and English translation, by Laurence, in the year 1820.[4] Laurence had access to only one codex, which was full of mistakes. Since his time several other manuscripts have been examined; and Hilgenfeld has been thereby enabled, with the help of Prætorius, to issue in his 'Messias Judæorum' a greatly improved edition of Laurence's translation.

The Armenian version, although it was published under the title of 'Third Ezra' in Zohrab's edition of the Armenian Bible in the year 1805, was first noticed by Ceriani.[5] At Hilgenfeld's request it was translated into Latin by J. H. Petermann. Four Venetian manuscripts, of which three at least are as late as the seventeenth century, were collated for this purpose. Hilgenfeld, therefore, has the merit of publishing the first complete translation in his 'Messias Judæorum.'[6]

The existence of the Syriac version was first made known by Ceriani.[7] It was found in a copy of the Peshito version of the Old Testament in the Ambrosian Library

---

[1] Ibid., 78. [2] *Das v. Ezrab.* S. 100.
[3] See Bensly, *The Missing Fragment*, 77–8.
[4] *Primi Ezræ Libri, qui apud Vulgatam appellatur quartus, Versio Æthiopica; nunc primo in medium prolata, et Latine Angliceque reddita, a* Ricardo Laurence LL.D. Oxoniæ, 1820.
[5] *Monum. Sacra et Profana*, tom. i., fasc. i. 1861. Præfatio, p. xiii. Mr. Bensly says it was published in the first edition of the Armenian Bible in 1666. See *The Missing Fragment*, p. 2, n. 2, where the authorities for his statement are given.
[6] See the *Mess. Jud.* pp. xxxv. and 378.
[7] *Mon. Sac. et Prof.*, tom. i. fasc. i. Præf. p. xiii.

at Milan. Ceriani published a Latin translation of it in 1866,[1] and the Syriac text itself in 1868.[2] Hilgenfeld has followed Ceriani's translation, with some modifications, and added most of his notes in the 'Messias Judæorum.'[3]

The possession of these versions, which were probably all taken independently from the original Greek,[4] is of great value, not only in enabling us to obtain a more trustworthy text of this particular book, but in confirming by distinct outward evidence the judgment which we formed in connection with the Book of Enoch, that it is not safe to rely on the purity of the text in the case of works of this class which have come down to us through Christian hands. As we have seen, four chapters of Christian composition, which were originally quite independent of 4th Ezra, were at first attached to and finally incorporated with it. Partly on the ground of one of these chapters, Fabricius believed that the whole work proceeded from a Jew converted to Christianity.[5] We now know from the Latin manuscripts themselves, as well as from the other versions, that this argument is baseless. The only other argument used by Fabricius rests upon a single word in vii. 28, where the Latin reads, 'My son Jesus shall be revealed.' The word 'Jesus,' however, is peculiar to the Latin. The Syriac and Arabic have 'my son Messiah;' the Æthiopic, 'my Messiah;' and the Armenian, 'the anointed of God.' The following words presented a statement not very acceptable to Christians. The Latin allowed the doctrine to stand that after four hundred years 'my son Christ shall die;' but the other versions have their several ways of escaping the difficulty. The Armenian omits the statement altogether; the Arabic, while allowing the

---

[1] *Mon. Sac. et Prof.*, tom. i. fasc. ii.   [2] Ibid. tom. v. fasc. i.
[3] *Mess. Jud.* p. xxxvii.   [4] See Hilg. *Mess. Jud.*, p. xxxviii. sq.
[5] *Codex Apocryphus Novi Testamenti*, Hamburgi, 1703, p. 936 sq.

Messianic period of four hundred years to remain, leaves out the death of the Messiah; the Æthiopic retains the death but omits the years; and the Syriac boldly changes the four hundred years into thirty, clearly in order to bring the period into agreement with the earthly life of Jesus. This instance will suffice to show us the necessity for closely scrutinising our authorities before we rely on them for single Messianic expressions.

We must now notice very briefly the contents of this interesting book. The scene is laid in Babylon thirty years after the destruction of Jerusalem; that is, in the year 558 B.C., just a century before the real Ezra came to Jerusalem. As Ezra lay upon his bed he was visited with troubled thoughts, owing to the contrast between the desolation of Zion and the prosperity of Babylon. God had chosen the Israelites for his own people; and though they had sinned, they had not sinned so grievously as other nations. How was it then that they suffered so fearfully, while the heathen triumphed? This question is proposed in an address to God. In reply, the angel Uriel is sent to Ezra, and the various difficulties connected with the fate of Israel are then resolved in a series of seven visions and revelations. In the first of these[1] Ezra is told that he cannot expect to understand the ways of the Most High, that the world is hastening towards its end, and that, though the time of the end is unknown, prodigies and troubles shall herald its approach. The second revelation[2] deals with the difficulty that God ought at least to have punished his people with his own hand. Ezra is again reminded of the limitation of his powers, and is assured that everything must proceed in a regular course, that the end will be brought about through God himself, and not through another, and that Esau

---

[1] iv. 1–v. 15. [2] v. 20–vi. 34.

shall be the end of the present age, and Jacob the beginning of the second. The third revelation [1] takes up the old difficulty in a new form—the world was created for the sake of the Israelites; how comes it that they have no inheritance in it? This leads to a discussion of various points connected with the appearance of the Messiah, the state of the dead, and the future judgment. The fourth revelation [2] is given under the image of a woman mourning for the death of her only son, who had been born after she had spent thirty childless years of married life. While Ezra was rebuking her for her excessive grief, suddenly her face flashed like lightning, the earth trembled, and in her place appeared a city. This woman represented Zion. The thirty fruitless years were three thousand [3] years during which no offering was presented. At the end of this period Solomon built the city and offered sacrifice. The death of the son symbolised the destruction of Jerusalem, and the city of the vision was the glorious city of the Most High. In the fifth revelation [4] the history of the fourth kingdom in Daniel and of the coming of the Messiah is exhibited through a vision of an eagle. As the date of the work must be determined from this vision, we may reserve it for fuller notice a little farther on. The sixth revelation [5] discloses the victory of the Messiah over the heathen powers, and the return of the Israelites to their own land. The last revelation [6] contains the story of Ezra's restoration of the books of Scripture. As these had all been burned, he

---

[1] vi. 35–ix. 24.   [2] ix. 25–x. 60.

[3] Not 'thirty,' as in our common version. See the readings at x. 45–6, in Hilgenfeld. Wieseler, however, defends the reading 'thirty,' and refers it to the thirty years of David's reign, counting from the conquest of Jebus. See his article, 'Das vierte Buch Esra, nach Inhalt und Alter untersucht,' in the *Studien und Kritiken*, 1870, S. 285.

[4] xi. 1–xii. 39.   [5] xiii.   [6] xiv.

was desired to take five swift writers, and to retire with them for forty days. A cup, filled as it were with water, which had, however, the colour of fire, was given to him, and when he had drunk it he was filled with wisdom, and his memory was strengthened. In the forty days ninety-four books were written. Of these twenty-four (evidently the canonical books) were to be given to the public, but seventy were to be reserved for the perusal of the wise. 'And Ezra, having written all these things, was removed and taken up to the place of the living who are like himself. And he has been called the Scribe of the knowledge of the Most High for ever and ever.'

We must next review the evidence in regard to the date of the work. We have already observed that our opinion upon this point depends on our interpretation of the vision of the eagle; but our choice of an interpretation (if, at least, we exclude the hypothesis of interpolation) is fixed within certain historical limits, and these we must notice before proceeding to the vision itself. The book is later than that of Daniel, which is expressly referred to in xii. 11. As sufficient time had elapsed for the fourth kingdom in Daniel to require a fresh interpretation (for this seems implied by verse 12, 'it was not interpreted to him in the way in which I now interpret it to thee'), we may safely say that the book is considerably later than the middle of the second century before Christ. Again, Clemens Alexandrinus quotes v. 35,[1] expressly ascribing the words to Ezra the prophet; and as some time must probably have passed before it could be quoted in this way, we must fix its latest date certainly before the time of Septimius Severus, that is, before 193 A.D. Lücke supposed that we might take the destruction of Jerusalem by the Romans as the latest limit,

[1] *Stromata*, iii. 16.

because this event is not distinctly mentioned, and because in the historical vision there is no reference to the rebuilding of the city.[1] It is evident, however, that the work was composed during a time of the deepest national humiliation; and the actual destruction of the Jewish capital might certainly be alluded to by the words, 'Thou didst take down the habitations of those who were prosperous, and lower the walls of those who injured thee not.'[2] Elsewhere it may be referred to, in connection with the last days, by the expression, 'When the humiliation of Zion shall have been complete.'[3] The coming of the heavenly Jerusalem is clearly indicated in the vision of the woman.[4] There is no allusion in this place to the historical rebuilding of Jerusalem after the Captivity; and this omission seems to me most easily explained by supposing that the writer unconsciously (or perhaps purposely) transferred Ezra to his own time, and that that was a time when only the ideal and heavenly Jerusalem was looked for. Leaving this, however, undetermined, we must seek the interpretation of the historical vision at least within the wider limits above indicated.

One or two attempts which have been made to bring these limits within a very narrow range deserve only a passing notice. The fact that Ezra is represented as seeing the visions in the thirtieth year after the fall of the city cannot, I think, be relied upon as evidence that the author wrote thirty years after either the capture of Jerusalem by Pompeius, in 63 B C., or its destruction by Titus in 70 A.D., for it is not pretended that more than an approximate date would be thus furnished, and 'the thirtieth year' might perhaps be borrowed from the first

---

[1] *Einl. in d. Off.* S. 202-3.   [2] xi. 42.
[3] vi. 19.   [4] x. 50 *sq.*

verse of Ezekiel. As little can we accept Hilgenfeld's confident appeal to the statement[1] that 'Esau is the end of this age,' as a proof that the book was produced under the Idumean Herod;[2] for Edom was used in the Rabbinical theology as an equivalent for Rome,[3] and a similar extended application may have been given to the name by the writer of 4th Ezra. It might, at all events, as Wieseler suggests,[4] and, as Hilgenfeld himself in his earlier work admits,[5] include the Herodian dynasty, and so allow us a period extending to the close of the first century.

The vision itself must now be described. Ezra saw in his dream an eagle, which had twelve wings and three heads, ascending out of the sea. It stretched its wings over all the earth, and all the winds of heaven blew upon it. From its wings were born others, which became very little wings. The heads remained quiet, and the middle head was larger than the others. The eagle flew on its wings, and reigned without contradiction over the world and its inhabitants. It raised itself on its claws, and said to its wings that they should not all keep awake together, but sleep each in its place, and waken at the proper

---

[1] vi. 9.   [2] *Mess. Jud.*, 55.

[3] See Buxtorf's *Lexicon Chaldaicum Talmudicum et Rabbinicum*, Basileæ MDCXXXIX, under the word אֱדוֹם. He says, 'Eo Hebræi *Regnum Christianorum, et Imperium Romanum* intelligunt. Apparet hoc ex infinitis testimoniis.' Instances are subjoined. Again, 'quicquid Prophetæ de *Edom* destructione in ultimis temporibus dicunt, id ipsi de *Roma* intelligunt et exponunt.' Among other reasons for this is the following,—'Alii volunt, Romanos vocari Edomæos, propter Titum Vespasianum, qui sanctuarium ipsorum desolavit. Nam scribunt Titum Vespasianum ab Esavo ortum esse.' If, as Ewald thinks, 4th Ezra was written under Titus, this last notion is not without significance in our present inquiry. See also Grätz, *Geschichte der Juden von den ältesten Zeiten bis auf die Gegenwart. Aus den Quellen neu bearbeitet.* Vierter Band, zweite Auflage, Leipzig, 1866, S. 17. My references to the third vol. will also be to the second edition, which appeared in 1863.

[4] *Stud. u. Krit.* 1870, S. 278.   [5] *Jüd. Apok.* S. 195.

time; and the heads should be kept till the end. The voice which said this proceeded not from the heads, but from the middle of the body. Ezra counted the little wings, and found that there were eight. Then on the right side one wing arose, and reigned over all the earth. But its end came, and it disappeared, so that its place did not appear. And the next one arose, and reigned for a long time. And its end came, and it disappeared like the first; but before this happened, a voice told it that none after it should rule for even half its time. The third reigned and vanished in like manner. And so it happened to all the wings one by one to hold rule, and nowhere to appear a second time. And Ezra saw that the little wings were raised, themselves also on the right side, in order to hold rule; and of these some held it, but immediately disappeared, while others rose up but did not hold rule. And after this, twelve wings and two little wings no longer appeared, and nothing remained in the body of the eagle but the three quiet heads and six little wings. Of these six little wings two detached themselves, and remained under the head at the right-hand side, while four remained in their place. These latter thought to rule; and one rose up and immediately disappeared, and a second disappeared more quickly than the first. While the other two were thinking of reigning the middle head awoke, and, taking the other two heads with it, devoured these aspiring little wings. This head terrified all the earth, and oppressed its inhabitants above all the wings that had been; but suddenly it disappeared. The two remaining heads reigned in like manner; but, lo! that on the right hand devoured that on the left. Then Ezra heard a voice bidding him look, and consider what he saw; and a roaring lion came from the forest, and addressed the eagle with the voice of a man, upbraiding him for his tyranny, and denouncing destruction upon him, that the earth might be refreshed. While the lion spoke, the remaining head vanished; and the two little wings which had gone over to it rose up to reign, but their reign was short, and full of tumult. And lo! they also disappeared, and the whole body of the eagle was burned, and the earth trembled greatly.

In answer to his prayer an interpretation of the dream is granted to Ezra. The eagle is the fourth kingdom that was seen by Daniel; but it was not interpreted to him as it is now interpreted. In this kingdom shall reign twelve kings, one after another. The second shall reign longer than any other of the twelve. This is the interpretation of the twelve wings. The voice from the midst of the body signifies that in the midst of the time of that kingdom [1] great contentions shall arise, and it shall be in danger of falling; but it shall not fall then, but be again restored to its original power. And this is the interpretation of the eight little wings: there shall arise in this kingdom eight kings whose times shall be short; and two of them shall perish when the middle time is approaching; [2] four shall be kept for the time when the end shall begin to approach; [3] but two shall be kept for the end. And this is the interpretation of the three heads: in the last times the Most High will raise up

[1] I follow here the Arm., 'in medio tempore,' which seems the most suitable, and is confirmed by the Syriac, 'inter tempus.' The Arabic has 'in tempore;' Æth. 'de medio corporis regni illius.' The Latin, 'post tempus,' seems clearly wrong.

[2] So the Latin has it, 'appropinquante tempore medio.' The Syriac has substantially the same, 'cum adveniet tempus quod medium erit.' But the Æth. reads, 'in mediis eorum temporibus constitutis;' the Arabic, 'appropinquante tempore eorum;' and the Arm., 'appropinquante tempore et veniente potestate ejus.' This variation at least renders the meaning somewhat doubtful.

[3] This seems the most probable meaning, though it is not very clear in all the versions.

three kings, and they will make many innovations, and tyrannise over the earth and its inhabitants more than all who have been before them. For this reason they are called the heads of the eagle, because they will bring its impieties to a head,[1] and accomplish its end. The disappearance of the largest head signifies that one of those kings shall die upon his bed, and, nevertheless, with torment. The sword shall devour the two who have remained; for the sword of one shall devour him who is with him, but, nevertheless, he also shall fall by the sword in the last times. The two wings that passed over to the right-hand head are those whom the Most High has preserved for the end, whose reign shall be short and full of trouble. And the lion is the Anointed, whom the Most High has reserved for the end.

Notwithstanding the apparent clearness of this vision and its interpretation, its exposition is beset with difficulties, and I know of none that seems in every respect satisfactory. The key to the interpretation might appear to be given by the reference to Daniel, and we might feel constrained, with Hilgenfeld, to seek for our solution among the Græco-Macedonian dynasties: but unfortunately the fourth kingdom of Daniel was in later times referred to the Romans,[2] and their empire is most readily suggested by the imagery of the eagle. We are therefore at liberty to look for the explanation of the details of the vision in either the earlier or the later period.

---

[1] Recapitulabunt. I have sought to preserve the play upon the word.
[2] See Josephus, *Ant.* x. 11, 7, with Lücke's note in his *Einl. in d. Off.* i. S. 196; also the Apocalypse of Baruch, c. 39, where, however, the 'fourth kingdom' is not expressly connected with Daniel; Matt. xxiv. 15; and Clem. Al. *Strom.* i. 21 (end), where, though the kingdoms are not mentioned, Daniel's prophecies are extended to the Roman Empire. See further in our Second Book, ch. vii.

Hilgenfeld has directed all his acumen to the discovery of the necessary facts under the Græco-Macedonian rule. In his 'Jüdische Apokalyptik,'[1] he found the requisite kings in the line of the Ptolemies, whom he took to correspond with the wings of the eagle, and in Cæsar, Antonius, and Octavianus, who, he supposed, were represented by the three heads. In an article[2] written at a later time, however, he abandoned the Ptolemies in favour of the Seleucids; and this later view has received the sanction of his maturest judgment in his 'Messias Judæorum.' He is thus led to fix the date of 4th Ezra soon after the battle of Actium, about 30 B.C. Hilgenfeld's is, so far as I am aware, far the ablest defence of the pre-Christian origin of this part of the book; but the following objections appear to me completely fatal to it. In the first place, if Alexander the Great is meant by the first wing, which 'reigned over the whole earth,' it is very strange that no notice is taken of the division of his kingdom, but we are left to suppose that the other kings succeeded to his full dominion. And not only so, but we are expressly told that the eagle stretched its 'wings' into all the earth, and that it flew on its wings, and reigned over the earth and everything under heaven. It is singular that Hilgenfeld, who is fond of noticing the resemblances to Daniel, has not observed the marked contrast in this respect; for there the division in the fourth kingdom is a prominent feature. Secondly, it could not be affirmed that none of his successors reigned half as long as Seleucus I., Nicator; for though his reign extended to forty-three years, Antiochus the Great occupied the throne for a period not much shorter, thirty-

---

[1] S. 217 *sq.*
[2] 'Die jüdische Apokalyptik und die neuesten Forschungen,' in the *Zeitsch. für wiss. Theol.*, 1860, S. 335 *sq.*

seven years. Hilgenfeld has two different ways of meeting this difficulty. In the article above referred to [1] he boldly treats '*sed nec dimidium ejus*' as an interpolation; but as the reading is sustained by all the versions, this is rather a hazardous conjecture, and it is not repeated in the ' Messias Judæorum.' He there [2] maintains that the words ' no one after thee ' must be limited to the four remaining wings on the right-hand side, a limitation for which there is no warrant whatever in the text, and which is in distinct contradiction of the statement that the second king shall reign longer than any of ' the twelve.' [3] Another grave objection is presented by the fact that the book itself does not contain the slightest intimation that the three heads belong to a different empire from the wings, but on the contrary implies the identity of the kingdom from first to last. Again, Antonius could not very well be spoken of as a king; and he did not perish by the sword of Octavianus, but by his own,—though this latter objection is perhaps not very serious. And once more, it was not Cæsar, but Pompeius, that put an end to the dynasty of the Seleucids; and we cannot suppose, with Hilgenfeld,[4] that a Jewish writer would pass over in silence the terrible conqueror who had captured Jerusalem, and ascribe his exploits to Cæsar merely because the latter happened to be consul at the time. Finally, Julius Cæsar did not die in his bed in torments; and to refer this to his death in his toga beneath the daggers of assassins appears to me one of the most whimsical pieces of interpretation that the ingenuity of modern criticism has produced.

[1] S. 344.   [2] P. 86.
[3] xii. 15 (18 in the Æth.). The number 'twelve' is retained in all the versions, and even in Hilgenfeld's own rendering into Greek:—αὐτὸς κρατήσει πλείονα χρόνον τῶν δώδεκα.
[4] Article, S. 354.

Laurence,[1] followed by Van der Vlis[2] and Lücke,[3] understood by the three heads Sulla, Pompeius, and Cæsar; but their varying attempts to adapt the wings to the period before Sulla have so little plausibility that we need not enter on a detailed refutation.

We are, then, driven to seek the solution of our riddle among the events of the post-Christian period. Of those who have had recourse to this later date the majority concur in recognising the three Flavian emperors, Vespasian, Titus, and Domitian, in the three heads of the eagle; and all without exception refer the second wing to Augustus, who, if we reckon from his first consulship, reigned fifty-six years, or more than twice as long as any of his successors down to the time of Constantine. There is, however, considerable variation in the mode by which the final result is reached, and we must briefly glance at the more important among recent opinions.

Gfrörer[4] understands by the twelve wings the nine emperors from Julius Cæsar to Vitellius, together with the three unsuccessful aspirants to the throne, Vindex, Nymphidius, and Piso Licinianus. For the eight little wings he has recourse to the petty kings and leaders in Palestine. The two that vanished first are Herod the Great and Agrippa I. The group of four is composed of the ringleaders of the Jewish insurrection, Eleazar, John of Gischala, Simon Bar-Giora, and perhaps John the Idumean. The two that went over to the right head are Agrippa II. and Berenice, who in the Jewish war attached themselves to the side of the Romans. The conclusion is thus reached that 4th Ezra was written before the death

---

[1] Prim. Ezræ Lib., p. 314.
[2] *Disputatio Critica de Ezræ libro apocrypho vulgo quarto dicto*: Amstelodami, 1839, p. 179, *sq.*, referred to by Hilg. *Mess. Jud.* p. lvii.
[3] *Einl in d. Off.* i. S. 204 *sq.*
[4] *Jahrh. des Heils*, i. S. 82 *sq.*

of Domitian, about 94 or 95 A.D. This explanation can hardly be accepted as satisfactory; for there is nothing in the vision itself to justify us in departing from the recognised line of Roman emperors in the case either of the great or of the little wings, and the selection of representatives of the latter seems very arbitrary. Even Dillmann,[1] who in other respects assents to this interpretation, suggests that the parts of the vision relating to the little wings may be a later interpolation, made in consequence of the non-fulfilment of the Messianic hopes at the time originally specified. This, however, is a violent remedy, not based on a criticism of the text itself, and to be adopted only as a last resource.

Wieseler[2] agrees with Gfrörer in his interpretation of the twelve wings and the three heads,[3] but proposes a fresh explanation of the eight minor wings. These, he believes, must represent kings dependent on the Roman Empire, and, as the work is Jewish, must be sought in the Herodian dynasty. This line supplies us with exactly eight rulers, Antipater, Herod I., his three sons, Archelaus, Antipas, and Philip, Agrippa I., and his two children, Agrippa II. and Berenice.[4] Though this view is more satisfactory than Gfrörer's, it is exposed to serious objections. It includes in the number of the great wings three pretenders, although it is expressly stated of these wings that they *all* exercised dominion.[5] Wieseler appeals to the statement in xi. 20, 21, that some of them rose up, but did not hold the sovereignty.[6] But it appears to me that the reference to the great wings clearly ends with verse 19, and that the sequentes pennæ (or, according to the Syriac, alæ modicæ) denote the eight little

---

[1] 'Pseudopig. des A. T.' in Herzog's *Encyk.* xii. S. 312.
[2] 'Das vierte Buch Esra, nach Inhalt und Alter untersucht,' in the *Studien und Kritiken*, 1870, S. 263-304.
[3] S. 270-1.   [4] S. 272.   [5] xi. 19; xii. 14.   [6] S. 271.

wings. It is not allowable to make the verse contradictory to other less ambiguous statements, and some allusion to the fate of the subordinate wings is required before verse 22, where it is said that the twelve great wings and two of the little wings had disappeared. The rendering is given so variously by the different versions that it is impossible to be certain about the meaning; but from the statement just referred to in verse 22, one cannot help suspecting that the Arabic is right in dealing here with only two of the little wings. If the Latin, Syriac, and Æthiopic are correct we have, on the contrary, a general statement affecting the minor wings as a class, preparatory to the following account of their separate fortunes. In any case the passage cannot be legitimately appealed to in favour of Wieseler's conclusion, and we are bound to discover twelve men who not only were aspirants to the throne, but actually held the reins of government. The difficulties attending the proposed interpretation of the little wings are even more serious. Their reigns were to be of short duration, '*quorum erunt tempora levia et anni citati*,'[1] a statement which would by no means apply to the reigns of the Herods. Wieseler endeavours to evade this objection by referring 'levia,' as he may fairly do, to the insignificance of the reigns in relation to the eagle-empire, and 'citati' (which is more questionable), not to the shortness of their duration, but to their restless character. But if we allow this interpretation to pass, the evidence of the brevity of their reigns is not exhausted by the verse which Wieseler criticises. When six of the little wings remained, and two of these were separated to be kept till the end, thus leaving a group of four, we are told that one was raised up, and immediately disappeared, and the second disappeared more quickly than the former.[2]

[1] xii. 20. [2] xi. 26, 27.

These two ought, according to the hypothesis, to be found among the sons of Herod the Great; but Philip and Antipas both had reigns of unusual length, and even of Archelaus, who ruled for more than nine years, it could hardly be said that he disappeared immediately. Wieseler, however, in utter defiance of the text, supposes that these two represent Archelaus and Agrippa I.[1] According to this interpretation the remaining two in the group of four must be Philip and Antipas. Yet they survive after the disappearance of the other two; that is, Philip and Antipas survived Agrippa I., and 'thought of ruling' after his death! Still further, these would be the two wings devoured by the head, that is Vespasian.[2] Wieseler does not notice these difficulties; but probably he was conscious of at least the latter, for, in contradiction of his whole exposition and of the plain meaning of the text, he suggests that the two devoured wings were Antiochus king of Commagene and his son Epiphanes.[3] One more weighty objection remains. The chronology is quite unsuitable. After the disappearance of the twelve wings six dependent wings still remain;[4] but six of the Herodian family had vanished long before the outbreak of the civil wars, leaving only two of their number, Agrippa II. and Berenice, to linger on into the Flavian period. We must therefore seek for some other solution of this difficult problem.

Volkmar's interpretation[5] is pronounced by Colani[6] to be a *chef-d'œuvre de sagacité*. He believes that the book was written in the reign of Nerva, in the autumn of the year 97, before the adoption of Trajan, which took

---

[1] S. 275. [2] xi. 28–31. [3] S. 277, Anm. b. [4] xi. 23.
[5] *Das vierte Buch Esra*, S. 338 sq., besides the commentary on the passage.
[6] *Jésus-Christ et les croy. mess.*, p. 52, n. 3.

place in October, had given a new support to the Empire.
He fancies that he has disposed of all difficulties by insisting that a bird must use a pair of wings at once, and
that therefore two wings must represent one emperor.
The twelve wings stand for the emperors down to Nero;
six of the little wings are Galba, Otho, and Vitellius;
and the other two are Nerva, who was reserved for the
throne from the time of Nero, with whom he was in high
favour, till after the death of Domitian. If this process
of division were admissible without violating the plain
meaning of the text, the vision would be brought thereby
into sufficiently close correspondence with the facts of
history, though it would be difficult to understand why
the writer should make a distinct epoch in the course of
events at the death, not of Nero, but of Galba, nor is it
very apparent how he could suppose that the Messiah had
already appeared in the reign of Domitian. But notwithstanding Volkmar's contempt for everyone who is so
unintelligent as not to agree with him, I think this explanation is contradicted by the express statements of the
author himself. There is no intimation that the wings
are to be taken in pairs, unless the doubtful reading of
the Latin in xi. 27, is to be construed as such, 'secundæ
velocius quam priores non apparuit (or comparuerunt),'
where the singular is given by the other versions, with
the exception of the Armenian, which omits the verse.
Not only is this the case, but the following expressions
might almost seem designed to exclude the theory in
question. In xi. 8, in order to mark the proper succession of reigns, the eagle says to his wings, 'Do not wish
all to be awake at the same time, but sleep each in his
place, and be awake at the proper time.' This surely
implies that they were to reign one at a time. But as if
to place the matter beyond doubt, it is said in verse 12,

'one[1] wing rose up on the right side, and reigned over all the earth.' To say that this means that a pair of wings rose up, one on each side, is a sort of criticism by which facts may be tortured into the mould of our own views. Again, in verse 19 it is said, 'and thus it happened to all the wings one by one[2] to exercise the sovereignty.' In verses 26 and 27, it is said of the little wings, 'one[3] was raised up, but immediately disappeared; and the second disappeared more quickly than the former.' This is said in relation to the group of four little wings; and after this two of the four are still left. Here, then, certainly the wings are not taken in pairs. It is strange that in the presence of this fact Renan, who adopts Volkmar's view, should say that in the combinations relating to the wings, uneven numbers are never introduced.[4] It is true that we do not find combinations of three, five, or seven; but in this instance the wings are unmistakeably taken one by one. Almost equally decisive is the interpretation of the twelve wings in xii. 14, 'in it shall reign twelve kings one after another' (unus post unum, confirmed by Syr. and Arm.), and of the little wings as representing eight kings, in verse 20. The latter statements, however, present no difficulty to Volkmar; for the 'intelligent reader' would at once perceive that the number must be halved. We must add that Volkmar supposes that the writer purposely veiled his meaning under a riddle, and did not wish it to be too evident in unfriendly quarters. This suggestion is not without its value; but the key to a riddle ought to fit express and unambiguous statements.

This idea that the author intentionally wrapped his

---

[1] Una, expressed in all the versions but the Æth.
[2] Singulatim, a specification omitted only in the Arm.
[3] Una, sustained by all the versions.
[4] 'L'Apocalypse de l'an 97,' in the *Revue des Deux Mondes*, 1875, p. 141.

revelations in a mystery, which could be resolved only by
the discovery of the right clue, may be of some service
to Ewald's opinion, which, notwithstanding one or two
difficulties, and the scant favour which it has received,
appears to me on the whole the most satisfactory that
has been proposed.[1] According to him the twelve wings
represent the twelve Roman emperors down to Domitian;
the eight little wings stand for the eight emperors among
them who reigned less than ten years, Domitian, for
whom a short reign was anticipated, being included
among these; and the three heads describe, under yet
another form, the three Flavian princes. The twelve
wings vanished from the vision at the death of Nero,
because with him passed away the genuine successors of
Augustus; the empire, like a maimed eagle, was crippled
by the civil wars; and the remaining emperors all came
under the class of little wings. At the same time disappeared two of the little wings, namely Julius Cæsar and
Caius. The two who separated themselves, to be kept
till the last time, were Titus and Domitian. The group
of four was composed of Galba, who quickly vanished,
Otho, who disappeared more quickly still, Vitellius and
Vespasian. But here occurs the main difficulty in this
explanation. Vespasian, the greatest of the three heads,
came and devoured the two contending wings. It seems
very harsh to represent him as devouring himself.
Ewald, in his pamphlet,[2] assumes that the reading is
corrupt, and that it ought to be, 'one of the two wings.'
This assumption he abandons in the text of his history,
merely suggesting it in a note;[3] but he offers no explanation of the difficulty. Is it not possible, however, that
the writer meant to imply that Vespasian as a little wing

---

[1] See his *Das vierte Ezrabuch*; and his *Gesch. d. V. I.* vii. S. 65 *sq.*
[2] S. 14.　　　　　[3] S. 81.

in conflict with Vitellius, and acknowledged as emperor only in the east, was, through his ultimate success, swallowed up in Vespasian the great and victorious head of the whole empire? The description of the three heads suits the Flavian dynasty. Vespasian died of an illness which may very well have been a painful one, though on that point we have no information; and the vindictive feelings of a Jew would gladly magnify the sufferings of his country's enemy. Titus did not perish by the sword of Domitian; and though there were suspicions of foul play, his death could hardly have been represented as the result of open violence. Ewald, therefore, thinks that the book was written during the reign of Titus, about 80 A.D.[1] The death of the Emperor at the hand of Domitian might be anticipated from the character and machinations of the latter,[2] while it was hoped that Domitian himself would perish through the advent of the Mess'ah.

This explanation is not to be disposed of by simply calling it 'gar wunderlich.'[3] I may add a few considerations which help to sustain it. There is nothing in the text to prove that the two classes of wings and the three heads all refer to different rulers, and Schürer is therefore not justified in laying it down as a fundamental canon for the interpretation of the vision that we must find twenty-

[1] This conclusion is, I think, unnecessary; for it is difficult to say what stories may have found credence at the time. Dion Cassius (in the abridgment of Xiphilinus, lib. lxvi.) says of Titus that 'he died in the same waters as his father; as report says, at the hand of his brother, . . . but as some write, through illness; for while he was still breathing, and might perhaps have recovered, Domitian threw him into a chest filled with a quantity of snow, that he might die more speedily. At all events, while he [Titus] was still living, he [Domitian] rode into Rome, and entered the camp, and took the name and the power of the emperor.'

[2] See Suetonius (Titus 9, Domit. 2), who refers to the incessant plots of Domitian against Titus.

[3] Hilgenfeld, in the *Zeitschr. für wiss. Theol.* 1860, S. 343, Anm. 2.

three successive kings or aspirants to royalty.[1] On the contrary, the connection in xii. 13, 14, seems to limit the total number of kings to twelve:—'There shall arise a kingdom upon earth, and it shall be more terrible than all kingdoms that have been before it. And there shall reign in it twelve kings, one after another.' This certainly reads like a general statement affecting the whole period of the kingdom; and this impression is not invalidated by the subsequent statement that 'this is the interpretation of the twelve wings.' Another point not without significance is this, that the general description of the eagle, and of his dominion over all the earth, is introduced before any notice is taken of the little wings; and these latter, instead of forming a separate group, are produced out of the large wings. They may, therefore, represent, not a distinct succession of kings from those symbolized by the larger pinions, but some of the same kings under a new aspect. Again, this explanation relieves the concluding scene from great apparent confusion. The heads were to be kept till the last time.[2] They were to accomplish its last events.[3] The Messiah was to appear in the time of the last head, and cause the whole eagle to perish at his rebuke.[4] All this surely implies that the heads were to be the last emperors; and the appearance of two little wings afterwards is quite unintelligible. We cannot, with Volkmar, regard them as descriptive of historical reality, for it is incredible that the writer can have placed the coming of the Messiah in the past, and supposed that an emperor had just perished

---

[1] See his *Lehrb. der neut. Zeitg.*, S. 557. Schürer makes up the number out of unknown competitors during the troubled period, 68-70 A.D., except the last two little wings, which he ascribes to the apocalyptic imagination of the writer, S. 562.
[2] xi. 9, in novissimo; xii. 23, in novissimis.
[3] xii. 25, perficient novissima ejus.   [4] xi. 36 *sq.*

under his rebuke; nor can we, with Schürer, treat them as apocalyptic creations, because they are utterly insignificant, and answer no apocalyptic purpose. Now the Latin version seems to imply that when the last head perished, the two little wings no longer appeared;[1] and this would exactly suit Ewald's explanation. The other versions, it is true, do not sustain this meaning; and if they are right in representing the two wings as rising up to rule after the appearance of the Messiah and the destruction of the third head, Ewald's view has, at this point, a fatal flaw. But the Latin may have preserved the truer conception; and the other translators (a slight modification of whose text would be sufficient to produce the required difference of meaning) may have been led astray by a very natural misunderstanding of the vision. It is a more serious difficulty that the two wings, instead of attaching themselves to two heads, place themselves under one, and of this I can give no adequate explanation, unless it be that the head which destroyed its fellow was regarded as the guilty cause of the shortness and disaster of both his own and the preceding reign. Notwithstanding this and the other difficulties which have been pointed out, I am disposed to accept the main features of Ewald's interpretation till one less open to objection can be discovered.

Thus far those who have placed the composition of 4th Ezra in the post-Christian period of the Roman Empire have agreed in referring the three heads of the eagle to the three Flavian emperors,—a conclusion which seems forced upon us by the general limits of its date mentioned above. Gutschmid, however, escapes from these limits by the supposition that the eagle-vision is a

---

[1] xii. 1, 2, et factum est, dum loqueretur leo verba hæc ad aquilam, et vidi, et ecce quod superaverat caput [non comparuit seems to be wanting] et non comparuerunt alæ duæ, quæ ad eum transierunt et erectæ sunt ut regnarent et erat regnum eorum exile et tumultu plenum.

later Christian interpolation.[1] In his view the six wings on the right hand are the first six emperors, down to Nero. Galba, Otho, and Vitellius are omitted from the list, as is the case also with the lists of Ptolemæus and Clemens Alexandrinus, but are pointed out in the allusion to civil wars which should endanger the existence of the empire. The six wings on the left-hand side are Vespasian, Domitian, Trajan, Hadrian, Antoninus, and M. Aurelius. Among these come the short reigns of Titus and Nerva, the two little wings which vanished along with the twelve. The group of four little wings is composed of Commodus, Pertinax, Didius Julianus, and Pescennius Niger. While the latter two rose up as rival emperors, Septimius Severus, the great head, appeared upon the scene, and, having destroyed his enemies, afterwards associated with himself in the empire the two smaller heads, his sons Caracalla and Geta. Severus died from an attack of gout, which was so painful that he is said to have asked, though in vain, for poison to terminate his sufferings. Geta was murdered by order of Caracalla, and the latter was assassinated five years later at the instigation of Macrinus. Macrinus was declared emperor; and he, along with his son Diadumenianus, whom he appointed Augustus, completed the number of the little wings. He was defeated by the general of Elagabalus on June 8th, 218 A.D.; and he and his son were put to death not long afterwards. Now, the downfall of Macrinus might have been anticipated from his defeat; but as, according to the vision, he was to be succeeded, not by another emperor, but by the Messiah, we must suppose that the prophecy was written before his death was known. Gutschmid has consequently no hesitation in assigning its composition to June, 218 A.D.

---

[1] See the article before referred to, S. 33 *sq.*

There is, however, an obvious difficulty which must be met. In the interpretation of the vision the Messiah appears after the reign of the last pair of little wings, which is quite in conformity with Gutschmid's view; but in the vision itself the lion comes forward under Caracalla, and Macrinus and his son follow. Now, no one writing under Macrinus could have supposed that the Messiah had come in the time of the previous emperor. Gutschmid is therefore driven to the conclusion that the vision was first written under Caracalla, between 212 and 217 A.D.; but when the tyrant perished, and no Messiah appeared, the author, in order to save his credit as a prophet, thrust in the reign of the two little wings. As we have thus reached a date later than the reference in Clemens Alexandrinus, the whole passage must be an interpolation; and as a Jewish interpolation could not have found its way into a book already esteemed among the Christians, the author must have belonged to the Christian Church.

To this interpretation there are some serious objections. The twelve wings do not reign 'one after another,' —a phrase which naturally suggests continuous succession, —but have no less than three interruptions. Again, Commodus reigned twelve years, and yet he is one of the little wings, while some other emperors who reigned a shorter time are among the greater wings. Gutschmid endeavours to meet this difficulty by pointing out that for eighty-two years each Cæsar had reigned for at least nineteen years; that the previous reigns had been wise and orderly compared with that of Commodus; and that the writer was obliged to be a little arbitrary in order to keep within the number twelve for the large wings, a number suggested by the six great feathers in each wing of the real eagle. Our critic, however, does not indicate the full force of the objection. Would it be possible to describe Commodus by the words, 'Lo! one was raised up, and immediately disappeared?' And though it is quite true that Pertinax 'disappeared more quickly,' would not this be a strange comparison between a period of less than three months and one of twelve years? I cannot but think that this circumstance is quite fatal to the proposed explanation.[1] The suggestion of a double date for the composition, and of such an imperfect rectification of the earlier state of the text, is not very easy to admit. Nor should we rashly have recourse to the idea of interpolation. The work, with its sevenfold arrangement, is more complete with than without the vision, and the analogy of other apocalyptic books leads us to expect an historical sketch of this kind. And I see no reason why a Christian should have expected the second coming of Christ so confidently in the time of Macrinus, or why he should have inserted a passage free from all tincture of Christian doctrine. And lastly, the vision is casually referred to in xiv. 17 (in all the versions),—'for already the eagle which thou hast seen in the vision is hastening

[1] I learn from Schürer (*Lehrb. d. n. Z.* S. 560) that Le Hir ('Du IVe livre d'Ésdras,' in *Etudes Bibliques*, Paris, 1869, i. 184-192) agrees in the main with Gutschmid, but, appealing to the list of emperors in Clemens Alexandrinus, assigns a single reign to M. Aurelius and Commodus, and then obtains another little wing by inserting Clodius Albinus after Pescennius Niger. If this arrangement were allowable, the difficulty stated in the text would be obviated. But though it may have been convenient for Clemens (*Strom.* i. 21), whose object it was simply to ascertain the number of years from Augustus to Commodus, to count the last two reigns together, it does not at all follow that he regarded them as one reign. On the contrary, it is quite clear that he treats Commodus as a distinct emperor. Not to do so in reckoning up, not the years, but the number of the Roman emperors would be quite arbitrary and unaccountable. In the same way, Clemens furnishes no excuse for the omission of Galba, Otho, and Vitellius; for he actually mentions Galba, and assigns to him one year, and as the three together did not make up two years, it was unnecessary to refer to the other two.

to come.' This of course might be also an interpolation; but interpolators are seldom so ingenious in their method.

In regard to the rest of the book Gutschmid agrees with Hilgenfeld, and fixes its date in the autumn of 31 B.C.[1] He makes an elaborate chronological calculation founded on the statement that Solomon built the Temple in the 3,000th year of the world, and on the division of the world's history into twelve parts, of which nine and a half had passed in the time of Ezra.[2] The principle of the argument may be briefly stated. By calculating the length of time from the building of the Temple to the date assigned to Ezra, thirty years after the Captivity, and adding this to three thousand, we obtain the number of years between Ezra and the Creation; and dividing this number by nine and a half we find the length of each of the twelve periods. Multiplying the number of years in a period by twelve, we determine the duration of the world's history; and deducting the 400 Messianic years, we reach the latest limit of the date of the book, reckoning from the Creation. The Christian era is found by adding 558 years to the date already fixed for Ezra, and thus the date of the work before Christ is readily ascertained. This argument is by no means so conclusive as it may appear at first sight. Its validity depends on the assumption that the writer of 4th Ezra placed the Captivity the same number of years before the Christian era that we do, and that he consistently maintained a false representation throughout his work. But we have no evidence that he was a good chronologist. He begins by misplacing Ezra one hundred years, and it is certainly not impossible that his reckonings may have been taken from the date of the real Ezra. Another source of uncertainty is found in the state of the text,

[1] *L. c.* S. 70.   [2] xiv. 11, 12.

which is far from accordant in the several versions; and while Gutschmid bases his reasoning on one conjectural emendation, Hilgenfeld proposes another, and has therefore to reach the same result by a different mode of calculation. For the present Latin, 'transierunt ejus decimam et dimidium decimæ partis,' Gutschmid suggests as the original Greek, καὶ παρῆλθεν (ὁ αἰὼν) εἰς τὸ δέκατον αὐτοῦ μέρος καὶ εἰς τὸ ἥμισυ τοῦ δεκάτου.[1] Hilgenfeld emends decimæ into ἐνδεκάτου, and supposes that ten and a half parts have passed; but the Æthiopic has, ' the world is arranged in *ten* parts, and it has come to the tenth, and half of the tenth remains.' The other versions do not enable us to decide between the Latin and the Æthiopic; for the Arabic has a general statement without numbers, and the Syriac and Armenian omit the verses. Out of the same oracular statement Volkmar joyously extracts his own post-Christian date. Further, the various calculations depend on a supposition which we are not justified in assuming, that the periods are of equal length. In the Apocalypse of Baruch[2] the world's history is also divided into twelve periods, which are determined, not by their duration, but by the nature of their events, so much so that Hezekiah, Manasseh, and Josiah constitute three distinct periods. The Captivity marks the eleventh epoch, thus confirming Hilgenfeld's emendation in 4th Ezra. The twelfth period extends indefinitely to the last troubled times in which the Messiah appears. If we admit the possibility that the twelve parts in Ezra were similarly determined, the chronological argument in all its forms becomes worthless. The general conclusion, then, which is forced upon us in regard to these investigations, is that they rest on such unstable ground as to be of no value in the way of evidence.

[1] S. 59.   [2] Chs. liii.-lxxiv.

Gutschmid further relies upon the reference to Esau, which we have already discussed. He appeals likewise to several of the occurrences mentioned among the signs of the last days in v. 1–12, vi. 18–28, and ix. 1–4. So far, however, as these may be legitimately singled out as actual events, in contradistinction from the mere prodigies amid which they are placed in the first two passages, they suit the reign of Titus as well as that of Herod. The mutual hostility of nations, generals, princes, friends, characterized not only the civil war between Octavianus and Antonius, but that in which Vespasian rose to power; and that such troubles in the Empire were not over in consequence of Vespasian's successes might be inferred from the conspiracy formed against him by his supposed friends Cæcina and Marcellus in the last year of his reign, and from the enmity of Domitian against Titus. If there was a terrible earthquake in Palestine in the year of the battle of Actium, several earthquakes preceded the eruption of Vesuvius. If there was a fire in Rome before the battle of Actium, Cremona was reduced to ashes in the time of Vespasian,[1] the Capitol was burned,[2] the event being regarded by the Gauls as a sign of the approaching downfall of the Empire;[3] and the Capitol, when rebuilt, was destroyed with a number of other public buildings by a terrible conflagration in the reign of Titus.[4] Besides these disasters, so alarming to Italy and Rome, several cities throughout the Empire were, in the reign of Vespasian, afflicted with earthquake or conflagration.[5] And if we are to descend to such trifles as the reported appearance of a wolf in Rome in explanation of the statement that 'wild beasts shall wander beyond their province,'

---

[1] Tacitus, *Hist.* iii. 33.
[2] Ibid. 71.   [3] Ibid. iv. 54.
[4] Suetonius, *Titus*, 8; and Xiphilinus, Dion Cassius, lib. lxvi.
[5] Sueton. *Vespas.* 17.

we may find a parallel in the multitude of foul birds which hid the day from Vitellius, a fact which illustrates the prediction, 'birds shall migrate.'[1]

On the whole, then, I think we may rest in the conclusion that 4th Ezra was written during the last quarter of the first century after Christ. A careful investigation leads us to this period; and the fact is not unimportant in estimating the force of the argument, that several critics who otherwise disagree concur in recognising Augustus under the figure of the second wing, and the Flavian emperors in the three heads.[2] The general tone of the book is admirably suited to a period when the Jewish nationality seemed hopelessly ruined, and piety could console itself only with Messianic dreams. The place of composition cannot be determined with certainty; but it may not improbably have been Rome, the mystic Babylon.[3]

SECTION VII.—*The Apocalypse of Baruch.*

The Apocalypse of Baruch was for the first time given to the modern world in 1866 by Ceriani.[4] As in the case of 4th Ezra, however, the original Greek has been lost; and we are indebted to Syrian industry for the preservation of this valuable relic. Ceriani did not at first publish the Syriac text, but contented himself with offering to his

[1] Tacitus, *Hist.* iii. 56; 4th Ezra v. 6 and 8.
[2] The following among the more recent critics, in addition to those already mentioned, assign the book to the closing years of the first century: Anger, *Synopsis Evangeliorum*, Lipsiæ, 1852, Prol. p. xix., and *Vorlesungen über d. Gesch. der mess. Idee*, S. 86; Keim, *Gesch. Jesu*, i. S. 248; Oehler, 'Messias,' in *Herzog*, S. 430; Schürer, *Lehrb. d. n. Z.* S. 561; Colani, *Jésus-Christ et les croy. mess.* pp. 52 3; Davidson, Introd. to O. T. iii. 362. Schenkel ascribes it to the Roman period before Christ, *Bibel-Lexikon*, 'Messias,' S. 206.
[3] Wieseler fixes upon Palestine or some neighbouring country, largely on account of the supposed references to the Herods: S. 280.
[4] *Monumenta Sac. et Prof.* tom. i. fasc. ii. 73-98.

readers a verbatim Latin translation. The original text was printed in 1871.¹ The work was discovered in a Syriac manuscript judged by Cureton to belong to the sixth century. In addition to the canonical books of the Old Testament according to the Peshito version, this manuscript contains several other works, namely 'The Book of the Revelation of Baruch;' 4th Ezra; 3rd Maccabees (published in the London Polyglott); 4th Maccabees (a version of the work, 'De Machabæis, sive de rationis imperio,' printed at the end of editions of Josephus); and 'Sermo de excidio postremo Jerosolymæ' (which forms the sixth book of the De Bello Judaico of the Hebrew Josephus or Joseph Ben-Gorion). We must slightly qualify our statement that our first knowledge of the Apocalypse of Baruch was derived from this manuscript; for the last few chapters, containing an Epistle of Baruch to the nine and a half tribes of Israel, had long been known. This epistle, though with some variations, was printed in the Paris and London Polyglotts, and has appeared since in Syriac and in various translations. It also finds a place as a separate work in the manuscript to which we owe the preservation of the entire Apocalypse.²

The composer of this work has, like the author of the Book of Baruch in the ordinary Apocrypha of the Old Testament, chosen as the fictitious writer of his revelations the friend and amanuensis of Jeremiah.³ The scene is laid in or near Jerusalem; and the supposed time is that immediately preceding and following the destruction of the city and the transportation of the people to Babylon. The author professes to give the exact year, 'the twenty-fifth of Jechoniah King of Judah.'⁴ Jechoniah must here

---

[1] *Mon. Sac. et Prof.* tom. v. fasc. ii.

[2] See *Mon. Sac. et Prof.* tom. i. fasc. i. 1861, præf. pp. xiii., xiv., and tom. i. fasc. ii. 1866, præf. p. i.

[3] Jer. xxxii. 12; xxxvi. 4, &c.   [4] Ch. i.

stand for Jehoiakim, and the twenty-fifth year ought to be the eleventh.[1] The book contains several passages of great value in our present inquiry, and these will be fully noticed in due time. Meanwhile the following brief synopsis of its contents may be sufficient.

The work divides itself into seven parts, if, with Ewald,[2] we treat the letter to the nine and a half tribes as a kind of appendix. Baruch is throughout represented as the speaker, referring to himself in the first person, except in the openings of chapters i. and lxxviii. which are of the nature of a title.

The first part (chs. i.–ix.) opens by telling how the word of the Lord came to Baruch, and warned him of the destruction impending over Jerusalem on account of the wickedness of its inhabitants The punishment should last only for a time, and the ruin of the city should not be accomplished by the hands of its enemies. The next day the army of the Chaldeans surrounded Jerusalem; and when the sacred vessels had been committed to the safe custody of the earth, to be kept till the last times, angels overthrew the walls, the enemy were admitted, and the people were led captive to Babylon. Then Baruch and Jeremiah rent their clothes, and fasted seven days.

In the second part (chs. x.–xii.) Jeremiah is sent to Babylon, but Baruch is told to remain amid the desolation of Zion, that God may show him what will come to pass at the end of days. So Baruch sits before the gates of the Temple, and utters a lamentation over the fate of Zion, and prophesies vengeance against the victorious land now so prosperous. Having thus given vent to his grief, he again fasts for seven days.

In the third part (chs. xiii.–xx.) he stands upon Mount Zion, and is told that he shall be preserved till the end of

---

[1] See 2 Kings xxiii. 36; xxiv. 1 sq.   [2] *Gesch. d. V. I.* vii. S. 80.

times, that he may bear testimony against the nations which oppressed his people. He answers that only few shall survive in those days to hear the words of the Lord, and complains that those who have not walked in vanity like other peoples have derived no advantage from their faithfulness. The Lord answers that the future world was made on account of the just; 'for this world is a contest and trouble to them in much labour, and therefore that which is to come is a crown in great glory.' In further conversation Baruch is advised not to estimate the blessings of life by its length, and to look rather to the end than the beginning. He is then desired to sanctify himself, and fast for seven days.

In the fourth part (chs. xxi.–xxx.) he comes from a cave in the valley of Cedron, whither he had withdrawn, to the place where God spoke with him before. It is sunset, and he begins to deplore the bitterness of life, and calls upon God to hasten the promised end. In reply he is reminded of his ignorance, and told that the predetermined number of men must be completed, but that the end is not far distant. Baruch then says that he does not know what will happen to the enemies of his people, or at what time God will visit his works. The signs of the end are accordingly enumerated, the last time being divided into twelve parts, each with its distinguishing characteristic. These parts, however, are to be mixed together, and to minister to one another. The specified signs shall affect the whole earth; 'and then Messiah will begin to be revealed.' A description of the Messianic period follows, on which we need not at present dwell. With this the conversation terminates; and though the usual fast is not mentioned, the section evidently comes to a close.

In the fifth part (chs. xxxi.–xliii.), having consoled the

people by telling them of the future glory of Zion, he goes and sits upon the ruins of the Temple. While he laments he falls asleep, and has a vision of a vine and a cedar, of which the interpretation is afterwards given to him. The vision relates to the triumph of the Messiah. Baruch then asks, 'To whom and to how many shall these things be? or who shall be worthy to live in that time?' for many of God's people have thrown away the yoke of the law; but others have left their vanity, and fled for refuge under God's wings. God answers him: 'To those who have believed will be the predicted good, and to those who despise will be the opposite of this.' Baruch is then commanded to go and instruct the people and afterwards to fast for seven days, preparatory to further communications.

In the sixth part (chs. xliv.–xlvii.) he calls together his first-born son, his friend Gadelii, and seven of the elders of the people, and tells them that he is going to his fathers, according to the way of all the earth. He exhorts them not to depart from the law, and promises that they shall see 'the consolation of Zion.' He dwells on the rewards and punishments of the future world, desires them to advise the people, and assures them that, though he must die, 'a wise man shall not be wanting to Israel, nor a son of the law to the race of Jacob.' He then goes to Hebron, and fasts for seven days.

In the seventh part (chs. xlviii.–lxxvi.) he prays for compassion on his people, the people whom God has chosen, and who are unlike all others. He is told that the time of tribulation must arise; and many of its circumstances are recounted. He deplores such sad consequences of the sin of Adam; and in answer to an inquiry he is informed about the Resurrection and its results. At last he falls asleep, and has a vision. As this vision (ch. liii.) and its interpretation (chs. lvi.–lxxiv.), though they bring us to no definite date, throw an interesting light upon the uncertain methods in which history was parcelled out into periods, we may notice them at more length than would otherwise be necessary. A cloud ascended from the great sea; and it was full of white and black waters, and a similitude of lightning appeared at its extremity. It passed quickly on, and covered the whole earth. Afterwards, it began to discharge its rain. But the waters which descended from it were not all alike; for first there were very black waters for a time, and afterwards the waters became bright, but of these there were not many. Black waters succeeded, and again gave place to bright, and so on for twelve times; but the black waters were always more than the bright. And at the end of the cloud it rained black waters; and these were darker than all that had been before, and fire was mingled with them, and they brought corruption and ruin. And after these things the lightning which he had seen in the extremity of the cloud, flashed so that it illumined the whole earth; and it healed those regions where the last waters had descended. After this twelve rivers ascended from the sea, and surrounded that lightning, and were made subject to it. At this point Baruch awoke through fear. In answer to his prayer for the interpretation of the vision the angel Ramiel was sent to satisfy his request. The cloud symbolised 'the length of the age.' The first black waters were the sin of Adam, with its consequences, including the fall of the angels and the flood. The second, the bright waters, were Abraham and his descendants, and those who were like them. The third (black) waters were the mixture of all the sinners after the death of these just men, and the iniquity of the land of Egypt. The fourth (bright) waters were the advent of Moses, Aaron, Miriam, Joshua, Caleb, and all who were like them, in whose time 'the lamp of the eternal law shone upon all who were sitting in darkness.' The fifth (black) waters were the works of the Amorites, and the sins of the Israelites in the days of the judges. The sixth (bright) waters were the time of David and Solomon. The seventh (black) waters were the perversion of Jeroboam, and the sins of his successors, and the time of the captivity of the nine and a half tribes. The eighth (bright) waters were the righteousness of Hezekiah. The ninth (black) waters were the universal impiety in the days of Manasseh. The tenth (bright) waters were the purity of the generations of Josiah. The eleventh (black) waters were the calamity which had just happened to Zion. The rest of the interpretation is of course given in the future tense. 'As for the twelfth (bright) waters which thou hast seen, this is the word. For the time shall come after these things when thy people shall fall into calamity, so as to be in danger of all perishing together. But, nevertheless, they shall be saved, and their enemies shall fall before them. And they shall for some time have much joy. And in that time, after a little, Zion shall be again built, and its oblations shall be again established, and the priests shall return to their ministry, and the nations shall again come to glorify it: but nevertheless not fully as in the beginning. But it shall come to pass after these things, there shall be the ruin of many nations. These are the bright waters which thou hast seen.' The other waters which were blacker than all the rest, after the twelfth, belonged to the whole world; and they represented times of trouble and conflict, which are described at some length; and all who survived these should be delivered into the hands of the Messiah. These last black waters are, in the interpretation, succeeded simply by other bright waters, representing the blessedness of the Messianic time. Baruch, having heard the words of the angel, expresses his wonder at the goodness of God. He is then informed that, though he must depart from the earth, he shall not die. But before his removal he must go and instruct the people.

We are next told (ch. lxxvii.) how Baruch went to the people, and admonished them to be faithful, holding out hopes that their brethren might return from the captivity. The people promised to remember the good that God had done to them, and requested him to write a letter, before his departure, to their brethren in Babylon. He promised to do so, and send the epistle by the hands of men, and also to forward a letter to the nine and a half tribes by means of a bird. Accordingly, he sat alone under an oak, and wrote two letters. One he sent by three men to Babylon, and the other to the tribes beyond the Euphrates by an eagle which he called. He charged the eagle not to pause till he reached his destination; and, to encourage him, reminded him of Noah's dove, of Elijah's ravens, and how 'Solomon, in the time of his reign, whithersoever he wished to send or to seek anything, commanded a bird, and it obeyed him as he had commanded it.' Then the letter is subjoined (chs. lxxviii.–lxxxvi.). It consists of a general exhortation to the captive tribes to be faithful, in hope of being soon restored to a happier lot. The last chapter (lxxxvii.) relates how he folded and sealed the letter, tied it to the eagle's neck, and despatched it.

The work whose contents we have thus summarised was, according to its title in the manuscript in which it has been preserved, 'translated from Greek into Syriac.' Notwithstanding the Hebraic colouring of its thought and language, it may very well have been written originally in Greek. This point, however, I cannot pretend to have examined with any care, for it is of no great importance in our present inquiry.

More material is it to determine the nationality and religion of its author. There can be no doubt that it was written by a non-Christian Jew. Though it is rich in Messianic passages, I have not observed a single expression which betrays a Christian hand. The book is also pervaded by the strong and exclusive feeling of a Jew, confident, amid the most terrible humiliations, in the divine election of his race. In support of this affirmation I may quote some of the most striking expressions, following simply the order of their occurrence. In ch. iii. Baruch says in his prayer, 'If thou destroy thy city, and deliver thy land to those who hate us, how shall the name of Israel be again mentioned? . . . or to whom will be unfolded that which is in thy law?' In ch. xli. he laments that many of God's people had thrown away the yoke of the law. In ch. xlviii. he pleads with God, 'For this is the people whom thou hast chosen, and these are the people of whom thou dost not find the like. But I will speak before thee now, and will say as my heart thinks. In thee we trust, because, lo! thy law is with us, and we know that we shall not fall, so far as we keep thy ordinances. We shall always be happy at least in this, that we have not been mingled with Gentiles. For we are all named one people, who have received one law from one [God, or law-giver], and the law which is among us will help us, and the excellent wisdom which is in us will aid us.' In ch. li. the wicked are condemned to punishment 'because they have despised my law, and stopped their ears that they might not hear wisdom or receive understanding.' The good, on the other hand, are 'those who have been saved in their works, and whose hope the law has now been.' In ch. lix. we are told that 'the lamp of the eternal law' was given in the time of Moses. In ch. lxvi. Josiah is commended because 'he alone was firm in the law in that time, so that he did not leave anyone uncircumcised, or who acted impiously, in all the land all the days of his life. But he is one who shall receive an eternal reward, and he shall be glorified before the Mighty One more than many in the last time.' In ch. lxvii. we are told that the calamity of Zion is a grief to the very angels, and that 'the smoke of perfumes of righteousness out of the law has been quenched from Zion.' In ch. lxxii. it is said that in the time of the Messiah 'men of all nations shall be subjected to thy people,' and that 'all those who ruled over you . . . shall be delivered to the sword.' In ch. lxxxiv. the nine and a half tribes are admonished to remember Zion and the law, the holy land also, and their brothers, and the testament, and their fathers, and the feasts and sabbaths, and to deliver 'the traditions of the law' to their sons; and in ch. lxxxv. they are reminded that while their fathers had 'prophets and saints' to intercede for them, 'now we have nothing but the Mighty One and his law.'[1] These expressions speak for themselves, and betray the hand of one who adhered to the narrowest Jewish position.

In considering by whom this book was written, we cannot fail to be struck with the remarkable resemblances, both in general structure and in particular thoughts and expressions, between it and 4th Ezra. When no more of it was known than the letter to the nine and a half tribes, Dillmann had already observed its relation to the

[1] For the importance attached to the law, see also chapters xliv., xlvi., liv., lvii.

period and the circle of thought from which 4th Ezra proceeded;[1] and when the complete text was at last open to investigation, Ewald ascribed these two apocalypses, without any misgiving, to the same author.[2] Without venturing to pronounce confidently on so delicate a point, we may safely affirm that, if they are not both from the same hand, one is an intentional imitation of the other, but nevertheless with such clear differences and so much originality as not to be fairly open to the charge of plagiarism. In order to gain a just impression upon this subject, one ought to read the two works consecutively; but declining the task of a minute comparison, we may notice here a few of the more striking resemblances. In each the general object is substantially the same,—to account for the present calamities of Israel, and awaken hopes of a more glorious future. In each the hero is an eminent man from the time of the Babylonian captivity, and the thoughts which he reveals are communicated in supernatural conversations and visions. The partition of the matter into seven scenes, divided for the most part from one another by intervals of seven days, is characteristic of each; and if Ezra has finally to devote forty days to the restoration of the Scriptures, Baruch must instruct the people for the same period, before his removal from the earth. The division of the pre-Messianic time into twelve parts (given in each instance in the seventh section), the interest in the lost tribes,[3] the address of the lion to the eagle in Ezra[4] compared with that of the vine to the cedar in Baruch[5] (each in the fifth part), the awakening through terror caused by a supernatural

---

[1] 'Pseudepigr. des A. T.' in *Herzog*, S. 316.
[2] *Gesch. des V. I.* vii. S. 83 *sq.*
[3] See 4 Ezra xiii. 39; Baruch, lxxvii.-lxxxvii.
[4] xi. 38-46. [5] xxxvi.

dream,[1] the appeal to human ignorance as a ground for accepting trustfully the mysteries of providence,[2] the idea that a predestined number of men must be completed before the end could come,[3] and that the souls of the good were kept in storehouses till the resurrection,[4] the importance attached to Adam's transgression, with the appeal beginning in each, 'O, what hast thou done, Adam?'[5] and many other points of resemblance, certainly indicate a very close relationship between the two books. This is not the place to institute an exact comparison of their doctrinal statements; but I may mention one or two differences. The period of the Messianic reign, instead of being limited, as in 4th Ezra,[6] to four hundred years, is in Baruch[7] left quite indefinite; and nothing is said in the latter about the death of the Messiah. In 4th Ezra[8] complaint is made that the people of God ought to be punished by God's own hands, instead of being trodden down by unbelievers, and[9] that the altar was demolished and the Temple destroyed, the ark of the covenant plundered and the holy things contaminated—where the context shows clearly enough that all this misery was supposed to have come from the hands of enemies. But in Baruch[10] the enemy are deprived of the greatest triumph; Jerusalem is overthrown by angels; and all the holy vessels are rescued by the same heavenly interference from the greed of the spoiler. This curious fancy may have been suggested by the dif-

---

[1] Ezra xii. 3; Bar. liii.
[2] Ezra iv. 3 *sq.*; v. 36, *sq.*; Bar. xxii., xxiii.
[3] Ezra iv. 36-7; Bar. xxiii.
[4] Ezra iv. 35; (vi.) 54, 60, 74, &c.; Bar. xxi., xxx.
[5] Ezra vii. 48; Bar. xlviii.
[6] vii. 28, 29.
[7] See xl. and lxxiii.
[8] v. 29, 30.
[9] x. 21, 22.
[10] v.-vii.

ficulty which is started in Ezra, and, if so, affords some evidence of later composition.

We must now endeavour to ascertain the date at which the book was written. Ewald assigns it to the reign of Domitian;[1] but as in his History he gives no arguments, but merely refers to the *Göttinger gel. Anzeigen*, which I have not been able to see, I can pronounce no opinion upon his reasoning. That the work was composed after the destruction of Jerusalem by Titus seems to follow conclusively from ch. xxxii., where this prediction is given:—' After a short time the building of Zion shall be shaken, that it may be built again. But that building shall not remain, but shall be rooted up again after a time, and shall remain desolate for a time. And afterwards it must be renewed in glory, and shall be crowned for ever.' This allusion to the destruction of the second Temple removes all possibility of doubt as to the meaning of the fourth kingdom in ch. xxxix. It is there said that the kingdom which formerly destroyed Zion should be itself destroyed, and made subject to one [that is, the Persian] that should come after it. Again, that also should be destroyed after a time, and a third [the Macedonian] should arise and rule for its time, and be destroyed. And afterwards a fourth kingdom should arise, which should rule for many times, and be lifted up more than the cedars of Lebanon; and when the time of its end approached, the Messiah should be revealed. Obviously the fourth kingdom is the Roman Empire; and that the author expected its speedy downfall is shown by some expressions in which he speaks from his own point of view, and for the moment forgets to adapt his language to the time of Baruch. In ch. xxiii. are the words, ' For truly my redemption is near, that it may come, nor is it

[1] *Gesch. des V. I.* vii. S. 84 and 86.

distant as formerly.' Again, in ch. lxxxii., in the letter to the lost tribes, is the statement, 'The consummation which the Most High will make, is extremely near . . . and by no means far off is the consummation of his judgment.' This expectation would probably suit the beginning of Domitian's reign as well as any later period to which we could reasonably ascribe the composition of the book. It does not appear to me very safe to place much dependence on general allusions to civil wars, disasters, and earthquakes, which, as we have seen in the case of 4th Ezra, may with a little ingenuity be adapted to different times. But that the destruction of Jerusalem was still fresh in the memory of the writer, may be gathered from the general tone of his work; and I cannot help suspecting a reference to one of the stories of that time in an incident which he connects with the Babylonian period. He says that, after the angels had overthrown the walls of Jerusalem, a voice was heard from the interior of the Temple, saying, 'Enter, O enemies, and come, O adversaries, for he who guarded the house has deserted it.'[1] Compare with this the story of Josephus, that the priests, when engaged at their ministrations in the Temple, heard a voice, saying, 'Let us remove hence.'[2] This tale is given also by Tacitus:—'suddenly the doors of the Temple were opened, and a voice louder than the human was heard, that the gods were departing.'[3]

There is, however, a passage[4] which may seem to afford us a more precise determination of date. Referring to the afflictions which should precede the appearance of the Messiah, Baruch asks, 'Will that tribulation which is to take place remain for much time, or will that necessity comprise many years?' He is told in reply, that

[1] Ch. viii. [2] Μεταβαίνωμεν ἐντεῦθεν, *Bell. Jud.* vi. 5, 3.
[3] Hist. v. 13. [4] Chs. xxvi.–xxviii.

that time is divided into twelve parts; and after a description of the characteristics of these parts, he is informed—'Now the measure and computation of that time will be two parts, weeks, of the seven weeks.'[1] 'The seven weeks' probably refer to the seven weeks of Daniel ix. 25. 'Two parts, weeks,' can hardly mean anything but two-sevenths of the whole period. This interpretation is defended by Hilgenfeld against Ewald, who formerly understood by the 'two parts' two-thirds.[2] The addition of 'weeks' to 'parts' seems decisive; and we therefore arrive at two weeks, that is, in all probability, fourteen years, as the period of the final tribulation. Hilgenfeld reckons this from the beginning of the Jewish war in 65 [? 66] A.D., and supposes that Baruch was written about the beginning of the second week, in the year 72. All this, however, is very uncertain. We might with equal propriety calculate from the destruction of Jerusalem, and all that we could venture to affirm would be that the book was published some time before the end of the second week, that is, before 84 A.D. But as Wieseler[3] points out, we ought to date, not the two, but the seven weeks from the destruction of Jerusalem, and then the two weeks immediately preceding the appearance of the Messiah would comprise 105–119 A.D. Hence Wieseler concludes that the book was written in the time of Trajan. There is, however, nothing to indicate that the two weeks were not still future to the author himself, and the argument can only avail to prove that the work appeared between 70 and 119 A.D. If it was composed after 4th Ezra, this extension of time for the appearance of the Messiah may have been due to the failure of the

---

[1] 'Erunt duæ partes hebdomades τῶν septem hebdomadarum.'
[2] *Mess. Jud.* p. lxiii. n. 2.
[3] 'Das vierte Buch Esra,' in the *Studien und Krit.*, 1870, S. 288.

prediction contained in the latter book; and if so, it must have been composed after the death of Domitian. This, however, is an insecure basis on which to rest, and we must be content with the conclusion that it was written after the destruction of Jerusalem, but not so long after as to impair in the author's mind the vividness of his memory or the freshness of his grief.

CHAPTER II.

LYRICAL LITERATURE.

The Psalms of Solomon.

THE eighteen Psalms which bear this title were first given to the modern world by the Jesuit J. L. de la Cerda, who in 1626 published them from the text of a single Greek manuscript.[1] Fabricius republished this text, with some emendations, in his 'Codex Pseudepigraphus Veteris Testamenti,' in 1713. The manuscript from which De la Cerda's edition was taken is, it seems, no longer to be found. Fabricius,[2] however, referred to one which was said to exist in the Imperial Library at Vienna; and Hilgenfeld, having procured a collation of this with the text of Fabricius, made use of it in preparing the new edition of the Psalms which appeared in his 'Messias Judæorum.'[3]

That these Psalms proceeded from a single author is evinced by the unity of their thought and style. That they were originally written in Hebrew is regarded as certain by Ewald[4] and Dillmann.[5] Hilgenfeld, however,

[1] Fabricius, *Cod. Pseud. Vet. Test.* i. pp. 914, 915.
[2] Ibid. p. 973, note.
[3] See his *Prol.* p. xii. *sq.* Since the appearance of this work editions have been published by Geiger (*Der Psalter Salomo's, herausgegeben und erklärt von P. Eduard Ephraem Geiger.* Augsburg, 1871), and Fritzsche (in his *Libri Apocryphi Vet. Testamenti*, Lips., 1871). The latter of these I have not had an opportunity of seeing.
[4] *Gesch. des Volk. Is.* iv. 392, Anm. 1.
[5] Herzog, *Encyk.*, art. 'Pseudepig. d. A. T.' S. 305.

contends for a Greek original, chiefly on the ground that the 'Wisdom of Solomon' seems to have been used by the author, and believes accordingly that they were composed in Egypt.[1] His references do not appear to me conclusive; but, on the other hand, the Hebraic structure of the language is no greater than we should expect in a writer whose Greek style was formed upon Biblical models.[2] There is a certain Hellenistic breadth in the spirituality of the author's thought and his very scanty reference to the specialities of the Jewish law; but nevertheless he speaks of the calamities of Jerusalem as though he had known them with the bitterness of a personal experience.[3] Perhaps we might reconcile these conflicting appearances by supposing that the writer was a native of Palestine, but had been driven away, partly by his animosity to the leading party at Jerusalem, and partly by the invasion which he regarded as a divine judgment on the sins of the people. The supposition derives some support from express indications in the Psalms. In xvii. 18, having spoken of the iniquity of the 'sons of the covenant' the author adds: 'Those who love the synagogues of the holy fled from them,' and were scattered. In verse 6 he declares that sinners 'thrust *us* out;' but in verse 23 he prays that God will 'raise up to *them* their king, the son of David,' as though he himself were no longer in the midst of them. Again, in viii. 33–35, though the words may bear a different interpretation, he seems to include himself in the dispersion of Israel:—'Turn, O God, thy compassion upon us, and pity us. Bring together the dispersion of Israel with compassion and kind-

---

[1] *Mess. Jud.* Prol. p. xvi.–xviii.

[2] Geiger shows that many readings may be explained on the supposition of a Hebrew original, S. 20–23. He thinks the work was translated as late as the third century.

[3] See especially ii. 23, 24; viii. 1–7; xvii. 13: τὴν γῆν ἡμῶν.

ness; because thy faith is with us, and we hardened our neck.' That our conjecture is not intrinsically improbable is proved by the statement of Josephus that at the time of the invasion of Judea by Aretas the principal men among the Jews left the country, and fled into Egypt;[1] for, as we shall see, the Psalms refer in all likelihood to the troubles of that period. It is not impossible, then, that it may have been to more than the *historic* eye of the author that God showed the body of the oppressor lying unburied beside the mountains and the waves of Egypt.[2]

Ewald,[3] with whom Oehler[4] and Dillmann[5] agree, believes that the Psalms were composed soon after Antiochus Epiphanes had taken and plundered Jerusalem in the year 170 B.C. F. C. Movers,[6] who is followed by Hilgenfeld,[7] Keim,[8] Schürer,[9] Hausrath,[10] and others, refers them to the period subsequent to the capture of Jerusalem by Pompeius in 63 B.C. The writers, however, who adopt the latter view differ from one another as to the number of years which elapsed between the fall of Jerusalem and the composition of the Psalms. In order to judge between these conflicting opinions we must review the evidence.

We need hardly observe that the title of the Psalms gives no clue to their real date. Whether it was adopted by the author or subsequently added by an editor, there seems to be no reason for its existence except the fact that one thousand and five songs are attributed to Solo-

[1] Ant. xiv. 2, 1.
[2] ii. 30, 31.
[3] *Gesch. d. V. I.* iv. S. 392.
[4] Herzog, *Messias*, S. 426.
[5] Herzog, *Pseudep. d. A. T.* S. 305.
[6] *Kirchen-Lexikon, oder Encyklopädie der katholischen Theologie und ihrer Hilfswissenschaften.* Herausgegeben von H. J. Wetzer und B. Welte. Freiburg im Breisgau, 1847-60. Art. 'Apokryphen-Literatur,' S. 340-1.
[7] *Mess. Jud.* Prol. and notes.
[8] *Gesch. Jesu,* i. S. 243.
[9] *Neutest. Zeitgesch.* S. 141 sq.
[10] *Neutest. Zeitgesch.* i. S. 168.

mon in 1 Kings iv. 32; for the work itself makes no allusion to the wise king, nor does it pretend to speak in his name—unless, indeed, the words in i. 3 *sq.*, and xvii. 6 are, as Hilgenfeld supposes, to be so construed.[1]

The date, then, must be determined solely by the references which the Psalms contain to circumstances of the time; and these, happily, are not deficient either in number or variety. Instead of arranging them in the order in which they occur in the Psalms, it will be best for our purpose to take them in their historical sequence.

The writer describes a time of great moral corruption.[2] This description is, in its general features, applicable to either of the periods between which we have to decide; but Ewald contends that the references to the defilement of the Temple by Israelites[3] are suitable only to the time of Epiphanes. These references, however, are not so explicit that they must be regarded as pointing to apostates from the Jewish faith; they may simply brand the wickedness of those who administered the sacrificial rites. On the other hand, there is one expression which it is difficult to reconcile with Ewald's view. The writer ends his account of the people of Jerusalem with the words: 'The king is in transgression, and the judge not in truth, and the people in sin.'[4] As there was no king of the Jews at the date which he prefers, Ewald boldly asserts that Epiphanes was the king intended; but it is surely more natural to seek the explanation, with Hilgenfeld, in the closing years of the Maccabean period. The description

---

[1] In the former the writer refers to his children, evidently meaning the Jews; in the latter he describes by ἡμᾶς the line of David; but in neither is Solomon mentioned.

[2] i. 7, 8; ii. 3, 9-15; iv. 1 *sq.* viii. 8 *sq.*

[3] i. 8; ii. 3; viii. 12-14.

[4] xvii. 22: ὁ βασιλεὺς ἐν παρανομίᾳ, καὶ ὁ κριτὴς [οὐκ] ἐν ἀληθείᾳ, καὶ [ὁ] λαὸς ἐν ἁμαρτίᾳ.

would suit Alexander Jannæus, who not only was unfriendly to the Pharisees, but shattered his constitution by drunkenness, and issued the most savage orders for the destruction of his enemies while he himself feasted among his concubines;[1] and in an adverse eye it would not seem inapplicable to his sons Hyrcanus and Aristobulus, whose quarrel for the sovereignty caused the intervention of the Roman power. And again, we learn from xvii. 5 *sq.* that the royal authority was in the hands of usurpers who did not belong to the line of David. This statement applies to the Levitical dynasty of the Maccabees. Against these rose up a man foreign to the Jewish race.[2] This expression may, as Hilgenfeld supposes, point to Antipater the Idumean, who was the chief instigator of Hyrcanus against his brother, and by his machinations led to the downfall of Aristobulus; or it may, as Schürer,[3] perhaps with more probability, suggests, refer to Pompeius.[4] The divine judgment on the usurpers and their seed,[5] if it denote anything more specific than the general collapse of the Maccabean rule, may, with Hilgenfeld, be referred to the death of Aristobulus, who in 48 B.C. was poisoned by the Pompeian party, and of his son Alexander, who suffered decapitation in the same year.

Notwithstanding the corruption of the age there had been a time of great prosperity; the people were wealthy and glorious, and 'were exalted to the stars.'[6] This description, which will hardly apply to the feeble period before Antiochus Epiphanes, is well suited to the vigour of the Maccabean kingdom. Josephus speaks of the Roman invasion as leading to a marked decline in the Jewish

---

[1] Josep. *Ant.* xiii. 14, 2, and 15, 5.
[2] xvii. 9. [3] *Neutest. Zeitg.* 142.
[4] Geiger also takes this view, S. 13. There is no occasion, with Movers, to have recourse to Herod.
[5] xvii. 11. [6] i. 4, 5.

fortunes;[1] and we may compare the expression of the Psalmist, 'they were exalted to the stars' [ὑψώθησαν ἕως τῶν ἄστρων], with that of the historian, ' a nation previously raised to a great elevation' [ἔθνος ἐπὶ μέγα πρότερον αἰρόμενον].

The peace, however, was broken by a sudden war[2]— a circumstance which is equally true of both periods. The leader of the enemy came 'from the extremity of the earth.'[3] This fact, in the opinion of Ewald, points to Epiphanes, who seized the throne of Syria immediately after his return from Rome, where he had been detained for several years as a hostage. But it may be questioned whether the writer would refer in this obscure way to Antiochus when he had already been king for more than five years, and though he attacked Jerusalem on his return, not from Rome, but from an expedition into Egypt. On the other hand, the language admits an unforced application to Pompeius. It may further be suggested that the comparison of the war to 'a hurricane of fire borne through a desert'[4] may refer to the invasion of Aretas, who came with his tempest of Arabian horse and foot, and besieged Aristobulus and the priests in the Temple.[5] The profanation of the Temple mentioned a little further on[6] may be connected with this event; and afterwards Pompeius arrived upon the scene from the extremity of the world.

In the course of the war Jerusalem was captured by the Gentiles.[7] The circumstances of this capture must determine for us by whom it was effected. The rulers of the land received the conqueror joyfully, and opened

---

[1] *Ant.* xiv. 4 § 4 and 5.
[2] i. 2; viii. 1.
[3] viii. 16.
[4] viii. 2.
[5] Joseph. *Ant.* xiv. 2, 1.
[6] viii. 12–14.
[7] ii. 20; viii. 18 *sq.*

to him the gates of the city. Yet he seized the wall and battlements. He destroyed the rulers and everyone wise in counsel, and shed the blood of the inhabitants as unclean water; and he carried off their sons and their daughters. Notwithstanding this betrayal of the city by a party favourable to the enemy, the conqueror threw down strong walls with a battering-ram, and foreign nations went up upon the altar.[1] Now this curious combination of events exactly suits the invasion of Pompeius. He was admitted into the city by the party of Hyrcanus. The followers of Aristobulus shut themselves up within the enclosure of the Temple, which was strongly fortified. Pompeius was obliged to bring up a siege-train from Tyre; and it was not till he had battered down the largest of the towers, and effected a breach, that he was able to carry the place by storm. The priests would not forsake their duties, but fell where they were. Some of the defenders leaped from the precipices; others set fire to their houses; and twelve thousand perished in the slaughter. Pompeius himself entered the holy of holies. Aristobulus and his sons and daughters were carried away captive.[2] To the theory of Ewald the facts are less pliant. In neither of the sieges under Antiochus Epiphanes is there any reason to suppose that there was a double process of capture. In the first Josephus[3] says that Antiochus took the city without fighting, a party favourable to him having opened the gates. The treason is not mentioned in 1st Maccabees;[4] and we know not from what source Josephus has derived his statement. At all events, if we admit the treason, there is nothing to show that it was followed by a regular siege. On the second occasion Antiochus obtained possession of the city by means of false professions

[1] ii. 1, 2.
[2] Joseph. *Ant.* xiv. 4.
[3] *Ant.* xii. 5, 3.
[4] i. 20.

of peace.[1] The allusions, therefore, in the Psalms to the capture of Jerusalem and of the Temple point clearly to the time of Pompeius, and not to that of Epiphanes. If any doubt still linger in our minds, we may turn to xvii. 14, from which we learn that the captives were sent off to the west—a statement which indicates Roman rather than Syrian victories.

There is one other important item of evidence. In ii. 30–33 the writer says: 'God showed me his [the oppressor's] insolence pierced on the mountains of Egypt, his body scorned on land and sea,[2] marred upon the waves with much indignity, and there was none to bury him; because he scorned him [$i.\,e.$ God] with dishonour; he considered not that he was a man, and considered not the future. He said, I will be lord of land and sea;[3] and he acknowledged not that God is great, mighty in his great power.' This is no description of the end of Epiphanes; and Ewald is obliged to regard it as the expression of a hope founded on the prophecy against the great dragon of Egypt in Ezekiel xxix. This is very far-fetched. Why should a prophecy against 'Pharaoh king of Egypt, the great dragon that lieth in the midst of his rivers,' remind anyone of the king of Syria, and cause him to anticipate for him so remarkable an end? The very natural comparison of the oppressor to a dragon in verse 29 lends but a feeble support to this explanation, though it may have suggested it. But the whole description,

---

[1] Joseph. *Ant.* xii. 5, 4; 1st Mac. i. 30.

[2] I omit the doubtful ὑπέρ ἐλαχίστου.

[3] Hilgenfeld says, 'haec soli Pompeio conveniunt, non Antiocho Epiphani.' See, however, 1st Mac. i. 17; 'he entered into Egypt with a great multitude . . . and a great navy [ἐν στόλῳ μεγάλῳ],' and 2nd Mac. v. 21, 'weening in his pride to make the land navigable, and the sea passable by foot [τὸ πέλαγος πορευτὸν θέσθαι].' The applicability of the words to the conqueror of the Pirates is obvious.

notwithstanding some slight want of coincidence in detail, must recall the death of Pompeius to the mind of every reader of history. He was really murdered near Mount Casius in Egypt; and though the fatal blow was not inflicted 'on the mountains,' his head was cut off and sent on shore, and it was there that the proofs of his end were exhibited to the world. His body was left to the buffetings of the waves:

> Litora Pompeium feriunt, truncusque vadosis
> Huc illuc jactatur aquis.[1]

It is not strictly true that there was none to bury him, for his faithful freedman performed such hasty and imperfect rites as the circumstances allowed. But the stealthy ceremony could hardly be called a burial, especially for one who might have hoped to be followed to an honoured pyre by his country's most distinguished men:—

> tumulumque e pulvere parvo
> Aspice Pompeii non omnia membra tegentem.[2]

That the event here narrated had actually occurred is further evident from the tone of satisfaction with which the Psalm closes. The great leaders of the world are called upon to behold the judgment of the Lord, and those who fear God are exhorted to bless him. This implies that the Jews were already avenged, and that at least one episode in the long series of their calamities had come to an impressive close.

The above survey justifies us in the conclusion that the Psalms of Solomon were completed not very long after the death of Pompeius, which took place in 48 B.C.

If the date thus reached on independent grounds be correct, it disposes of the dictum of Grätz in regard to these Psalms, that 'their Christian character is unequi-

---

[1] Lucan, *Pharsalia*, viii. 698-9.   [2] Ibid. x. 380-1.

vocal.'¹ In support of this allegation he merely refers to xvii. and xviii. 8, that is, to the Messianic passages. In these I see nothing specifically Christian, unless it be the expression χριστὸς κύριος in xvii. 36, where perhaps the reading is open to suspicion. On the other hand, the exclusively Jewish character of the very passages which are appealed to is strongly marked. The purification of Jerusalem from the Gentiles is the great object of patriotic hope.² Israel is throughout the one favoured people. The Messiah is their king.³ They are the servant (or child, παῖδα) of God.⁴ Upon them God's love rests, and his chastening is upon them as upon a first-born, only-begotten son;⁵ and it will be their privilege to have no foreigner dwelling any more among them.⁶ When we add that the Messiah is nothing higher than a 'son of David,'⁷ and that there is not the faintest trace of any acquaintance with the facts of Christian history, we need have little scruple in rejecting Grätz's hypothesis as without foundation.

[1] *Gesch. der Juden*, lil. S. 439, Anm.
[2] xvii. 25, 33.   [3] xvii. 47.   [4] xvii. 23.
[5] xviii. 4.   [6] xvii. 31.   [7] xvii. 23.

CHAPTER III.

HAGGADISTIC LITERATURE.

The Book of Jubilees, or Little Genesis.

LIKE some other works, the 'Book of Jubilees,' or 'Little Genesis' was, up to a recent period, known to us only by references to it in ancient writers. It was supposed to be irretrievably lost, till the missionary, Dr. Krapff, presented an Æthiopic copy of it to the University Library of Tübingen in 1844. This copy had been very inaccurately made by an Abyssinian secretary of Dr. Krapff's. Dr. Dillmann, correcting its errors as far as he could, translated it into German, and published his version, divided by him into fifty chapters, and accompanied by notes, in Ewald's 'Jahrbücher der biblischen Wissenschaft,' in 1850 and 1851.[1] A second Æthiopic manuscript was afterwards obtained, and from a comparison of the two Dillmann was enabled to publish an edition of the Æthiopic text in 1859. In 1861 Ceriani, as has been previously mentioned, printed copious fragments, embracing nearly one-third, of an old Latin translation of this work.[2] In 1874 Rönsch published a revision of this Latin text, and side by side with it a Latin translation made by Dillmann from the corresponding sections

---

[1] Bd. ii., 1850, S. 230-256, and Bd. iii., 1851, S. 1-96. It is from this version that most of our citations must be made, and as the chapters are not divided into verses I shall generally give the page as well as the chapter.

[2] *Monum. Sac. et Prof.*, tom. I. fasc. i.

of the Æthiopic.[1] The text is only a small part of an elaborate volume, which forms an introduction and commentary upon the work. It is much to be regretted that this edition was not furnished with a revised copy of the complete German translation, in place of which we have only a brief synopsis of the several chapters.[2]

The contents of the book may be briefly described as a haggadistic[3] reproduction of the Biblical history from the creation of the world to the institution of the passover. This fact accounts for its name of 'Genesis,' to which the epithet 'Little' is prefixed, as applicable, not to its bulk, which is greater than that of the canonical Genesis, but to its inferior authority. The history, however, is related in the form of a revelation made to Moses on Mount Sinai by the angel who went before the camp of the Israelites; and in this way the author seeks to secure a divine sanction for the additions which he makes to the Biblical narrative. The other name of the work, the 'Book of Jubilees,' is derived from its peculiar chronological arrangement. The recurrence of the year of Jubilee every forty-nine years is taken as the basis of division into periods. Fifty of these, that is 2,450 years, are assumed as the length of time from the creation to the entrance of the Israelites into Canaan.[4] The Jubilee period is divided into seven weeks of years, and these again into single years. According to this division the dates of the several events are given in Jubilees, weeks, years, and months.

One leading purpose of the author was to carry the

---

[1] *Das Buch der Jubiläen oder die kleine Genesis*, &c.
[2] For the subject of the above paragraph, see Ewald's *Jahrb. der bib. Wiss.* Bd. ii. S. 230, and Rönsch S. 1–8.
[3] The meaning of this term will be explained in the chapter on the Talmud.
[4] Ch. 1., S. 69.

Jewish cultus back into the patriarchal period, and thus invest it with a new sanction, and emphasise the eternity of its obligation. Thus he relates that about the time of the birth of Isaac, Abraham built an altar, and erected tabernacles for himself and his servants, and this was the first feast of tabernacles that was celebrated upon earth; and having described the ceremonies, he adds, 'For this reason it has been decreed in the tablets of heaven concerning Israel, that they shall celebrate the feast of tabernacles joyfully for seven days in the seventh month, acceptably before the Lord, established by law for ever in their generations, year by year. Nor for this is there any end of time; for it has been enjoined upon Israel for ever that they should do that, and sit in tabernacles, and put crowns upon their heads, and take leafy branches and willow from the torrent.'[1]

The original language of the 'Book of Jubilees' was Hebrew, as we know from the testimony of Hieronymus, who says that he has met with certain Hebrew words 'in an apocryphal book which is called by the Greeks Μικρογένεσις.'[2] The Æthiopic version, however, is proved by the retention of Greek words to have been made from a Greek translation; and Rönsch has shown by a careful examination of the text that the Latin also has come to us through a Greek medium.[3]

That the author lived in Palestine may be reasonably inferred from his adoption of the Hebrew language; and this inference is supported by other indications, such as the constant demand for complete separation from the Gentiles, which would have been impracticable anywhere

[1] Ch. xvi. I follow the Latin and Dillmann's Latin translation in the one or two points in which these differ from the German.
[2] *Epist.* 127 (al. 78) ad Fabiolam, mansiones 18 and 24. The passages are quoted by Rönsch, S. 265-6.
[3] S. 439-444.

but in Palestine, and the introduction of Palestinian haggadah rather than Alexandrine allegory.[1] The author certainly belonged to the class of men learned in the Scriptures; but it is difficult to fix his position as a member of any of the sects. He approaches most nearly to the Pharisees, but differs from them on some important points.[2]

From the absence of chronological notices it is unfortunately impossible to determine the date of the book with any degree of precision. We need, however, have no hesitation in placing it before the destruction of Jerusalem; for it is assumed throughout that that city is the centre of the Jewish religion. Rönsch[3] appeals to a passage in the first chapter as clearly proving that the Temple was still standing:—'From the first creation till the time when my sanctuary shall be built among them for ever and ever ... and everyone shall acknowledge that I am the God of Israel ... and the king on Mount Zion from eternity to eternity.' This, however, seems to refer to the ideal temple; and the destruction of the sanctuary by Nebuchadnezzar is just as little mentioned as its destruction by Titus. More conclusive is the ordinance respecting the Passover—'it is not permitted to eat it outside the sanctuary of the Lord'—an injunction which is insisted on at some length.[4] This could hardly have been written after the Temple was no more, and, taken in connection with several other passages pointing in the same direction, may be considered satisfactory evidence that the book was written before the destruction of the city by the Romans. But how long before, it is less easy to say. Rönsch thinks that he detects in the work an anti-

---

[1] See Rönsch, S. 524–7.
[2] See Rönsch, S. 529 *sq.* and Schürer, *Lehrb. der n. Z.* S. 402–3.
[3] S. 528.   [4] Ch. xlix., the latter part.

Christian tendency.[1] The allusions are too obscure to justify more than a conjecture. The strongest evidence, to my mind, is found in the insistance on the eternal obligation of the Law, and the endeavour to trace it back to the patriarchal period, which might seem to be intended as an attack on the Pauline position; but in the absence of direct allusion we cannot look upon this as very convincing. Rönsch supposes that some ten or fifteen years must be allowed for the influence of Christianity to have made itself felt; and further, that before the work could have appeared with any prospect of success, the ground for the seed of hatred against the Romans which it was intended to plant[2] must have been broken up and made susceptible through a continually deepening sense of oppression during a period of about the same length; and hence he arrives at the conclusion that it was published from fifty to sixty years after Christ.[3] Dillmann contents himself with the vaguer statement that 'it was composed in the first Christian, perhaps as early as the first pre-Christian century.'[4] His principal reason is founded on the references which it contains to the 'Book of Enoch,' and the references to itself in the 'Testaments of the Twelve Patriarchs,' which prove that it was written between the dates of these two works.[5] Hilgenfeld, believing that the hatred of Esau manifested by the author points to Herod the Great, is of opinion that it was published during the closing years of that monarch's reign.[6] I fear we must be content with a less precise determination; but we may fairly accept the book as representing one phase of Jewish thought in a period not very remote from the time of Christ.

[1] S. 518–20. [2] S. 517–18. [3] S. 528–9.
[4] Herzog's *Encyk.*, 'Pseudepig. des A. T.' S. 317.
[5] *Jahrb. der bib. Wiss.* iii. S. 90 *sq.*
[6] *Zeitschr. für wiss. Theol.* 1874, S. 440.

CHAPTER IV.

THE TARGUMS.

It might well seem superfluous for one who has no pretensions to Rabbinical scholarship to write a chapter on the Targums, when the admirable article of the late lamented Mr. Deutsch, in Dr. Smith's 'Dictionary of the Bible,'[1] is accessible to every student of theology. But such important materials are contributed to our present subject by these ancient paraphrases that it is necessary, for the sake of completeness, to remind the reader of the most essential points. The question of date is the one with which we are here chiefly concerned.

The word Targum, תרגום, a translation or explanation, is used specifically to denote the Chaldee or Aramaic versions of the Old Testament. For the remote origin of these versions we must go back to the Babylonian captivity. This violent break in the national life had its effect upon the language; and the mass of the Jewish people gradually lost the use of their ancient tongue, and became unable to understand their own Scriptures. Accordingly, whenever the custom of reading lessons in the synagogues may have grown up, it was found necessary in course of time to accompany these lessons with a translation into the kindred Aramaic, the

---

[1] Reprinted in *Literary Remains of the late Emanuel Deutsch. With a brief Memoir.* London, 1874. Pp. 319-403. My references will be to this volume.

ordinary dialect of the people :[1] and it was thought advisable, in the case of obscure passages, to modify the translation into a paraphrase or a comment. Hence grew up a regular class of interpreters (מְתוּרְגְּמָן, drago-man), whose business it was to translate the verses read from the Hebrew by the reader. For a considerable period these interpreters were required to dispense with at least the public use of a manuscript, and it is quite uncertain at what time Targums were first reduced to writing. Zunz affirms that there were written Aramaic translations of most of the Biblical books as early as the Asmonean period;[2] but the earliest written Targum about which we have direct information appears to have been one of Job, and of that we can only say that it was written before the destruction of the Temple.[3] But at whatever date writing was first resorted to for the preservation of the Targum, the translator was still expected, in Palestine at least, to rely on his memory rather than the codex. It is related in the Jerusalem Talmud that 'a reader wished to make use of a written Targum, but he was told that this was not allowed; what was given in writing (the Bible) must remain in writing, but what was given orally must remain oral.'[4] This prohibition

---

[1] Eichhorn supposes that, at least till after the time of Christ, translations were not in use, but the lesson was followed by an explanatory discourse, and that it was not till the later centuries that for this discourse was substituted an extemporaneous translation. See his *Einleitung in das Alte Testament*. Vierte Ausg. 1823, ii. S. 15-17 and 21.

[2] *Die gottesdienstlichen Vorträge der Juden, historisch entwickelt. Ein Beitrag zur Alterthumskunde und biblischen Kritik, zur Literatur- und Religionsgeschichte.* Berlin, 1832, S. 61.

[3] Zunz, S. 61-2. Geiger, *Urschrift und Uebersetzungen der Bibel in ihrer Abhängigkeit von der innern Entwickelung des Judenthums*. Breslau, 1857. Excurs ii. 'Das jerusalemische Thargum zum Pentateuch.' S. 452. On the needlessness of written Targums till after the time of Christ, see Eichhorn, S. 15 *sq.*

[4] *Megillah* 4, quoted by Frankel, *Zu dem Targum der Propheten.* Breslau, 1872. S. 19.

is not found in the Babylonian Talmud, and there may perhaps have been a different practice among the Eastern Jews. But in whatever way it was used, the Targum acquired a character of fixity, which prevented it from adapting itself to the changes of thought and interpretation brought about by the labours of the Rabbinical schools in the post-Christian centuries; and in time the divergence between the popular paraphrases and the explanations of the learned became so marked as to occasion the necessity of revision.[1] This was thoroughly carried out only in Babylonia, where it resulted in the production of the Targums which have come down to our own time under the names of Onkelos and Jonathan ben Uzziel. In Palestine the difficulty was met by the insertion of corrections and additions, thus leading to a strange blending of old and new materials. Of the edition thus produced we possess, in part, two recensions, the Jerusalem Targum, and that of Pseudo-Jonathan. In order to see the evidence for these statements we must quit our more general treatment of this branch of literature, and attend to its separate representatives.

THE TARGUM OF ONKELOS comprises the Pentateuch, and is confessedly the oldest of the existing Targums. Its language is on the whole a pure Chaldee, and for the most part it adheres faithfully to the sense of the original. It is careful, however, to soften anthropomorphic expressions, and in a few passages it indulges, though with unusual care and delicacy, in that expansion of the literal meaning which is known by the name of haggadah. It is of course in these portions, where the translator becomes the commentator, that we must look for traces

[1] See Geiger, *Urschrift*, &c. Exc. ii., S. 452–3. Nöldeke, *Die alttestamentliche Literatur in einer Reihe von Aufsätzen dargestellt*. Leipzig, 1868. S. 255–6.

of later Jewish belief. But the use which we are entitled to make of the book in this respect clearly depends upon its date; and on the question of its date and authorship the most conflicting opinions have prevailed.

The earliest Jewish writing in which Onkelos is mentioned represents him as a proselyte, and a disciple of Gamaliel the elder.[1] The name does not occur in the Jerusalem Talmud, or in the early Christian writers. The scanty references to him in the Babylonian Talmud[2] are not easily reconciled with the earlier account; and if we are to follow traditional statements, all we can say is, that he was a proselyte, of uncertain date and country.

What, then, is the evidence upon which the Targum of the Pentateuch is assigned to his authorship? If we omit the title in the manuscripts, it amounts to no more than a single passage in the Babylonian Talmud, where the following words are found:—'R. Yeremyah, and, according to others, R. Chiyya bar Abba, said, "the Targum of the Torah [the Pentateuch] was made by Onkelos the Proselyte from the mouth of R. Eli'ezer and R. Yehoshua."'[3] Our doubt about the trustworthiness of this tradition is at once awakened by the fact that it bears a curious resemblance to the statement in the Jerusalem Talmud, that Aqilas [Aquila] the proselyte made the Targum of the Torah before R. Eli'ezer and R. Yehoshua';[4] and we cannot help suspecting that the later writer confused the Greek and the Chaldee translators.

---

[1] *Tosiphtah*, drawn up soon after the Mishnah. See the passages in Deutsch, p. 335.
[2] See them brought together in Eichhorn ii. S. 36, Anm. *q*, and in Deutsch, pp. 335-6.
[3] *Megillah* 3a; quoted by Deutsch and others. The original is given by Eichhorn ii. S. 36, Anm. *q*.
[4] *Megillah* i. 11. The original words are in Eichhorn, ibid.

This suspicion is confirmed when we find that in other instances similar circumstances are related in regard to each, and that the name of Onkelos may be only a Babylonian form of Aqilas.[1] The two accounts might, nevertheless, appear to confirm one another if it could be supposed that Aquila was the author not only of the Greek, but of the Chaldee version. But of this there is no evidence whatever, and Frankel takes perhaps unnecessary pains to refute such an hypothesis. That Aquila is not the author of the Targum is proved by comparing with it the surviving fragments of the Greek translation; by the language, which is East-Aramaic, whereas the Jews in Palestine had acquired the West-Aramaic dialect; and by the fact that the Onkelos-Targum is never cited in the Jerusalem Talmud.[2] Our sole item of external evidence, therefore, completely fails us, and we must endeavour to ascertain the origin of the Targum from other indications.

All the evidence points to the Babylonian schools as its birthplace. It is quoted several times in the Babylonian Talmud;[3] but instead of being cited, like 'the version of Aqilas,' under the name of its supposed author, it is referred to as 'our Targum,' and the quotations are introduced with the expression, 'as we translate.' This clear and direct evidence is confirmed, if we may trust

---

[1] אקילס or עקילס. The pronunciation of the ע may have contributed to the introduction of the n. See Eichhorn ii. S. 37–8; Deutsch p. 330; Geiger, Jüd. Zeitsch. 1871, S. 86–7; Frankel, Zu dem Targ. der Pr. S. 4 sq. Geiger, in his Urschr. u. Uebers. S. 163–4, thinks that Onkelos stands for Nikolaus, a name which belonged to a proselyte soon after the destruction of the Temple, but that it was substituted, as a more current designation, for Aquila, a name unknown to the Babylonian Jews. Grätz, Gesch. der Juden iv. S. 437–9, identifies Onkelos with the Aquila whom the Christians falsely, as he thinks, and in defiance of chronology, represented as a companion of Paul's.

[2] Zu dem Targ. der Pr. S. 5–6 and 45 sq.

[3] See the passages collected in Zunz, S. 63, Anm. e.

the confident affirmation of Geiger, by the nature of the language, which is not, as was formerly supposed, the genuine Chaldee, but the Babylonian dialect of the fourth century.[1] This judgment is, as we have seen, confirmed by Frankel. But Zunz pronounces the language to be West-Aramaic,[2] and Nöldeke, while admitting that the final redaction of the Targum was made in Babylonia, declares that its dialect, which was a rather more recent development of the Palestinian Aramaic employed in some books of the Old Testament, has generally been preserved intact, and has not been replaced by the common Babylonian dialect which is known to us from the Talmud.[3] Between these conflicting judgments I am not competent to pronounce; but perhaps a Babylonian revision of a Palestinian Targum would exhibit phenomena favourable to either view. This would seem to follow from the opinion of Deutsch,[4] who ascribes to Palestine 'the substance itself, i.e. the words,' but thinks that 'many grammatical and idiomatical signs' point to Babylon. However this may be, there seems to be no reason to doubt that the work in its present form emanated from Babylonia.[5] But if so, it cannot well be earlier than the third century; for then for the first time the Rabbinical schools in that country rose into importance, and needed a version revised in conformity with the more recent thought. To this period, accordingly, it is assigned by Frankel.[6] Deutsch places it about the end of the third or the beginning of the fourth century.[7] Geiger, with great confidence, ascribes it to the fourth century, and maintains that this date is guaranteed by its whole linguistic character, by its mode of procedure, and by the acquaintance

---

[1] *Jüd. Zeitsch.* 1871, S. 93.   [2] *Die Gott. Vortr.* S. 65.
[3] *Die alttest. Lit.* S. 257.   [4] P. 343.
[5] This is also the judgment of Eichhorn, *Einl. in das A. T.* S. 42-47.
[6] *Zu dem Targ. der Pr.* S. 9.   [7] P. 342.

which it exhibits with the later development of the halakhah and haggadah.[1]

I am not aware of any serious objection which can be urged against this view. Gfrörer,[2] who claims both for the Targum of Onkelos and for that of Jonathan a pre-Christian origin, rests his argument chiefly upon certain paraphrastic explanations of the Hebrew text which were suitable only while the Temple was still standing This argument, however, assumes that the interpretation did not seek to give what was honestly, though uncritically, believed to be indicated in the Hebrew, but was always adapted to the circumstances and wants of the time. He himself furnishes the answer to his inference in the case of one of the most striking examples. Genesis xlix. 27 is thus rendered:—'In the land of Benjamin will dwell the divine majesty, and in his portion will be built the sanctuary. Morning and evening will the priests offer oblations, and in the evening will they divide the remainder of their portions, from the remnants which have been sanctified.' There is here an unquestionable reference to the Temple and its sacrifices; but then, as Gfrörer himself points out,[3] this same explanation is retained in the Jerusalem Targum, which he admits to be as late as the sixth century.[4] He accounts for this by saying that 'people were for a long time accustomed to the old explanation of the words of Jacob.' The same reasoning will apply to the Targum of Onkelos, and the most that we can infer from the instances adduced by Gfrörer is that the traditional interpretation was sometimes faithfully preserved. Quite in conformity with this result is Geiger's conclusion that the Targum is a final redaction from the earlier freer

---

[1] *Urschrift und Uebers.* S. 164; *Jüd. Zeitsch.* 1871, S. 86, and 93 *sq.* and 1872, S. 199.
[2] *Jahrh. des Heils,* i. S. 36 *sq.*
[3] S. 57.
[4] S. 58.

Targums in accordance with the principles which had become prevalent in the Babylonian schools;[1] for in a redaction many older elements would be inevitably retained.

It only remains for us to inquire how the Targum came to be ascribed to Onkelos. The simplest explanation might seem to be that of Eichhorn, who believes that the real translator was so called, and that the cause of confusion between him and Aquila was due to the similarity of their names, combined with the fact that Onkelos was a private man, and when his translation was at last invested with authority nothing was known about him, and the Talmudists were glad to supply the deficiency by borrowing from the history of the Greek translator.[2] The more recent critics, however, have inclined to the opinion that it was called the Aquila- or Onkelos-Targum out of compliment to its merits, and especially on account of the unusual strictness with which, like Aquila's version, it adhered to the original text. But as it is only the later Rabbis who cite it by that name, it may almost seem more probable that its ascription to Onkelos was entirely owing to an accidental confusion on the part of those who were familiar with the Chaldee, but not with the Greek translation.

The Targum of Jonathan ben Uzziel, or 'the Targum of the Prophets,' comprises Joshua, Judges, Samuel, Kings, Isaiah, Jeremiah, Ezekiel, and the twelve minor Prophets. As we might expect from the character of the books which it translates, it indulges much more freely in paraphrase and amplification than that of Onkelos, and is therefore richer in the portraiture of Jewish beliefs and hopes.

According to the Rabbinical tradition Jonathan, the

---

[1] *Jüd. Zeitsch.* 1871, S. 87-93.   [2] *Einl. in das A. T.* S. 38-9.

reputed author, was a disciple of Hillel's, and consequently lived before Christ, and wrote before Onkelos. 'Our Rabbis hand down,' says the Talmud; 'there were eighty disciples of Hillel the elder, of whom thirty were worthy of having the Shechinah dwelling above them, as it did above Moses our master (peace be on him!); thirty were worthy of having the sun to stand still for them, as it did for Joshua the son of Nun; twenty, in fine, were in the middle between these. The greatest of all was Jonathan ben Uzziel, and the least of all Yochanan ben Zakkai. . . . They say of Jonathan ben Uzziel that, when he sat and worked at the Law, any bird flying over him was immediately burned.'[1] The Targum which now bears his name is, however, confessedly later than that of Onkelos, with which it indicates some acquaintance.[2] This may prepare us for the further fact that the evidence on which it has been ascribed to him is of the slenderest character. It consists of a single statement in the Talmud, given in continuation of the passage already quoted respecting Onkelos:—'The Targum of the Prophets was made by Jonathan ben Uzziel from the mouth of Haggai, Zechariah, and Malachi. And in that hour was the land of Israel shaken three hundred parasangs. . . . And a voice was heard, saying, "Who is this who has revealed my secrets unto the sons of man?" Up rose Jonathan ben Uzziel and said: "It is I who have revealed thy secrets to the sons of man. . . . But it is known and revealed before thee, that not for my honour have I done it, nor for

---

[1] *Baba Bathra*, 134a, quoted, among other works, in De Wette's *Lehrbuch der historisch-kritischen Einleitung in die Bibel Alten und Neuen Testaments*. Erster Theil. *Die Einleitung in das Alte Testament*. Neu bearbeitet von Dr. Eberhard Schrader. Achte Ausg. Berlin, 1869, § 70 Anm. a. S. 126. The original, as far as 'ben Zakkai' is given in Eichhorn, *Einl. in d. A. T.* S. 62, Anm. l.

[2] See Zunz, S. 63. One passage is cited from Onkelos without alteration, and another almost without alteration.

the honour of my father's house, but for thine honour; that the disputes may cease in Israel." . . . And he further desired to reveal the Targum to the Hagiographa, when a voice was heard:—"Enough!" And why? Because the day of the Messiah is revealed therein.'[1] It is clear that no reliance can be placed on this account. It seeks to derive the authority of the Targum from the Prophets themselves, and at most it represents a vague tradition that Jonathan was the first to publish what had previously been confined to the secret line of oral transmission. Our historical facts must be sought elsewhere.

In neither the Jerusalem nor the Babylonian Talmud is a single passage cited from this Targum under the name of Jonathan. On the other hand, this Targum contains all the passages cited in the Babylonian Talmud under the name of R. Yoseph.[2] The inevitable inference is that the compilers of the Talmud believed the real author to be this R. Yoseph, who was at the head of the school of Pumbeditha in Babylonia in the earlier part of the fourth century. It is most probable, as Deutsch[3] and Frankel[4] suppose, that he acted as editor of older translations, which he revised and brought into a form finally accepted as authoritative.

Why, then, was the work ascribed to Jonathan? Geiger's explanation is rather far-fetched. He thinks that as this Targum was only a revision, like Theodotion's emendation of the LXX., it was called after the Greek reviser, just as the Targum of the Pentateuch was called after Aquila. Then for Theodotion was substituted the

---

[1] *Megillah 3a*, quoted by Deutsch (whose translation I adopt) pp. 364–5, and others. The original, down to 'it is I who have revealed thy secrets to the sons of man,' is given in Eichhorn, S. 62, Anm. *k*.

[2] See them collected in Zunz, S. 63, Anm. *e*.   [3] Pp. 366–7.

[4] *Zu dem Targ. der Pr.* S. 10–41. See also Geiger, *Urschr. und Uebers.* S. 165.

corresponding Hebrew name, Jonathan; and finally, as there had been a scholar of Hillel's of this name, he was assumed to be the translator of the Prophets.[1] To this hypothesis Frankel objects that there is no evidence that the translation of Theodotion was known even in Palestine, and much less can it have been known in Babylon.[2] He himself adopts the view that the old translations of difficult passages which were worked up in the new edition were Jonathan's, and that therefore the whole Targum was named from him; but he suggests that perhaps the title ת"י, standing for תרגום יוסף, was resolved into תרגום יונתן.[3] We need not pause to determine among these different views. It is sufficient for our present purpose to have learned that the Targum of the Prophets, instead of being pre-Christian, belongs to the fourth century of our era.

PALESTINIAN TARGUMS.—There are in existence two other Targums of the Pentateuch, one complete, the other fragmentary. The former has gone, during the last few centuries, under the name of Jonathan ben Uzziel, and is frequently referred to as that of Pseudo-Jonathan; the latter is called Yerushalmi or Jerusalem Targum. These were both known down to the fourteenth century under the designation of Jerusalem, and probably the ascription of the former to Jonathan was due to the error of a transcriber, who mistook the meaning of the abbreviation ת"י.[4] The relation to one another of the two Targums thus bearing the same title has, however, been variously interpreted. Zunz believed that they were simply different recensions of the same work.[5] Geiger thought that

---

[1] *Urschr. und Uebers.* S 162–3 and 165.
[2] *Zu dem Targ. der Pr.* S. 11, Anm. 1.   [3] Ibid. S. 11.
[4] This was the opinion of Zunz, S. 71, who is followed by later writers.
[5] S. 66 *sq.*

the Jer. Targum was never more than a collection of single glosses on the original Palestinian Targum, set down at first in the margin of a manuscript.[1] Deutsch and others, following Frankel, have adopted the conclusion that 'Jerushalmi is a collection of emendations and additions to single portions, phrases, and words of Onkelos, and Pseudo-Jonathan a further emendated and completed edition to the whole Pentateuch of Jerushalmi-Onkelos.'[2] However this may be determined, it is the opinion of competent scholars that the Palestinian Targums, as we now possess them, do not contain the results of a thorough-going revision, but have preserved unaltered many earlier elements, and so exhibit in strange juxtaposition ideas old and new.[3] Apparently no very long time elapsed between the two publications, and historical references in Pseudo-Jonathan point to the second half of the seventh century as the date of their completion.

In these Targums the literal sense is much more widely departed from than in those of earlier date; but the ampler view which might thus seem to be opened into the domain of Jewish thought is impaired, for our present purpose, by the lateness of the period in which they assumed their final shape.

We need not dwell upon the Targums to other books of the Old Testament; for though their exact dates are unknown, they are undoubtedly of very late origin. Deutsch places them vaguely at about 1000 A.D.[4]

From the above survey it is evident that even the earliest Targums can no longer be appealed to as direct witnesses of Jewish belief in the time of Christ. At best

---

[1] *Urschr. und Uebers.*, S. 455.   [2] Deutsch, p. 383.
[3] Geiger, *Urschr. und Uebers.* S. 165 and 455, and *Jüd. Zeitschr.* 1871, S. 93. Nöldeke, *Die alttest. Lit.* S. 259.
[4] P. 394.

they represent a traditional interpretation ; but if we see reason to believe that certain Messianic ideas developed themselves along the two lines of Christianity and Judaism, we may make a guarded use of these utterances of the schools in the illustration of earlier conceptions.

CHAPTER V.

THE TALMUD, AND OTHER RABBINICAL WORKS.

In coming to the Talmud we pass from the region of apocryphal or half-authorised works to that vast compilation which, though never formally sanctioned as a binding rule, became the accepted standard of Jewish faith and practice. In order that we may correctly estimate its value in our present inquiry, it is necessary to give a brief account of its origin and nature. But in doing so I must once more disclaim all pretence of independent Rabbinical knowledge. I can only follow those who have made a special study of this department of learning, and present to the reader some of the more important results which have been won by their labours.

The remote origin of the Talmud must be sought in the peculiar character which was impressed upon the Jewish nation by the bitter experience of the Babylonian captivity. After the return to the land of their forefathers, it was the predominant aim of those to whom the direction of affairs had been entrusted to establish a polity based upon a strict observance of the Mosaic Law. That this end might be accomplished it was necessary to make provision for instructing the people in the Law, and for applying the ancient rules to the altered circumstances of the time and to the varying needs of a progressive life. Hence arose a class of men learned in the Scriptures (Sopherim, scribes), under whose influence the Canon was gradually formed, and a body of interpretation was accumulated, which, being orally transmitted, formed a traditional law side by side with the written code.[1] According to the fancy of later times, Moses himself had given with each commandment an explanation which was to be committed to memory and handed on to succeeding generations; and in this way, although doubtful cases still remained which were to be solved by certain rules of exegesis and settled by the voice of the majority, a mass of tradition was preserved which had no feebler claim to divine authority than the text of the Pentateuch itself.[2] The recipients of this tradition after the captivity are said to have been the 'men of the great synagogue,' —a term which occurs for the first time in Pireqé Aboth,[3] about the close of the second century of our era. It is not necessary to discuss here the various opinions which have been held respecting the nature and functions of this supposed corporation.[4] Whatever these may have been,

---

[1] See the origin and course of this development treated, among other works, in Jost's *Geschichte des Judenthums und seiner Sekten*: Erste Abth. Leipsig, 1857, Erstes Buch. Kuenen's *Relig. of Israel*, chs. viii. and ix.

[2] See the whole process described in the preface of Maimonides to Seder Zera'im, translated by Pressel, article 'Thalmud,' in Herzog's *Encyk.*, S. 647 sq.

[3] i. 1.

[4] Up to a recent period the most plausible view was, I think, that of Jost. He supposed that the men of the great synagogue were all who presided over the study of the law in Judea down to the time of Simeon the Just, and that the Jerusalem synagogue received the name of 'great' because the less important synagogues throughout the country looked to it for direction in the regulation of their public services (*Gesch. d. Jud. und s. Sekt.* i., S. 42). Kuenen, by a fresh investigation of the subject, has completed the labours of previous critics, and obtained results possessing a high degree of probability; and as his pamphlet is not very accessible to the English reader, a brief sketch of his line of argument may be found interesting. (The pamphlet is entitled, *Over de mannen der groote synagoge*. Bijdrage van A. Kuenen. Overgedrukt uit de Verslagen en Mededeelingen der Koninklijke Akademie van Wetenschappen, Afdeeling *Letterkunde* 2de Reeks, Deel vi. Amsterdam, 1876). From the history of

the words attributed to its members admirably sum up the labours of those earnest men who wrought the Mosaic institutions so deeply into the national life: 'Be deliberate in pronouncing judgment; train up many disciples; and make a hedge for the law.'[1] Simeon the Just, who was high-priest in the time of Alexander the Great or somewhat later, is said to have been one of the last survivors of the great synagogue, and to have handed on the tradition to Antigonus of Socho; and he in turn transmitted

the word Cenéseth, with its Greek equivalent συναγωγή, he infers that the writer who first invented the term Cenéseth haggedolah had in his mind the idea of some definite assembly, in all probability that of a religious meeting (pp. 20–22). Among the assemblies mentioned in the Old Testament, that whose proceedings are recorded in Neh. viii.–x. could alone be referred to under this name, and would moreover by this name be exactly described (pp. 23, 24). Now 'the men of the great synagogue' are actually identified with this assembly in Midrash Ruth, fol. 45 c. (pp. 25, 26). Certain expressions, moreover, contained in Neh. ix. 5–37 are ascribed by Rabbinical writers to the same set of men (pp. 26, 27). Further, the number of the men is variously given by the Rabbis as 85 or 120. Now the men who subscribed the covenant in Neh. x. amount to 84; and as the list of the Levites begins with a *vau*, it is probable that a name has fallen out, and that the original number was 85. To obtain the larger number we may add 35 names from viii. and ix., or else resort to the list of families that returned from Babylon, in Ezra ii. and viii. This agreement can hardly be accidental (pp. 28, 29). It seems, then, that this was the assembly which was in the first instance denoted by the term 'the great synagogue.' Hence it must follow that the Talmudical representation is unhistorical; for the assembly in the time of Nehemiah was not legislative, and was not organised into a permanent corporation (pp. 30, 31). An obvious difficulty arises from the fact that in Pireqé Aboth it is said that Simeon the Just was of the remnants of the great synagogue; for the meeting convened by Ezra and Nehemiah was held about 440 B.C., whereas Simeon was high-priest, at the earliest, about 300 B.C. (p. 34). To this two answers may be given. First, before the time of the redactor of the Mishnah the original meaning of the expression may have been somewhat modified (p. 35). Secondly, the Jewish chronology placed the destruction of the Temple 112 years before the Seleucid era, leaving only 52 years for the period of subjection to the Persians. The Talmudists repeatedly represent Simeon the Just as a contemporary of Alexander the Great; and therefore, according to this chronology, Simeon may very well have been a member of the assembly held in the time of Nehemiah (pp. 36, 37).

[1] Pireqé Aboth, i. 1.

it to the five 'pairs,' who in succession presided over the schools of scriptural learning.[1]

A new epoch is reached with the distinguished Hillel, who is pronounced by Grätz[2] to be 'the first founder of Talmudical Judaism.' The dates of his birth and death are uncertain; but he lived till a few years after the beginning of the Christian era. He was born in Babylonia, and although, according to tradition, deriving his lineage on the mother's side from the house of David, is said to have spent his youth in needy circumstances. In course of time he removed to Jerusalem, and became an ardent hearer of Shemaiah and Abtalion, who stood at the head of the Pharisaic school. Graced with a sweetness of temper which won the heart, and equipped with a learning that ensured respect, he attained at last, about 31 B.C., the highest dignity to which he could aspire, and was appointed president, it is said, of the Sanhedrin, but more probably of the school of law. In this office he was associated first with Menahem, but, after the retirement of the latter, with Shammai. Shammai was a man of harder character than Hillel, and more rigid in his interpretations of the law; and the divergent tendencies which appeared, though without mutual estrangement, in the leaders, manifested themselves in their successors in two bitterly hostile schools. It is, however, with the activity of Hillel in promoting the development of legal tradition that we are here concerned. He is said to have introduced greater method into the study of the law by collecting under eighteen titles the regulations which

---

[1] According to Jost the Sanhedrin derived its origin from the time of Simon the Maccabee, and first assumed a definite form under John Hyrcanus (*Gesch. d. Jud. u. s. Sekt.* i. S. 123-4, 231, 272). From this time he dates the distinct beginning of the oral law, although it rested upon earlier usage (S. 128, 273).

[2] *Gesch. d. Juden,* iv. S. 16.

had hitherto been distributed under 613, viz., 365 prohibitions according to the number of days in a year, and 248 positive commandments according to the number of parts in the human body.[1] The mass of traditional enactments he endeavoured to reduce to system, and to bring under the application of general principles. He sought to mediate between the Pharisaic and Sadducean positions by establishing a relation of dependence between the written and the traditional code. On the one hand he conceded to the Sadducees that nothing was valid which had not its foundation in Scripture; but on the other hand he contended that the full scope of Scripture was not to be ascertained by a hard and literal exegesis. He accordingly devised seven rules of interpretation, in conformity with which the Rabbinical development of the law ought to proceed; and he thereby not only provided a higher sanction for the existing tradition, but paved the way for that method of discussion and inference which properly bears the name of Talmud.[2]

Hillel was succeeded by his grandson Gamaliel, through whom his influence passed to the Apostle Paul. Gamaliel's son and successor, Simeon, perished at the siege of Jerusalem. A distinguished disciple of Hillel's, however, Yochanan ben Zakkai, still survived. Inheriting the broad principles of his school, he was opposed to the war party, whose ill-directed zeal he foresaw would only bring about the destruction of the city and temple. He therefore sought and obtained the friendship of the

---

[1] See these collected in Jost, *Gesch. d. Jud. u. s. Sekt.* i. Anhang, S. 451 *sq*.

[2] For the above see especially Grätz, *Gesch. d. Jud.* iii. S. 172 *sq*. and Jost, *Gesch. d. Jud. u. s. Sekt.* i. S. 254 *sq*. The reader who is limited to English may see the account in *Lectures on the History of the Jewish Church* by A. P. Stanley, D.D., Dean of Westminster, Third Series, London, 1876, p. 447 *sq*.

Romans; and having caused himself to be conveyed out of Jerusalem in a coffin, thereby eluding the vigilance of his enemies, he withdrew with his disciples to Jamnia. On the fall of the temple and the cessation of the sacrifices he was the one to prove that the essence of Judaism need not perish with its ritual, and he consoled his disciples with the remark that beneficence might take the place of the sacrifices, as it was said in the Scriptures, 'I will have mercy, and not sacrifice.'[1] He succeeded in collecting a school, which soon afterwards assumed the constitution of a Sanhedrin, at Jamnia, and thus provided a new centre of religious life for the scattered and despairing Jews; and from this time the authority of the priesthood was finally superseded by that of the Rabbis. Yochanan and his successors, whose labours resulted in the formation of the Mishnah, are known by the name of Tannaim,[2] or teachers of the traditional law. Among these it may be sufficient to mention here the famous Akiba, who acknowledged the Messianic claim of Bar Cochba, and perished in the persecution which followed the ruin of his hopes; and Yehudah the holy, who brought their labours to a close by the reduction of the Mishnah to its permanent form. Before the middle of the second century the leading Rabbinical school had been transferred to Galilee; and it was here that R. Yehudah devoted himself to the important task of codifying the oral law.

The chronology of R. Yehudah's life is rather uncertain; but according to Jost he was born shortly before 140 A.D., and lived to 220 A.D.[3] He endeavoured,

---

[1] See Grätz, iv. S. 13, 14.

[2] תַּנָּאִים, from תְּנָא, tradere, docere: Buxtorf.

[3] *Gesch. d. J. u. s. Sekt.* ii. S. 114–115, 118. According to Grätz he was born about 150 and died about 210 A.D.: *Gesch. d. Jud.* iv. S. 210 and 480 *sq.*

through the instruction of several teachers, to extend his knowledge and his thought beyond the limits of a single school. Eminent alike for his learning and his wealth, he attained at an early age (about 170 A.D.) to the office of president or patriarch. In this capacity he succeeded in making himself almost the sole fountain of authority; and towards the disciples who assembled round him at Sepphoris, where he had fixed his residence for the sake of his health, he was austere and irritable.

The great work of R. Yehudah was the arrangement of the Mishnah, a work which had not before been brought to a successful issue. He took as his basis the previous labours of Akiba. His edition was at first distinguished as that of R. Yehudah; but, owing to his own high reputation and the zeal of his scholars, it gradually superseded the older compilations, and rose to the position of the sole recognised authority. The precise date of its completion is uncertain. Pressel places it as late as 230 A.D.;[1] Grätz prefers 189;[2] and Deutsch contents himself with the vaguer statement, 'about 200 A.D.'[3]

The word Mishnah (מִשְׁנָה) was used to denote the oral in contradistinction from the written law, and is derived either from שָׁנָה 'to repeat,' or (with Grätz) from שֵׁנִי 'second,' i.e. second in addition to the written doctrine. In handing down the traditional law three modes of instruction were observed. The first was the communication of precepts in the driest and briefest form, so that the very words might be unalterably impressed on the memory. These precepts were given in the name of the authority from which they proceeded, and in the

---

[1] Herzog, *Thalmud*, S. 662.
[2] *Gesch. d. J.*, iv. Note 1.
[3] Article on the Talmud in the *Quarterly Review* for October, 1867, pp. 440-1. Reprinted in the *Literary Remains*, pp. 1-58. For the statement in the text see p. 32.

earlier period were not classified, but simply strung together, without connection of subject, under the names of the teachers whose utterance they were. They were known by the name of Halakhah (הֲלָכָה), from הָלַךְ 'to go;' i.e., according to Deutsch, 'rule, norm;'[1] according to Pressel, what is current in regard to the law, and therefore, like Mishnah, expressive of the tradition itself. The second mode of instruction was called Midrash (מִדְרָשׁ, 'commentary, interpretation,' from דָּרַשׁ 'to study'). In this it was pointed out how, in accordance with certain rules of interpretation, the traditional laws might be derived from the Scriptures.[2] A further stage was reached when it became necessary to apply the accepted laws to new cases, and to draw fresh inferences from what had been previously acknowledged. This process, which called into exercise the powers of thought and logical dexterity, was known by the designation Talmud.[3] Distinct from these formal modes of legal instruction contained in the Mishnah was the Haggadah (הַגָּדָה), something said, the homiletic and edifying expansion and illustration of the Halakhah, seeking its ends through parable and allegory, startling and wayward inferences, history and myth, philosophy and science. 'The Haggadah,' says Deutsch, ' in general transforms Scripture, as we said, into a thousand themes for its variations. Everything being bound up in the Bible—the beginning and the end—there must be an answer in it to all questions. Find the key, and all the riddles in it are

---

[1] Lit. Rem. p. 17.
[2] On Midrash see Jost, Gesch. d. J. u. s. Sekt. ii., S. 212 sq. He extends its meaning so as to include Haggadah. Zunz says that Midrash originally was divided into Halakhah and Haggadah (S. 42), but afterwards was used as synonymous with Talmud or Gemarah to denote the study of the Law, whether in the Scripture or the Mishnah (S. 43).
[3] On the meaning of this term see also Jost ii., S. 125.

solved. The persons of the Bible—the kings and the patriarchs, the heroes and the prophets, the women and the children, what they did and suffered, their happiness and their doom, their words and their lives,—became, apart from their presupposed historical reality, a symbol and an allegory. And what the narrative had omitted, the Haggadah supplied in many variations. It filled up these gaps, as a prophet looking into the past might do; it explained the motives; it enlarged the story; it found connections between the remotest countries, ages, and people, often with a startling realism; it drew sublime morals from the most commonplace facts. Yet it did all this by quick and sudden motions, to us most foreign; and hence the frequent misunderstanding of its strange and wayward moods.'[1]

The Mishnah, as edited by R. Yehudah, consists in the main of Halakhah. Haggadistic elements, however, are not wanting, and it has been computed that they occur pretty abundantly in twenty-six treatises, more sparingly in twenty-two, while from only thirteen are they entirely absent. Haggadah appears most copiously in the treatises entitled Aboth (which contains moral precepts of the early teachers) and Middoth (which deals with the measurements of the Temple and its different parts). The language of the Mishnah is Hebrew, which is as pure as one could expect to find at that late period. It is enriched by words borrowed from Greek and Latin, and by new technical expressions.[2] It would be tedious to give an analysis of its contents, and it will be sufficient to describe the general plan upon which it has been compiled. The

---

[1] Art. on Talmud, p. 452, *Lit. Rem.* p. 45. For a fuller treatment of Haggadah see Zunz, fourth and following chapters. In the distinctions above given I have followed Grätz, *Gesch. d. Jud.* iv. pp. 16-19 and Note 2 at the end of the volume.

[2] See Jost, ii. S. 124.

whole work is divided into six books, called Sedarim (סְדָרִים), or 'Orders,' which deal respectively with the produce of the soil; with festivals and the observance of special days; with women, marriage, divorce, and kindred subjects; with injuries, and the suitable punishments; with holy things; and with the defilement and purification of vessels, garments, and other objects. Each Seder is subdivided into treatises, called Massikhtoth (מִסְבְּתוֹת), or 'Webs.' Each treatise, again, is divided into chapters, Peraqim (פְּרָקִים, from פְּרַק to rend), or 'Sections.' And lastly, each Pereq contains a certain number of Mishnayoth, the separate items of the oral law.[1]

Grätz says that this Mishnah, like the older collections, was not preserved in writing, but was for many centuries communicated orally, as it was considered a sin to write down the traditional teaching.[2] Jost, also, while expressing himself more cautiously, believes that it was still transmitted orally, though the custom of making a note of particular points had already begun.[3]

From the above account of the Mishnah it is evident that it is a most valuable authority for the study of Rabbinical opinion in the two centuries immediately succeeding the birth of Christ. A system of orthodoxy naturally retains its main features through a considerable period, and the Jewish orthodoxy seems to have been handed down with peculiar care. Still the most stable system of belief is liable to insensible modifications; and while we

---

[1] For a summary of the 525 Peraqim see Pressel's article on the Talmud, in *Herzog*, S. 620-630. For a more compendious one of the 63 Massikhtoth see Schürer's *Lehrb. d. neut. Zeitg.* S. 39-42; and *The Ethics of the Fathers collected by Nathan the Babylonian, Anno Domini* cc. *Translated from the original Hebrew Text, with an Introduction to the Talmud.* Edinburgh: Robert Young [no date], pp. 52-71.

[2] *Gesch. d. Jud.* iv. S. 221.

[3] *Gesch. d. J. u. s. Sekt.* ii. S. 122, Anm. 3, and S. 123-4.

may safely study in the Mishnah the general character of the thought in the midst of which Christ first planted his seeds of truth, we must not too hastily assume that opinions recorded in it are of pre-Christian origin. Each must be examined upon its own merits; and only when we have distinct grounds for so doing, such as the mention of pre-Christian authorities or corroborative evidence from other sources, can we be justified in treating it as a portion of the current opinion in the time of Christ.

The reduction of the oral law to system did not check, but only gave a new direction to the dialectics and casuistry of the Rabbis. The Mishnah itself presented difficulties and required illustration, and the grounds on which its decisions rested were open to the play of conflicting opinions; and accordingly it now became the central object of intellectual activity. The teachers who devoted themselves to the explanation of the Mishnah were called Amoraim (אֱמוֹרָאִים), a Chaldee word signifying originally the same as Methurgeman, i.e. interpreter, expounder;[1] and the process of discussion itself was called Amarah (אֲמָרָה), or in Chaldee, Gemarah (גְּמָרָה).[2] Of the latter word other explanations have been given, of which the commonest are the two kindred ones, 'supplement,' and 'completion,' expressive of its relation to the Mishnah. In process of time the freshly accumulated material itself required to be classified and arranged. This work was undertaken both in Palestine and in Babylonia, giving rise to the two recensions of the Gemarah which have been preserved to our own time. As the Gemarah was based upon the Mishnah, and follows its order section by section in the manner of a commentary, the two were combined into a

---

[1] See Grätz, *Gesch. d. Jud.* iv. S. 253 Anm.
[2] Pressel, *Thalmud*, S. 639, Anm.**, and S. 646.

single work, which bears the name of Talmud, a designation which is, however, sometimes applied separately to the Gemarah.

The Jerusalem Talmud, as the Palestinian recension was called, is of uncertain origin and date. Under the pressure of adverse circumstances the schools in Palestine gradually declined; and they finally lost their pre-eminence when, stung to a revolt through the oppression of the so-called Christian emperors, they rose against the power of Gallus, the cruel Cæsar of Constantius. The rising was speedily crushed with imperial ferocity; and in 352 A.D. Sepphoris, Tiberias, Lydda, and other towns were laid even with the ground.[1] It seems natural to assume that the work must have been completed before this time;[2] but is it not possible that its compilation was due to the interruption in the work of the Schools, and the consequent need of writing for its continued preservation?[3] If this were the case, it might account for its being named from Jerusalem instead of Tiberias.[4] Be this as it may, the absence of allusion to events of a later time may justify us in placing its final elaboration in the last third of the fourth century.[5]

Regarding the origin of the Babylonian Talmud we

[1] Grätz, *Gesch. d. J.* iv. S. 341. Jost, *Gesch. d. J. u. s. Sekt.* ii. S. 107-8.

[2] So Schürer, *Lehrb. d. n. Z.* S. 44.

[3] Zunz, S. 53, says that Julian is mentioned in Jer. Nedarim iii. 2; and as Julian was emperor 361-363 A.D., it seems necessary to place it after the revolt.

[4] Jost supposes that it was the work of the Babylonian scholars who had studied in Palestine, or of their successors. Thus owing its origin to the Palestinian tradition, it was received in Palestine, while it soon lost its authority in Babylonia. He thus explains the want of acquaintance with Roman history which it exhibits: *Gesch. d. J. u. s. Sekt.* ii. S. 165, Anm. 8, and S. 170, Anm. 2.

[5] Gfrörer's argument that it was known to Hieronymus does not seem to me very sound, as I think it rests on a misunderstanding of the words which he quotes: *Jahrh. d. H.* i. S. 22.

are more fully informed. While the learning which had flourished in Palestine was sinking into decay, its seeds, transplanted to the freer soil of Babylonia, sprung into a luxuriant growth. Two of the disciples of R. Yehudah founded the famous schools of Nahardea and Sura; and somewhat later that of Pumbeditha was established on the further side of the Euphrates. In these academies the traditional learning was discussed, and decisions accumulated, till the memory refused to retain the enormous and ill-digested mass, and it became necessary to arrange it into an orderly system. This work was undertaken by Rab, or, to give him his usual title of honour, Rabbana (our teacher) Ashi, who lived from about 350 A.D. to about 430. He was early chosen to preside in the academy of Sura, and his talents and character raised him to that pre-eminence which was needful for the accomplishment of his task. The plan on which he proceeded was the following. Every year, at the two great festivals of the Passover and the Atonement, he assembled round him a band of students from all quarters. On each occasion he took one treatise of the Mishnah, and went through its several subdivisions, questioning those present upon each, and thus learning the various forms which the tradition had assumed in different places. By taking a few of the treatises together he brought under review the whole number, sixty-three, in the course of thirty years. He then began to revise the entire work upon the same plan, and nearly completed his gigantic task before his death.

According to Grätz this recension, which became the accepted standard of the Talmud, was not yet committed to writing, as the Jews wished to preserve their secret doctrine from the Christians, who had already appropriated their Scriptures.[1] Jost leaves the question undecided, but thinks it most probable that copies were circulated during the reigns of Jesdigird I. and Behram Gais, extending to 442 A.D.[2]

Not long after the death of Ashi a persecution was raised against the Jews by the Persian king, and for a time the schools were closed. On the cessation of the persecution in the year 485 [3] the schools of Sura and Pumbeditha were reopened under the presidency of Rabina and R. Yosé. These men devoted themselves to the completion of R. Ashi's work; and through their influence the Talmud became a closed canon of law, to which no further additions should be made. It is not, indeed, altogether free from later interpolations; but these may be readily detected by a skilful eye. Grätz says that the work was finally closed in the year of Rabina's death, 499 A.D.;[4] but others prefer a somewhat later date.

The language of each Gemarah is a corrupt Chaldee; but that of the Babylonian is purer and more flowing than that of the Jerusalem.[5] Neither, in its present form, extends over the whole of the Mishnah. In the Jerusalem Talmud the Gemarah is wanting to two treatises ('Eduyyoth and Aboth) in the fourth Seder, to the whole of the fifth, and to the sixth, with the exception of the treatise Niddah. The Babylonian is defective in the first Seder, with the exception of Berakhoth; in the treatise Sheqalim in the second; in 'Eduyyoth and Aboth in the fourth; in Middoth and Qinnim and half of Tamid in the fifth; and altogether in the sixth with the exception of Niddah. The Jerusalem Gemarah accordingly

---

[1] *Gesch. d. Jud.* iv. S. 381.
[2] *Gesch. d. J. u. s. Sekt.* ii. S. 199 and 201.
[3] According to the computation accepted by Grätz, iv. S. 407.
[4] iv. S. 409.   [5] Pressel, *Thalm.* S. 642.

embraces thirty-nine treatises, the Babylonian thirty-six and a half. Twenty-eight treatises are found in both, eleven only in the Jerusalem, eight and a half only in the Babylonian, and fifteen and a half in neither. The Babylonian is nevertheless at least four times as voluminous as the Jerusalem.[1]

As an evidence of the state of Jewish opinion in the time of Christ it is obvious that the Gemarahs, and especially the Babylonian, must be used with much more reserve than the Mishnah. Still they may sometimes throw back an explanatory light upon the more obscure allusions of an earlier period: and it cannot be without advantage to trace the growth of kindred or identical beliefs along different lines of descent, and to compare their variations according to the genius of the people among whom they were transmitted.[2]

It remains for us to notice very briefly a few other works of kindred nature to the Talmud. The Mishnah of R. Yehudah did not embrace all the existing laws, because some appeared to lack the needful authority, others were virtually included under more general formulæ. His successors, accordingly, addressed themselves to the completion of the Mishnah; but, owing to the preponderant authority of his work, they did not venture to add to it, but

---

[1] Schürer, *Lehrb. d. n. Zeitg.* S. 44.

[2] I may refer the reader to Jost's *Geschichte der Israeliten seit der Zeit der Maccabäer bis auf unsre Tage, nach den Quellen bearbeitet.* Vierter Theil, Berlin, 1824. Excursus, 'Ueber den Thalmud als historische Quelle,' S. 264-294.

It may save the beginner some trouble if I state that the Mishnah is generally referred to by the name of the Treatise, followed by numbers denoting the Pereq and the Mishnah. The Jerusalem Gemarah is cited similarly, according to the Pereq and Halakhah, but with the prefix Jer. to distinguish it. The Babylonian Gemarah is quoted by the name of the Treatise, followed by the number of the folio page, and a letter to indicate the part of the page.

formed independent collections, which were known by the distinguishing name of Baraitha, 'external,' i.e. outside the principal compilation. Still later collections, of which we possess fifty-two treatises, were called Tosiphta, or 'supplement,' generally explained as supplement to the Mishnah, but supposed by Grätz [1] to be only another term for Mishnah, and to denote therefore a supplement to the Torah or written law. This work is generally ascribed to the third century—an opinion which is confirmed by its being written for the most part in Hebrew; but Dünner believes that it received its present form in the post-talmudical period, on the ground that several Halakhahs which occur in it seem to have been unknown to the compilers of the Talmud.[2]

Another valuable source for the study of Rabbinical teaching is found in the earlier Midrashim, or commentaries upon portions of Scripture. The older Midrashim, which took their origin in the period devoted to the formation of the Mishnah, are principally composed of Halakhah;[3] those of later date consist almost exclusively of Haggadah. The former are the three following —Mekhilta, on a part of Exodus; Siphra, on Leviticus; and Siphri, on Numbers and Deuteronomy. These were probably reduced to their present shape in the third century. The later Midrashim range from the sixth century to the twelfth.

A work named Seder 'Olam Rabbah is an exposition of Biblical history from Adam to the time of Alexander the

---

[1] *Gesch. d. Jud.* iv. S. 419.

[2] 'Halachisch-kritische Forschungen,' in the *Monatsschr. f. Gesch. u. Wissensch. d. Judenth*, 1870, S. 298-308 and 355-364. Referred to in Schürer, *Lehrb. d. n. Zeitg.* S. 42, Anm. 3.

[3] Siphri, however, contains Haggadah to the extent of ⅔ of the whole work: Zunz, *Gottesd. Vortr.* S. 84 sq.

Great, and is ascribed to the second half of the second century.[1]

Yalqut Shime'oni, ascribed to R. Shime'on haddarshan, is a collection of interpretations of the whole Hebrew Bible. In connection with each passage the explanations of older works are strung together into a catena. Zunz assigns this work to the first half of the thirteenth century.[2]

Some of the works above enumerated are so remote from the origin of Christianity that they can be used only by way of illustration. I need not even refer to the later mystical writings, as appeal cannot legitimately be made to them where they deviate from earlier sources.

[1] Zunz, *Gott. Vort.* S. 85.
[2] Ibid. S. 298 *sq.* I learn from Dr. Schiller-Szinessy that clear evidence proves it to be as early as the eleventh century.

BOOK II.

HISTORY.

CHAPTER I.

INTRODUCTORY.

HAVING now completed our survey of the literature on which we must principally rely for information respecting the Messianic idea in the centuries nearest to the time of Christ, we must next proceed to unfold the contents and trace the development of the idea itself. In entering upon this task different methods lie open to our choice. We may take the several books in their probable chronological order, and endeavour to present in one view the picture of the Messianic time which each contains; or we may at once resolve the expectation into its component elements, and follow each of these separately through its historical changes. The latter method, which is the one I propose to adopt, will have the advantage of greater system, and will save us from some needless repetitions; and if it is exposed to the objection that it will exhibit no complete representation of the Messianic belief at any given time, this will be sufficiently obviated if, under each head, we are careful to keep the pre-Christian distinct from the post-Christian authorities, and at the conclusion of our survey give a brief summary of the conceptions certainly or probably held before Christian teaching can have exercised any modifying influence upon Jewish thought.

The origin of the Messianic idea, no less than its permanent spiritual elements, must be sought in that hope of an ideal future which animated the noblest minds of the Israelites and belonged to the purest part of their inspiration. For them the divinest portion in the world's history was not behind, but before; and the prophetic conviction of a grand destiny for the people of God remained unconquerable through the most terrible crises in the national fortunes. The imagery in which this expectation was expressed was inevitably borrowed to a large extent from the past; but the king or prophet or legislator that was to come was glorified beyond the proportions of the past, and was to realise the aspirations which the olden time had kindled only to disappoint. This forward look of the Hebrew people was the inevitable result of their faith in divine providence, as it was the source of heroic, though too often misdirected endeavour; and those who pray that the kingdom of God may come, and toil hopefully for human good, do but take up in its modern form the burden of the ancient prophets. In regard to the expectation of a personal Messiah it may be less easy to detect a universal principle; but we must remember that the Messiah, under whatever form conceived, was to be the highest expression of Jewish life, the purest realisation of Jewish hope. This was the truth that lay hidden in the troubled imagination of the people; and, however wild and fanatical dreams may have clustered together in the popular conception of the Messiah, we cannot treat that conception as altogether visionary till we are prepared to deny that a supreme embodiment of Hebrew inspiration has ever appeared upon the stage of history, and failed to obtain the recognition of his countrymen because they themselves no longer felt the living breath of that inspiration in their hearts.

With the noblest conception, however, when committed to the custody, not of a select few, but of a whole people, it is inevitable that low and selfish thoughts should mingle. While times of calamity answer a holy purpose in raising men's minds to the contemplation of a divine order to which the world must ultimately be conformed, yet they are times when men of inferior spirit are prone to dream dreams, and to see visions in which the products of a higher faith are fantastically blended with imagery born from the terror of defeat, the rage of helpless suffering, and the lust of revenge. In such times false prophets abound, and ready credence is given to what satisfies the dominant passion. Josephus relates that at the siege of Jerusalem a multitude of six thousand people, including women and children, perished in a porch connected with the Temple, owing to the proclamation of a false prophet, who had desired them to go up to the sacred enclosure to receive there the signs of their deliverance. He adds that there were many prophets of this kind 'suborned by the tyrants' to prevent the people from deserting, and that 'a man in misfortunes is soon persuaded.'[1] A similar instance of credulity was witnessed at the capture of Constantinople by the Turks. 'From every part of the capital' there 'flowed into the church of St. Sophia . . . the multitude of fathers and husbands, of women and children, of priests, monks, and religious virgins: the doors were barred on the inside, and they sought protection from the sacred dome . . . Their confidence was founded on the prophecy of an

[1] *B. J.* vi. 5, 2.

enthusiast or impostor, that one day the Turks would enter Constantinople, and pursue the Romans as far as the column of Constantine in the square before St. Sophia; but that this would be the term of their calamities: that an angel would descend from heaven, with a sword in his hand, and would deliver the empire, with that celestial weapon, to a poor man seated at the foot of the column. "Take this sword," would he say, "and avenge the people of the Lord." At these animating words, the Turks would instantly fly, and the victorious Romans would drive them from the West.'[1] Amid the great upheaval of thought at the time of the Reformation wild fanatics arose, filled with disordered longings for a redeemed and renovated world. The prophets of Zwickau professed to have special revelations, and laid claim to the power of predicting future events. Strange visions haunted their sleep, and were not wholly absent from their waking moments. With the same confidence as the writer of 'Fourth Ezra,' they foretold the speedy termination of the present order of things. The Turk would soon seize upon Germany. All priests (even married ones) would be slain. In five, six, or seven years such general destruction would take place that not a single sinner would be left. And then the kingdom of God would come, and there would be one baptism, one faith.[2] Even by English rustics, in their abhorrence of the papal proclivities and despotic measures of James II., it was fondly believed that 'their beloved Monmouth,' though his treason had been terminated by the scaffold, 'would

---

[1] Gibbon, *Decline and Fall*, ch. lxviii. In Dr. Smith's edit. of 1854–5 vol. viii. pp. 172–3.

[2] See Ranke's *Deutsche Geschichte im Zeitalter der Reformation*. Vierte Auflage, 1869, ii. S. 15 *sq*. The original authorities are quoted in Gieseler's *Lehrbuch der Kirchengeschichte*. Dritten Bandes erste Abth. 1840, Cap. i. Anm. 87, S. 101 *sq*.

suddenly appear, would lead them to victory, and would tread down the King and the Jesuits under his feet.'[1] But not to multiply instances, we may borrow an example from our own time. Amid the excitement produced in France by the disasters in the Franco-German war the imagination of many was exalted into the intensity of belief, and a ready ear was given to stories of miracle and prophecy. Monseigneur Dupanloup, Bishop of Orleans, in an address to his brethren of the Catholic Church in France, relates how a person had said to him with full confidence, 'God will work a miracle; God will strike a great blow.' He asked him how he knew, and the reply was, 'You will see; I have no proof to give, but I am sure of it.' He mentions that at the time of writing he had before him more than twenty volumes of pretended prophecies, of all sizes and countries, but chiefly from France and Belgium. One of these was called 'Le Grand Avènement, Preceded by the Great Prophecy.' This great advent was to take place on February 17, 1874, and a Paris bookseller stated that before that date fifty thousand copies had been sold.[2] This example, borrowed from a neighbouring country which boasts of being the leader of civilisation, may enable us to enter more sympathetically into the wild hopes and longings of the struggling and oppressed Jews, and may also save us from laying undue stress upon a class of literature which, in some of its aspects, may represent rather the passion of an hour and of a party than the per-

---

[1] Macaulay's *History of England*, ch. viii. In fourth edition, vol. ii. p. 367. Similarly, the victims of the Bloody Assizes believed that Christ would soon come to the rescue. Ibid. ch. v.

[2] This is taken from the French correspondent of the *Times*. I have not got the exact reference; but a portion of the correspondent's letter was quoted in *The Inquirer*, April 25, 1874.

manent conviction of a nation. But through all its vagaries the reader to whom the human soul, even in its errors, is dear, will discern a love of righteousness which no oppression could crush, and the aspirations of a faith which no suffering could extinguish.

CHAPTER II.

SKETCH OF THE MESSIANIC IDEA AS EXHIBITED IN THE PROPHETS.

It does not belong to our present subject to give a full and critical account of the Messianic idea as it is presented in the pages of the Old Testament. But as it is desirable to have a general view of the Scriptural basis on which the belief of a later time was supposed to rest, we must briefly notice the picture of the ideal future exhibited to us by the successive prophets; and here, for the sake of conciseness, we shall follow the former of the two methods indicated in the last chapter, and sketch at once the entire view of each writer or group of writers. In doing so I must not pause on disputed points of criticism and interpretation, a discussion of which would be inconsistent with the subsidiary character of the present survey.[1]

We may confine our attention to the prophetical books, in which the great lines of Messianic thought are clearly and unmistakably traced. Among these we may

---

[1] I must acknowlege my indebtedness, among other works, particularly to Anger's *Vorlesungen über die Gesch. der mess. Idee*, which is chiefly occupied with the Old Testament, and gives a careful and neatly arranged synopsis of the subject; and to Oehler's article 'Messias' in Herzog. References to other works may be seen in Anger, S. 17. I may refer here to *Il Messia secondo gli Ebrei studio di David Castelli*. Firenze, 1874. The Old Testament view is treated in the First Part. I unfortunately procured the work too late to avail myself of the numerous Rabbinical references in the Second Part.

class together Joel (about 870 B.C.),[1] Amos (about 800 B.C.), and Hosea (about 784 B.C.); for their descriptions of the future, though varied to suit the occasion and purpose of their prophecies, are essentially similar, and agree in the total absence of a Messiah, or personal mediator, in the inauguration of the ideal blessedness. Notwithstanding this deficiency, the main features of the Messianic expectation, as it existed in later times, are sketched with sufficient distinctness. First must come a time of judgment, called by Joel and Amos 'the day of Yahveh.'[2] According to Joel's glowing imagery, 'the sun shall be turned into darkness, and the moon into blood' before that day come;[3] and then, the troubles of Judah being over, the heathen will be assembled for judgment in the Valley of Jehoshaphat—here, probably, only a symbolical name for the place where 'Yahveh judges.'[4] Amos denounces approaching punishment not only against the heathen,[5] but also against Judah,[6] and at far greater length against Israel;[7] and Hosea, who belonged to the northern kingdom, directs his warnings throughout against Israel, though Judah is not altogether overlooked.[8] Turning in penitence to God is the condition on which a more blessed future is promised. 'Therefore also now, saith the Lord, turn ye to me with all your heart, and with fasting, and with weeping, and with mourning: and rend your heart, and not your garments, and turn unto the Lord your God: for he is gracious and merciful, slow to anger and of great kindness, and repenteth him of the

---

[1] Hilgenfeld places him some 400 years later; and the opinion which assigns to him a late date has recently been gaining ground. See Hilg.'s view in Schrader's *De Wette*, Einleit. § 285, Anm. c.
[2] Joel i. 15; ii. 1, 32; iii. 12, 14; Amos v. 18, 20.
[3] ii. 31.   [4] iii. 2, 12.   [5] i. 3–ii. 3.
[6] ii. 4, 5.   [7] ii. 6–ix. 10.
[8] v. 5, 10; xii. 2.

evil.'¹ As I have already said, no personal mediator is introduced; and the language of Hosea,² speaking in the name of Yahveh, fairly represents the view of the three prophets: 'I will be thy king: where is any other that may save thee in all thy cities?' Yet the times of David serve already to prefigure the future glory:—'In that day will I raise up the tabernacle of David that is fallen, and close up the breaches thereof; and I will raise up his ruins, and build it as in the days of old;'³ 'afterwards shall the children of Israel return, and seek the Lord their God, and David their king.'⁴ By none of these prophets is the expected salvation extended beyond Judah and Israel, and Joel dwells with satisfaction on the hope that no stranger shall any more pass through Jerusalem.⁵ It is true that Joel also speaks of the Spirit's being poured out upon all flesh;⁶ but this expression seems limited by the connection to the 'children of Zion,' and therefore denotes, not the universality of a spiritual dispensation, but the general diffusion of the divine gift among the members of the chosen race. This prophecy, together with the call to repentance already alluded to, shows that the moral and religious aspect of the future was not overlooked; and Hosea dwells fondly on the love that shall exist between Yahveh and his people:—'In the place where it was said unto them, Ye are not my people, there it shall be said unto them, Ye are the sons of the living God.'⁷ But the external prosperity of the people enters even more largely into the prophetic vision:—'Behold, I will send you corn, and wine, and oil, and ye shall be satisfied therewith;' 'and it shall come to pass in that

---

¹ Joel ii. 12, 13. See also i. 14; ii. 14-18; Amos v. 4-6, 14-15, 24; Hosea iii. 5; vi. 1-3, 6; x. 12; xii. 6; xiv. 1-3.
² xiii. 10.   ³ Amos ix. 11.   ⁴ Hos. iii. 5.
⁵ iii. 17.   ⁶ ii. 28.
⁷ i. 10. See also ii. 16-23; xiv. 4 *sq.*

day, that the mountains shall drop down new wine, and the hills shall flow with milk, and all the rivers of Judah shall flow with waters;'[1] 'and in that day I will make a covenant for them with the beasts of the field, and with the fowls of heaven, and with the creeping things of the ground: and I will break the bow, and the sword, and the battle out of the earth, and will make them to lie down safely.'[2] Zion will still be the centre of the people's religious life:—' So shall ye know that I am the Lord your God dwelling in Zion, my holy mountain.'[3] There is no very clear indication of time. Hosea says vaguely that ' the children of Israel shall abide many days without a king,' and afterwards they shall return and seek the Lord.[4]

We now proceed to another group of three prophets, who lived during the period of the Assyrian invasions of Palestine, namely Isaiah, the elder Zechariah,[5] and Micah. The prophecies of Isaiah extend from 759 to about 713 B.C. Zechariah is supposed to have written about 740 B.C., the year in which Tiglath-pileser, king of Assyria, invaded the north of Palestine.[6] Micah prophesied in the reigns of Jotham, Ahaz, and Hezekiah,[7] and was accordingly a younger contemporary of Isaiah. The general description of the Messianic period in the writings of these prophets agrees with that of the previous group; but it is distinguished from it by two important particulars. In the first place, the person of the ideal king is distinctly introduced and portrayed. In Zechariah[8] he comes as a just and peaceful king, riding on the unwarlike ass. 'His dominion shall be from sea to sea, and from the river

---

[1] Joel ii. 19; iii. 18.
[2] Hos. ii. 18. See the whole passage; also Amos ix. 11–15.
[3] Joel iii. 17. See also ii. 32; iii. 21; cf. Amos i. 2.
[4] iii. 4, 5.   [5] Zech. ix.–xi.
[6] See 2 Kings xv. 29.   [7] Mic. i. 1.   [8] ix. 9, 10.

to the ends of the earth,'—a hope which may have been derived from recollections of the reign of David. In Micah[1] his Davidic descent is plainly implied in the reference to the antiquity of his descent, and to Bethlehem as its source; and Isaiah derives him in express words from the stem of Jesse.[2] The fullest description of his high endowments, and of the glory of his reign, is given by Isaiah.[3] I must not enter on the controversies which have been raised respecting the nature of his person, but content myself with stating my own belief that a sound interpretation does not carry us higher than an ideal man, whom the Spirit of God has furnished with amplest gifts for the fulfilment of his office. Whether immortality is included among these, or he is regarded simply as the first in an everlasting succession of kings, may admit of reasonable question. The time of the Messianic kingdom is vaguely described as 'in the last days;'[4] but in one passage Isaiah seems to expect it 'in a very little while.'[5] The second point which distinguishes these prophets from the preceding is the fact that they extend the anticipated blessedness beyond the limits of their own people. In Zechariah, indeed, this feature is extremely obscure; but in ix. 7, he seems to expect a portion of the Philistines to share in the happiness of Judah. Micah is much more explicit:—' In the last days it shall come to pass, that the mountain of the house of the Lord shall be established in the top of the mountains, and it shall be exalted above the hills, and people shall flow unto it. And many nations shall come, and say, Come and let us go up to the mountain of the Lord, and to the house of

---

[1] v. 2.   [2] xi. 1.
[3] ix. 1-7, xi. See also Mic. v. 2, 4, and iv. 1-7, in which last, however, God alone is spoken of as king.
[4] Isai. ii. 2; Mic. iv. 1.   [5] xxix. 17.

the God of Jacob; and he will teach us of his ways, and we will walk in his paths: for the law shall go forth of Zion, and the word of the Lord from Jerusalem.'[1] He adds that it shall be a time of universal peace. The same passage occurs in Isaiah,[2] but with this difference, that, instead of saying 'people,' he says, 'all nations shall flow unto it.' Compare also his statement, 'the earth shall be full of the knowledge of the Lord, as the waters cover the sea. And in that day there shall be a root of Jesse, which shall stand for an ensign of the people; to it shall the Gentiles seek: and his rest shall be glorious.'[3] Amongst these nations Egypt and Assyria are selected for especial honour:[4]—'In that day shall Israel be the third with Egypt and with Assyria, even a blessing in the midst of the land; whom the Lord of hosts shall bless, saying, Blessed be Egypt my people, and Assyria the work of my hands, and Israel mine inheritance.'[5]

Zephaniah flourished during the reign of Josiah, and his prophecies were probably uttered between 630 and 624 B.C. 'The great day of Yahveh' is with him also 'a day of wrath, a day of trouble and distress, a day of wasteness and desolation, a day of darkness and gloominess, a day of clouds and thick darkness, a day of the trumpet and alarm against the fenced cities, and against the high towers.'[6] He leaves no doubt about the time of its coming:—'It is near, it is near, and hasteth greatly.'[7] He makes no mention of a Messiah, for God is 'the king of Israel.'[8]

Jeremiah prophesied from the thirteenth year of Josiah

---

[1] iv. 1, 2.   [2] ii. 2-4.
[3] xi. 9, 10.   [4] xix. 18-25.
[5] Verses 24, 25. The genuineness of this whole passage has been called in question; but in the absence of decisive reasons I retain it as an evidence of Isaiah's breadth of sympathy.
[6] i. 14-16.   [7] i. 14. See also 7.   [8] iii. 15.

till after the beginning of the Babylonian captivity in 588 B.C., and therefore witnessed the appearance of the formidable Chaldeans in Palestine, 605 B.C., and the successive calamities which culminated in the destruction of Jerusalem. To the picture of the Messianic period already sketched he adds some touches of his own. He predicts for the Babylonian exile a duration of seventy years.[1] Afterwards the people shall be gathered together in their own land once more, and God will make 'a new covenant,' 'an everlasting covenant,' with them, and will write his law in their hearts, and all shall know him from the least unto the greatest.[2] He expects a king of the line of David, 'a righteous branch,' whose name shall be 'Yahveh is our righteousness.'[3] This name is in another passage ascribed to Jerusalem, and the prophet evidently looks, not for a single Messianic ruler, but for a perpetual succession of kings upon the throne of David—'David shall never want a man to sit upon the throne of the house of Israel.'[4]

To the period of the Captivity belong Ezekiel, probably Obadiah,[5] and, in the view of recent critics, Isaiah xxiv.-xxvii., and the so-called later Isaiah, xiii. 1-xiv. 23, xxi. 1-10, xxxiv., xxxv., and xl.-lxvi.[6] Obadiah, who may have written soon after the beginning of the captivity, offers little of a Messianic character. He anticipates a speedy judgment upon all the heathen, when 'upon Mount Zion shall be deliverance, and there shall be holiness,' and 'the kingdom shall be the Lord's.'[7] Isaiah xxiv.-xxvii. perhaps falls within this period, though

---

[1] xxv. 11-14; xxix. 10.
[2] xxxi. 31-34; xxxii. 40; l. 5.   [3] xxiii. 5, 6.
[4] xxxiii. 15-17.
[5] The date of Obadiah is disputed. See Schrader's *De Wette*, § 290.
[6] Kuenen, *Rel. of Isr.* ii. pp. 120-1, classes these passages together.
[7] 15, 17, 21.

placed by Ewald somewhat later.[1] Unless we resort to figurative interpretation, this prophet expects for his own people a resurrection of the dead,[2] while this hope is expressly denied to those who had tyrannised over them.[3] He even declares that death will be destroyed for ever.[4] The blessedness of the future is described under the figure of a feast on Mount Zion.[5] The destruction of leviathan is mentioned;[6] but it is evident that the prophet refers under this name to the hostile nations whom he may not have thought it prudent to indicate more clearly. The trumpet also is introduced:—'It shall come to pass in that day, that the great trumpet shall be blown, and they shall come which were ready to perish in the land of Assyria, and the outcasts in the land of Egypt, and shall worship the Lord in the holy mount at Jerusalem.'[7] There is throughout no trace of a Messiah.

Ezekiel prophesied shortly before the exile, and during its earlier years. In his Messianic expectations he closely resembles Jeremiah, but adds some features of his own. Unless we treat the passage about the dry bones as figurative throughout, he expects his people to rise up out of their graves, and be restored to their own land.[8] The scattered people shall all be brought together to the holy mountain,[9] and shall again be united into a single nation.[10] They shall be under one king, David, the servant of the Lord, who shall be 'their prince for ever.'[11] But when the people are dwelling safely and without walls, 'Gog,

---

[1] *Die Propheten des Alten Bundes.* Zweite Ausg., 1867-8, iii. S. 164.
[2] xxvi. 19.   [3] xxvi. 14.
[4] According to Ewald's translation, xxv. 8.
[5] xxv. 6.   [6] xxvii. 1.   [7] xxvii. 13.
[8] xxxvii. 1-14. I must confess that the argument drawn from this passage and that of Isaiah in favour of a belief in the resurrection seems to me very precarious.
[9] xx. 34-44.   [10] xxxvii. 21, 22.
[11] xxxiv. 23, 24; xxxvii. 24, 25.

the land of Magog' (probably the king and people of Scythia), shall come like a storm, like a cloud to cover the land, 'all of them riding upon horses, a great company, and a mighty army.' But then there shall be a great shaking in the land, and 'every man's sword shall be against his brother,' and the Lord will plead against Gog 'with pestilence and with blood,' and 'will rain upon him, and upon his bands, and upon the many people that are with him, an overflowing rain, and great hailstones, fire, and brimstone;' and thus will the Lord be known in the eyes of many nations. They shall fall upon the open field, and the birds and beasts shall assemble at the great sacrifice thus prepared for them on the mountains of Israel; and for seven months shall the house of Israel be burying Gog and his host in the valley of Hamongog; and the weapons of the slain shall serve for firewood for seven years.[1] The measures of the new Jerusalem and Temple, and the divisions of the land, are stated with great minuteness.[2] This prophet, with his stern patriotism, has no word of hope for other nations.

The later Isaiah, if we accept the modern critical view, prophesied immediately before the end of the Captivity. Notwithstanding his idealising temperament, he adds little beyond beauty of description to the Messianic picture which we have already obtained. He declares that the old heaven and earth shall pass away, and be replaced by new.[3] No Son of David appears as the leader of a brighter lot; and it is more than doubtful whether any Messiah is alluded to. Cyrus, indeed, is spoken of as the Lord's 'anointed.'[4] The name 'Messiah,' or anointed, however, is nowhere else used in the Prophets to designate the ideal mediator; and to say nothing of

[1] xxxviii., xxxix.
[2] xl.–xlviii.
[3] li. 6, 16; lxv. 17; lxvi. 22.
[4] xlv. 1.

the improbability of a Jew's fixing on a foreign potentate to fill this supreme position, it seems clear that the Prophet regards him only as an unconscious[1] instrument in the hands of God, and at best as preparing the way for the Messianic period. The 'servant' of the Lord spoken of so often in xl.–liii. is probably a collective name for those who remained faithful among the Israelites;[2] and though these chapters contain passages of wonderful spiritual depth, and capable therefore of a very exalted application, they have no certain reference to an expected Messiah.

Haggai and Zechariah (i.–viii.) came forward in the year 520 B.C. to assist Zerubbabel and the High-priest Joshua, who were then engaged in the work of rebuilding the Temple. These later Prophets offer little on which it is necessary for us to pause. For the most part they are content to follow the lines marked out by earlier writers, simply adapting their ideals to the special circumstances of their own time. It is interesting to observe that the cruel experiences of the Captivity did not quench in the Prophets a longing for a wider than a merely national good. 'Many nations,' says Zechariah, 'shall be joined to the Lord in that day, and shall be my people.'[3] 'Yea, many people and strong nations shall come to seek the Lord of hosts in Jerusalem, and to pray before the Lord.'[4] The same Prophet, following the imagery of Jeremiah, speaks of a servant of the Lord named the Branch, who shall build the Temple, and bear the glory, and sit and rule upon his throne.[5] The reference to the building of the Temple shows that this Branch, whom the

---

[1] xlv. 5.
[2] See especially xli. 8; xliv. 1, 2; xlix. 3. See Kuenen's *Rel. of Isr.* ii. pp. 130–1.
[3] ii. 11.   [4] viii. 22.   [5] iii. 8; vi. 12, 13.

Lord brings in,[1] is Zerubbabel, because it is expressly said of him that his hands 'have laid the foundation of this house; his hands shall also finish it.'[2]

Malachi was probably contemporary with Nehemiah, about 430 B.C. His indignation was roused by the corruptions of the priesthood; and he accordingly announces a 'great and dreadful day of the Lord,'[3] in which the wicked shall be burned up as stubble, but to those who fear the Lord's name ' the sun of righteousness shall arise with healing in his wings.'[4] But instead of the royal mediator of the older Prophets, 'the messenger of the covenant' shall be sent to prepare the way before Yahveh himself, and he shall suddenly come to his temple, and purify the sons of Levi.[5] This messenger is named after the great destroyer of idolatrous priests, Elijah the Prophet.[6] But the Prophet's ideal extends only to the observance of the law of Moses,[7] and the restoration of the ceremonial which prevailed ' in the days of old.'[8]

[1] iii. 8. [2] iv. 9.
[3] iv. 5. I follow the divisions of the Authorised Version.
[4] iv. 1, 2.   [5] iii. 1-3.   [6] iv. 5.
[7] iv. 4.   [8] iii. 4.

CHAPTER III.

THE SON OF SIRACH, TOBIT, AND BARUCH.

THE three apocryphal works indicated by the above names require a separate notice, because they probably represent, at least to some extent, the period intermediate between the last of the Prophets and the beginning of the Maccabean struggle. There is, however, anything but a consensus of opinion as to their dates. As regards the Wisdom of Jesus the son of Sirach, we may reasonably accept the opinion of De Wette, who ascribes the original work to 180 B.C.[1] The dates assigned to Tobit range from the close of the Persian period to the time of Trajan; but as some high authorities place it before the time of the Maccabees, we may notice here the few passages that concern us.[2] The Book of Baruch, also, is of most uncertain date;[3] but as it throws little light on our subject, and cannot safely be used to illustrate the views of a later time, we may venture, for convenience, to class it with the two other apocryphal works already mentioned.

'The Wisdom of the Son of Sirach,' in common with the rest of the Apocrypha, makes no allusion to a personal Messiah, though hopes known as Messianic appear in different parts of the book. The writer expects the Lord to take vengeance on the Gentiles,[4] and to gather together

---

[1] Schrader's *De Wette*, § 383.
[2] Ibid. § 378.
[3] Ibid. §§ 390, 391.
[4] xxxii. 22-24; xxxiii. 1-12; xxxix. 23.

'all the tribes of Jacob.'[1] He prays for blessings on Jerusalem, and on Israel whom God had made like a 'first-born.'[2] 'The days of Israel are without number,'[3] and 'their seed shall remain for ever.'[4] The Lord 'exalted' David's 'horn for ever, and gave him a covenant of kings and a throne of glory in Israel.'[5] There is also an obscure allusion to the return of Elias, as foretold by Malachi, and in connection with it an intimation that 'we also shall live with life' (= shall surely live), from which some suppose that the writer expected Elias to appear in his own lifetime.[6]

The expression of Messianic hopes in Tobit is not quite so indefinite. The scattered Israelites will be once more assembled together.[7] The second Temple, inferior to the first, shall stand 'until the times of the age be fulfilled,' and afterwards 'the house of God shall be built gloriously' in Jerusalem 'as the Prophets spake concerning it,' and the city itself shall be built of precious stones, and 'all its streets shall cry hallelujah.'[8] And 'many nations shall come from far to the name of the Lord God, having gifts in their hands, even gifts for the King of heaven,'[9] and 'all the nations shall turn truly to fear the Lord God, and shall bury their idols; and all the nations shall bless the Lord, and his people shall confess to God, and the Lord will exalt his people; and all who love the Lord God in truth and righteousness shall rejoice, showing mercy to our brethren.'[10]

This hope of universal blessedness changes in Baruch into longing for vengeance on the enemies of Zion : 'The enemy persecuted thee, and thou shalt see his destruction speedily, and mount up upon their necks;'[11] 'wretched

[1] xxxiii. 13. [2] xxxvi. 17–22. [3] xxxvii. 25.
[4] xliv. 13. [5] xlvii. 11. [6] xlviii. 10, 11.
[7] xiii. 5; xiv. 5. [8] xiv. 5; xiii. 16–18. [9] xiii. 11.
[10] xiv. 6, 7. [11] iv. 25.

are those who injured thee, and rejoiced in thy fall; wretched the cities to which thy children were in bondage; wretched she who received thy sons; for as she rejoiced at thy fall, and was glad at thy ruin, so shall she be grieved at her own desolation.'[1] The sufferings of the Israelites are, as usual, represented as due to their sins,[2] but speedy succour is expected from the eternal Saviour,[3] and they shall be restored to Jerusalem for ever, and rejoice in the glory of God.[4] Then Jerusalem itself shall put off the garment of sorrow, and 'put on the comeliness of the glory that is from God, for ever,' and its 'name shall be called by God for ever, The peace of righteousness and the glory of God's worship.'[5]

An argument from silence is always more or less doubtful; but we can hardly help inferring from their total silence on the subject that the authors of these works had no belief in the coming of a Messiah. It cannot be said that their subjects did not lead them to speak of this belief; for the above references show how fully they shared the prophetic aspirations after the future glory of their race; and when they describe the magnificence of the Jerusalem that is to be, or dwell upon the covenant made with David, or picture all nations turning from their idolatry to the fear of God, it is inconceivable that they should omit the central figure, through whose agency every blessing was to come, if such a personality really entered into their belief. We cannot of course conclude that the belief had altogether died out of the hearts of the Jewish people; for as we observed in the writings of the Prophets that the person of the Messiah advances and recedes as we turn from one to another, so a difference of opinion may have prevailed at the later time of which

---

[1] iv. 31–35.   [2] iv. 6 *sq.*   [3] iv. 22.
[4] iv. 23, 36, 37; v. 5. See also ii. 27–35.   [5] v. 1 *sq.*

we are treating. But from the little, and in part doubtful, evidence that remains to us it would seem that in the period between the Captivity and the rise of the Maccabees the Messianic hope resolved itself into vague anticipations of a glorious and happy future, in which the presence of God would be more manifest, but of which a Messiah would form no essential feature.

CHAPTER IV.

DIVISIONS OF TIME.

WE must now proceed to unfold systematically the elements of the Messianic idea as it existed in the period which begins with the tyranny of Antiochus Epiphanes. If we except from this the transient glories of the Maccabees, it was marked by an ever-deepening gloom. The crushing power of Rome proved more formidable than the sway of Persians and Greeks, and, after provoking once and again a violent but fruitless resistance, culminated in the entire and permanent overthrow of the Jewish polity. Despair of the present, combined with an unconquerable faith in providence, awakened passionate hopes for the future; and these, building on insecure interpretations of the ancient Scriptures, gradually reared, if not a precisely dogmatic, yet a grandly indefinite and richly coloured eschatology.

As a sad present transfigures itself in hope into a glorious future, it is only what we should expect when we find the world's history divided into two great periods. This division is apparent in the Book of Daniel. First is the transitory period, in which the heathen powers hold dominion successively, and then comes the eternal period in which 'the saints of the Most High shall take the kingdom, and possess the kingdom for ever, even for ever and ever.'[1] Between these two periods a judgment is to

---

[1] vii. 18.

take place, in which sentence shall be passed upon the heathen.[1] The time immediately preceding this change is spoken of as 'the latter days,'[2] and 'the time of the end;'[3] and this end was to be brought in at a divinely appointed time.[4]

A similar distinction between a transitory and an eternal period is recognised in the Book of Enoch: and there also the two are marked off by the 'great judgment' which is to take place 'in the last time.'[5] Here too the days are under divine appointment, so that men need not disturb themselves about the times; for in due course the righteous will rise up from sleep, and God will be gracious to them, and give them everlasting righteousness and dominion.[6] The same trustful thought, that God knows the time when the better state of things will begin, occurs in the Psalms of Solomon;[7] and the author of the Assumption of Moses expects the Lord to have regard to his people 'in the consummation of the end of days.'[8]

The post-Christian book, Fourth Ezra, adopts the above view, simply giving it a more explicit utterance:—'The Most High did not make one age, but two.'[9] If by Esau we may understand the heathen powers generally, though especially Rome which was the dreaded enemy of the time, the writer adopts the view of Daniel, when he says, 'Esau is the end of this age, and Jacob the beginning of the following,'[10] and 'the Most High made this age on account of many, but the future on account of few.'[11] With him also 'the day of judgment will be the end of this age, and the beginning of the future immortal age, in which corruption will pass away.'[12] No less

---

[1] vii. 9 sq.   [2] x. 14.   [3] viii. 17; xi. 40; xii. 4, 9.
[4] viii. 19; also generally implied in the explanations of the visions.
[5] x. 12; xxv. 4; xxvii. 3.   [6] xcii. 2-4.
[7] xvii. 23.   [8] i. 4.   [9] (vi.) 25.
[10] vi. 9.   [11] viii. 1.   [12] vii. 43.

clearly does he insist that God has pre-arranged the age which he has created, and has weighed and measured, and numbered the times, and will wait till the predicted measure be filled.[1]

From the Rabbinical authorities it may be sufficient to quote one illustrative passage :—'Rabbi Ya'aqob said, This age (הָעוֹלָם הַזֶּה) is like a vestibule in comparison with the age to come (הָעוֹלָם הַבָּא). Get thyself ready in the vestibule, that thou mayest enter the dining-room. He used to say, One hour in penitence and good works in this age is fairer than the whole life of the age to come; but one hour of refreshment of spirit in the age to come is fairer than the whole life of this age.'[2]

The former of these two ages was, no doubt with a view to determine its ulterior limit, frequently divided in a manner more or less artificial. The beginning of this kind of division is found in Daniel. It there assumes two forms, the first of which is purely historical, being founded on the known succession of heathen empires. By Nebuchadnezzar's dream, in which he saw an image composed of four metals, with a mingling of clay in the feet, are typified four kingdoms.[3] At an early period the fourth of these kingdoms was referred to the Roman Empire,[4] and those in modern times who consider them-

[1] iv. 36–42; v. 46–49; (vi.) 48.
[2] Pireqé Aboth, iv. 16, 17. Compare the New Testament expressions, ὁ αἰὼν (or καιρὸς) οὗτος, ὁ νῦν αἰών, and αἰὼν ὁ μέλλων, or ἐκεῖνος, or ὁ ἐρχόμενος, Matt. xii. 32; xiii. 22, 40; Mark x. 30; Luke xvi. 8; xviii. 30; xx. 34, 35; Rom. xii. 2; 1 Cor. i. 20; ii. 6, 8; iii. 18; 2 Cor. iv. 4; Eph. i. 21; ii. 2, 7; 1 Tim. vi. 17; 2 Tim. iv. 10; Tit. ii. 12; Heb. vi. 5. As expressions answering to 'the latter days' of Daniel compare ἐν ὑστέροις καιροῖς, 1 Tim. iv. 1, ἐν καιρῷ ἐσχάτῳ, 1 Peter i. 5; ἐπ' ἐσχάτων τῶν χρόνων, 1 Peter i. 20; ἐπ' ἐσχάτου τῶν ἡμερῶν, Heb. i. 1; 2 Pet. iii. 3; ἐν ἐσχάταις ἡμέραις, 2 Tim. iii. 1; James v. 3; τὰ τέλη τῶν αἰώνων, 1 Cor. x. 11; ἐπὶ συντελείᾳ τῶν αἰώνων, Heb. ix. 26.
[3] ii. 31 sq.
[4] See the authorities in *Speaker's Com.* vi. p. 332.

selves bound to accept the traditional exegesis are strenuous in the defence of this explanation. According to this view the three preceding kingdoms must be the Chaldean, the Medo-Persian, and the Greek. If, however, we do not feel constrained to follow traditional opinion, we can have little hesitation in regarding the fourth kingdom as the Greek; and then the three earlier kingdoms may be the Chaldean, the Median, and the Persian, though Hitzig would here understand by the first the reign of Nebuchadnezzar himself, by the second 'inferior' one that of Belshazzar, and by the third the Medo-Persian.[1] Daniel's vision of four beasts in ch. vii. also symbolises four kingdoms; and here, as Nebuchadnezzar is now supposed to be dead, it is admitted by Hitzig that these four are the Chaldean, Median, Persian, and Greek.[2]

[1] Against Hitzig's view Dr. Pusey has nothing to allege but 'its dullness;' but as even this allegation is grounded on the assumption that the theory in question makes the 'bear' of ch. vii. represent Belshazzar, it only shows that Dr. Pusey had not made himself fully acquainted with the view which he undertook to criticise.

[2] See Hitzig in the *Kurzgefasstes exeget. Handbuch zum A. T.* Dr. Pusey, overlooking Hitzig's view, says 'it is allowed on all hands, that the four beasts in Daniel's vision in the first year of Belshazzar correspond exactly to the four empires represented in the image exhibited to Nebuchadnezzar,' (*Daniel the Prophet*, p. 65). See this whole question well discussed by 'R. M.' in the *Theological Review*, September 1865, p. 491 *sq.* There are undoubtedly difficulties connected with the interpretation of the four kingdoms on the hypothesis of the later date of the book, and these are pointed out with considerable force by Dr. Pusey in Lecture III.: but he seems quite to forget that literary judgments must depend on a *balance* of probabilities. The differences of opinion at which Dr. Pusey is so jubilant, appear, as we have seen, in the interpretation of the uncanonical apocalyptic books; and if anyone chose to maintain that such books contained real prophecies, he might make much capital out of these differences, to the great discomfiture of the 'unbelievers.' But even among the defenders there are different opinions; for, to go no farther, Dr. Westcott maintains that the four kingdoms are the Babylonian, Median, Persian, and Grecian (*Dict. of Bible*. Daniel, Book of, § 12), and the same view is urged with great force by Delitzsch (*Herzog*, Daniel, S. 279 *sq*); so that concessions extorted by 'conscience' are not all

The other mode of division adopted in Daniel[1] is less simple, and begins the practice of seeking to discover the time of the expected deliverance through an artificial interpretation of ancient writers. The author appeals to the prophecy of Jeremiah that the Lord 'would accomplish seventy years in the desolations of Jerusalem.'[2] Now if the seventy years were understood literally, the prophecy had been only partially fulfilled; and therefore not only seventy years, but seventy 'weeks,' or groups of seven, must be the period intended. From a comparison of xii. 7 with xii. 11 we learn that three and a half *times* are the equivalent of twelve hundred and ninety days, and must therefore represent three and a half *years*. Now this same period is treated in ix. 27 as half a week; and hence it is evident that the weeks are to be regarded as weeks of years. The seventy weeks are divided into periods of seven, sixty-two, and one. The points of time indicated by this division will be considered in a subsequent chapter.

The mystic number seventy recurs in two different connections in the Book of Enoch. Instead of seventy weeks of years we now have seventy shepherds to whose power the Israelite sheep were committed.[3] But the same number is adapted to the whole course of the world's history up to the final judgment. The bad angels are represented as bound under the hills for seventy generations, till the last judgment shall be held for all eternity.[4] Gfrörer endeavours to prove that the period of each of these generations comprises one hundred years. In a later portion of the book the first age is divided into ten weeks.[5] Now Enoch begins his account

on one side. See different opinions discussed in Hitzig, and in *Speaker's Com.* vi. Excursus on the Four Kingdoms, p. 332 *sq.*

[1] ix. 24–27.   [2] ix. 2.
[3] lxxxix. 59 *sq.*   [4] x. 12.   [5] xciii. and xci. 12 *sq.*

of this division by saying that he was born as the seventh in the first week, and after him, in the second week, great wickedness should arise. It is a natural inference that he is supposed to have been born on the seventh day; and as the date of his birth is given in Genesis [1] as 622 after the Creation, it follows that each day, answering to a generation in the previous passage, consists of one hundred years, and the whole of the first age consequently embraces seven thousand years.[2] This inference, however, rests on an assumption which cannot be verified. Dillmann has shown conclusively that the author cannot have intended by his weeks to denote equal periods. The flood, which according to the chronology in Genesis took place in the year 1656 after the Creation, is placed within the second week. Again, the Law is given at the end of the fourth week, and the Temple built at the end of the fifth. The fifth week, therefore, comprises less than 480 years, for according to 1 Kings vi. 1, the Temple was begun in the 480th year after the Exodus. It is therefore more probable that the writer reckoned by generations, counting seven to each week, or fourteen in the later periods when the generations became shorter.[3]

The Assumption of Moses presents a different kind of division. If, as there can be little doubt, the lacuna at the beginning ought to be filled up with a reference to the 120th year of Moses, the death of the lawgiver is placed in the year 2500 from the creation of the world;[4] and from this date till the time when God will appear in order to punish the Gentiles and glorify Israel will be 250 times.[5] Hilgenfeld understands by these 'times'

[1] v. 3–18.   [2] *Jahrh. d. II.* ii. S. 202 sq.
[3] *Das Buch Henoch*, S. 298 sq.
[4] i. 1.   [5] x. 29.

weeks of years, and thus obtains 4,250 years for the duration of the first age.[1] One is strongly tempted, however, to multiply by ten instead of seven, and thus reach a period of 5,000 years, of which the central point is marked by the death of Moses. The date assigned to Moses by the writer of this work is only slightly altered in the Book of Jubilees. In order to preserve the even fifty jubilees the 2,500 years from the Creation are reduced to 2,450.

Coming to the post-Christian period we find a continuation of the same kind of artificial division. The fourth book of the Sibylline Oracles divides the course of history into eleven generations,[2] of which, however, no use is made in determining the duration of the present state of things. It is said that the judgment of the world will take place in the 'tenth' generation, according to the reading of the manuscripts,[3] but probably we may adopt the emendation of Fabricius and Bleek, and read 'eleventh.'[4]

In Fourth Ezra we are told that 'the age has been divided into twelve parts, and there have passed already ten and the half of the tenth part.'[5] This is the reading of the Latin. The Æthiopic, however, reads as follows:— 'For the world has been arranged in ten parts, and it has come to the tenth, and there remains half of the tenth.' This is certainly more intelligible, and Gfrörer pronounces it to be unquestionably correct.[6] He is mistaken, how-

---

[1] *Mess. Jud.* p. 468.
[2] Verse 20. See also 47, 50, 55, 66, 86.   [3] 47.
[4] See Friedlieb, S. xxxix. Anm. 2.
[5] xiv. 11. The reading hitherto has been, 'et transierunt ejus decimam et dimidium decimæ partis.' Mr. Bensly's new MS. A reads, however, 'decem iam,' and Mr. Bensly says that he can detect the erasure of an *i* before the *a* in cod. S (*Missing Fragment*, p. 29). I have, therefore, no hesitation in adopting 'decem jam' as the true reading.
[6] *Jahrh. d. H.* ii. S. 204 Anm.

ever, in supposing that the division of Ezra would thus be brought into coincidence with the ten weeks of Enoch; for in the latter the eighth, ninth, and tenth weeks all belong to the ideal period. It is possible that the Greek text was corrupt, for the Syriac, Arabic, and Armenian all omit this verse; and the Æthiopic translator may have chosen his own way of rendering it perspicuous. The Latin becomes intelligible, if for 'half of the tenth part' we read 'half of the eleventh part.' With this correction Fourth Ezra is brought into complete agreement with the Apocalypse of Baruch, with which it has otherwise so close an affinity; for there the Babylonian captivity falls within the eleventh period.[1] The time said to have already elapsed would then indicate, not, as Hilgenfeld supposes,[2] the date when the work was composed, but, as we should expect, the date assigned by the author to the real Ezra. As we have already seen in noticing Baruch, the twelve divisions represent by no means equal periods.

Several opinions about the length of the first age are collected in the Babylonian Talmud:[3] 'Rab Qatina says, The world [strictly age] will last for 6,000 years, and in 1,000 it will be destroyed, for it has been said, "And the Lord alone shall be exalted in that day." [4] Abbayé says, For 2,000 years it will lie waste, for it has been said,[5] "He will vivify us after two days, on the third day he will raise us up, and we shall live in his sight."' The opinion of Rab Qatina is then supported as follows: 'As in the period of seven years there is one year of remission,[6] so likewise in the age there will be a remission of a thousand years in seven thousand years, for it has been said, "And the Lord alone shall be exalted in that day," and it

[1] Ch. lxvii. [2] *Mess. Jud.* pp. 103-4. [3] *Synhed.* 97a.
[4] Isa. ii. 11. [5] Hosea vi. 2. [6] See Levit. xxv. 1-7.

has been said,[1] " A psalm of singing for the sabbath-day," a day which shall be altogether sabbath, and it is said,[2] "A thousand years in thy sight are but as yesterday when it is past."[3] It was taught in the house of Eliyahu :[4]— Out of the six thousand years of the world two thousand years have passed in emptiness, two thousand years are [the time of] the Law, and two thousand years are the days of the Messiah[5] . . . Eliyahu said to Rab Yehudah, brother of Rab Salla, the pious one, The age will not last less than eighty-five jubilees, [*i.e.* 4,165 years], and in the last jubilee the Son of David will come.' . . . Rab Chanan bar Tachalipha sent [word] to Rab Yoseph that he had met a certain man having in his hand a volume written in the excellent[6] character and in the holy language, which was said to have been found among the treasures of Persia; and in this book it was written that after 4,291 years from the Creation, the world should cease; some of the intervening years should be spent in the wars of the dragons, and some in the wars of Gog and Magog, and the rest should be the days of the Messiah; and God would not renew the world except after seven thousand years. It is added, however, that ' Rab Acha bar Raba says, After five thousand years.' These extracts show that there was no settled opinion upon this point, even in the schools of the learned, and Rab went so far as to say, ' All the [prescribed] limits [of time] have ceased, and the thing depends only on penitence and good works.'

---

[1] Ps. xcii. 1.   [2] Ps. xc. 4.

[3] See this argument fully given in the Epistle of Barnabas, xv., and in later Christian writers cited by Gfrörer, *J. d. II.* ii. S. 207 *sq.*

[4] The meaning of this expression is disputed.

[5] This last statement is also made in '*Abodah Zarah*, 9a.

[6] Often translated ' Assyrian,' but probably a word referring to the beauty of the character.

CHAPTER V.

SIGNS OF THE LAST TIMES.

From the survey in the preceding chapter it appears that the first age of the world was divided according to the fancy and the skill of each writer; and though the ground is here prepared on which the more precise, but equally fallacious, calculations found in the Christian Fathers were based, we have discovered no generally acknowledged system on which popular hope could be made to rest as on a secure foundation. It was the more natural, therefore, that the imagination should stray in quest of signs, whether mundane or supernatural, by which the approach of the last times might be recognised.

These signs in the Book of Daniel are not spoken of as such, and being derived from the circumstances of the writer's time can only be regarded as a basis for some of the later speculations. His historical sketch, leading up to the triumph of the people of God, can hardly come under this head, though there are features in it, such as the desecration of the Temple, which were easily translated into Messianic signs.[1] In xii. 1 there is a more general statement, which was adopted as a characteristic of the approaching end:—'There shall be a time of trouble, such as never was since there was a nation even to that same time.'[2] In verse 7 the assurance is added,—

---

[1] See Matt. xxiv. 15.
[2] This also is adopted in Matt. xxiv. 21.

'When he shall have accomplished to scatter the power of the holy people, all these things shall be finished.' Through this process of suffering 'many shall be purified, and made white, and tried; but the wicked shall do wickedly: and none of the wicked shall understand; but the wise shall understand.'[1]

The Sibyl, as becomes her poetic style, deals with more marvellous tokens:—'I will tell thee a very clear sign, so that thou mayest perceive when the end of all things is to come upon the earth. When swords are seen at night in the starry heaven towards the west, and towards the east, and dust is in a moment borne down from heaven to all the earth, and the light of the sun shall be eclipsed from heaven in the midst [of its course], and the beams of the moon shall appear and come again to the earth, and a sign shall arise from the rocks with blood and drops, and ye shall see in a cloud a battle of foot-soldiers and horse-soldiers, as a hunt of wild beasts, resembling mists; this end of war God who dwells in heaven will accomplish.'[2] This book of the Oracles throughout regards the sins of various nations as productive of the calamities which are to be succeeded by the last great crisis in mundane affairs. A sufficient idea of its tone may be given by quoting the passage just before the description of this crisis:—'But do thou [O mortal] guard against the wrath of the great God, when the fulfilment of pestilence shall come upon all mortals, and being subdued they shall fall into fearful punishment, and king shall capture king, and take away his territory, and nations shall desolate nations, and tyrants [desolate] tribes, and leaders shall all flee into another land, and the land of mortals shall be changed, and a barbarous empire shall lay waste all Greece, and drain the fat land

[1] xii. 10.   [2] iii. 795 *sq.*

of its wealth, and they shall come into their strife in the land of others for the sake of gold and silver,—covetousness shall be fostering evils for cities. But all shall be unburied, and vultures and wild beasts of the earth shall mar their flesh; and when these things are accomplished, the huge earth will consume the remains of the dead. But it itself shall be all unsown and unploughed, proclaiming in its wretchedness the abomination of innumerable men, many lengths of times in revolving years, light bucklers and great shields, javelins, arms of every kind; nor from the oak thicket will wood be cut for the shining of fire.[1] And then from the sun will God send a king.'[2] The Sibyl's descriptions are in part borrowed from the circumstances of the time; but, as we shall see, signs which were first delineated in conformity with historical suggestion came to be regarded as characteristic of the latter days, at whatever unknown period these might at last present themselves.

The Book of Enoch describes still more fully the state of things preceding the judgment which is to divide the two ages. Great changes are to take place in the course of nature:—'In the days of the sinners the years will be shortened, and their seed will become late in their lands and on their pastures, and all things on earth will change, and not appear at their [proper] time. The rain will be held back, and the heaven will stop it. And in those times the fruits of the earth will be late and not grow at their [proper] time, and the fruits of the trees will be stopped in their time. And the moon will change her order, and not appear at her time. And in those days one will see in the heaven how a great unfruitfulness comes, on the outermost of the carriages in the west; and

---

[1] Meaning that the arms of the dead would serve for firewood.
[2] 632-652.

it will shine more brightly than agrees with the [usual] regulation of light. And many heads of the stars appointed to preside will wander, and these will pervert their ways and occupations, and those subject to them will not appear in their times. And the whole regulation of the stars will be closed against sinners, and the thoughts of those who dwell upon earth will wander on their account, and will be alienated from all their ways, and transgress, and hold them for gods. And many evils shall come upon them, and a penal judgment shall come upon them in order to destroy them all.'[1] As, in this book, the flood is regarded as the first grand example of the judgment of the world, the wickedness by which it was preceded is expected to recur before the second and final judgment takes place:—'Again will the unrighteousness repeat itself, and all the deeds of unrighteousness, and the deeds of violence and of crime will be fulfilled for the second time upon the earth, and . . . then will a great penal judgment from heaven come upon them all.'[2] 'And in those days will the peoples be moved, and the races of the people will lift themselves up in the day of destruction. And in those days will the fruit of the womb miscarry, and they will mangle their own children; they will drive their children from them, and miscarriages will take place; and they will drive sucklings from them, and will not return to them and have compassion on their beloved. Again, I swear to you sinners that sin is ready for a day of ceaseless bloodshed. And they will adore stones, and others will form images of gold and silver and wood and clay, and others will adore unclean spirits and demons, and all kinds of idols, even in the idol-temples, while one nevertheless

---

[1] lxxx. 2-8. Compare Matt. xxiv. 29; Luke xxi. 25, 26.
[2] xci. 6, 7.

can find no sort of help in them. And they will sink into ignorance on account of the foolishness of their heart, and their eyes will be blinded through the fear of their heart, and through their visions in dreams. Through them will they fall into ignorance and fear, because they do all their works in falsehood, and adore stone; and they shall perish at once.'[1]

The picture exhibited by the post-Christian books is very similar in its character. In the Book of Jubilees[2] we are told that from the time of Abraham till the day of the great judgment human life should be shortened, and made subject to increasing infirmity and suffering, till these evils should come in their most aggravated form 'upon the wicked generation which fills the earth with guilt through the impurity of fornication and defilement and the abomination of its deeds.' 'And in that generation the children will quarrel with their fathers and gray-haired men on account of sin and unrighteousness and the speech of their mouth, and on account of the great wickedness which they do, and because they forsook the covenant which the Lord had made between them and Himself that they should observe and keep all his commandments and ordinances, and his whole law, without swerving to the left or to the right.' 'See, the earth will go down on account of all their works, and there will no more be any seed of wine and oil, because their works are mere ungodliness; and they shall all go down together, the wild beasts, and the cattle, and the birds, and all the fishes of the sea, on account of the children of men; and they will contend with one another, these with those, the young with the oldest, and the oldest with the young, the poor with the

---

[1] xcix. 4-9. Compare generally the exhortations and denunciations in xciv. sq.
[2] Ch. xxiii.

rich, and the mean with the great, and the beggar with princes, namely, about the law and the covenant, for they have clean forgotten his commandments and the covenant, and the festivals, and the new moons, and sabbaths, and jubilees, and everything. And they will arise with swords and bows to bring them back to the way, but they will not be converted till much blood has been shed upon the earth. One will be against another, and those who remain over will not be converted to the way of righteousness from wickedness. For they will all arise to seek after wealth by robbery, and to take what belongs to another, and to make themselves a great name, but not so in reality and truth; and they will pollute that which is most holy with the impure corruption of their defilement. And a great penal judgment shall come from the Lord on account of the deeds of that generation.'

In Fourth Ezra and the Apocalypse of Baruch also the prevailing token of the approaching crisis is found in the calamities and wickedness of the time. The representations of the latter are couched in a higher strain than those of the former; and as they are not so easily accessible, I will quote them at length. 'This, then, shall be the sign: when amazement shall seize the inhabitants of the earth, and they shall fall into many tribulations, and again shall fall into great torments. And it shall come to pass, when they shall say in their thoughts by reason of their great tribulation, "the Mighty one remembers the earth no more,"—and it shall come to pass, when they shall despair,—then will the time awake. And I answered and said, Will that tribulation which is to take place remain for a long time, or will that necessity comprise many years?' And he answered and said to me, That time is divided into twelve parts, and each of these is reserved for that which has been appointed for it. In the first part will be the beginning of disturbances; and in the second part, the slaughter of nobles; and in the third part, the falling of many into death; and in the fourth part, the issuing of desolation; and in the fifth part, famine and the stoppage of rain; and in the sixth part, earthquakes and alarms; and in the eighth part [the seventh is wanting in the MS.], a multitude of apparitions and meeting of the Sciade;[1] and in the ninth part, the falling of fire; and in the tenth part, much rapine and oppression; and in the eleventh part, iniquity and incontinence; and in the twelfth part, a confused simultaneous mixture of all the things that have been already mentioned. But these parts of that time are reserved, and will be mixed one with another, and will minister to one another.'[2] 'That time of tribulation will arise. For it will come and pass by in vehement rush, and coming in the fury of indignation will be full of disturbance. And it shall come to pass in those days that all the inhabitants of the earth shall rest one upon another, because they shall not know that my judgment has drawn near. For not many wise shall be found in that time, and men of understanding shall be only a few individuals; but also those who shall know will be very silent. And there will be many rumours, and not a few messengers, and works of apparitions will be shown, and not a few promises will be uttered, of which some shall be vain, and others shall be confirmed. And honour will be turned into ignominy, and strength will be humbled into contempt, and firmness will be dissolved, and beauty

---

[1] On this and some other names in ch. x. Ceriani has the following note:—'Nomina servavi, quia in his vix, ac ne vix quidem quae exacte referant, reperire licet' (*Mon. Sac. et Prof.* I. ii, p. ii, n. 10).
[2] xxv.-xxvii.

become a thing to be despised. And many will say to many in that time, Where has the abundance of intelligence concealed itself, and whither has the abundance of wisdom removed? And while they reflect upon these things, jealousy will arise against those about whom they were not thinking, and suffering will seize him who was at rest, and many will be moved in anger to injure many, and will stir up armies to shed blood, and in the end shall perish with them. And it shall come to pass at that time that the change of times shall appear manifestly to every man, because in all those times [in the past time] they were contaminated, and exercised oppression, and walked everyone in his own works, and did not recollect the law of the Mighty one. Therefore, fire shall devour their thoughts, and in flame shall the cares of their hearts be examined; for the judge will come, and not be slow, because everyone of the inhabitants of the earth knew when he was acting unrighteously, and it was on account of their own pride that they did not know my law.'[1] 'Lo! the days shall come, and it shall be when the time of the age shall have become ripe, and the harvest of its bad and good seeds shall have come, the Mighty one will bring upon the earth and its inhabitants, and upon its governors, disturbance of spirits and amazement of heart, and they shall hate one another, and challenge one another to battle, and the mean shall lord it over the honourable, and the petty shall be exalted over the glorious, and the many shall be delivered to the few, and those who were nothing shall lord it over the powerful, and the poor shall abound above the rich, and the impious shall be exalted above heroes, and the wise shall be silent and fools shall speak, nor shall the thought of men nor the counsel of the Mighty one be confirmed at that

[1] xlviii.

time, nor shall the hope of hopers be confirmed. But it shall come to pass that, when the things which have been predicted shall have taken place, confusion shall fall upon all men, and some of them shall fall in battle, and some of them shall perish in distress, and some of them shall be hindered by those who are theirs. But the Most High will make manifest to those peoples whom he prepared before, and they will come and wage battle with the leaders who shall then be left. And it shall come to pass, whosoever shall have escaped from war shall die in an earthquake, and he who shall have escaped from the earthquake shall be burned in fire, and he who shall have escaped from the fire shall perish in famine. And it shall come to pass, whosoever shall have escaped and fled from all those things that have been foretold, of those who have conquered and have been conquered, shall be delivered into the hands of my servant Messiah. For every land shall devour its inhabitants; but the holy land shall have pity on its own, and shall protect its inhabitants in that time.'[1]

In Fourth Ezra we are told that 'in proportion as the world shall become weak from old age, evils will be multiplied upon its inhabitants.'[2] Truth and faith shall fail, and unrighteousness increase; understanding shall be withdrawn into its storehouses; hope shall be baffled; the very stature of men shall be diminished; friends will fight against friends as enemies, and there shall be 'disturbance of peoples, plottings of nations, inconstancy of generals, disturbance of princes.'[3] One shall reign whom the inhabitants of the earth expect not. Various prodigies, intended to produce an impression of horror, are also mentioned among the signs of the end. The sun

---

[1] lxx. lxxi.   [2] xiv. 16.
[3] The quoted words are in ix. 3.

shall shine at night, and the moon by day. Blood shall drop from wood, and stone give forth its voice. Birds shall migrate, and wild beasts remove from one place to another. Salt water shall be found in sweet. Infants a year old shall speak. Women shall bring forth monsters; and untimely infants, of three or four months, shall live. Sown places shall suddenly appear unsown, and full storehouses shall suddenly be found empty. The Dead Sea shall cast out fish, and utter a voice at night, which all shall hear. As supernatural portents of a higher order, the books shall be opened before the face of the firmament, and all shall see them together; and the trumpet shall sound, and all hearing it shall suddenly tremble.[1]

The same idea of degeneracy and calamity as characteristic of the times immediately before the Messiah finds no doubtful expression in the Talmud. In the Mishnah [2] the gradual national decline, as celebrated Rabbis passed away, is mournfully depicted; and then occur these words: 'In the footprints of the Messiah [3] impudence will increase, and there will be dearness [scarcity]. The vine will produce its fruit, but wine will be dear. And the kingdom [*i.e.* the government, the dominant worldly power] will turn itself to heresy, and there will be no reproof. And the house of assembly will be for fornication. Galilee [the boundary, 'haggalil'] will be de-

---

[1] See v. 1-13, 54, 55; vi. 7-28; viii. 63-ix. 6; xiv. 15-17.

[2] *Sotah*, ix. 15.

[3] That is, a little before the arrival of the Messiah, as Surenhusius renders it, explaining the expression of the time 'quo pedes quasi ad iter ingrediendum jam promovet.' This interpretation is confirmed by the parallel passage in Synhedrin. (*Mischna sive totius Hebræorum juris, rituum, antiquitatum, ac legum oralium systema, cum clarissimorum Rabbinorum Maimonidis et Bartenoræ commentariis integris. Quibus accedunt variorum auctorum notæ ac versiones in eos quos ediderunt codices. Latinitate donavit ac notis illustravit Guilielmus Surenhusius.* Amstelædami 1698-1703, vol. iii. p. 319, note 29.)

stroyed, and Gablan [the 'beautiful province'] laid waste, and men of Gebûl [the 'limit']¹ will go from city to city, and find no favour. And the wisdom of scribes will stink, and those who fear sin will be despised, and truth will fail. Boys will whiten [*i.e.* make pale, confuse] the faces of old men. Old men will rise up before the young. The son will treat the father shamefully, and the daughter will rise up against her mother, and the daughter-in-law against her mother-in-law, and a man's foes will be those of his own household.² The face of that generation will be as the face of a dog; the son will have no shame before his father. Upon whom, then, are we to trust? Upon our Father who is in heaven.' Part of this passage is repeated in the Babylonian Gemarah.³ The account is there referred to the authority of Rabbis Yehudah, Neborai, and Nechemyah. Other opinions are quoted in the same place: 'Rabbi Yochanan says, In the generation in which the Son of David shall come, the disciples of the wise shall diminish, and of the rest the eyes shall be consumed by trouble and groaning, and afflictions shall be multiplied, and vexatious decrees shall be renewed. Whilst the first is being ordered the second will hasten to come. The Rabbis have taught: In the cycle of seven years in which the Son of David shall come, in the first year this text shall be confirmed, " I shall cause rain to come upon one city, and upon another city I shall not cause the rain to come;"⁴ in the second the arrows of famine shall be sent; in the third there shall be a great famine, and men and women and children, pious people and men of deed [according to some, miracle-workers] shall die, and

---

[1] Notice the play upon the words.
[2] Quoted from Micah vii. 6; applied by Christ to the results of his own teaching, Matt. x. 35.
[3] *Synhed.* 97*a*. [4] Amos iv. 7.

the Law shall be forgotten by those who have studied it; in the fourth shall be satiety, but it shall not be satiety; in the fifth shall be great satiety, and they shall eat and drink and rejoice, and the Law shall return to those who had learned; in the sixth, uproar; in the seventh, wars; in the end of the seventh the Son of David will come. Rab Yoseph says, There have been many septennial cycles of this kind, and he has not come.' The answer is given by his disciple Abbayé that the sixth and seventh signs have not happened, and that events have not occurred in the specified order. Some, however, seem to have objected to this theory of premonition. Rabbi Zera says, 'Three things come unexpectedly; these are the Messiah, a finding (treasure-trove &c.), and a scorpion.'[1] Again (as we have already seen) 'Rab says, All the limits have ceased, and the thing depends only on penitence and good works.'[2] 'Rabbi Eli'ezer says, If Israel repent, they shall be redeemed; if they do not repent, they shall not be redeemed. To him said Rabbi Yehoshua', If they do not repent, they shall not be redeemed, but God raises against them a king whose decrees shall be hard as Haman's, and the Israelites repent, and become good. . . . Yet it has been said, "ye have been sold for nought," for idolatry, and "ye shall be redeemed without money," but not with penitence and good works.'[3] Several passages are cited in support of these opposite opinions.[4] A little farther on various views of different Rabbis are quoted, which may be presented together, without naming the authorities: 'The Son of David will not come until a fish shall be sought for a sick person, and shall not be found; for it is said,[5] "I will sink their waters deeply, and I will bring their rivers as oil." . . . The Son of David will

---

[1] *Synhed.* 97a. Compare 1 Thess. v. 1, 2; Matt. xxiv. 36 sq.
[2] *Synhed.* 97b.
[3] See Isa. lii. 3.
[4] *Synhed.* 97b sq.
[5] Ezek. xxxii. 14.

not come until the despicable government [the last remnant of the semblance of government] be destroyed from Israel. . . . The Son of David will not come until the proud be destroyed out of Israel. . . . The Son of David will not come until all judges and ministers perish from Israel. . . . Jerusalem shall not be redeemed except by righteousness. . . . If thou shalt see a generation which continually diminishes, expect him.[1] . . . If thou shalt see a generation on which many afflictions come like a stream, expect him. . . . The Son of David will not come except in a generation in which either all are righteous or all are sinners.'[2]

We have only to add that the calamities which are to indicate the coming of the Messiah are sometimes spoken of as חֶבְלֵי הַפָּשִׁיחַ, or, as the phrase stands in the Talmud, חבלו שלכישח, the birth-pains of the Messiah.[3]

[1] Founded on 2 Sam. xxii. 28.
[2] Founded on Isai. lx. 21 and lix. 16. *Synhed.* 98a.
[3] Shabbath 118a, and other references in Bertholdt, *Christologia Judæorum Jesu Apostolorumque ætate*, &c. Erlangæ, 1811, p. 48. Bertholdt very appropriately refers to Matt. xxiv. 8, πάντα δὲ ταῦτα ἀρχὴ ὠδίνων. For wars and other calamities compare Matt. xxiv. 6, 7.

CHAPTER VI.

FORERUNNERS OF THE MESSIAH.

HAVING described the signs which were to indicate the coming of the Messiah, we must now notice that great event which was immediately to precede his appearance. In Matthew xvii. 10, 11 we are told that his disciples asked Jesus, 'Why then say the scribes that Elias must first come?' and that he answered, 'Elias truly shall first come and restore all things.' The expectation which is here referred to was founded on the prophecy of Malachi,[1] and may very probably have existed in pre-Christian times. If I am not mistaken, however, the first allusion to it as an element in Jewish thought, outside the New Testament, is found in Justin Martyr's dialogue with Tryphon. The Jew there urges as an objection against the Christian belief that 'Christ, if he has even come into being, and exists anywhere, is unknown, and does not yet even know himself, nor has he any power until Elias shall come and anoint him, and make him manifest to all.'[2] This function of anointing the Messiah is, I believe, nowhere else assigned to Elijah. It corresponds, however, with his commission to anoint Hazael, Jehu, and Elisha, referred to in the Old Testament,[3] and suits the character of high-priest which is ascribed to him by the Targums.[4]

---

[1] iv. 5, (iii. 23 in the Hebrew).
[2] Ch. 8: φανερὸν πᾶσι ποιήσῃ may be compared with John i. 31, ἀλλ' ἵνα φανερωθῇ τῷ Ἰσραὴλ διὰ τοῦτο ἦλθον ἐγὼ κ. τ. λ. See also Justin, *Dial.* 49.
[3] 1 Kings xix. 15, 16. [4] Lam. iv. 22; Pseudo-Jon., Exod. vi. 18; Deut. xxx. 4.

Several references to the great forerunner are found in the Rabbinical writings. A vague allusion to his office is made in Seder 'Olam Rabbah: 'In the second year of the reign of Ahaziah Elijah became hidden and seen no more until King Messiah shall come, when he will be again seen, and hidden a second time, and not seen again until Gog and Magog come. And now he writes down the work of all the generations.'[1] According to this it would seem that he would come to proclaim the Messiah, and then withdraw until his aid was required against the last enemies of Israel.

In the Mishnah[2] his functions are thus described:— 'Rabbi Yehoshua' said, I have received from Rabban Yochanan ben Zakkai, who heard from his teacher, and his teacher from his teacher, an halakhah of Moses from Sinai, that Elijah will not come to declare anything unclean or clean, to remove to a distance or to bring nearer, except to remove those who were brought near by force, and to bring near those who were removed by force. . . . Rabbi Yehudah says, To bring near, but not to remove to a distance. Rabbi Shime'on says, To settle controversies. And the wise men say, Not to remove, and not to bring near, but to make peace in the world [or age], as it is said, "Behold I send you Elijah the prophet &c., and he shall bring back the heart of fathers to the sons, and the heart of sons to their fathers."' Bartenora ['Obadyah of Bertinoro] says, in explanation of this rather obscure passage, that to 'remove and bring near' refers to the purification of families from those who were defiled by incestuous descent, and the decision whether a family is mixed in this way or not.[3] Different views are expressed

---

[1] Ch. xvii. Referred to by Gfrörer *J. d. II.* ii. S. 228.
[2] *'Eduyyoth*, viii. 7.
[3] See the Latin translation of his commentary in Surenhusius, iv. p. 362.

upon this subject; but, according to the most merciful, Elijah will restore those who have been violently dispossessed of their privileges, but will not disturb those whose position in the commonwealth of Israel has been violently obtained, and he will act as a general peace-maker. As the prophet was thus to settle all controversies, it became a saying that in cases of dispute, when an agreement could not be arrived at, the final determination must be left 'until Elijah comes.'

At the end of the passage already quoted from the Mishnah,[1] describing the troubles before the Messianic time, we find at present the words, 'Rabbi Pinchas ben Yair says, . . . the Holy Spirit brings to the revivification of the dead, and the revivification of the dead comes by the hands of Elijah.' This clause may perhaps be of later date. Surenhusius says that it is found only in the copies of the Mishnah which have not the Gemarah, and thinks it probable that it did not belong to this place, but was borrowed from 'Abodah Zarah 20b, where a similar statement occurs, and that it was copied into the codices of the separate Mishnah in order that the treatise might not break off in the midst of ill-omened words.[2]

In the New Testament we have plain intimations that other forerunners of the Messiah were expected as well as Elijah. According to John i. 21, 22, John the Baptist was asked, not only 'Art thou Elias?' but 'Art thou the prophet?' Some light is thrown upon this reference to 'the prophet' by Matthew xvi. 13, 14, where the disciples tell Jesus that some people thought he was John the Baptist, and some that he was Elias, and others that he was Jeremiah or one of the prophets. In the accounts of the transfiguration also Moses appears along with Elijah. We have no statement of purely

---

[1] *Sotah*, ix. 15. [2] iii. p. 321, n. 30.

Jewish origin that Jeremiah was to appear before the Messiah; but in 2nd Maccabees this prophet is twice mentioned in a way which connects him with the later destinies of his people. In ii. 4–8 we are told how Jeremiah commanded the tabernacle and the ark to accompany him to the mountain where Moses climbed up and saw the heritage of God, and how he hid these and the altar of incense in a cave which was to remain unknown until God gathered his people together, and became gracious to them; and then the Lord would show these things. Again, in xv. 12 *sq.* it is related that Judas Maccabæus had a dream, in which he saw, besides Onias the high priest, 'a man with gray hairs, and exceeding glorious, who was of a wonderful and excellent majesty. And Onias answered and said, This lover of the brethren is he who offers many prayers for the people and the holy city, Jeremiah the prophet of God.' Jeremiah then gave Judas a golden sword, and told him to accept it as a gift from God wherewith to wound the adversaries. The transition would not be difficult from these conceptions to a belief in the reappearance of Jeremiah in the last days. There may possibly be some allusion to an expected company of prophets in Fourth Ezra vii. 28, where it is said that the Messiah 'shall be revealed along with those who are with him.' In Debarim Rabbah [1] it is said that Moses should appear in the future world along with Elijah. The scantiness of this evidence shows that the return of any of the ancient prophets besides Elijah can have occupied no very prominent place in the Messianic hope of the Jews.

---

[1] (Midrash on Deut., before 900 A.D.) 'Eqeb, towards end. Referred to by Gfrörer, *J. d. H.* ii. S. 230.

CHAPTER VII.

CONCEPTION OF THE IDEAL KINGDOM WITHOUT A MESSIAH.

It is now time to inquire into the character of the Messianic kingdom itself. At our very entrance upon this subject a preliminary question meets us which demands our careful consideration. While our authorities concur in the recognition of a future ideal kingdom, it is, to say the least, extremely doubtful whether they all recognise a Messiah as standing at its head. It will be best to consider first the cases in which this uncertainty exists, and then, whichever way our decision may turn, we may appeal to our authorities in the chronological order whenever they throw light on the particular subject of which we may be treating.

The Book of Daniel is the first which asks for an impartial investigation; but how to secure impartiality in the present instance it is not so easy to determine. It is not fair to charge a critic with partiality because he believes, as he thinks upon sufficient grounds, that the book contains a prediction of several historical events which took place centuries after its composition, and that we are bound to accept all interpretations which are found in the New Testament. But it is evident that such a judgment may very seriously affect the meaning which we attach to the text, and so far as we are swayed by it, we may be led quite unconsciously to repudiate a sense which we should otherwise derive from the words before us. It therefore seems more truly impartial to take the book simply as we find it, and endeavour to learn by a literary procedure what it was that the author meant to communicate to his readers. If the result prove to be inconsistent with the above assumptions, then it is, so far as it goes, an evidence against their truth; while if it prove to be favourable to them, it will be a stronger support than an interpretation which has been avowedly made in subjection to their restraints. Hengstenberg, however, wishes to throw the blame of partiality upon those who question the traditional interpretation. He says,—'So far as the rationalistic commentators were concerned, besides their general inclination to limit the number of Messianic prophecies as far as possible, there were special reasons why they should reject a Messianic explanation in the present case, if they could find any possible excuse for doing so. They assign its composition to as late a date as the period of the Maccabees. But according to the current theory, which I have shown to be erroneous in my work ' für Beibehaltung der Apocryphen,' there is not a single trace of the expectation of a personal Messiah to be found in the apocryphal books. This belief is said to have been altogether extinct in the days of the writers of the Apocrypha. If therefore there is any Messianic prophecy in the Book of Daniel, according to this theory it must be altogether erroneous to assign it to a Maccabean origin.'[1] Now Hitzig undoubtedly uses the assumed date of the book as conclusive against the Messianic interpretation,[2] and so far as this consideration affected his judgment in inter-

---

[1] *Christology of the Old Testament: translated by James Martin:* Clark, Edinburgh, 1858, vol. iii. p. 87. My references will be to this edition and volume.
[2] S. 116.

preting the text, he was, though on the opposite side, under the influence of precisely the same kind of partiality as more orthodox critics. This, however, is no reason for refusing to adopt the purely literary method, and to interrogate the book without reference to external conditions. We shall not be exposed to the bias which Hengstenberg points out, if we consider Hitzig's argument unsound; and for my own part I cannot see why, even if the Messianic belief had died out as completely as he supposes, the writer of Daniel might not have endeavoured to revive it in the minds of his countrymen.

The first passage for which a Messianic meaning is claimed is at the end of Daniel's vision of the four beasts, and runs thus: 'I saw in the night visions, and, behold, [one] like a son of man [not '*the* son of man,' as in the Authorised Version] came with the clouds of heaven, and came to the Ancient of days, and they brought him near before him. And there was given him dominion, and glory, and a kingdom, that all people, nations, and languages, should serve him: his dominion is an everlasting dominion, which shall not pass away, and his kingdom that which shall not be destroyed.'[1] Now when we refer to the context to enable us to interpret this passage, we may guide our judgment both by the parallelism of the vision itself and by the explanation of it which is given in the succeeding portion of the chapter. In the vision four beasts are seen, which represent the brutal might of four successive heathen kingdoms; and as these beasts are altogether symbolical, we naturally expect the higher power which is to take their place to be also symbolically represented. What more suitable to succeed the savage beasts than the human form, drawing its life from heaven, and receiving its dominion from the Ancient

[1] vii. 13, 14.

of days? The vision itself, therefore, suggests that the 'son of man' stands for the ideal Israel, for whom the empire of the world was destined in the counsels of God. But no, says Hengstenberg,[1] 'on the contrary the analogy favours the Messianic interpretation. The four beasts do not represent kingdoms without heads, but " four kings." '[2] 'Hence, according to the analogy, we are not to look in this instance for a kingdom (ver. 27) without a king, a sovereign people.'[3] This remark of Hengstenberg's really strengthens the case against himself. How is it that Daniel is content to speak of the four heathen monarchies as ' four kings,' although the individual kings were of no importance, while in the case of the people over whom he is supposed to place a superhuman head, the pre-existent Messiah, he changes his mode of description, and says not a word about a king? This surely suggests to us the notion, not altogether foreign to Old Testament thought, of a pure theocracy, in which the Ancient of days would himself come and dwell as sole king upon his holy mountain; and we have in this suggestion a sufficient answer to Oehler's not very astute remark that in any case 'the kingdom is not to be thought of without its king.'[4]

In these observations we have partly anticipated our notice of the interpretation of the dream. In this the beasts are expressly referred to, but unfortunately the 'son of man' is not again mentioned. There are, however, three different verses in which the concluding part of the vision is explained,[5] and in all of these the dominion

---

[1] Hengstenberg's treatment is so copious and elaborate that in the following discussion I have taken him as the representative of the traditional interpretations, and have guided my arguments by reference to his. Some other views will, however, be noticed as we proceed.
[2] vii. 17.   [3] P. 89.
[4] Herzog, *Messias*, S. 416.   [5] Verses 18, 22, 27.

is assigned to 'the saints of the Most High,' without the faintest allusion to a Messiah; and accordingly, if we are to allow the author to be his own interpreter, we must believe that the 'son of man' and 'the saints of the Most High' are identical. The only answer which Hilgenfeld makes to this argument is, 'but surely the Messiah is precisely the head of this people,'[1] a remark which merely takes for granted the thing to be proved. Hengstenberg says, 'The error committed in the statement of this argument is, that the passage under review is severed from the entire course of prophecy, and no attention is paid to the relation in which Daniel himself declares that he stood to the prophets who preceded him; compare ix. 6 . . . and 10. It was a fundamental idea of prophecy that the future salvation was to be bestowed upon the people of the saints of the Most High, through the medium of the Messiah; that it did not belong to the people as a body, but to the people as united under Christ their head. . . . If Daniel could assume that this was already known, he had no reason to fear that he would be misunderstood, when he afterwards attributed to the people of the saints of the Most High, what he had previously written of the Messiah. No true Israelite would have misunderstood him, even if he had not expressly mentioned the Messiah before, and thus guarded against any misapprehension.'[2] In this reply Hengstenberg scarcely meets the point of the adverse argument. The question is not whether Daniel could have attributed to the saints of the Most High what he had previously written of the Messiah, but whether he had previously written anything of the Messiah; and the argument is that the total failure to notice the Messiah throughout a long interpretation of the dream, although there is a reiterated recurrence to

[1] Jüd. Apok. S. 46.   [2] Pp. 88-9.

its supposed Messianic portion, is an evidence in favour of the non-Messianic explanation. Hengstenberg has given no reason for this failure, which is the more extraordinary if we say, with Hilgenfeld,[1] that 'it was the principal aim of the author to bring this [the Messianic kingdom] livingly before the soul of his compatriots.

Our surprise is not diminished when we look more closely at the vision and its interpretation. If the 'son of man' be the Messiah, he is here presented in a way which, so far as we know, is wholly new. The imagery of the ancient prophets, towards whom Daniel is said to have so carefully maintained his relations, is discarded, and instead of one sprung from the stem of Jesse, heir to the throne of David, we have a mysterious being, coming in cloudy grandeur to rule over the whole world, while the people of Israel are passed by without the most cursory notice. Now if anything required explanation, surely this did, especially as Hengstenberg was not at hand to point out that the second coming of the Messiah was intended, a fact which is studiously concealed in the vision itself. The presumption which is thus created that this mysterious allusion could not be left without elucidation is strengthened when we find that the fourth beast, with his ten horns and his little horn, receives such ample notice. How is it that the impiety of the little horn, the type of Antichrist, is portrayed with such individual features, while on the opposite side the great mediator vanishes utterly from view, and the Ancient of days and the chosen people completely fill the scene? This silence in regard to the Messiah Hengstenberg does not so much as pretend to explain.

It may be said, however, that Daniel's connection

[1] *Jüd. Apok.* S. 46.

with the prophets renders it improbable that he can have been without the Messianic belief. In this consideration there is some weight. But we have already seen that the prophets are by no means unanimous in what Hengstenberg is pleased to lay down as 'a fundamental idea of prophecy;' and as the writer has certainly not followed the old prophetic type, there is no difficulty in believing that he may have reverted to the still older idea of a pure theocracy, in which, though human leaders might be necessary, none should be distinguished with special Messianic dignity. Whether he did so or not must be judged simply from his own statements. The passage to which appeal is made with the greatest confidence yields to those who do not thrust into it a meaning derived from other sources a picture of world-wide dominion exercised by the saints under the immediate government of the Almighty himself; and this interpretation is confirmed by the two parallel passages in which the kingdom is referred to. In ii. 44 we are told that 'in the days of these kings shall the God of heaven set up a kingdom which shall never be destroyed: and the kingdom shall not be left to other people, but it shall break in pieces and consume all these kingdoms, and it shall stand for ever.' There is nothing in this inconsistent with the Messianic conception; but had the Messiah been a prominent figure in the writer's thoughts, he would probably have been alluded to on so suitable an occasion. It is of more consequence, however, that in the other passage we find a mediator actually named, and that this is not the Messiah, but the archangel Michael. Having stated that the king of the north [Antiochus Epiphanes] should come to his end, and none should help him, the writer proceeds, 'And at that time shall Michael stand up, the great prince which standeth for the children of thy people;'[1] and it is evident from the whole scope of the passage, and particularly from the reference to the resurrection, that here also 'the time of the end' is described. It is surely incredible that if the writer believed in a supernatural Messiah, he could be content to accord to him only an obscure description, occupying a couple of verses, and then at the close of his book not only omit to say a word about him, but introduce Michael by name as the heavenly mediator to whom the Israelites were to look for deliverance.

Hengstenberg, however, produces arguments on the opposite side, which appear even to Hilgenfeld pretty much to the point,[2] and it is possible that these may more than counterbalance the evidence already adduced. In the first place he appeals to the 'history of Biblical interpretation.' 'It was supported by the whole of the early Christian Church with very few exceptions.'[3] As the early Christian Church had no better means of interpreting the passage than we have ourselves, and as it was the most natural thing possible for them to give it a Messianic interpretation, I do not see that there is any force in this argument. But he adds, 'the Jews were certainly interested in opposing it, as Christ had so expressly declared himself to be the Son of Man. Yet with the exception of Abenezra, they are unanimous in supporting this exposition.'[4] When the Messianic idea was fully developed, and when sound principles of interpretation were systematically disregarded, it is not surprising that the Jews adopted this into the number of Messianic passages. They may have done so before the time of Christ, though in support of this supposition we cannot appeal to the Book of Enoch, the

---

[1] xii. 1.   [2] 'Ziemlich treffend:' *Jüd. Apok.* S. 46, Anm. 2.
[3] Pp. 86-7.   [4] P. 87.

passages in that work relating to the Son of man being probably of later date. But even in this case the question is whether the national point of view may not have been altered after the power of the Romans began to make itself felt, and whether the Book of Daniel may not have been forced by a new interpretation into conformity with the changed circumstances of the people. As this is part of the question at issue, it is irrelevant to appeal to Jewish exegesis which does not go back beyond the Roman period. In regard to the bias of the Jews Hengstenberg is clearly wrong. The Messiah coming in the clouds presented so marked a contrast to the crucified Jesus that the passage in Daniel was used in refutation of the Christian claim; and the recourse to a second coming, however satisfactory to Christians, could appear to a Jew little better than a makeshift. In the dialogue with Tryphon [1] Justin Martyr quotes this passage at length to illustrate the glory of Christ; and what is the Jew's reply? [2] 'These and similar scriptures compel us to expect in glory and greatness him who as a son of man receives the eternal kingdom from the Ancient of days; but this so-called Christ of yours has been dishonoured and inglorious, so that he even fell under the extreme curse that is contained in the law of God, for he was crucified.' I think, therefore, that we need not abandon our own judgment in deference to that of the Talmudists.

In support of the presumption which he thinks is created by the 'history of Biblical interpretation' Hengstenberg adduces four 'positive arguments.'

'1. The ideal personality of the nation would have been more particularly pointed out at the very outset; otherwise everyone would understand the passage as referring to the actual person of the Messiah. The elevation of the

[1] Ch. 31. [2] Ch. 32.

people had hitherto been inseparably connected with the royal house of David; and earlier prophets had invariably pointed to the Son of David as the author of its future glory. If, therefore, Daniel ascribed this future exaltation first to the Son of man, and then to the nation, he could only intend that the former of these should be understood as referring to the Messiah.'[1] This argument conveniently assumes the very point which is under discussion, namely that the Messianic belief was existing in full vigour at the time when the book was written. And we may venture to say on the other hand, that it was only under the suggestion of a pre-existing belief that a Messianic interpretation could possibly have arisen. But in addition to this *petitio principii* the argument is strangely inconsequential:—the people always expected the Messiah to appear in the person of one of the royal house of David; therefore they could not possibly suppose that one like a son of man coming with the clouds of heaven could be other than the Messiah. Where is the identity or resemblance between these two ideas? Even in the Talmud, where the Messianic sense is admitted, the contrast between this and an earlier view is felt to require explanation:—'Rabbi Yehoshua' ben Levi threw two verses against one another: " Behold he will come in the clouds of heaven as the Son of man," and "He is poor, sitting on an ass."—If they [the Israelites] are deserving, [he will come] on the clouds of heaven; if they are not deserving, poor, sitting on an ass.'[2] I think, therefore, that the Messianic interpretation is not the first which would occur to an Israelite who had always expected the Messiah to rise out of the stem of Jesse; and Hengstenberg's argument consequently falls to the ground.

'2. His coming in the clouds of heaven is decisive. The anti-Messianic expositors have not only to explain,

[1] P. 89.   [2] *Synhed.* 98a.

how Israel could be in heaven, . . . but how it could become possessed of omnipotent judicial power. For it is this that is indicated by his coming with the clouds.'[1] We have here two arguments in the form of one. The first, that Israel could not be in heaven, seems to me, I must be excused for saying, 'decisive' of nothing but the inconceivably prosaic character of the man who can resort to it; as though the glowing dreams of a prophet and poet were to be as dry and literal as the dreary lucubrations of a modern theologian. Will, then, Hengstenberg explain how the Lord could 'cast down from heaven unto the earth the beauty of Israel,'[2] if Israel had never been in heaven, and how Babylon could have 'fallen from heaven,'[3] and how Capernaum can have been 'exalted unto heaven'?[4] He must also explain how kings could be beasts, and come up from the sea. But leaving this trifling, let us look at the writer's own thought. First he sees the four winds of heaven striving upon the great sea, and four great beasts coming up from the sea, and exercising successive dominion till the Ancient of days appears, and passes judgment upon them; and then, in contrast to these beasts, born from the wilderness of ocean amid tumult and tempest, and wielding their brute power in a selfish and impious tyranny, another form, bearing the mild and devout lineaments of a man, comes with the pomp and glory of heaven to receive from the Ancient of days an eternal kingdom. The heaven is the proper contrast to the sea, as the human form is to the bestial, and the beauty and significance of the vision would be seriously marred if this feature were removed.

As to the second portion of the argument, it is a pure assumption to say that coming with the clouds denotes

---

[1] Pp. 89-90. See also Pusey, p. 85 *sq.*   [2] Lam. ii. 1.
[3] Isai. xiv. 12.   [4] Matt. xi. 23.

'omnipotent judicial power.' A few pages farther back, indeed, Hengstenberg says that 'in the symbolical language of the Bible the clouds represent judgment,'[1] and again, 'the Messiah appears upon the clouds of heaven; he is, therefore, an almighty judge, even *before* the dominion is given to him.'[2] It is a strange principle of exegesis which ascribes an unalterable meaning to the figurative language of poetry, and it may seem hardly worth while to refer to one or two other ideas represented by clouds. As one might expect in a hot climate, the word is used to symbolise refreshment and coolness; 'The Lord will create upon every dwelling place of mount Zion . . . a cloud and smoke by day,'[3] *i.e.* to serve as a welcome shade. Again, as something transient, though dark and threatening, the cloud becomes a symbol of forgiven sin: 'I have blotted out, as a thick cloud, thy transgressions, and, as a cloud, thy sins.'[4] And in reference to God himself it denotes that He is for a time inaccessible to the petitions of men: 'Thou hast covered thyself with a cloud, that our prayer should not pass through.'[5] That from the magnificence of cloudy scenery it should be used to symbolise the divine majesty, and from the terrors of the thunder-storm be mingled with the concomitants of divine judgment, is only what we should expect; but to say that therefore anyone who seems in a night-vision to come with the clouds must be an omnipotent judge is merely idle assertion. That the language in Daniel is intended to indicate the heavenly exaltation of the 'one like a son of man,' and the solemn inauguration of a divine kingdom upon earth, is evident without going beyond the limits of the passage itself; but we must observe that the Son of man is not represented as coming

[1] P. 83.   [2] P. 84.   [3] Isai. iv. 5.
[4] Isai. xliv. 22.   [5] Lam. iii. 44.

down to earth, as we should expect a judge to do, but as coming to the Ancient of days; and therefore, if we may venture to follow the leading of the words themselves instead of a traditional theology, the idea presented is not that of an almighty being coming in his own right to rule the world, but rather that of one who has been raised up from the earth, and is borne along with the clouds to the throne of the Eternal, in order to receive by divine grant a kingdom which others had claimed by their own lawless force. As Hengstenberg is fond of Jewish interpretation, we may appeal in support of this view to Fourth Ezra, in which the being like a man comes up 'out of the heart of the sea,' and afterwards flies 'with the clouds of heaven;' and his goal is 'the top of mount Zion,' which, we may remember, was believed to be the dwelling-place of God.[1] This view is further confirmed by the fact that the judgment is supposed to have already taken place,[2] and if the writer meant to imply that this judgment was conducted by the Son of man, he has certainly expressed himself with the most studied obscurity. The conception which we have thus reached, though not inconsistent with the Jewish belief in the Messiah, is perfectly suitable to the ideal Israel. Hengstenberg's 'decisive' argument, therefore, can satisfy only those who are already convinced.

Before leaving this argument, however, it may be worth while to hazard a further remark. If the plea could be sustained that coming with the clouds represents judicial power, then we have only to turn to verse 22 to find that 'judgment was given to the saints of the Most High.' Though this may perhaps mean that justice was

---

[1] xiii. 3 (in all the versions but the Latin, in which there is evidently a lacuna), 5, 25, 35.
[2] Verse 10.

done to the saints, something may be said on behalf of the idea that the power of judgment was committed to them. The word here used is דִּינָא; and as the same word is twice used in this very chapter to denote the supreme judgment,[1] we might expect the same sense to be preserved throughout.[2] In this case the saints would be expressly invested by the writer himself with that judicial power the supposed possession of which by the ' son of man ' is regarded as such a conclusive proof that he cannot be identical with them. That the idea was not foreign to Jewish thought, that judgment, in a subordinate sense, might be committed to the Israelites, we learn from the Book of Enoch: 'Afterwards there will be another week, the eighth, that of righteousness, and there shall be given to it a sword, in order that judgment and righteousness may be exercised on those who act violently, and the sinners shall be given over into the hands of the righteous.'[3] The final judgment is not to take place till the tenth week; but at an earlier time the sword of judgment is entrusted to the righteous. Thus, even if we admit Hengstenberg's statement that the ' clouds represent judgment,' his conclusion is invalid.

'3. Israel could not appropriately be compared to a son of man. Such a comparison presupposes that there was a difference as well as a resemblance.'[4] If we are in this way to press the particle of comparison, כ, the argument is directly opposed to the purpose for which it is used. Christ was a *real* son of man, as Hengstenberg of course admits; and therefore, whatever he may have

---

[1] Verses 10 and 26.
[2] So Mr. Fuller understands it, explaining it by the rule, 'quod facit per alterum, facit per se.' *Speaker's Com.* vi. p. 330.
[3] xci. 12. See also xcv. 3, 'that you [the righteous] may exercise judgment on them [the sinners] as you will.'
[4] P. 90.

been besides, we cannot say that he *resembled* a son of man. A man is a great deal more than a biped; yet it would be absurd to say that he resembled a biped. The description, accordingly, though not inconsistent with the idea of a wholly supernatural Messiah, who was not a true son of man, completely excludes Hengstenberg's Messiah. On the other hand, it precisely suits a personified people, who are not a son of man, but only *as it were* a son of man. In the passage already quoted from Fourth Ezra, in the Æthiopic, Arabic, and Armenian versions, it is the wind which rises up from the sea like a man, though after this has occurred the mysterious being is spoken of as a man. This suggests the thought that perhaps the writer of Daniel may have meant by his comparison that it was not a real man of flesh and blood that appeared in the clouds, but rather a grand cloudy form that shaped itself out of the ascending vapours, till it seemed the glorified heavenly reflection of ideal humanity. On the other hand, if he meant the Messiah, I have seen no satisfactory reason for his using the particle of comparison at all. It would have been more natural to have said simply, 'I saw the Son of man.'

'4. In the other passages of this book, in which anyone is described as being like the children of men, it is not an ideal person, but a real person, who is spoken of. The same remark applies to Ezek. i. 26.'[1] The analogy of four passages, even if they were like the present one, could hardly establish a rule. But in all four instances the expression is quite different. And here again the argument turns against Hengstenberg; for the comparison is invariably used in reference to those who were in no sense men—to God in Ezekiel, and to angels in Daniel.[2]

[1] P. 90. [2] viii. 15; x. 16, 18.

Such are the arguments by which the Messianic interpretation is defended, and which appear satisfactory even to such a critic as Hilgenfeld. To my own mind they appear simply worthless; and therefore the considerations which led us to assign a different meaning to the passage remain unimpaired.

The next passage in which the Messiah is by some critics supposed to appear is viii. 15 *sq.* At the end of the vision of the ram and the goat Daniel 'heard one saint speaking, and another saint said unto that certain saint which spake, How long shall be the vision concerning the daily sacrifice?' When Daniel had heard the answer, there stood before him 'as the appearance of a man [גָבֶר]. And I heard a man's voice between the banks of Ulai, which called, and said, Gabriel, make this man to understand the vision.' Oehler [1] and Hilgenfeld [2] think that this person with the man's voice can be no other than the Son of man of vii. 13. With the interpretation, however, which we have given to the latter passage, all plea for this opinion falls away. There is nothing in the narrative itself to suggest anything but the presence of two angelic beings, one of whom assumed the visible appearance of a man, and is evidently Gabriel, while the other is known to be at hand only by the voice which is heard above the middle of the river. To assume that the owner of this voice is the Messiah is indeed to build one's theories in the air.

This passage is, however, connected with a later vision, which Daniel saw 'by the side of the great river, which is Hiddekel.' [3] Here appeared 'a certain man clothed in linen, whose loins were girded with fine gold of Uphaz.' Now the linen dress denotes the priestly

---

[1] Herzog, *Messias*, S. 417. [2] *Jüd. Apok.* S. 47.
[3] x. 4 *sq.*

office, and the gold indicates the rank of a prince; and thus, according to Hilgenfeld,[1] is indicated a character precisely suited to the Messianic conception in the Maccabean time, when the high-priest had so long presided over the nation. These tokens, however, are not inconsistent with the dignity of an archangel. Michael also is 'one of the chief princes,'[2] and if we have no other reference in Daniel to the priestly functions of the angels, it would not be unsuitable to ascribe them to those who stood nearest to the throne of God.[3] With these articles of dress all resemblance to the Messiah ceases. This being, whoever he is, belongs wholly to the celestial realm. He is there engaged in conflict with the angel-prince of the kingdom of Persia. With the help of Michael he was able to leave the contest for a time, in order to make revelations to Daniel; but when this duty is accomplished, he must return to the fight. His revelation is long and minute, and extends to the time of the resurrection; yet nowhere does he give the faintest hint of any personal participation in the earthly fortunes of Israel. The people are Daniel's people,[4] and Michael is their heavenly prince.[5] How anything could be more unlike the Messiah it is difficult to conceive; and indeed the total absence of Messianic promise throughout this elaborate description of 'what shall befall thy people in the latter days'[6] seems to me to be conclusive evidence that, if the writer believed in a Messiah at all, he regarded him as so subordinate to the general glory of Israel that it was not worth while to introduce him on the scene; and it is most probable that the Messianic idea had lost all

---

[1] *Jüd. Apok.*, S. 49. [2] Verse 13.
[3] Hitzig appropriately refers to Rev. viii. 2, 3.
[4] x. 14; xii. 1.   [5] x. 21. xii. 1.   [6] x. 14.

hold on the mind of the people, and had not yet re-shaped itself from the pictures in the ancient prophecies.

We come now to a passage the interpretation of which is beset with difficulties, ix. 24–27.[1] To this Hengstenberg devotes all his strength in a laboured exposition and argument, which occupy, in the translation, more than 170 pages. As it is not necessary for us to imitate this minuteness in order to arrive at rational grounds for deciding between the Messianic and non-Messianic interpretations, I propose to start by presenting Hengstenberg's translation, and accepting it with the exception of a few points which seriously affect the decision of the controversy.

The following, then, is his rendering, a few of his explanations which are needed to make the sense clear being given in brackets:—' Seventy weeks are cut off [definitely and precisely determined] upon thy people and upon thy holy city, to shut in [forgive, cover up] transgression, and to seal up sins [remove them from the sight of God], and to cover iniquity, and to bring eternal righteousness; and to seal up vision and prophet [not, as most suppose, to fulfil or confirm them, but to put them aside as no longer necessary], and to anoint a Holy of Holies. And thou shalt know and understand: from the going forth of the word to restore and to build Jerusalem unto an anointed one, a prince, are seven weeks and sixty-two weeks: the street is restored and built, and firmly determined;[2] but in narrow times. And after the sixty-two weeks an anointed one will be cut off; and there is not to him [Christ, owing to his rejection, has no

---

[1] Various opinions on this passage may be seen collected in the *Speaker's Commentary*, 'Excursus on the Seventy Weeks,' vi. pp. 360–365. They are given with candour and good taste; but the Excursus can hardly be said to contribute anything to the criticism of the subject.

[2] Dr. Pusey prefers 'street and wall shall be restored and builded,' p. 173.

rule over the covenant-people];[1] and the city and the sanctuary the people of a prince, the coming one, will destroy; and it will end in the flood,[2] and to the end there is war, decree of ruins. And one week will confirm the covenant to the many [or, he will confirm the covenant to the many one week], and the middle of the week will [or, in the middle of the week will he] cause sacrifice and burnt-offering to cease, and the destroyer comes over the summit of abominations, and indeed until that which is completed and determined shall pour down upon the desolate places.'[3]

According to the view of the Messianic interpreters we have here a literal prophecy of the coming of Christ, of his death, and of the destruction of Jerusalem by the Romans. By the anointing of a holy of holies Hengstenberg understands the communication of the Spirit to Christ. He frankly admits that 'in the whole Bible קֹדֶשׁ קָדָשִׁים is never applied to a person, but only to things;'[4] but he thinks that 'Christ is here represented as a most holy thing,' and that this interpretation is justified by 1 Chron. xxiii. 13, where he believes that the expression is used of Aaron and his sons,[5] and by Luke i. 35, where Christ is described as τὸ γεννώμενον ἅγιον.[6]

---

[1] Or, as Dr. Pusey explains it, 'the city and the sanctuary shall be his no more:' pp. 176 and 184-5.

[2] The words 'the end thereof shall be with a flood' (as the A. V. has it) Mr. Fuller refers to the destruction, not of the city, but of the prince, and he thinks they should be rendered 'the prince that shall come and shall find his end in the (not "a") flood,' the flood being used for the 'army,' or as typical of divine punishment. P. 358.

[3] Mr. Fuller thinks that the last word in 27, whether it be taken as 'a desolate one' or as 'desolator,' refers to the Nagid (the prince). He who had been a desolator becomes desolate. P. 360.

[4] P. 123.

[5] Translating, 'Aaron was set apart to sanctify him as a most holy one, he and his sons for ever.' P. 119.

[6] 'The Greek Versions . . . distinctly understand the words in dispute in a personal sense.' Speaker's Com., where the words are cited, vi. p. 361.

He refers 'an anointed one' in each instance to Christ, and 'a prince, the coming one,' to Titus. He adopts as the beginning of the seventy weeks the year in which Nehemiah offered his prayer for the restoration of Jerusalem, on the ground that the actual restoration of the city was not commenced before that time.[1] It was in answer to this prayer that the divine decree went forth to rebuild the city. Now this event took place in the 20th year of Artaxerxes, that is, as Hengstenberg endeavours to prove, in the year 455 B.C.[2] The last clause in verse 25, he believes, must describe the events of the seven weeks just mentioned, and he infers that 'the restoration of the city is said to occupy the whole seven weeks, and to be completed when they close.' The year 455 B.C. corresponds with 299 from the foundation of Rome. Add to this sixty-nine weeks, or 483 years, and we reach 782 A.U.C., the year in which Christ began his ministry. Arguments are adduced to show that Christ's ministry really lasted three years and a half,[3] at the close of which he put an end, by his death, to the Jewish sacrifices, in conformity with verse 27.

The principal points in the non-Messianic interpretation may be briefly stated. The seventy weeks are adopted by the writer as an interpretation of the seventy years of Jeremiah, and terminate in the time of Antiochus Epiphanes. If we take as the earliest point of departure for our calculation the year 606 B.C., when Judæa fell under the Chaldean power, we reach the year 116 B.C., which is half a century too late. We thus encounter a

---

[1] P. 202 *sq.*
[2] Dr. Pusey assigns to this event the year 444 B.C. (pp. 169–170, with note 6). He dates, in preference, from the commission of Ezra in the seventh year of Artaxerxes, 457 B.C. (pp. 169 and 172), so that in his initial point of reckoning he differs only by two years from Hengstenberg.
[3] P. 240 *sq.*

serious chronological difficulty, which must be brought under discussion farther on. 'An anointed one, a prince,' is Cyrus who is to appear at the end of seven weeks, this period being separated by the punctuation from the sixty-two weeks. The second 'anointed,' who is to be 'cut off,' is either Seleucus IV., who died in 175 B.C., or the high-priest Onias III., who was killed most probably in 171 B.C. The last week terminates in 164 B.C.; and in the midst of this period of seven years Antiochus Epiphanes captured Jerusalem and put a stop to the sacrifices.

Before proceeding to the evidence which must guide our judgment in deciding between these two views, we must make a remark about the method of inquiry. Hengstenberg tries to create a prejudice against the non-Messianic interpreters by using these words :—'There is a hint at the genesis of these views in the words of Hitzig: "after the death of Jesus the Son of man (vii. 13), it was inevitable that those who regarded him as the Messiah, should interpret the words 'the anointed one shall be cut off' as pointing to him." It was necessary at any price to set aside the exposition which owed its origin to faith; for the simple reason that they had got rid of faith itself.'[1] This insolent speech (as I must term it) does not tend to awaken our confidence in the candour of the critic who makes it. Men are not to be charged with want of faith because they see no reason to believe that the minute prediction of the chronology of future events is an element in real prophecy. Whatever difficulties stand in the way of such a supposition are opposed to the Messianic interpretation; and if these difficulties be considerable, they certainly impose upon honest men the duty of freshly examining the passage, to see whether the old interpretation be the only one that is tenable. At the

[1] P. 250.

same time we must be careful not to allow this reflection to bias our exegetical judgment. We must endeavour to determine simply from the book itself and its correspondence with historical facts what it was that the writer meant, and for the time being maintain an attitude of indifference towards the theory of special prediction. On the other hand we must be equally careful not to be biassed by the traditional interpretation; for Hitzig's very just remark shows that, on the supposition of its being wrong, we can fully account for its existence. With these remarks we may proceed to an investigation of the evidence.

We must notice, in the first place, certain phrases to which appeal is made, but which seem to me to afford no evidence either way. The first is, 'to anoint a holy of holies.' We have already seen the way in which Hengstenberg applies this to Christ. On the other hand it is referred to the temple or to the altar, and to the restoration of the national worship, after the victories of Judas Maccabæus. The expression here used is applied to the altar in Exodus xxix. 37; and in Leviticus viii. 11 it is said that this was consecrated by anointing with oil. To this Hengstenberg replies that the term is much more extensive than the temple or the altar, and therefore could not be used alone to denote either of these. 'It would be only by a mere guess, and without any foundation whatever, that the expression could be understood as referring to the temple itself,' or to the altar.[1] '*Every interpretation which is based upon a mere conjecture must for that very reason be rejected.*'[1] Now it may be quite true that the term would not at once suggest either of these meanings to a reader remote from the scenes to which it relates; but, I imagine, some such meaning would

[1] P. 120.

immediately occur to those who had either just witnessed or were eagerly expecting the reconsecration of the temple amid popular rejoicing and thanksgiving.[1] The expression, however, need not be limited, but may refer to the dedication of all that the Jews considered most holy in connection with the temple-worship. In any case Hengstenberg's interpretation must fall before his own canon. Was any reader not previously biassed likely to think of the Messiah when his eye lighted on the anointing of a most holy *thing*? Nowhere else is the Messiah so called, and it is only by a process of forcing that the words can be made to suit him. Hengstenberg further objects that 'the outward dedication of the outward temple and altar is not in harmony with the other communications of divine grace, promised in the context. They are all of a spiritual nature,' &c.[2] To this it is a sufficient answer to say that the expression and embodiment of spiritual blessings in an outward temple is not inconsistent with Jewish thought, and we know from the history of the Maccabees how strong was the attachment of the religious party to the sanctuary and its worship. Hengstenberg's other objections, founded on the chronology, and on the supposed prediction of the total destruction of the temple, as they have a bearing on the whole passage, will be considered in another connection.

The expressions, 'an anointed, a prince' in verse 25, and 'an anointed' in verse 26, do not necessarily refer to the Messiah. The former might certainly be applied to Cyrus, who was called the Lord's anointed by the later Isaiah;[3] and if it be doubtful whether the latter could denote a heathen king who had conferred no benefits upon Israel, it would be a suitable designation of a high-

---

[1] See the description in 1 Mac. iv. 52 *sq.*
[2] P. 121.
[3] xlv. 1.

priest. Hengstenberg's arguments to prove that these terms must signify the Messiah have so little force that we need not pause to notice them. On the other hand, it may very fairly be contended that the absence of the article furnishes no light argument against the Messianic interpretation, and that especially its absence in the second instance, together with the want of any term answering to 'prince,' shows that the two anointed ones are not the same. This difficulty, however, might perhaps be got over, if the preponderant evidence pointed to a different conclusion.

Hengstenberg lays great stress on the general Messianic character of the opening verse. But this is not disputed. The writer undoubtedly looks forward to an ideal kingdom as earnestly as any of the prophets. The only question in this respect is whether he places a Messiah at the head of that kingdom.

We must now turn to the more general considerations which may be alleged in favour of each view.

We may notice first those which render it probable that the fulfilment of the prophecy is to be sought in connection with Antiochus Epiphanes. The ample description in chapters xi. and xii. seems to me almost decisive of the question. There, as we have seen, there is not only no mention of the Messiah, but the great consummation of the world's history is connected with Antiochus, and the last solemn prophecy in the whole book relates to the suspension of the daily sacrifice in his time. How could the ultimate limit of the author's view be more clearly indicated? Again, how are we to believe that the author could dwell at such great length and with such reiteration on the brief episode of Antiochus, and yet confine himself to the most meagre and obscure allusions to the Messiah? There is something utterly grotesque in the supposition that a man should be miraculously commissioned hundreds of years before to predict such ample details about an ephemeral tyrant, and to tell about the world's great Redeemer that he should come in a certain year, and that he should be cut off, that he should confirm the covenant for one week, and cause sacrifice to cease, and not another word about a life so rich in everlasting results. Surely so wonderful a gift can never have been so eccentric in its action.

Once more, there are certain obvious correspondences between this passage and the prophecies which confessedly relate to Antiochus, and these make it probable that we are to seek the solution in the same events. In verse 27 we are told that sacrifice should cease in the middle of the seventieth week. Three years and a half, therefore, are left before the bringing in of everlasting righteousness. Now this is the period elsewhere assigned to the suspension of the sacrifices under Antiochus.[1] This is certainly a singular coincidence, if different events are really referred to. Certain characteristic expressions also are here used. וְעַל כְּנַף שִׁקּוּצִים מְשֹׁמֵם ('over the summit of abominations [comes] a desolator,' or, if we are guided by the corresponding phrases, and admit a slight change of reading, 'over the summit of abominations of the desolator') reminds us of הַפֶּשַׁע שֹׁמֵם ('the transgression of the desolator') in viii. 13, הַשִּׁקּוּץ מְשֹׁמֵם ('the abomination of the desolator') in xi. 31, and שִׁקּוּץ שֹׁמֵם ('the abomination of the desolator') in xii. 11. These resemblances might no doubt point to a parallelism between the Syrian and the Roman invasions; but taken by themselves they would certainly lead us to suppose that the writer was referring to the same event throughout.

---

[1] vii 25; viii. 14; xii. 7, 11. In the statements in these passages there are minor differences; but as they do not affect the general conclusion, we need not pause to discuss them.

The above reasons, viewed in combination, appear to me to possess great force; but we must now see how far they are counterbalanced by objections to the view which they seem so firmly to support. Hengstenberg advances no fewer than eleven arguments against the Maccabean interpretation, of which, while some are of slight importance, one or two possess considerable weight. These we must now survey in their order.

1. He says, 'We cannot see how the supposed Pseudo-Daniel could possibly regard the prophecies of Jeremiah as unfulfilled, and so be induced to make them the subject of a parody. These prophecies contain no Messianic elements whatever.'[1] It is quite possible, however, that the writer may have believed that the prophecy had been literally fulfilled, and yet have supposed that it contained a deeper sense in which it had not yet found its accomplishment.[2] Jeremiah certainly connects the return from the Captivity with the most glowing anticipations of the Messianic time in chapters xxx. and xxxi.; and it would not have been at all inconsistent with ancient modes of interpretation to conclude that, while the seventy years literally ended with the return from Babylon, they must be mystically extended to embrace the happier period. It seems evident also that there must have been some connection in the writer's mind between the seventy years of verse 2 and the seventy weeks of 24, and that the recurrence of the seventy is not a mere coincidence. Indeed there is no apparent reason for his mentioning the prophecy of Jeremiah at all except as a ground on which to erect his own. These remarks may serve at the same time as a reply to the next argument.

---

[1] P. 251.
[2] This supposition sufficiently meets Dr. Pusey's appeal to Ezra i. 1 as evidence that the Jews regarded the prophecy as fulfilled. Pp. 192–3.

2. 'A mystic interpretation like this, "for seventy years write quickly 490," is so evidently a mere caprice, that no author could have adopted it, unless he intended to make fun of Jeremiah.' According to this criticism a good many Jewish interpreters must have wished to make fun of their Scriptures. But perhaps Henstenberg is only making fun of himself.

3. The initial point of the seventy weeks ought to be the same as that of Jeremiah's seventy years, and this is conceded by many anti-Messianic expositors; but then the difficulty arises that no divine command to rebuild Jerusalem was given at that time. If appeal is made, as it is by Hilgenfeld,[1] to Jeremiah xxv., where the prophecy is assigned to the fourth year of Jehoiakim, 606 B.C., the rejoinder is made that the prophet in that passage says nothing about the rebuilding of the city. To escape this difficulty Hitzig appeals to Jeremiah xxx. and xxxi., where the rebuilding of the city is expressly mentioned;[2] but he thus lays himself open to the objection that he adopts a different initial point for the seventy weeks, namely 588 B.C. I believe the solution of the difficulty is to be found in identifying the 'commandment,' or rather 'word,' of verse 25 with the 'word of the Lord' in verse 2; for limiting the desolations of Jerusalem to a period of seventy years is tantamount to a promise to restore it when that period has elapsed. When Dr. Pusey ridicules the idea of thus calling the 'prophecy of that temporary desolation *a word* or promise *to restore and rebuild it*,'[3] he forgets that this is the very view presented by Ezra i. 1-2, where the decree of Cyrus to build the house of the Lord is represented as the fulfilment of 'the word of the Lord by the mouth of Jeremiah.' That the prediction about the seventy years is the one

[1] *Jüd. Apok.* S. 20. [2] xxx. 18; xxxi. 4, 38. [3] P. 195.

here referred to is evident from the parallel passage in 2 Chronicles xxxvi. 21–23, where it is expressly mentioned. It is clear, therefore, that the words of Jeremiah were understood not so much as a prophecy that Jerusalem should lie waste as in the sense of a promise that it should be restored after a certain time.

4. 'The fact that, in ver. 24, there is an evident antithesis to ver. 2, where it is said that seventy years are to be accomplished upon the ruins of Jerusalem, militates against the assumption, that the destruction is taken as the point of commencement. How can the years, which are to be accomplished *upon the ruins*, be included in those which are to be accomplished *upon the city*?' The antithesis between the two verses is not evident except to those who agree with Hengstenberg; to those who take the other view it is the parallelism that is evident. That the 'desolations' and 'the city' are not antithetic is sufficiently proved by verse 18, 'open thine eyes, and behold our desolations, and the city which is called by thy name.'

5. 'דָבָר, without the article, cannot properly be referred to the definite announcement made by Jeremiah.' In a passage where the article is so often omitted, when, if Hengstenberg be correct, we should expect it, this difficulty can have but little weight. The indefiniteness is peculiarly appropriate here, if, as I have suggested, the 'word' in question was rather implied than distinctly announced by Jeremiah. Dr. Pusey strangely says, '*a decree to restore and build Jerusalem* is, according to these theories, not to be any decree or commandment of God, but a prophetic promise.'[1] But surely a prophetic promise is at least as divine as the decree of an eastern despot; and what God has promised, he may very well

[1] P. 194.

be said to have decreed. When Dr. Pusey says there is 'no more ground to select a prophecy of Jeremiah . . . than one of Micah or Isaiah,'[1] he seems quite to forget that the chapter opens with a reference to the דְבַר־יְהוָֹה that came to Jeremiah.

6. The two periods ought to terminate with the same event; but 'of the blessings, which are spoken of in ver. 24, . . . not one is mentioned by Jeremiah.' On the contrary, the most essential blessings are fully mentioned by Jeremiah, not indeed in immediate verbal connection with the seventy years, but in connection with the return from the Captivity: 'I will forgive their iniquity, and I will remember their sin no more.'[2]

7. We come now to the most serious objection. If we count the seventy weeks from the earliest admissible date, 606 B.C., they carry us about half a century too far. Hitzig endeavours to escape this difficulty by regarding the seven weeks as included within the sixty-two, and reckoning them from 588 to 539 B.C. It is not a serious objection to this that Cyrus did not restore the Jews till the year 536; for the author may not have thought it necessary to introduce fractions into his longer periods, although he does so in the last week, where the division was of more importance. The inclusion of the seven weeks is recommended by the fact that the sixty-two weeks, reckoned from 606 B.C., exactly suit the chronology. But this suitability is qualified by the following consideration. According to Hitzig's punctuation the city is to be rebuilt during the sixty-two weeks; and therefore we should expect them to begin with the return from the Captivity. And again, it is a very arbitrary and artificial way of dealing with the seventy weeks to treat them as not continuous. No one could possibly imagine such an

---

[1] P. 195.   [2] xxxi. 34. See the whole chapter.

interpretation from a simple study of the passage itself; and it is difficult to suppose that the writer can have intended that of which he gives not the slightest hint. The same objection applies to the variation of Hilgenfeld, who reckons the seven weeks and the sixty-two weeks from the same initial point, 606 B.C., ending the seven weeks with the victory of Cyrus over Astyages the Median in 558 B.C.[1]

Ewald escapes from these difficulties, but in a manner which seems no less arbitrary. He supposes that the author, having arrived at the idea of seventy weeks, acts on the belief that the week was the divine measure of time, and that every week must have its sabbath of divine peace and favour. From the midst of the seventy weeks, therefore, must be withdrawn seventy years representing the sabbaths, leaving the remainder as the time of affliction. Having thus curtailed the period given by the writer himself, Ewald starts with the year 588 B.C. Seven weeks, or forty-nine years (for here the sabbaths are not omitted), bring us to 539. The sixty-two weeks, or 434 years, extend to 105 B C. Subtract seventy years, and we are carried back to 175. The remaining week ends with 168 B.C; and the half-week, which Ewald regards as a lucky hit on the part of the author, represents a short transition period before the Messianic time comes in. Of this curious shortening of the time there is not a hint in the text; but this is no difficulty to Ewald: if there is not, there ought to be; it is evident that the passage must originally have had some closing words, and these no doubt made everything clear.[2] All this is to imagine rather than to interpret.

Delitzsch, following Hofmann and Wieseler, thinks the seven weeks are to be placed at the end, not at the

[1] *Jüd. Apok.* S. 30.   [2] *Proph. d. A. B.* iii. S. 423 *sq.*

beginning of the seventy, and that they consequently come after the time of Epiphanes, and indicate the interval between him and Christ. But this not only seems quite opposed to the plain meaning of the text, but introduces the insuperable difficulty that the seven weeks must equal at least 160 years.[1]

Can we, then, suppose that the author made a serious chronological mistake? This supposition is not easily admitted, for, as Ewald points out,[2] the succession of the high-priests, and the observance of the festivals, and of the sabbatical years, must have caused the preservation of a correct chronology. It seems evident, however, that the author did not choose the period of seventy weeks purely on chronological grounds; and it is quite possible that amid the excitement of national disaster he had neither the wish nor the opportunity to estimate with precision the lapse of time. Dr. Pusey appears to treat the supposition of error as something impious. In eking out his own theory it no doubt would be so. But if the work be of Maccabean origin, and if its inspiration concern itself with great principles, and not with the dry details of history, we may reasonably expect a certain amount of error and difficulty, such as we find in other apocalyptic books. To conclude that the Book of Enoch was written by Enoch because, on the supposition of its late date, it presents difficulties in the solution of which critics are by no means agreed, would be obviously absurd; yet Tertullian, had he known what variety of opinion critics would express, might, like Dr. Pusey, have indulged in some cheap merriment at their expense. On the other hand, a single error, however minute, is incom-

---

[1] Herzog, *Daniel*, S. 283 *sq.* Other attempted explanations may be seen in Dr. Pusey's work, p. 195 *sq.*
[2] *Proph. d. A. B.* iii. p. 423.

patible with the theory of miraculous prediction; and this must not be forgotten in estimating the force of objections urged from the opposite sides.

We, have then, in the chronology the one serious objection to the Maccabean interpretation. The question whether this objection is to be considered fatal, or to be treated merely as a difficulty the solution of which is uncertain, depends upon another question yet to be examined, whether any better interpretation is open to our choice.

We may notice in this connection an objection insisted upon by Hengstenberg in regard to the sixty-two weeks.[1] He correctly maintains that the only legitimate translation, if these weeks be connected with the building of the city, is, 'during sixty-two weeks;' and he asks 'how could the restoration of the streets, which was accomplished, according to the testimony of history, in a much shorter time, . . . be described as occupying the whole period of 434 years?' In reply to this we may observe, in the first place, that Hengstenberg himself makes the rebuilding occupy exactly forty-nine years,[2] for which there is no historical warrant whatever. Jerusalem must have been made a habitable city in a much shorter time. The building of a town, however, is a continuous process, which we cannot say has been finished at any particular moment. The restoration of Jerusalem might very well be spoken of as continuing, though 'in troublous times,' throughout the whole period from the Captivity to the reign of Antiochus Epiphanes, who again overwhelmed it in ruin.

8. 'If the prophecy relates to the Maccabean era, how is it that it contains no allusion whatever to an event

---

[1] P. 138 *sq.*
[2] Dr. Pusey, with his different initial point, manages to extract the same time. Pp. 174–5.

which is mentioned in all the other prophecies of Daniel connected with this period, the restoration of the state and temple?' It would be well if Hengstenberg had pointed out the passages on which he relied for this statement. In the prophecy in xi. and xii. I cannot find any express assertion that the temple will be restored. The vision of the ram and the goat also, in viii., ends with the abolition of the daily sacrifice, though Daniel then hears one saint telling another that after a certain time the sanctuary should be cleansed. On the other hand, in the present passage verse 24 surely implies that all the calamities of the people and the holy city will be over at the end of seventy weeks, and it was not necessary to repeat this at the conclusion of the prophecy.

9. Hengstenberg points out some difficulties in the way of applying the words, 'an anointed one shall be cut off,' to either Alexander or Seleucus Philopator; but he says nothing about their application to Onias.

10. He appeals to the unanimous testimony of Jewish tradition. But the Jews must, at a very early period, have been forced to adopt a non-Maccabean interpretation; for they saw that the everlasting righteousness had not come; and they were not prepared to admit that the writer was mistaken. This remark might apply even to the time when the first Book of Maccabees was written, though the alleged references of that book to the other prophecies of Daniel, while this is not alluded to, might be sufficiently explained by the greater clearness and fulness with which they dwell on the disasters of the time.[1]

---

[1] Mr. Fuller, however, understands 1 Mac. i. 54, as referring to this passage, and says, 'the LXX. by its [sic] curious reading of v. 26—μετὰ ἑπτὰ καὶ ἑβδομήκοντα καὶ ἑξήκοντα δύο, i.e. "after 139 years" (139 Seleucid æra or B.C. 174)—refer [sic] the passage to the same period:' Excursus on the

11. The 'non-Messianic interpretation will continue false, so long as the word of Christ is true,—that is, to all eternity.' This statement is made on the ground that Matthew xxiv. 15 and Mark xiii. 14 contain an allusion to this prophecy, and 'it is quoted by the Lord as an actual prophecy which had still to be fulfilled, so far as the destruction of the city and temple was concerned.' I must not shrink from noticing this objection, though I cannot but regret that that great and holy name is dragged into a mere critical discussion. If this appeal to authority is to prohibit the exercise of our own judgments, why has Hengstenberg wearied himself and his readers with such a dreary quantity of superfluous matter? The fact is that, when it suits him, 'he does not trouble himself about the authority of the Lord' any more than Hitzig, whom he treats with such contempt. On philological grounds he renders מְשֹׁמֵם 'destroyer,' although Christ renders it τῆς ἐρημώσεως, 'desolation,' and he does not think it incumbent on him to maintain that שִׁקּוּצִים is in the singular number because in the New Testament it is translated τὸ βδέλυγμα. To the argument, however, there are even for Christians three answers. First, it is possible to acknowledge and revere the spiritual authority of Christ without supposing that it was any part of his office to pronounce ex-cathedra judgments upon questions of

Seventy Weeks, *Speaker's Com.* vi. p. 360. According to this the *oldest* Jewish interpretation supported the modern view. The reading referred to, however, is not what is generally found in editions of the LXX. Those of Wechelius (Frankfort, 1597), of Grabe (1707–1720), of Reineccius (Leipzig, 1730), of Holmes (fourth vol. Oxford, 1827), and of Tischendorf (Leipzig, 1850) all read μετὰ τὰς ἑβδομάδας τὰς ἑξηκονταδύο, and none of them mentions the other reading. That the text of the ordinary printed LXX. agrees here with the Codex Vaticanus is confirmed by the recent fac-simile edition of that MS. by Vercellone and Cozza (Rome, 1868–72). I have found the 'curious reading' only in a work entitled *Daniel secundum Septuaginta ex tetraplis Origenis nunc primum editus e singulari Chisiano codice annorum supra* IƆCCC. Romæ, CIƆ IƆ CCLXXII.

interpretation and criticism. Secondly, Christ does not really express any opinion about the original meaning of the prophecy. He *applies* it no doubt to the destruction which was still future; but it is quite conceivable that he may have regarded the passage as descriptive of the time of Epiphanes, and yet have gathered from it the wider conviction that the 'abomination of desolation' in the holy place was the sure sign of national ruin. And lastly, the passage in which the reference to Daniel occurs is one of those in which we can least be certain that his words have been correctly reported.

The general conclusion, then, at which we arrive is that the Maccabean interpretation is supported by arguments of great strength, but is opposed by a serious chronological difficulty. We must now turn to the other interpretation, and see what can be urged for and against it.

Let us look first at the more general considerations which arise from the position of the passage in the book. These are all opposed to the Messianic exposition. In addition to those already noticed we may observe the following. The chronology which is given would be utterly valueless to Daniel; for the seventy weeks would be reckoned from an undetermined point in the future. This hardly corresponds with the profession of Gabriel, that he came to give Daniel 'skill and understanding.' Again, the prayer to which this revelation is an answer is opposed to Hengstenberg's idea that the writer fully accepted the literal and complete fulfilment of Jeremiah's prophecy. Had he done so, and been the real Daniel, he would have believed that the 'desolations of Jerusalem' had nearly reached their allotted term. But of this there is not a sign in the prayer:—'Let thine anger and thy fury be turned away from thy city Jerusalem, thy holy mountain;' 'O my God, incline thine ear and hear; open thine eyes, and behold our desolations, and the city which is called by thy name. . . O Lord, forgive; O Lord, hearken and do; defer not, for thine own sake, O my God.' These are not the words of one who is calmly trusting in the speedy fulfilment of a divine promise; but they exactly suit the state of mind of one who felt that the prophecy in its plain sense did not harmonise with the facts, and who longed to extract from it some gleam of present hope. And yet again, the revelation made by Gabriel is obviously intended as an answer to the prayer for the speedy restoration of Jerusalem; but on the Messianic interpretation it leaves undetermined the one thing that Daniel wanted to know, and deals instead with things that he had not referred to. It consoles him by telling him that the city will be irretrievably ruined, and the sacrifices abolished for ever; and the bald allusions to the Messiah are not calculated to impart either comfort or hope. Thus the evidence in favour of the Messianic view must be found wholly within the passage itself, and in the precision with which its various parts accommodate themselves to historical facts.

There are only two points in which the Messianic interpretation seems at first sight to possess a decided advantage, and one of these vanishes on a closer examination. The first is the accuracy with which the sixty-nine weeks fit themselves into the real chronology, if at least Hengstenberg be right in his elaborate calculations, and if we are content to ignore the decree of Cyrus. These particulars we need not criticise, but leave him in the full enjoyment of his one telling argument. The second point is that, according to this prophecy, the city and temple are to be 'irremediably destroyed,' whereas in the time of Epiphanes they were 'merely subjected to a severe visitation.'[1] Now there is no statement whatever that the destruction of the city is final, and Hengstenberg's conclusion is merely an inference from the usage of certain words. On the other hand, verse 24, especially when taken in connection with the preceding prayer, seems to imply in no doubtful way that the people and the city were, on the expiration of seventy weeks, to enter into the enjoyment of everlasting righteousness; and if we have been right in our explanation of 'a holy of holies,' the reconsecration of the temple is expressly referred to. We cannot escape from this plain inference by appealing to poetic phrases, especially as Hengstenberg himself does not deny the applicability of these phrases to the Babylonian destruction, which was certainly not 'irremediable.' But it may be worth our while to turn to 1st Maccabees to see whether the proceedings of Antiochus were of such an innocuous character that the language of Daniel could not be properly applied to them. We are there told that 'when they [the people of Jerusalem] had given him credence, he fell suddenly upon the city, and smote it very sore, and destroyed much people of Israel. And when he had taken the spoils of the city, he set it on fire, and pulled down the houses and walls thereof on every side. But the women and children took they captive, and possessed the cattle.'[2] The 'sanctuary was laid waste like a wilderness.'[3] This disaster was regarded as a judgment. The dying Mattathias said to his sons, 'Now hath pride and rebuke gotten strength, and the time of destruction, and the wrath of indignation,' and he therefore exhorts them to be 'zealous for the law;'[4] and Judas turned 'away wrath from Israel' by 'destroying the ungodly.'[5]

[1] P. 263. [2] i. 30–32. [3] ἠρημώθη ὡς ἔρημος, i. 39. See also ii. 12.
[4] ii. 49. [5] iii. 8.

Meanwhile 'Jerusalem lay void as a wilderness,[1] . . . the sanctuary also was trodden down.'[2] The people looked upon this as a terrible affliction. On their return to the ruined city, ' when they saw the sanctuary desolate,[3] and the altar profaned, and the gates burnt up, and shrubs growing in the courts as in a forest or on one of the mountains, yea, and the priests' chambers pulled down; they rent their clothes, and made great lamentation, and cast ashes upon their heads.'[4] As the altar had been defiled, they thought it best to pull it down, and build a new one,[5] and 'new holy vessels' had to be made.[6] The rebuilding of the fortifications is also expressly mentioned.[7] It is clear, therefore, that the Syrian treatment of Jerusalem was not a mere temporary occupation, which could not be justly compared with the Babylonian and Roman destructions. It aimed at the utter ruin of the Jewish polity;[8] the fortifications of the city were levelled with the ground, the houses were burned or pulled down; and if the shell of the sanctuary was left standing amid its desolations, it was only that it might be 'trodden down' with unholy feet, and 'profaned' with the heathen 'abomination of desolation.'[9] There is nothing, then, in the language of Daniel which is too strong to describe

[1] Ἔρημος.
[2] iii. 45. See also 51.
[3] Ἠρημωμένον.
[4] iv. 38, 39.
[5] iv. 44-7.
[6] iv. 49.
[7] iv. 60; vi. 7.
[8] i. 41-53.
[9] i. 54; see also vi. 7. Yet all this becomes with Dr. Pusey,—' shall fire some houses in the city, yet leaving it, as a whole, unhurt and inhabited as before [for which he refers to i. 38 and 55], and displacing not one stone or ornament of the temple, nay nor touching it; for the idol-altar was built on the brazen altar outside' (p. 228). On this I forbear to remark, beyond stating that the account of i. 38 is that ' the inhabitants of Jerusalem fled on account of them, and it became a habitation of foreigners.' But before this we are informed that the enemy, after their destruction of the houses, ' built the city of David with a great wall,' and placed there a sinful nation, apparently to act as a garrison : i. 33, 34. That is, part of the city was spared for military purposes.

this invasion, which in its purposes was the most formidable that the Jews ever experienced, and in its actual results was fraught with calamities, which 'poured down' upon the desolate sanctuary, and had come upon the city with the sudden violence of a 'flood.'[1] Hengstenberg's argument therefore falls to the ground.

We must now ask how far the Messianic interpretation really answers to the statements in the text. The following considerations seem to me completely fatal to it. In order to estimate them at their full value we must remember that, by the hypothesis, this is a miraculous prophecy, and therefore, if its claims are to be sustained, it must be perfectly accurate in every part. You cannot defend your prophet by pleading errors which might be venial in an historian.

1. The Messianic kingdom did not begin, as stated in verse 24, nor was Christ anointed at the end of seventy weeks, but at the end of sixty-nine. It is no answer to say, with Hengstenberg,[2] that the prophecy was not fulfilled till 'the people of the covenant' personally appropriated the proffered reconciliation, and that Christ's anointing must be extended to the opening period of the Christian Church. This sort of answer would be equally good if the seventy had been seven hundred or seven thousand. What was there exactly seven years after Christ's baptism that we should say he had not been really anointed till then? Is it an orthodox dogma that Christ was anointed three years and a half after the ascension?

2. There is nothing in the text to account for the division of the sixty-nine weeks into seven and sixty-two. It is very easy to assume that the seven weeks are meant

---

[1] I am content to leave Hengstenberg the benefit of the doubt as to the reference of 'the flood.'
[2] P. 127.

for the building of the city; but there is not a word to that effect, and there is no historical reason for assigning to it exactly that time.

3. Christ was not cut off till some time had elapsed after the expiration of the sixty-two weeks, but it is certainly implied in the text that 'an anointed' was to be cut off at the close of that period. Thus verse 26 makes his death contemporaneous with his appearance, and 27 makes it three years and a half later. Dr. Pusey, oblivious of the difficulty which he thus creates, says, 'Once, in the future, at the end of the seventy weeks, there should be an atoning for all iniquity.'[1] Yet according to his own interpretation, the atoning took place, not at the end of seventy weeks, but in the middle of the seventieth.

4. The destruction of Jerusalem by the Romans did not take place at the end of the sixty-two weeks, or indeed till a considerable time after the close of the seventy. To say that 'when Christ was put to death Jerusalem ceased to be the holy city,'[2] is no answer; for that is not what the prophecy is supposed to affirm, but that the army of Titus will come and destroy the city; and this event was not coincident with Christ's death, and still less with his baptism. This interpretation, therefore, makes Daniel a false prophet.

5. Christ did not cause the sacrifices to cease at the time of his death. Here it may be said with some plausibility, that the sacrificial rites ceased 'so far as everything essential was concerned.'[3] But the prophecy has all the appearance of relating to the objective fact; and we cannot suppose that a prophet who knew the exact time of Christ's death would indicate it only by connecting it, to the great confusion of his readers, with an event which took place long afterwards. The sacrifices

[1] P. 179.   [2] Hengst. p. 166.   [3] Ibid.

were stopped by the soldiers of Titus; and if we are to judge from the rest of the book, this kind of hostile stoppage is the only one which Daniel could have anticipated.

6. Hengstenberg can assign no meaning whatever to the second half of the last week. He tries to account in a sort of way for sixty-nine and a half weeks; but the prophecy speaks of seventy, and as no intelligible reason can be given for fixing on the middle of the fourth year after Christ's death as the moment when everlasting righteousness should be brought in, the interpretation breaks down hopelessly in a most essential point. Hengstenberg's lame suggestion is that 'the terminal point of the confirmation of the covenant is, more or less, a vanishing one, and therefore does not admit of being chronologically determined, with any minute precision.'[1] But unfortunately the prophet does determine it with minute precision, and fixes on a point of time distinguished by no historical event. Dr. Pusey thinks 'the remaining $3\frac{1}{2}$ years probably mark the time during which the Gospel was preached to the Jews, before the preaching to the Samaritans showed that the special privileges of the Jews were at an end, and that the Gospel embraced the world. We have not,' he adds, 'the chronological data to fix it.'[2] Those who think that the grand climax of Daniel's prophecies was 'the preaching to the Samaritans' are probably beyond the reach of argument.

7. It is, as we have already observed, clearly implied in verse 24 that the people of Daniel and the holy city, and, for anything that appears, they alone are to enjoy the blessings which are promised after the lapse of seventy weeks.

[1] P. 240.   [2] P. 170.

These objections, which singly are very weighty, appear to me, when taken in combination, to be perfectly conclusive. The Maccabean interpretation, therefore, is left without a rival; and accordingly we are justified in accepting it, even though we cannot satisfactorily dispose of the chronological difficulty.

Our general conclusion, then, is that the Book of Daniel, though it portrays an ideal kingdom, fails to place its sovereignty in the hands of a Messiah.

In the Book of Wisdom there is one passage to which a Messianic interpretation has been given. It is that in which the treatment of the righteous man by the wicked is described.[1] Bad and unbelieving men are represented as expressing their hatred of one who is just, because he reproves their evil ways; and this just person has been supposed to be the Messiah. The closing verses[2] are the most significant :—' He pronounceth the end of the just to be blessed, and maketh his boast that God is his Father. Let us see if his words be true : and let us prove what shall happen in the end of him. For if the just man be the son of God, he will help him, and deliver him from the hand of his enemies. Let us examine him with despitefulness and torture, that we may know his meekness and prove his patience. Let us condemn him with a shameful death.' It is not surprising that these words were applied to Christ; but it is quite evident that in the original connection the righteous man is simply the representative of a class, and that no particular individual is alluded to. The absence of the Messiah from this book might seem to be less significant than in the case of Daniel, because the future glory of the righteous appears in a much less definite shape. Nevertheless that glory is so

[1] ii. 10-20. [2] 16-20.

distinctly alluded to that a writer who held the Messianic hope could hardly have failed to utter it. He insists on the immortality of the righteous, and predicts that 'they shall judge the nations, and have dominion over the people, and their Lord shall reign for ever,'[1] and that they shall 'receive a glorious kingdom, and a beautiful crown from the Lord's hand.'[2] Nothing would have been more natural than to blend with these anticipations some allusion to the coming of the Messiah and the establishment of his rule; and we must therefore suppose either that the author did not entertain the Messianic hope, or that it occupied such a subordinate place in his mind that he did not think it worth mentioning.

In the first Book of Maccabees we similarly fail to discover the Messiah. Appeal has been made to ii. 57, where Mattathias, in reminding his sons of ancient examples of virtue, says, 'David in his mercy inherited the throne of a kingdom for ever;' but the most that we could infer from this is that Mattathias expected the royal line of David to be restored, and to rule without further interruption, and he might not unsuitably have referred to the Messiah as the great restorer, had he believed in him. Two other passages also are cited, in which reference is made to the future coming of a prophet. In the first[3] it is said that the people put away the stones of the old altar, which they had pulled down on account of its defilement, 'until a prophet should come to give answer concerning them.' In the second[4] we are told that 'the Jews and the priests were well pleased that Simon should be governor and high-priest for ever until a faithful prophet should arise.' In both instances the word 'prophet' is without the article, and the passages express nothing

---

[1] iii. 8. [2] v. 16.
[3] iv. 46. [4] xiv. 41.

more than the hope that the gift of prophecy, which had passed away, might be at some time restored.

Equally silent about the Messiah is the second Book of Maccabees, though the author expresses his earnest hope that the scattered Israelites will soon be brought together, through the divine pity, into the sacred place.[1] We shall see farther on that the Messianic idea was not altogether unknown to the Maccabean period; but it is certainly remarkable that it should appear only in a couple of dreamy or poetic books, the Book of Enoch and the Sibylline Oracles, while it is conspicuously absent not only from historical and didactic works, but from the great prophetical utterance of the age. We must conclude that it was just beginning to shape itself dimly in enthusiastic minds, and had not yet been accepted as a popular faith. The speedy triumph of the Maccabees satisfied for a time the aspirations of the people; and a longer period of suffering and disappointment was needed to develope the hope of a Messiah into a passion among the masses of the nation, and into a doctrine in the schools of the learned.

The Assumption of Moses is another book where we look in vain for the belief in a Messiah; for Hilgenfeld's notion that he is to be found in Taxo[2] is too whimsical to require serious notice.[3] We cannot, of course, tell what the author may have said in the portion of the work which has not survived; but in x. 26–28 he declares that God's kingdom will appear, and that God will come and take vengeance on the Gentiles, and exalt Israel to the stars, so that he could not have had a more suitable place for introducing the Messiah. We may with much probability conclude that he was not one of those who accepted the Messianic belief.

[1] ii. 18.   [2] ix. 24, 25.   [3] *Mess. Jud.* p. 467.

The Book of Jubilees is equally destitute of all traces of the Messiah. It is remarkable that the writer omits the blessings which Jacob pronounced upon his sons, though these would have opened to him a fine field for eschatological excursions. He just touches the tempting theme, but makes no disclosure of future events:—'Israel blessed his sons before he died, and told them everything that should happen to them in the land of Egypt, and that should come upon them in the last days; he told them everything, and blessed them.'[1] It is extremely disappointing that we have not his exposition of the prophecy about Judah, and one cannot but suppose that there was some purpose in the omission. I can hardly help suspecting that he passed over this portion of Genesis on account of its accepted Messianic meaning, which he did not approve, and yet was not willing openly to contradict, and on account of its curse on Levi; for he invents blessings of his own for Levi and Judah, and, to avoid the obvious inconsistency with Genesis, puts them into the mouth of Isaac. In these, Levi takes the first place. His descendants are to be 'lords and princes and presidents to the holy seed of the children of Jacob.' They are to 'speak the word of the Lord,' and to tell his ways to Jacob, and are to stand nearest to the Lord. Judah also is to take a high position, but one political rather than religious. He is to tread down all who hate him. He is to be a lord over the sons of Jacob, he and one of his sons. His name, and the name of his sons, is to overspread the earth, and he is to be the terror of the Gentiles. Through him help and deliverance are to come to Israel, and, when he sits on the throne of honour, his righteousness shall be great.[2] This is certainly like a deliberate omission of the Messianic doctrine.

[1] Ch. xlv.   [2] Ch. xxxi.

There are also several other passages relating to the future of Israel in which the author, had he accepted this doctrine, might have been expected to introduce it.[1]

Turning to a different class of literature, we must notice two passages of Philo's, in which some have supposed that there is a reference to the Messiah. The first is in the *De Exsecrationibus*, § 9. Philo is speaking of the sudden reformation of the Israelites scattered among their enemies in all parts of the world, and their consequent return to their own land; and he says that they will be 'led by an appearance[2] more divine than the naturally human, invisible indeed to others, and manifest to those only who are being saved.' Dähne assumes that this superhuman leader is the Messiah; and from the analogy between the appearance here described, and the pillar of cloud and fire which led the Israelites through the wilderness, and which Philo allegorized into the Logos, he thinks it not improbable that the Logos is referred to in the present passage, and that thus the identification of the Logos with the Messiah was made by Philo.[3] Gfrörer is much more confident that the Logos is intended, but does not admit that he was identified by Philo with the Messiah.[4] It seems to me that the true effect of this passage is to induce a doubt whether Philo believed in a Messiah at all. If he entertained such a belief, this is certainly an occasion on which we should expect to find it clearly expressed. But this vision,

[1] Ch. i. S. 232; ch. xix. S. 16; ch. xxi. S. 19; chs. xxii., xxiii., and ch. xxxii. S. 42. Among the apocalyptic works the fourth book of the *Sib. Oracles* also is without a Messiah, notwithstanding its eschatological passages, which will be noticed farther on. This is the more remarkable as it belongs to the same period as Fourth Ezra and the Apoc. of Baruch.

[2] Ὄψεως.

[3] *Geschichtliche Darstellung der jüdisch-alexandrinischen Religions-Philosophie*, 1834, i. S. 437–8.

[4] *Philo u. d. al. Theos.* i. S. 528–530.

apparently of human form, but supernatural in its lineaments, and invisible to all but the sons of Israel, fulfilling moreover the sole function of guide to the Holy Land, does not correspond with any accepted type of the Messiah.

The other passage to which appeal is made seems at first sight to offer a more certain testimony. It occurs in the course of a long eschatological description in the *De Praemiis et Poenis*, § 16. Referring to the final overthrow of those who disturb the world's peace, Philo says, 'For a man shall go forth, says the oracle, leading an army and waging war, and shall conquer great and populous nations,[1] God having sent upon his saints a fitting help. Now this is undaunted courage of soul and the mightiest strength of body, of which either is terrible to enemies, but, if both be united, they are absolutely irresistible.' In this conquering warrior Gfrörer[2] and Schürer[3] find the Messiah. But it should be observed that the individual warrior is mentioned only in the quotation from Numbers; and if, with Oehler,[4] we regard what follows as an explanation of the oracle, he is immediately allegorized into a mere symbol of courage and strength. Throughout the whole passage there is not, in Philo's own words, a single allusion to the Messiah; and I must therefore regard it as the most probable conclusion that, while Philo shared in the ideal hopes of his race, he did not expect these hopes to be concentrated and fulfilled in any supreme personality.

Even among the later teachers the belief in the Messiah encountered some opposition. It is related that when R. Akiba acknowledged the Messiahship of Bar-

---

[1] This is taken loosely from the LXX.; Num. xxiv. 7.
[2] *Philo u. d. al. Theos.* i. S. 530.
[3] *Lehrb. d. n. Zeitg.* S. 575.   [4] Herzog, *Messias*, S. 425.

Cochba, Rabbi Yochanan ben Toretha said to him, 'Grass will grow on thy cheeks, and the Son of David will not have come.'[1] At a still later period R. Hillel (that is, Hillel II. who lived in the time of Constantine[2]) said, 'There will be no Messiah for Israel, because they have enjoyed him already in the days of Hezekiah.' Rab Yoseph, however, refuted this:—'May God pardon R. Hillel. When was Hezekiah? In the first house [during the time of the first Temple]; but Zechariah prophesied in the second house,' allusion being made to the prophecy that Israel's king should come sitting on an ass.[3]

The above evidence, when fairly construed, seems sufficient to prove that the belief in a Messiah was far from being universally entertained among the Jews, especially before the time of Christ. Nor can we say that it was rejected only by some particular party; for we have failed to discover it in apocalyptic, haggadistic, didactic, historical, and philosophical works, and have found it disputed even in the schools of the Rabbis. But now we must turn our attention to those books in which it receives a more or less complete recognition.

---

[1] Jer. Ta'anith iv. 8 (5 in the modern editions).
[2] The accuracy of this statement is open to question, but need not be here discussed.
[3] *Synhed.* 99a.

CHAPTER VIII.

THE TIME OF THE MESSIAH'S APPEARANCE.

WE have already noticed the grand division into the present and the future age, and our first duty is to determine within which of these periods the Messiah was expected to establish his rule.

Our first witness is the Sibylline Oracles, if the view generally entertained be correct, that the king mentioned in III. 652 is intended for the Messiah. This view, however, has been called in question. Holtzmann believes that the reference is to Simon, the Maccabean high-priest, 143–135 B.C.[1] The Sibyl's words are the following:—
'Then God will send from the sun a king who will stay the whole earth[2] from evil war, slaying indeed some, and to others confirming faithful treaties. Nor will he do all these things by his own counsels, but relying on the good decrees of the great God.' This description of the king's rule certainly answers with remarkable exactness to the historical work of Simon. He crushed the remnants of the Syrian party in Palestine; he renewed the treaties with Sparta and Rome; and during the greater part of the time in which he held the office of high-priest the land enjoyed a profound peace, which is described in glowing terms by the writer of 1st Maccabees.[3] The time also suits the date of the oracle, as determined

---

[1] Judenth. u. Christenth. S. 199.
[2] Perhaps 'land,' γαῖαν.
[3] xiv. 4 sq.

by Hilgenfeld on quite independent grounds. But on the other hand Simon was not a 'king,' βασιλεύς. This might seem a matter of small importance, as he was invested with all the powers of a king, were it not that his titles, Chief, High-priest, General, and Ethnarch,[1] were expressly conferred upon him, and that of king appears to have been purposely avoided. Moreover at this point the Sibyl passes from the domain of history into that of poetic imagination; so that we may perhaps conclude that the king is idealised from Simon, and represents the writer's anticipations at least as much as his retrospect. If this interpretation be rejected, we must add this Book of the Sibylline Oracles to the number of those which recognise no Messiah; and certainly our doubts upon this point are not removed when we find that in the kingdom which God is to raise up for ever over all men,[2] instead of a single Messianic head, the Prophets are to be the 'judges and just kings of mortals.'[3] If, however, we accept the usual explanation, it is evident that the Sibyl places the Messiah wholly within the limits of the first age, and makes him simply instrumental in preparing the way for a more glorious future.

In the Book of Enoch the Messiah, though not so designated, appears, in the historical vision of the sheep and the wild animals, under the figure of a white bull.[4] If we followed the order of the narrative, which but for a single sentence has all the appearance of being consecutive, we should be obliged to place him in the future age. When the suffering of the sheep has reached its climax, their Lord presents himself upon the scene, erects his throne, and conducts the final judgment, which, as we have learned, marks the division between the two ages.

---

[1] Ἡγούμενος, ἀρχιερεύς, στρατηγός, and ἐθνάρχης. 1 Mac. xiv. 41, 42, 47.
[2] 766-7.   [3] 780-1.   [4] xc. 37.

He then establishes for himself a new house. And 'afterwards' Enoch was brought and set down in the midst of the sheep, 'before the judgment took place;'[1] and then he watched till 'a white bull was born.' If the words 'before the judgment took place' are genuine, the Messiah belongs to the first age; but they are open to suspicion, because they make the verse in which they occur self-contradictory, and the time of the Messiah is obviously coincident with that of the world's final peace and blessedness. Notwithstanding these perplexing words, therefore, I think that this passage places the Messiah in the future age.

The Psalms of Solomon contain nothing explicit upon this subject; but they seem to expect the Messiah to come before any great crisis in the world's history.[2]

The Sibyl of the time of the triumvirs looks for the Messiah in the midst of ordinary mundane events: 'When Rome shall rule Egypt, . . . then shall appear upon men the supremely great kingdom of the immortal King And a pure sovereign will come, to conquer the sceptres of the whole earth unto all ages.'[3] Farther on[4] is mentioned the 'judgment of the immortal God, the great King;' so that, though the distinction is not noticed, we may say that this writer places the Messiah in the first age.

Fourth Ezra is fuller and more explicit in its statements. At the end of four hundred years after his advent the Messiah and all men are to die, and the world is to return to its pristine silence for seven days, and afterwards the new age will awake, and the corrupt one die.[5] Similarly, in the explanation of the historical vision of the eagle, it is said that he will liberate the

---

[1] xc. 31. [2] xvii. 23 *sq*. [3] iii. 46–50.
[4] 56. [5] vii. 28 *sq*.

remainder of the people of God, and give them joy until the day of judgment.[1] The same view is presented in the Apocalypse of Baruch, where we are told that the Messiah's 'dominion shall stand for ever, *until the world of corruption be ended*, and until the times predicted be fulfilled.'[2]

Among the Rabbinical authorities the general opinion is that the Messiah is to come in the present age, or at most to mark a kind of transition period; but some remove him into the future world. The statement of Rabbi Yochanan is very explicit: 'All the good that the prophets prophesied was only prophesied about the times of the Messiah; as for the days of the future age, "no eye has seen."'[3] The middle view is implied in the saying of Shemuel:—'There is no difference between this age and the days of the Messiah except the subjection to the kingdoms' (meaning that Israel should no more be subject to Gentile kingdoms in the time of the Messiah.)[4] Similarly in the Targum of Pseudo-Jonathan[5] it is said that 'King Messiah shall be revealed in the end of days,' that is, at the close of the first age. The same view is given in the Jer. Targum[6] and time is left for his dominion over the Gentiles.[7] In one passage, however, it is said that he is to appear, along with Moses, just before the termination of the present world. In Exodus xii. 42 it is stated that the night in which the Israelites went out of Egypt is 'to be observed by all the children of Israel in their generations.' On this the Targum remarks: 'For there are four nights written in the book of records. The first night was when the word of the Lord was

---

[1] xii. 34.
[2] Ch. xl.
[3] *Synhed.* 99a.
[4] Ibid.
[5] Gen. xxxv. 21.
[6] Gen. iii. 15
[7] Gen. xlix. 10–12. See also Num. xi. 26.

revealed upon the age [or world] to create it. . . . The second night was when the word of the Lord was revealed upon Abraham . . . The third night was when the word of the Lord was revealed upon the Egyptians in the middle of the night. . . . The fourth night shall be when the age shall come to its end to be dissolved [? or, redeemed], the cords of the wicked shall be exterminated, and the iron yokes broken; Moses shall go forth from the midst of the desert, and King Messiah from the midst of Rome [1]; the one shall speak on the top of the cloud, and the other shall speak on the top of the cloud, and the word of the Lord shall speak between them.' [2] The Targum of the Prophets, without making any explicit statement, seems generally to sanction the prevalent view; but in one passage [3] it says that Solomon 'prophesied concerning the kings of the house of David who were destined to rule in this age and in the future age of Messiah.'

A few other authorities which place the Messiah in the future age are very late; and we may therefore regard it as the predominant, if not the universal view in the earlier period that the work of the Messiah was to belong to the present order of things, though it was generally supposed that it would prepare the way for and immediately precede the dissolution of this perishable world.

---

[1] Or, 'the high place,'—רוֹמָא.

[2] The Messianic passages of the Targums may be seen collected in *Christology of the Targums, or the Doctrine of the Messiah, as it is unfolded in the ancient Jewish Targums . . . . Hebrew, Chaldee, and English.* Edinburgh: Robert Young.' No date. This little book has saved me much labour in collecting passages, and I have sometimes followed its closely literal translations.

[3] 1 Kings v. 13: (iv. 33 according to the division in the *A. V.*)

CHAPTER IX.

THE BIRTH-PLACE, CONCEALMENT, AND DESCENT OF THE MESSIAH.

THE accounts of the Messiah's expected birth-place, or of the place where he should be first revealed to men, are not very numerous or very early. The Book of Enoch, if we are to judge from the context, fixes on Jerusalem as the place of his birth:—'I saw that that house [*i.e.* Jerusalem] was great and very full; and I saw that a white bull was born.'[1] Later writers, however, follow the suggestion of Micah v. 2, and give the preference to Bethlehem. The following is the Targum upon that passage:—[2] 'And thou, Bethlehem-Ephratha, hast been little to be numbered among the thousands of the house of Judah; out of thee, before me, shall come forth Messiah to be made a ruler over Israel, whose name is spoken of from of old, from the days of eternity.' This view is also adopted in the following story, which is told in the Jerusalem Talmud.[3] 'An incident happened in connexion with a certain Jew, who was engaged in ploughing. His ox bellowed. An Arab passing, and hearing the ox bellow, said, Son of a Jew, son of a Jew, loose thy oxen, and loose thy ploughs, for the Holy House

---

[1] xc. 36-7. [2] v. 1 in the original.
[3] Berakhoth, ii. 4. This is quoted in Lightfoot's *Horæ Hebraicæ et Talmudicæ*, Matt. ii. 1. I have made his translation in many points more literal. There is a parallel passage in Ekhah Rabbathi (Midrash on 'Lamentations'), on i. 16.

[temple] is laid waste. The ox bellowed a second time. The Arab said to him, Yoke thy oxen and fit thy ploughs; for King Messiah has just been born. But, said the Jew, what is his name? Menachem, said he. And what is the name of his father? Chizqiyyah, said the Arab. To whom the Jew, But whence is he? The other answered, From the palace of the King of Bethlehem-Judah. Away he went, and sold his oxen and his ploughs, and became a seller of infants' swaddling clothes. And he went about from town to town till he came to that place. There all the women bought of him, but the mother of Menachem bought nothing. He heard the voice of the women saying, O thou mother of Menachem, thou mother of Menachem, come and buy bargains for thy son. But she replied, I would rather strangle the enemy of Israel [the child], because on the day that he was born the temple was laid waste. To whom he said, But we trust that, as it was laid waste at his feet, so at his feet it is being built again. She said, I have no money. To whom he replied, What matters it? Buy bargains for him, and if you have no money to-day, after some days I will come back and receive it. After some days he returned to that place, and said to her, How is the child doing? And she said, After the time you saw me last, winds and tempests came and snatched him away from me.'

The latter part of this story is connected with a belief that the Messiah existed somewhere in concealment until the time when he should be revealed to the world. This belief is expressed in Fourth Ezra, xiii., where the Messiah is seen in a vision ascending out of the sea, and the explanation is given that 'this is he whom the Most High reserves for many times, through whom He will save his creation;'[1] and it is added,

[1] 26.

'When the signs take place which I have showed thee before, then my Son will be revealed.'[1] Here the sea is apparently chosen to denote the indefinite and unknown character of the region where the Messiah was hidden away.[2] The same idea is given without the figurative language, though only as an hypothesis, in Justin Martyr's Dialogue with Tryphon,[3] in a passage already quoted. The Jew is represented as saying, 'Christ, even if he has been born and exists anywhere, is unknown and does not yet even know himself, until Elias shall come and anoint him, and make him manifest to all.'[4] The Targum of Micah iv. 8 gives the reason for this concealment:—'Thou Messiah of Israel, who art concealed on account of the offences of the congregation of Zion, to thee the kingdom is to come.'

Out of his concealment he will be revealed at the proper time. According to Fourth Ezra[5] he will take his stand upon the summit of Mount Zion; but according to the Jer. Targum of Exodus xii. 42, already quoted, he is to go forth from the midst of Rome.[6] The same curious notion is found in the Bab. Talmud,[7] which represents him as sitting at the gate of Rome among the poor and sick:—'He [Rabbi Yehoshua' ben Levi] said to him [Elijah], When comes Messiah? So he said to him, Go and ask himself. And where does he sit? At the gate of the city [Rome]. And what is his sign? He sits between poor ones that are suffering from sickness; and while all of them open and bandage again all their

---

[1] 32. Cf. vii. 28.

[2] See 52. Schürer explains this passage as a reference to the pre-existence of the Messiah: *Lebrh. der n. Zeity.* S. 584. This view will be examined farther on.   [3] Ch. 8.

[4] See also ch. 110, where this statement is alluded to.

[5] xiii. 35. Cf. *Apoc. of Baruch*, ch. xl.

[6] But see before, p. 278, note 1.   [7] *Synhed.* 98a.

wounds at once, he only opens one and closes one, saying, Perhaps I may be wanted at the very minute, so that there should be no delay.' Another view is presented in the Targum of Pseudo-Jonathan on Gen. xxxv. 21, where it is said that the Messiah will be revealed at the place where Jacob spread his tent after the death of Rachel, beyond the tower of 'Eder. This, I presume, is founded on the prophecy of Micah:—[1] 'And thou, O tower of 'Eder [עֵדֶר as in Genesis, rendered 'flock' in the Authorised Version], the stronghold of the daughter of Zion, unto thee shall it come, even the first dominion.' The expectation that the Messiah would appear first in Galilee is found only in very late authorities.[2]

The descent of the Messiah from David had been so clearly announced by the Prophets that it was simply taken for granted in later times. It is explicitly asserted in the Psalms of Solomon,[3] Fourth Ezra,[4] and the Targums.[5] The view of the Talmudists is given in the title 'Son of David,' to be presently noticed.[6]

[1] iv. 8.
[2] See the passages in Gfrörer, *Jahrh. d. II.* ii. S. 231.
[3] xvii. 5 *sq.* and 23.
[4] xii. 32, in all the versions but the Latin.
[5] See Isai. xi. 1; xiv. 29; Jer. xxiii. 5; xxxiii. 15; and for his descent from Judah, Zech. x. 4, and Jer. Targ. Gen. xlix. 11.
[6] For the concealment of the Messiah compare John vii. 27: 'When Christ cometh no man knoweth whence he is.' For his earthly manifestation see John i. 31, and for his revelation, connected by the Christians with his second coming, see 1 Cor. i. 7; 2 Thess. i. 7; 1 Peter i. 7, 13; iv. 13.

CHAPTER X.

TITLES AND NAMES OF THE MESSIAH.

THE future and ideal Ruler of Israel is referred to under various designations. That which has supplied a name to the religion of the most cultured races—Messiah, Christ, Anointed—occurs in its special sense for the first time in the Psalms of Solomon. In xvii. 36 he is called, according to the present text, 'Christ the Lord, χριστὸς κύριος, but we cannot help suspecting that we ought to have the genitive κυρίου, 'the Lord's Anointed.' The same expression occurs in xviii. 8 ; but as both words are in the genitive, this does not help us to a decision. In xviii. 6, however, we have χριστοῦ αὐτοῦ, where αὐτοῦ refers to θεός, and this may give some support to the suggested emendation. Hilgenfeld[1] believes the reading to be genuine. His appeal to Christian writers is hardly relevant, and may be disregarded; but he refers to one instance in the LXX., where the words משיח יהוה are rendered by χριστὸς κύριος.[2] It is difficult to suppose that any Jew can have seriously adopted this translation; but if the reading be not in both instances due to an error of transcription, it is probable that the words in the Psalms of Solomon are, like those in the LXX., due to a misunderstanding of the Hebrew expression. The name 'Messiah' (but without the addition) occurs also in Fourth Ezra[3]

---

[1] *Mess. Jud.* p. 32.   [2] Lament. iv. 20.
[3] vii. 28, 29, (where the Latin, however, with an obvious falsification, reads 'Jesus' in 28; and 29 is omitted by the Arab. and Arm.), and xii. 32 (according to the Lat., Syr., and Arm.)

and the Apocalypse of Baruch.[1] In the Targums and the Talmud it is found so frequently that it is unnecessary to cite particular passages. In the former it is often preceded by the title of 'King.'

The designation 'Son of David' is used only once in the pre-Christian writings, Psalms of Solomon xvii. 23. Among the Targums it is found in Canticles iv. 5, where it is employed to distinguish him from the other Messiah, the 'Son of Ephraim.' In the Talmud it occurs several times.[2]

The title 'Son of man,' if we have been right in our criticisms on the Book of Enoch, is adopted only in Christian literature. If any adhere to the Messianic interpretation of Daniel vii. 13, I may remark that the expression is not there used as an appellative, but only by way of comparison.

The title 'Son of God,' however, which might seem more distinctive of Christianity, is met with a few times in our present texts. In the Book of Enoch cv. 2 we read, 'I and my Son will unite ourselves with them [the sons of earth] for ever.' We have seen how little dependence can be placed on the accuracy of the text in regard to isolated expressions of this kind, and I am inclined to suspect that we have here a Christian interpolation; for there is nothing in the context to indicate who is meant by 'my Son.' In saying that the expression might be understood from the Old Testament, Dillmann[3] is right to this extent, that it finds some support in the Old Testament; but unless current use had already sanctioned it (and of this we have no evidence), I doubt whether it would have been intelligible, and the writer

---

[1] Chs. xxix. xxx. xxxix. xl. lxx. lxxii.
[2] See, for instance, the passage already quoted, pp. 220–1.
[3] *Das Buch Henoch*, S. 325.

would probably have added some further epithet to explain its meaning.

The case is different in Fourth Ezra; for there, in the first passage in which the title occurs, the addition of the word 'Messiah' removes the obscurity. Other circumstances, however, seem to me to excite a just suspicion that in this book also the term may be due to the tampering of Christian transcribers. In order to judge of this we must examine the passages one by one.

The first is in vii. 28, 29. In the Latin the text stands thus: 'For my Son Jesus will be revealed with those who are with him, and will rejoice those who have been left, for four hundred years. And it shall come to pass after these years, my Son Christ shall die, and all men who have breath.' Here the word 'Jesus' proves that a Christian hand has been at work, and raises the question whether the word 'Son' may not have been inserted in both verses. We turn, then, to the Syriac, and we find 'my son Messiah' in each verse; but here too the Christian copyist betrays himself by the change of 'four hundred' years into 'thirty.' The Æthiopic has in the first verse 'my Messiah,' without 'Son.' In the second verse it has 'my servant Messiah.' I am obliged to depend upon the Latin translation; but it is suggestive. Laurence's 'famulus' is corrected in Hilgenfeld's edition into 'puer.' This must no doubt represent the Greek παῖς, and this again answers to the Hebrew עֶבֶד, as in Isaiah xlii. 1, where עַבְדִּי is rendered by the LXX. ὁ παῖς μου. Παῖς, again, might easily be translated 'filius,' in which sense, whatever may be the case in the Book of Acts, it certainly seems to be used of Christ at a later time.[1] If this suggestion be correct, 'my Son' may

---

[1] Cf. Hippolytus, *Ref. Om. Hær.* x. 33, τὰ δὲ πάντα διοικεῖ ὁ λόγος ὁ θεοῦ, ὁ πρωτόγονος Πατρὸς παῖς.

represent ultimately the Hebrew עַבְדִּי 'my servant,' the author having very naturally adopted the LXX. rendering of a term which he would most probably apply to the Messiah. We should then have an exact parallel with the Apocalypse of Baruch, where we read 'my Messiah' in chapters xxxix., xl., and lxxii., and 'my servant Messiah' in lxx. The Æthiopic, however, is not without evidence of intentional alteration; for it omits the 'four hundred years.' The Arabic has 'my Son Messiah' in the first verse, but omits the second altogether. The Armenian also omits the second verse, and in the first has simply, 'then will appear the Anointed of God.'

The next passage is in xiii. 32, where the Latin has, 'Then shall be revealed my Son, whom thou didst see as a man ascending.' The Syriac and Arabic have the same reading; but the Æthiopic has, 'Then shall be revealed that man,' while the Armenian has, 'The Most High will appear with great strength; this is that man whom thou didst behold.' Here, then, we have two of the versions opposed to the reading of the other three. Again, in verse 37 the Latin has these words, 'But my Son himself will convict the nations which have come.' The Syriac and Arabic confirm this reading; but the Æthiopic has, 'He, therefore, is that Son who will convict the peoples of their sins,' where the expression 'that Son' is so devoid of meaning that one must suppose the original to have been, 'He, then, it is who will convict.' This conjecture is confirmed by the Armenian, which simply carries on the previous nominative, 'he.' The expression recurs in verse 52, where the Latin reads, 'No one upon earth will be able to see my Son, or those who are with him, except in the time of the day [appointed].' The Syriac alone follows exactly the same reading. The Æthiopic has, 'None of those who are in the earth can have knowledge of the Son,' (or according to some manuscripts, 'the Son of man,') which has certainly a Christian sound about it. The Arabic has another variation, 'No one upon earth can see the mystery of my Son, since his works are marvellous, except in the time of his days.' The Armenian exhibits a totally different reading, 'No one upon earth will be able to learn or to know the thoughts of the Most High, except in the time of his glorious revelation.'

Lastly, in xiv. 9 the Latin has these words, 'For thou shalt be received from men, and shalt dwell the rest of the time with my Son, and with those who are like thee, until the times be finished.' This is confirmed by the Syriac, Æthiopic, and Arabic; but in the Æthiopic several manuscripts read, ' my sons.' The Armenian has, 'shalt be with me.'

It thus appears that in the six instances the Latin, Syriac, and Arabic are in substantial agreement, except that the Arabic omits one of the verses. On the other hand, the Armenian in not a single instance sanctions the reading ' my Son,' and the Æthiopic adopts the reading 'Son' in only three cases, and in two of these it has a not unimportant variation from the Latin. If, therefore, we looked only to the number of authorities, we should have to admit the genuineness of the words. But how can we explain the total silence of the Armenian and the partial silence of the Æthiopic? Such words were not likely to be omitted or altered; whereas, considering the evident traces of Christian revision, we could not be surprised at their insertion. When we add to this uncertainty of text the possibility that, if in any instances the word 'Son' be not an interpolation, it may only represent the Greek παῖς in the sense of 'servant,' we cannot attach much weight to the evidence afforded by

Fourth Ezra that the Jews applied to their Messiah the title of 'Son of God.'

This exhausts the testimonies in favour of the use of the title. In opposition to them an explicit statement of Origen's may be quoted. He says, 'A Jew would not confess that any prophet said that God's Son would come; for what they say is that the Christ of God will come. And often they raise questions against us about the Son of God, as though no such person existed or had been prophesied.'[1]

Among the personal names ascribed to the Messiah, about which the Rabbis differed, may be mentioned Shiloh, Menachem the son of Chizqiyyah, and Yinnon. The last is derived from Psalm lxxii. 17, 'As long as the sun remains, *his name shall flourish*' [ינון שמו], or, '*his name is Yinnon.*'[2]

In connection with this part of our subject we may notice a few titles which are applied to the Israelites as the people of God, and which remind us of Christian phraseology in relation to Christ. In the Sibylline Oracles those who are to enjoy the final blessedness are called 'sons of the great God.'[3] In the Psalms of Solomon it is said, 'they are all sons of their God;'[4] and again, 'thy love is on the seed of Abraham, the sons of Israel, and thy correction is upon us as a first-born only-begotten son.'[5] In the Assumption of Moses, also, the Israelites are spoken of as the 'sons of God.'[6] In the Book of Jubilees we find these words, 'I will be their father, and they shall be my son, and shall all be named sons of God;'[7] and again, 'I have chosen the seed of

---

[1] *Cont. Celsum*, i. 40.
[2] *Bab. Tal. Synhed.* 98b.
[3] iii. 702.
[4] xvii. 30.
[5] xviii. 4, ὡς υἱὸν πρωτότοκον μονογενῆ.
[6] x. 27.
[7] Ch. i. S. 233. See also ch. xv. S. 10.

Jacob, . . . and have written it down as my first-born son, and hallowed it to me for ever and ever.'[1] Fourth Ezra repeats the language of the Psalms of Solomon,— 'We are thy people whom thou didst honour, and call first-born and only-begotten.'[2] These instances are not, it is true, very numerous; but they may be sufficient to show that the Jews, about the time of Christ, if they thought it impious to apply such exalted language to a particular individual, saw no impropriety in using it both collectively and distributively of the chosen race. Those who regarded the Messiah as the promised seed would not shrink from its more limited application.

[1] Ch. ii. S. 235. See also ch. xix., S. 16.
[2] vi. 58. Compare Ex. iv. 22, 'Thou shalt say unto Pharaoh, Thus saith the Lord, Israel is my son, even my first-born.' See also Deut. xiv. 1.

CHAPTER XI.

THE NATURE OF THE MESSIAH.

IN our inquiry into the nature of the Messiah we may start from the very explicit statement of Justin Martyr, which undoubtedly represents the prevailing view. He puts these words into the mouth of Tryphon the Jew,— 'We all expect that the Christ will come into being as a man from men.'[1]

Certain authorities, however, are alleged as indicating the existence of a different opinion. Gfrörer appeals to a few passages in the LXX. to show that the translators believed in the pre-existence of the Messiah. The first is Psalm lxxi. 5: συμπαραμενεῖ τῷ ἡλίῳ, καὶ πρὸ τῆς σελήνης γενεὰς γενεῶν, which he strangely translates, 'He will live as long as the sun, he was already in existence before the moon, and endures from generation to generation.'[2] Even if the meaning were not determined by the Hebrew לִפְנֵי יָרֵחַ, it would be obvious that the πρό must refer to place, and not to time. Again, in Psalm cix. 3 the Greek version, deviating from the Hebrew, reads, ἐκ γαστρὸς πρὸ ἑωσφόρου ἐγέννησά σε. The expression is a very strange one. The addition of ἐκ γαστρός shows that we must understand the begetting in quite a figurative sense; and the translators may have

---

[1] *Dial.* ch. 40, ἄνθρωπον ἐξ ἀνθρώπων.
[2] 'Er wird so lange leben als die Sonne, er war schon vor dem Monde und dauert von Geschlecht zu Geschlecht.'

thought only of an ideal pre-existence. The last passage is in Isaiah ix. 6, 'Unto us a child was born, ... and his name is called μεγάλης βουλῆς ἄγγελος.' Gfrörer regards this as a statement that the Messiah was 'the angel of the great (heavenly) council, one of the rulers above.' But in order to arrive at this meaning Gfrörer, though professedly quoting the Greek continuously, quietly leaves out καὶ καλεῖται τὸ ὄνομα αὐτοῦ, thus bringing ἄγγελος into apposition with παιδίον, and changing it from a title of honour into a description of the child's nature.[1] I think, therefore, that, in the absence of other evidence, this appeal to the LXX. is not very convincing.

An expression in the Sibylline Oracles III. 652, might seem at first sight to point to a supernatural Messiah,—'Then from the sun [ἀπ' ἠελίοιο] will God send a king.' But this expression 'from the sun' may either denote 'from the east,' or be used figuratively to indicate the splendour of the Messiah's appearance and its providential character. In line 286 it is said, in reference to Cyrus, 'then God will send a king from heaven [οὐρανόθεν];' and in 745 and following lines, honey and fruits, flocks and herds are characterised as 'from heaven.' These examples show that we must not press too closely the exalted language of the would-be prophetess; and if the writer expected the Messiah literally to descend from the sun, he could hardly have failed to describe his advent and his work with greater elaboration.

In the Book of Enoch, if we reject the Similitudes, there is nothing to suggest a supernatural character in the Messiah. He appears indeed among the sheep, in the historical vision, as a 'white bull;'[2] but this signifies nothing more than a return to the primitive greatness of

---

[1] See *Jahrh. des Heils*, ii. S. 295-6. [2] xc. 37.

man, as we learn by reference to the first part of the vision; and all the beasts and birds are accordingly changed into white bulls. The Messiah is distinguished only by his size, and by his great black horns. It is expressly said that he 'was born,' evidently in the usual course, and there is no allusion, as in some later books, to his being 'revealed,' as though from some mysterious hiding-place. It is clear, therefore, that his nature is regarded as simply human.

The Psalms of Solomon contain a far fuller and more interesting portrait of the Messiah. He is to be a son of David, a righteous king taught by God, the anointed of the Lord. He will not place his trust in horse and bow, or multiply gold and silver for war; but his hope will be in God, and he will smite the earth with the word of his mouth. He will be pure from sin, strong in the Holy Spirit, and wise in counsel, with strength and righteousness. He will be mighty in the fear of God, feed the flock of the Lord in faith and righteousness, and lead them all in holiness. This is the beauty of the king of Israel. His words are as words of saints in the midst of sanctified peoples.[1] In this description there is nothing that transcends the human. The Messiah is simply one of the house of David, richly endowed for his high office.

The 'pure king' [ἁγνὸς ἄναξ] of the later Sibyl,[2] though the delineation is not finished, suggests to us a ruler of the same kind. In the pre-Christian books, therefore, we have no certain traces of a supernatural or pre-existent Messiah.

Fourth Ezra is believed by some to give no doubtful expression to the doctrine of the Messiah's pre-existence.[3]

---

[1] xvii. 23, 35–49. [2] iii. 49.
[3] See Gfrörer, *Jahrh. d. H.* ii. S. 295, and Schürer, *Lehrb. d. n. Zeitg.* S. 584.

First, appeal is made to xii. 32 and xiii. 26, in which the Messiah is spoken of as kept or reserved [reservavit, conservat] unto the end.¹ That this 'reserving' of the Messiah was intended to imply his personal existence may be inferred from xiv. 9, where it is said to Ezra, 'Thou shalt be received from men, and live the rest of the time with my Son, and those who are like thee, until the times be ended.' We have seen reason, however, to doubt the genuineness of this reading, the Armenian having 'with me' instead of 'with my Son,' and several Æthiopic manuscripts having 'with my sons.' A similar uncertainty rests upon xiii. 52, where the concealment of the Messiah is supposed to be taught. The statement that the Messiah 'shall be revealed,'² seems to involve the same idea. With this last we may compare the passages in the Apocalypse of Baruch where the same term is used.³ It seems to me, however, that the idea of the Messiah's concealment, of which we have already spoken, contains the key to all the passages to which reference is made. If the ordinary reading be genuine, still they do not bring before us a supernatural Messiah, but only imply the belief that he should be withdrawn after his birth into a place of concealment, from which he should return when the proper time arrived for his revelation. Ezra was to be not only with the Messiah, but with others like himself, including no doubt Enoch, Moses, and Elijah. In the same way Baruch was to depart from the earth, but not to death; he too was to be reserved till the end of times.⁴ This kind of pre-existence was a necessity of thought to those who expected the Messiah to appear

¹ The Arm. reads in both instances *mittet*. We may, however, allow the majority of versions to be decisive in the present case.
² vii. 28.   ³ Chs. xxix. and xxxix.
⁴ *Apoc. of Bar.* chs. xiii. and lxxvi.

immediately as a triumphant king; but there is nothing in it inconsistent with the possibilities which they ascribe to human nature; and the fact that the writer of Fourth Ezra makes the Messiah die like all other men, shows that the qualities which he attributed to him, however marvellous, were not in his judgment beyond the attainment of saintly men.

The Targums have only faint and dubious traces of anything transcending the human in the Messiah. It is said in several passages[1] that he shall be 'revealed,' perhaps in the sense just explained, and in Micah v. 1, that 'his name is spoken of from of old, from the days of eternity.' The latter statement need not imply more than an existence in the purposes of God and in prophecy; and indeed it may seem to have been the express purpose of the Targumist to convey this idea by his change of the original, 'his goings forth,' into 'his name is spoken of.' The Targum of Isaiah ix. 5 has been sometimes thought to imply a more exalted nature. This is translated by Young as follows:—'To us a child is born, to us a son is given, and he shall receive the law upon him to keep it, and his name is called from eternity Wonderful, Counsellor, Mighty God, Continuing for ever, The Messiah; for peace shall be multiplied upon us in his days.'[2] מן־קדם, however, which Young translates 'from eternity,' commonly means 'from before' a person.[3] The Targum may therefore be translated thus:—'his name is called (before him who is wonderful in counsel, the

---

[1] Jer. xxx. 21; Zech. iii. 8; iv. 7; vi. 12; *Pseudo-Jon.* Gen. xxxv. 21; Cant. viii. 1.

[2] *Christol. of Targ.* p. 23.

[3] See for examples of its use Dan. ii. 6, 15; v. 24; vi. 27; vii. 10; Targ. Isai. x. 27; liii. 10; Jer. xviii. 5, &c. In Micah iv. 8, it means 'on account of.' For the sense ascribed to it by Young the Targum uses מלקדמין, as in Micah v. 1.

mighty God, continuing for ever,) Messiah.' This rendering is considered the more probable by Oehler;[1] and as there is nothing answering to מִקֶּדֶם in the Hebrew original, we can hardly avoid supposing that the Targumist inserted this phrase with the distinct intention of removing from the Messiah a series of epithets which appeared unduly exalted. Elsewhere the Targums represent the Messiah simply as a human king, of the house of David.

The Talmud also brings before us a human Messiah, one indeed who may appear 'unexpectedly,'[2] and whose reign shall last far beyond the natural term of human life,[3] but not separated in nature from the race which he is to bless.

The more mystical view of the Messiah belongs to later books, and cannot be here noticed. Whatever germs of it may appear in the works which we have examined, we have found nothing to set aside the emphatic testimony with which this chapter opened.

---

[1] Herzog, *Messias*, S. 437.   [2] *Synh.* 97a.
[3] Ibid., to be noticed farther on.

CHAPTER XII.

THE LAST ENEMIES.

ON the appearance of the Messiah the enemies of the Israelites and of God will muster their forces for a last decisive conflict. The picture which Ezekiel drew of the armies of Gog and their destruction, and the representation given by the writer of Daniel of the terrible invasion by Antiochus Epiphanes, are abundantly reproduced in the literature which we are reviewing.

The Sibylline Oracles, having mentioned the God-sent king, proceed thus :—'But the people of the great God shall again be loaded with very beautiful riches, with gold and silver and purple adornment; and the earth shall be fruitful, and the sea full of good things. And kings shall begin to be angry with one another, cherishing evil in their soul—envy is not a good thing for wretched mortals. But again kings of the Gentiles will hasten in crowds against this land, bringing doom upon themselves. For they will wish to destroy the shrine of the great God, and the best men. When they have come to the land, polluted kings will sacrifice around the city, each having his throne and a people disobedient [to God].'[1]

The Book of Enoch also anticipates a combined assault of all the hostile powers prior to the establishment of the final blessedness. It, however, introduces the Messiah after the destruction of the enemies, and re-

[1] iii. 657-668.

presents the attack as being made on one of the sheep with a great horn, probably John Hyrcanus. 'All the eagles,' it says, 'and vultures and ravens and kites [*i.e.* the various heathen adversaries] assembled themselves, and brought with them all the sheep of the field [*i.e.* apostate Israelites, the Hellenizing party of the time], and they all came with one another, and in combination helped to break that horn of the young [sheep].'[1]

In Fourth Ezra a similar event is described in the vision of the man ascending from the sea:—' I saw afterwards, and lo, an innumerable multitude of men assembled from the four winds of heaven, to war against the man who had ascended from the sea.'[2] This circumstance is fully explained in the interpretation of the vision:—' Some will think to wage war against others, state against state, and place against place, and nation against nation, and kingdom against kingdom. And it shall come to pass, when these things take place, and the signs happen which I have shown thee before, then shall be revealed my Son, whom thou didst see as a man ascending. And it shall come to pass, when all nations have heard his voice, each will leave in its own region the war which they have against one another; and there shall be assembled together an innumerable multitude, as thou didst see, wishing to come and take him by storm.'[3]

The Targums contain abundant allusions to this expectation; but as the passages for the most part are not easily separated from their context, it will be best to reserve them till we speak of the overthrow of the enemies by the hands of the Messiah. We may, however, refer in this connection to Psalm ii. 2, which, even without the slight expansion of the Targum, sufficiently indicates

---

[1] xc. 16   [2] xiii. 5.   [3] xiii. 31-34.

the uprising and combination of the Gentile kings against the Messiah.

It was sometimes supposed that these enemies were to be commanded by one great leader, the Antichrist, who was to be the impersonation of the world's antagonism to God. One of the earliest passages relating to this subject is found in the Sibylline Oracles, III. 63–74. It is, however, doubtful whether these verses can be safely referred to the time of the second triumvirs, because the derivation of Beliar from the line of Augustus points to a date subsequent to the reign of Nero. Hilgenfeld, accordingly, supposes that they do not belong to the connection in which they are at present found.[1] Gfrörer, following the suggestion of Bleek, escapes from the difficulty by omitting two lines, and thus bringing the first part of 61 into connection with the end of 63, and inserting κατὰ γῆν to fill up the metre, thus :—πᾶσιν ἐν ἀνθρώποις [κατὰ γῆν] Βελίαρ μετόπισθεν.[2] This is rather a violent remedy; and considering the fragmentary character of the opening of this book, we cannot but regard Hilgenfeld's conjecture as the more probable. Friedlieb, indeed, understands by Σεβαστηνῶν simply the Roman rulers,[3] but does not explain how such a term could have been used before the assumption of the title of Augustus. In accordance with this view he thinks the author must have meant by Beliar either Antonius or one of his contemporaries. Leaving these questions undecided, we may quote the passage as representing one view of the last adversary :—
'From the line of Augustus will afterwards come Beliar, and he will set the height of the mountains, and set the sea, the great fiery sun and brilliant moon, and he will set [raise up] corpses, and perform many signs for men.

---

[1] *Jüd. Apok.* S. 241, Anm. 2. [2] *Philo u. d. al. Theos.*, ii. S. 134-5.
[3] Einleit. S. xxvi.

But there will be in him no completion, but [only] error; and he will lead astray many men, both faithful and elect Hebrews,¹ and lawless men and others who have not yet heard the word of God. But when the threats of the great God draw near, and flaming power shall come with swelling flood upon the earth, he will burn both Beliar and all haughty men, as many as reposed faith in him.'

In the Apocalypse of Baruch a 'last leader' is mentioned, though without having a name assigned to him, who, after the destruction of his armies, shall be brought bound to Mount Zion, and there convicted by the Messiah of all his impious deeds, and put to death.²

In the Targums and the Talmud Gog and Magog appear so often as the last enemies of the chosen people that it is unnecessary to cite particular passages. Some of them will be referred to farther on. Another monster named Armilûs,³ or Armilaus, is mentioned in the Targum of Isaiah xi. 4, as one who shall be slain by the Messiah by the word of his mouth. According to the later notions this adversary was to appear after Gog and Magog, as the leader of the Christian forces. He was to triumph over and slay the Messiah ben Ephraim (who will be spoken of farther on), but was finally to be destroyed by the Messiah ben David. Philip Aquinas derived his name from the Greek ἐρημόλαος.⁴ Gfrörer, accepting this derivation, regards the name as the equivalent of Balaam, בִּלְעָם, which he derives from בֶּלַע עָם, a devouring of the people. Balaam, as the adversary of Moses, is, in his opinion, one of the types of Antichrist.⁵

From the dangers which will thus gather round them

---

¹ Cf. Matt. xxiv. 24.   ² Ch. xl.   ³ אַרְמִילוֹס.
⁴ See Buxtorf, *Lex. Chal. Talm. and Rab.* sub voc.
⁵ *Jahrh. d. H.* ii. S. 401 sq. 'This has been earlier and better said by the Rabbis (Tal. Bab. *Synh.* 105a. Cf. the reading of 'Arukh, s. v.).'— Dr. Schiller-Szinessy.

the Israelites are to be delivered by the signal destruction of their foes. This destruction is fully related in the Sibylline Oracles. Here the Messiah is not introduced, and the overthrow is ascribed to the immediate agency of God alone; but as the attack is provoked by the appearance of the Messiah, and the consequent prosperity of his people, it is not unreasonable to suppose that he was regarded as the occasion of the divine interference. The Sibyl's description is as follows:—'God will speak with a great voice to all the uninstructed, empty-minded people, and judgment shall come upon them from the great God, and all shall perish by the immortal hand. And from heaven shall fall fiery swords to earth, and great torches shall come, shining into the midst of men. And the all-producing earth shall be shaken in those days by the immortal hand; and the fishes in the sea, and all the beasts of the earth, and the countless tribes of birds, and all souls of men, and all the sea shall shudder with awe before the immortal face, and fear shall be [upon them]. He will break lofty peaks, and heights of huge mountains, and dark Erebus shall appear to all. And misty ravines in the high mountains shall be full of corpses; and rocks shall stream with blood, and the whole torrent fill the plain. And all the well-built walls of ill-disposed men shall fall to the ground, because they knew not the law, nor the judgment of the great God; but with senseless mind, all rushing to the attack, ye lifted spears against the temple. And God will judge all by war, and sword, and fire, and deluging rain. And brimstone shall fall from heaven, and stone, and hail abundant and dreadful; and death shall be on four-footed animals. And then shall they know the immortal God, who judges in this way. And groaning and lamentation of perishing men shall come upon the boundless earth; and all, speechless, shall bathe in blood; and the earth itself shall drink of the blood of the perishing, and the wild beasts shall glut themselves with flesh.'[1] Farther on it is said that the faithful will gather the arms of the enemies for seven years, and have no need to cut firewood in the forest.[2]

The Book of Enoch also predicts a terrible destruction for the assembled enemies of Israel; but, as has been already observed, it places this portion of the final drama before the appearance of the Messiah. The following passage is the continuation of the one last quoted from this work:—'And I saw that man who wrote the book according to the commandment of the Lord, until he opened that book of the destruction which the last twelve shepherds had inflicted, and showed that they had destroyed far more than their predecessors, before the Lord of the sheep. And I beheld until the Lord of the sheep came to them, and took the rod of anger in his hand, and smote the earth so that it rent, and all the beasts and the birds of heaven fell away from the sheep, and sank in the earth, and it closed over them. And I beheld until a great sword was given to the sheep, when the sheep marched out against those beasts of the field to slay them, and all the beasts and the birds of heaven fled before their face.'[3] One or two other passages must be quoted, which refer to these final catastrophes, and which show how deeply the spirit of revenge was eating into the heart of at least a portion of the people:—'Woe unto you who love the works of unrighteousness; why do you hope good for yourselves? Know that you shall be given into the hands of the righteous; they shall cut off your necks, and slay you, and have no pity on you.'[4]

---

[1] iii. 669-697.

[2] 727-731. As the text stands, this action is ascribed to the converted Gentiles; but I can hardly help suspecting that these lines are misplaced.

[3] xc. 17-19.   [4] xcviii. 12.

'Again I swear unto you sinners, that sin is ready for a day of ceaseless bloodshed.'[1] 'Woe to those who do unrighteousness, and help violence, and slay their neighbour, until the day of the great judgment; for he will cast down your glory, and lay to heart your wickedness, and stir up the spirit of his wrath, that he may destroy you all with the sword; and all righteous and holy beings will remember your sin. And in those days shall fathers be slain along with their sons in one place, and brothers shall fall with one another in death, until their blood streams like a river. For a man will not compassionately withhold his hand from his sons and from his grandsons, to slay them; and the sinner will not withhold his hand from his most honoured brother; from the blush of morning till sunset will they kill one another. And the horse shall walk up to its breast in blood, and the chariot sink up to its top.'[2]

The Psalms of Solomon breath a much less sanguinary spirit. Under the Messiah Jerusalem is indeed to be purified from the Gentiles, and sinners to be thrust away from the inheritance; but he will not have recourse to instruments of war, but smite the earth, and destroy lawless nations, 'by the word of his mouth.'[3]

Philo, too, as we might expect from a philosophical Alexandrine, hopes for a milder solution of the evils of war. First of all, the wild beasts are to lay aside their ferocity; and then men, endowed as they are with reason, will be ashamed to be more savage than irrational animals. But if any, insanely yielding to the passion for war, indulge in the rage of battle, they shall find that they make an empty boast; for they shall be chased in various directions, and some, though none pursues, will turn their backs in terror upon their foes. For a man

[1] xcix. 6. [2] xcix. 15–c. 3. [3] xvii. 25–27, 37, 39.

shall go forth, says the oracle, who shall subdue great and populous nations. But some of the enemies, Scripture says,[1] will be unworthy of being defeated by men, and shall be destroyed in the most disgraceful way by swarms of wasps, which will war on behalf of the saints; and thus a bloodless victory will be obtained.[2]

The Book of Jubilees is no less explicit upon this point:—'In that time the Lord will heal his servants, and they shall lift themselves up, and shall see ever more a deep peace, and again pursue their enemies. And they shall see it, and give thanks, and rejoice with joy for ever. And they shall see upon their enemies all their penal judgments and all their curse.'[3]

The post-Christian Sibyl, taking a milder view, allows at least an opportunity of repentance :—' Wretched mortals, repent of these things, and bring not the great God to all kinds of anger; but, having put away swords, and groanings, and slaughters, and insults, wash your whole body in perennial rivers, and stretching forth your hands to the sky ask pardon for your past works, and heal your bitter impiety with acts of piety. . . . But if, of evil mind, you do not obey me, but loving impiety receive all these things with evil ears, there shall be fire through the whole earth, and a very great sign, swords, trumpets, at the rising of the sun. All the world shall hear a roar and tremendous sound, and he will burn all the earth, and destroy all the race of men, and burn up all cities and rivers and seas together; all these things shall be burnt-out ashes.'[4] I quote this passage here as presenting a different view from that of most of our authorities. Not only does the Messiah not appear, but there is nothing to show that Israel is not included in these

---

[1] Ex. xxiii. 28: Deut. vii. 20.
[2] *De Præmiis et Pœnis*, § 16.
[3] Ch. xxiii.
[4] iv. 161–177.

world-wide threats. The destruction of the world by fire is moreover placed immediately before the resurrection and judgment, thus leaving no room for the Messianic reign, at least within the bounds of the present age.

In Fourth Ezra we find the fullest account of the Israelitish triumph combined with its direct ascription to the Messiah. This victory is predicted first in the historical vision of the eagle, in which a lion comes and rebukes the eagle for all its wickedness, and, while he speaks, the remaining head and wings disappear, and the whole body of the eagle is burned. Of this occurrence the following explanation is given:—' The lion which thou didst see roused up from the forest, and roaring, and speaking to the eagle, and convicting it and its deeds of injustice, by means of all its words as thou didst hear,—this is the Anointed whom the Most High reserved unto the end of days, who will arise from the seed of David, and come and speak to them, and according to their impious deeds will convict them, and will rebuke them for their wickedness, and heap up retribution before them. For he will set them alive in judgment; and it shall come to pass, when he has convicted them, then he will destroy them.'[1] In the vision of the man ascending out of the sea, the idea which we have already met in the Psalms of Solomon is repeated with greater elaboration. Ezra saw the man carving out a great mountain for himself, and flying upon it, but was unable to discover the region from which the mountain had been carved. Then 'all who were assembled against him, to take him by storm, were greatly afraid; nevertheless they ventured to fight. And lo! when he saw the assault of the coming multitude, he did not lift his hand, nor hold a spear or any

[1] xii. 31–33. I have not followed quite verbally any single version; but the general sense is the same in all.

implement of war, but I only saw how he sent out of his mouth as it were a wave of fire, and from his lips spirits of flame, and from his tongue he emitted sparks of tempest; and all these were mingled together, waves of fire and spirits of flame and a multitude of tempest. And he fell upon the multitude which was ready for the assault, and burned them all, so that suddenly nothing was perceived of the innumerable multitude, save only dust of ashes and an odour of smoke.'[1] The following explanation is given:—'But he himself will stand upon the summit of Mount Zion. And Zion shall come and be shown to all, prepared and built, as thou didst see a mountain carved without hands. But he [or, my Son] himself will convict of their impiety the nations which have come—those nations which were likened unto a storm—and will array before them their evil works, and the tortures with which they are to be tortured, which were like a flame, and he will destroy them without trouble by the law, which was like fire.'[2]

The Apocalypse of Baruch conveys the same idea under a different figure. As Baruch sat lamenting among the ruins of Jerusalem, he fell asleep, and had a vision. 'Lo! a forest of trees planted in a plain; lofty mountains and steep rocks surrounded it, and the forest occupied much room. And lo! opposite to it a vine grew up, and from beneath it tranquilly came forth a fountain. But that fountain came to the forest, and was made into great waves, and the waves inundated the forest, and suddenly rooted up a multitude of that forest, and overturned all the mountains around it. And the height of the forest was brought down, and the top of the mountains was made low, and the fountain greatly prevailed, so that it did not leave anything of that multitudinous forest except

[1] xiii. 6-11.   [2] xiii. 35-38.

one cedar only. When it had thrown down even this, and had destroyed and rooted up the multitude of that forest, so that nothing was left of it, and its place was not known, then that vine itself came with the fountain in great quietness and tranquillity, and came up to a place which was not far from the cedar; and the overthrown cedar was brought to it. And I saw, and lo! that vine opened its mouth, and spoke and said to the cedar, "Art not thou the cedar which has been left of the forest of wickedness? And in thy hand wickedness was persevering, and was exercised all these years, and goodness never. And thou didst grow powerful upon that which was not thine, nor didst thou ever feel pity upon that which was thine, and thou didst extend thy power over those who were far from thee, and those who drew near to thee thou didst detain in the nets of thy impiety, and didst always lift up thy soul as one that could not be rooted out. But now thy time has hastened, and thy hour is come. Go, therefore, even thou, O cedar, after the forest which has gone away in thy presence, and become with it dust, and let your earth be mingled together. And lie ye down now in distress, and rest ye in torment, until thy last time arrive, in which thou shalt come again, and be more tormented." And after these things I saw that cedar burning, and the vine growing, itself and all that was around it, a plain full of unfading flowers.' An interpretation of this vision was vouchsafed in answer to Baruch's prayers. The kingdom which formerly destroyed Zion [the Babylonian] should be itself destroyed, and made subject to one [the Medo-Persian] that should come after it. Again, that also should be destroyed after a time, and a third [the Greek] should arise, and rule for its time, and be destroyed. And afterwards a fourth kingdom [the Roman] should arise, whose power should be harder and more oppressive than those which went before it; and it should rule for a long time, and be lifted up more than the cedars of Lebanon. And all the wicked should fly to it, as wild beasts creep into the forest. 'And it shall come to pass, when the time of its end, that it should fall, shall have approached, then shall be revealed the dominion of my Messiah, who is like a fountain and a vine; and when he has been revealed, he will root out the multitude of its assembly. And as for the fact that thou didst see a lofty cedar which was left of that forest, and that the vine spoke with it words which thou didst hear, this is the explanation: the last leader who shall be left alive when the multitude of his assembly is destroyed, shall be bound, and they shall bring him to Mount Zion, and my Messiah will convict him of all his impious deeds, and will collect and set in his sight all the works of his hosts. And afterwards he will slay him, and will protect the rest of my people who shall be found in the place which I have chosen. And his dominion shall stand for ever, until the world of corruption be ended, and until the predicted times be fulfilled.'[1]

The Targumists also believe in the final destruction of the enemies of Israel. According to the view presented in one passage, God will destroy them, and take vengeance on Magog, and so magnify the kingdom of the Messiah.[2] Elsewhere Edom, or Rome, is threatened with destruction at the hands of the Persians.[3] Pseudo-Jonathan represents the Messiah as a king of the house of Judah, who shall wage war against his enemies, slaughter kings and rulers, and redden the mountains with blood.[4] He takes advantage of the prophecy of

[1] Chs. xxxv.–xl.
[2] 1 Sam. ii. 10.
[3] Lam. iv. 22.
[4] Gen. xlix. 11.

Balaam to enlarge on the same subject. The Moabites and Amalekites, Gog and all the children of the east, shall perish for ever; and the ships of war from Lombardy and Italy, and the legions from Constantinople, shall fall by the hand of king Messiah.[1]

Such were the hopes with which an oppressed and persecuted people consoled their misery. In the diviner providence of history their enemies are being gradually vanquished, and turned into friends, by the world-wide humanity and compassion of a far different Messiah.

[1] Num. xxiv. 17-20, 24.

CHAPTER XIII.

GENERAL CHARACTER OF THE MESSIANIC REIGN.

It now devolves upon us to look at the Messiah in the exercise of the sovereignty which is to be established by the overthrow of his enemies. But before proceeding to the discussion of the various questions which arise in connection with this subject, we may briefly survey the general character of his government.

We have already quoted the short notice in the Sibylline Oracles,[1] and have seen that, according to the view there presented, the Messiah is to establish a universal peace, relying, not on his own counsels, but on the commandments of God. We have also seen the character of the king as pourtrayed in the Psalms of Solomon. We have only to add a few words as to the nature of his kingly office. He is to 'rule over Israel,'[2] and to 'judge the tribes of a people sanctified by the Lord his God.'[3] He is to 'tend the flock of the Lord in faith and righteousness, and not suffer any to be infirm among them in their pasture.'[4] 'No stranger and foreigner shall dwell any more among them. He will judge peoples and Gentiles in the wisdom of his righteousness; and he shall have peoples of the Gentiles to serve beneath his yoke,'[5] and Gentiles will come from the extremity of the earth

---

[1] iii. 652-656. [2] xvii. 23.
[3] xvii. 28. [4] xvii. 45. [5] xvii. 31, 32.

to see his glory.¹ Thus 'he will bless the people of the Lord in wisdom with gladness.'²

Fourth Ezra notices in the briefest way the relation of the Messiah to the Jews:—'He will liberate with compassion the rest of my people, who have been saved upon my boundaries, and will gladden them until the end come, the day of judgment of which I spoke to thee from the beginning.'³ In the Apocalypse of Baruch it is said that he will preserve alive every people that does not know Israel, and has not trodden down the seed of Jacob; that all nations shall be subjected to Israel; and that when the Messiah has humbled whatever is in the earth, he will sit in peace upon the throne of his kingdom.⁴

The character of the Messiah's rule is very clearly indicated in the Targums. He is to be 'a king,' who 'shall hereafter rise and rule in the fear of the Lord.'⁵ He 'shall prepare his throne in goodness, and shall sit upon it in truth, in the city of David, judging and seeking judgment, and executing truth.'⁶ He 'shall reign and prosper, and execute the judgment of truth and righteousness in the earth. In his days they who are of the house of Judah shall be saved, and Israel shall dwell safely.'⁷ And 'they shall bring tribute to the Messiah of Israel, who shall have dominion over those who are in the wilderness.'⁸

Gfrörer appeals to the Targum of Zechariah, vi. 12, 13, as an evidence that in one view the regal and priestly offices were to be united in the Messiah.⁹ I think, however, that his translation is open to question, and it would have been more satisfactory if he had given the

---

¹ xvii. 34.   ² xvii. 40.
³ xii. 34. See also vii. 28, where the same expression, *jucundabit*, is used.
⁴ Chs. lxxii., lxxiii.   ⁵ 2 Sam. xxiii. 3.
⁶ Isai. xvi. 5.   ⁷ Jer. xxiii. 5.
⁸ Isai. xvi. 1.   ⁹ *Jahrh. d. II.* ii, S. 345.

whole passage. He renders thus :—' "Behold, a man, Messiah is his name—he shall sit upon his throne and rule (as king), also he shall be a high priest upon his throne" and so on.' Without omissions the text stands thus :—' Behold, a man, Messiah is his name, who shall hereafter be revealed and magnified, and build the temple of the Lord. For he shall build the temple of the Lord, and shall bear the weapon [sceptre], and shall sit and rule on his throne; and there shall be a high priest by his throne, and the counsel of peace shall be between them both.' The concluding words, which adhere closely to the original Hebrew, show that two persons are intended; and if this be so, the Messiah is expressly distinguished from the priest. The words which I have translated, 'there shall be a high priest by his throne,' ויהי כהן רב על כסאוהי, would of course admit of the other rendering; but the added words, omitted by Gfrörer, appear, both here and in the original, to be decisive.

CHAPTER XIV.

PLACE, EXTENT, AND DURATION OF THE MESSIAH'S KINGDOM.

JERUSALEM is invariably regarded as the centre of the future kingdom. 'The sons of the great God,' says the Sibyl, 'shall all live quietly around the temple;'[1] and again, 'From all the earth shall they bear frankincense and gifts to the houses of the great God; and there shall be no other house among future men in which to enquire, but only that which God gave to faithful men to honour.'[2] In the Book of Enoch it is implied that the white bull will live in the house of the Lord, that is, Jerusalem,[3] and if this is to be 'a new house,' it is expressly stated that it will be in the same place as the first.[4] In the Messianic picture in the Psalms of Solomon, again, Jerusalem occupies the foremost place.[5] Psalm xi. is devoted to the glory of Jerusalem as the place to which its children shall come with joy from east and west, from the north and the distant isles :—' Put on, O Jerusalem, the garments of thy glory, make ready the robe of thy sanctuary; for God has spoken good concerning Israel for evermore.'[6] The Book of Jubilees, though without a Messiah, assigns an eternal pre-eminence to Jerusalem. One passage will suffice :—' Write it down for Moses from the first creation till the time when my sanctuary shall be built among

[1] iii. 702-3. [2] iii. 771-4. [3] xc. 36-7.
[4] xc. 29. [5] xvii. 25. [6] xi.

them for ever and ever, and God will appear to the eye of everyone, and everyone shall recognise that I am the God of Israel, and the Father of all the children of Jacob, and the King upon Mount Sion from eternity to eternity.'[1] We have already seen that Fourth Ezra and Baruch place the Messiah on Mount Zion; and the view of the Targumists has been illustrated by the passage recently quoted from Isaiah xvi. 5.

The extent and duration of the future kingdom are plainly stated in Daniel:—'There was given him dominion and glory and a kingdom, that all people, nations, and languages should serve him: his dominion is an everlasting dominion, which shall not pass away, and his kingdom that which shall not be destroyed.'[2] The same universality of dominion is probably implied in the passage already quoted from the Sibylline Oracles,[3] where it is said that they shall bring gifts 'from the whole earth;' and this, combined with eternal duration, is promised a few lines before:—'Then will he raise up a kingdom for ever over all men.'[4] The Book of Enoch likewise extends the power of the Messiah over 'all the beasts of the field and all the birds of heaven,' *i.e.* over all the heathen nations.[5] How far the time of eternal blessedness[6] is connected with the Messiah does not appear. The Psalms of Solomon also recognise the Messiah's sovereignty over Gentiles,[7] but in respect to the duration of his kingdom say vaguely, 'he will smite the earth with the word of his mouth for ever.'[8] The later Sibyl is no less wide-sweeping in her vision:—'A pure king shall come, to subdue the sceptres of all the earth unto all ages.'[9] The promise made to Jacob in the Book of Jubilees is to the same effect:—

[1] Ch. i. S. 233.   [2] vii. 14. See also ii. 44; vii. 18, 27.
[3] iii. 771.   [4] 766-7.   [5] xc. 30, 33, 37.
[6] xci. 17.   [7] xvii. 32, 34.   [8] xvii. 39   [9] iii. 49, 50.

'I am the Lord thy God, who has made heaven and earth. I will cause thee to grow, and multiply thee exceedingly, and kings shall go forth from thee, and shall rule everywhere, where only a foot of the children of men doth tread. And to thy seed will I give the whole earth which is under heaven, and they shall rule as they please over all peoples; and accordingly they shall draw the whole earth to themselves, and inherit it for ever.'[1] If the expressions relating to time in the above passages are to be construed literally, they present a different view from that of the later books, according to which the reign of the Messiah is to be of limited duration. The term 'for ever' does not, however, necessarily denote unending time, but may imply nothing more than unbroken continuance up to a natural and inevitable termination. We shall presently meet with an instance of this in the Apocalypse of Baruch. In Daniel and Enoch we need not hesitate to take the words in their more extended significance; for there the kingdom is represented as coming after the judgment, and as belonging therefore to the final and eternal order, and this is undoubtedly opposed to the prevailing view that the Messianic reign was to come before the judgment, and to fall within the present system of the world. In regard to the other books the question must remain undecided.

In Fourth Ezra the Messiah's reign is expressly limited to a period of four hundred years.[2] This number, indeed, occurs only in the Latin and Arabic; but the reasons for its omission or alteration in the other versions are so obvious that we can have no hesitation in accepting it as genuine, especially as it corresponds with one of the views held by the Rabbis. The origin of this limitation we shall see farther on. In the same passage it is

---

[1] Ch. xxxii. S. 42.   [2] vii. 28.

intimated that the Messiah's death will take place at the close of the present world. This terminal point of his reign is again mentioned in xii. 34. The Apocalypse of Baruch assigns the same limit to the Messianic rule, but without attributing to it any precise duration:—'his dominion shall stand for ever, until the world of corruption be ended.'[1] We must use this passage to limit the statement which is made farther on,[2] that he shall sit in peace for ever upon the throne of his kingdom. The world-wide character of his sovereignty is implied rather than affirmed in Ezra; but in Baruch it is expressly said that men of all nations shall be subjected to Israel, and that Messiah will humble whatever is in the world.[3]

The Targumists extend his power over 'all kingdoms,' or 'all the children of men.'[4]

An account of the different views held by the Rabbis as to the duration of his kingdom, and of the curious mode of Biblical interpretation on which these views were founded, is given in the Babylonian Talmud:[5]—'Rabbi Eli'ezer says, The days of the Messiah will be forty years, because it is said,[6] "forty years long was I grieved with this generation."' The applicability of this quotation depends on the principle that the blessedness under the Messiah must be an exact compensation for previous misery. This principle was founded on Psalm xc. 15, 'Make us glad according to the days wherein thou hast afflicted us, and the years wherein we have seen evil.' 'Rabbi El'azar ben 'Azaryah says, Seventy years, because it is written,[7] "It shall come to pass in that day, that Tyre shall be forgotten seventy years, according to the days of

---

[1] Ch. xl.   [2] lxxiii.   [3] Chs. lxxii., lxxiii.
[4] See Zech. iv. 7; Onkelos Num. xxiv. 17; Jerus. Gen. xlix. 10. In Micah v. 1, only Israel is referred to; but this is not inconsistent with a wider sway.
[5] *Synhedrin*, 99a.   [6] Ps. xcv. 10.   [7] Isai. xxiii. 15.

one king."' The king is, of course, the Messiah. 'Rabbi says, Three generations, as it is said,[1] "They shall fear thee as long as the sun and moon endure, from generation to generation."' The Hebrew of the last expression is דּוֹר דּוֹרִים, that is, according to the Rabbinical interpretation, one generation and two generations. . . . 'Rabbi Dosa says, Four hundred years, because it is written,[2] "They shall afflict them [the seed of Abraham] four hundred years."' This conclusion is founded on the principle of compensation already explained. 'Rabbi says, Three hundred and sixty five years, according to the number of the days of the sun, for the Scripture teaches,[3] "The day of vengeance is in mine heart, and the year of my redeemed is come."' Here, in Gfrörer's opinion, 'year,' being parallel to 'day,' must be equivalent to it, and therefore a divine day is equal to three hundred and sixty-five common days, and the divine year accordingly answers to three hundred and sixty-five ordinary years.[4] 'Abimi, the son of Rabbi Abuhu, teaches, The days of the Messiah for Israel are seven thousand years, because it is written,[5] "As the bridegroom rejoiceth over the bride, so shall thy God rejoice over thee."' The reasoning here is not very obvious; but no doubt Rashi (*in loco*)[6] gives the right solution: a marriage festival lasts for seven days, and one day of the Lord is a thousand years. 'Rab Yehudah says, Shemuel

---

[1] Ps. lxxii. 5. [2] Gen. xv. 13. [3] Isai. lxiii. 4.

[4] *Jahrh. d. II.* ii. S. 253. I owe to Dr. Schiller-Szinessy the old, and no doubt correct, explanation :—'The day is equivalent to a year because the Israelites were condemned to wander in the wilderness forty *years* for the forty *days* of the spies (Num. xiv. 34).' I learn from the same scholar that Rashi knew here of a reading 'thousand,' as God's day is a thousand years. What Rabbi here states is a different version of the same story, or he would contradict the opinion already ascribed to him.

[5] Isai. lxii. 5.

[6] For this reference I am indebted to Dr. Schiller-Szinessy. See also Gfrörer, S. 254.

says, The days of the Messiah are as many as from the time in which the world was created unto this time, as it is said,[1] "That your days may be multiplied, and the days of your children, in the land which the Lord sware unto your fathers to give them, as the days of heaven upon the earth." Rab Nachman bar Yitzchaq says, As from the days of Noah down to this time, for it is written,[2] "For this is as the days[3] of Noah unto me: for as I have sworn that the waters of Noah should no more go over the earth, so have I sworn that I would not be wroth with thee, nor rebuke thee."' Some other opinions are contained in an earlier passage of the same treatise,[4] which I have already quoted. We there learn that, in the opinion of Rab Qatina, there will be a thousand years of rest in the world's period of seven thousand years; and this millennium we may, no doubt, assign to the reign of the Messiah. The teacher of the house of Eliyyahu, however, allowed two thousand years to the Messiah. According to another opinion he was to come in the year of the creation 4291, and to reign, according to different views, till the year 5000, or till 7000, when the present world should come to an end. Equally fluctuating opinions on this subject are collected in a much later work, the Yalqut:[5]—'Rabbi Berekhyah says, in the name of Rabbi Chiyya, The days of the Messiah last six hundred years, because it is written,[6] "As the days of a tree are the days of my people." The Sedan[7] tree lasts six hundred years. Rabbi Eli'ezer says, One thousand years, because it is said,[8] "The day of

---

[1] Deut. xi. 21. [2] Isai. liv. 9.
[3] So the Rabbis, instead of 'waters.' [4] 97a.
[5] Paragraph 806, on Psalm lxxii. 5, referred to by Gfrörer, *Jahrh. d. H.* ii. S. 254–5.
[6] Isai. lxv. 22.
[7] A peculiar kind of tree. Sedan also means 'a block;' and Gfrörer, nverting the genitive, translates, 'the trunk of a tree.'
[8] Isai. lxiii. 4.

vengeance is in my heart." A day of the blessed God is a thousand years. Rabbi Yehoshua' says, Two thousand years, because the Scripture teaches,[1] "Make us glad according to the days wherein thou hast afflicted us." The word "days" signifies at least two days of God.'

From the above survey it is evident that the doctrine of a millennium was very far from being a settled dogma among the Jews. We have met with very few representatives of it, and by the side of it we have seen periods varying from forty up to seven thousand years assigned, on the most arbitrary grounds, to the Messianic kingdom. This particular view was adopted by the writer of Revelation,[2] and, no doubt under his influence, became the prevailing opinion among those Christians who looked forward to a temporal reign of Christ.

[1] Ps. xc. 15.
[2] xx. 4-7.

CHAPTER XV.

HAD THE KINGDOM A DISTINCTIVE NAME?

In answer to the question placed at the head of this chapter, the two titles so common in the New Testament at once occur to the mind: 'the kingdom of God,' and its equivalent 'the kingdom of heaven.' The former of these expressions is found in the Psalms of Solomon;[1] but there is nothing in the context to show that it is used technically of the time of the Messiah. The Son of David is introduced much later in the Psalm, and though to him is assigned the duty of perfecting the divine rule upon earth, yet that rule is not restricted in time, but is eternal as He who wields it:—'Lord, thou thyself art our king for ever and ever.'[2] The Sibyl, varying the expression to suit her poetry, approaches more nearly to a technical use of the words:—'Then shall appear the greatest kingdom of the immortal king,'[3] and immediately afterwards it is said, 'a pure king [the Messiah] shall come.' In the Assumption of Moses, though there is no Messiah, this designation is used in reference to the time which corresponds with the Messianic. The passage occurs immediately after the account of Taxo, who resolved to die rather than transgress the commandments of the Lord. 'Then,' it is said, 'shall his kingdom appear in all his creation;'[4]

---

[1] xvii. 4.
[2] xvii. 1 and 51.
[3] iii. 47, 48.
[4] x. 26.

and a few lines farther on, 'For the heavenly one will rise up from the throne of his kingdom, and go forth from his holy habitation in indignation and anger on account of his sons.' From the last sentence it seems evident that the kingdom of God is regarded, not as a particular institution on earth, but as God's eternal sovereignty, which is, however, to be at some time made gloriously manifest among men. This interpretation will apply also to the language of the Sibyl. Although, therefore, the reign of the Messiah is very naturally referred to as a revelation of the kingdom of God, I see no warrant in the Jewish writings for identifying the two expressions; and still less is there any evidence to show that 'the kingdom of God' had become a current and accepted designation of the Messianic time.

In the Wisdom of Solomon the expression is used in a simply religious sense:—'She [Wisdom] led in right paths the just man [Jacob] when he fled from the wrath of his brother, showed him the kingdom of God, and gave him a knowledge of holy things.'[1] There is no reason to suppose that a prophetic revelation of the future kingdom is meant, and the phrase seems parallel to the following words, 'a knowledge of holy things.'

The other expression, 'the kingdom of heaven,' מַלְכוּת שָׁמַיִם, is very probably, as Lightfoot, who is followed by more recent writers, supposes, derived from Daniel vii. 13, 14, although the words do not there occur in juxtaposition;[2] and if so, it must be intended to stand in contrast with the rule of wicked earthly powers. But even then it might denote the eternal rule in heaven, which should descend into a delegated manifestation among the Israelites. The transition might seem easy from this to its application as a specific title of the

---

[1] x. 10. [2] *Heb. and Talm. Exerc.* Matt. iii. 2.

Messianic reign; but there is, so far as I am aware, no evidence that the transition was made. The expression is frequently used by the Rabbinical writers, but not as a designation of the kingdom of the Messiah. In all the passages cited by Lightfoot [1] it is employed in a spiritual sense, referring evidently to the reign of God within the heart, or, as Lightfoot himself says, to 'the inward love and fear of God.' Men are said to take the kingdom of heaven upon them, or to lay it aside, or to break its yoke and take upon themselves the yoke of flesh and blood; and, according to Lightfoot, it was in this sense that the Jewish writers 'most ordinarily applied this manner of speech.' He adds, however, that 'they used it also for the exhibition and revelation of the Messiah in the like manner as the Evangelical History doth;' but in proof of this he appeals only to passages in the Gospels themselves, and to two verses in the Targum of Isaiah. In xl. 9 it is said, 'the kingdom of your God is revealed;' but reference to so remote a place as liii. 10, where 'the kingdom of their Messiah' is referred to, can hardly identify the two expressions.

Two or three passages cited by Wetstein [2] will serve to illustrate the spiritual use of the words:—'Ye fools, this is an impious kingdom which does not take upon itself the yoke of the kingdom of heaven and the yoke of the law.' 'The sons of Eli were sons of Belial, because they shook off from themselves the kingdom of heaven, and said, there is no kingdom in heaven.' 'When any-one prays while walking, it is necessary for him to take up the kingdom of heaven standing. What is that kingdom of heaven? The Lord our God is one God.' The repetition of this great confession of faith seems to have been what was technically meant by taking upon oneself the

---

[1] Ibid., principally from Berakhoth. [2] Nov. Test. Mt. iii. 2.

kingdom of heaven. For the Messianic meaning of the phrase Wetstein can refer only to the Targum of Isaiah xl. 9, which has been already noticed, and of Micah iv. 7–8. The latter passage, which is clearly Messianic, runs thus: 'And the kingdom of the Lord shall be revealed upon them in Mount Zion henceforth and for ever. And thou, O Messiah of Israel, . . . to thee hereafter is the kingdom to come.' But even here there is nothing to show that 'the kingdom of the Lord' is a proper name for the kingdom of the Messiah. Rather is it the wider kingdom, existing from eternity, of which the Messianic is only a particular, though glorious and abiding revelation.

Schoettgen [1] also says that 'the more common notion in the writings of the Jews' was that the kingdom of heaven meant 'the cultus of the Church of the Old Testament as exercised by pious Jews.' Whether this is an adequate definition may be doubted; but what is more to our purpose is his confession that, though he has diligently attended to that phrase, he can cite only one passage in which it means the kingdom of Christ, and that one is the Targum of Micah which we have just noticed. Like Lightfoot, however, he relies upon statements in the Gospels to prove that this was an interpretation of it which was well understood by the Jews. This is not the place to comment on the Gospels, and consider whether the expression may not in them have a more purely spiritual meaning; what at present it concerns us to remark is that, at all events in the purely Jewish literature, there is no satisfactory evidence that 'the kingdom of God,' or 'the kingdom of heaven,' was ever used by the Jews as synonymous with the kingdom of the Messiah.

[1] *Horæ Hebraicæ et Talmudicæ in universum Novum Testamentum &c.*, 1733, p. 1147 *sq.*, where there is a Dissertatio de Regno cœlorum.

CHAPTER XVI.

MORAL NATURE OF THE KINGDOM.

WE have already seen, in sketching the general character of the Messianic government, that the future kingdom was to be one of righteousness; but the subject is so important as to deserve a separate and fuller treatment, and we may advantageously bring together some passages which indicate more directly the Jewish aspirations in this direction.

We may notice, first, two places in the Sibylline Oracles in which, though there is no allusion to the Messiah, the righteousness of a future time is depicted:—
'For all good order shall come upon men from the starry heaven, and righteous dealing, and with it holy concord, which for mortals excels all things, and love, faith, hospitality. And from them shall flee lawlessness, blame, envy, anger, folly. From men shall flee poverty, and necessity shall flee, and murder, and pernicious strifes, and mournful quarrels, and thefts by night, and every evil in those days.'[1] According to the Sibyl this triumph of righteousness would manifest itself in the sacrificial rites of the temple:—' Again shall there be a sacred race of pious men, devoted to the counsels and mind of the Most High, who, round about it, will glorify the temple of the great God with libation and savour of victims, and with sacred hecatombs, and sacrifices of well-fed

[1] iii. 373-380.

bulls, and perfect rams, and firstlings of the sheep, and purely presenting on a great altar fat flocks of lambs as whole burnt-offerings.' Their office as teachers of the people is not forgotten. The passage continues:—'And in righteousness, having obtained the law of the Most High, they shall dwell happily in cities and rich fields. And they themselves, exalted by the Immortal, shall be prophets and bringers of great joy to all mortals. For to them alone the great God gave prudent counsel, and faith, and most excellent understanding in their breasts.'[1]

In the Book of Enoch, as we have seen, the time of blessedness comes after the judgment. The evil spirits, who in the days before the deluge seduced mankind, and have since been bound under the hills, will at the judgment be consigned to the fiery abyss, and shut up in torture for ever,[2] and then the earth shall be cleansed 'from all violence, and from all unrighteousness, and from all sin, and from all ungodliness, and from all impurity,'[3] and 'sin shall not be named any more for ever.'[4] God 'will be gracious to the righteous, and give him eternal righteousness, and give him dominion, and he shall be in goodness and righteousness, and walk in eternal light. And sin shall go down into darkness for ever and ever, and shall no more appear from that day for ever.'[5] 'Over all the righteous and holy will he set holy angels as watchers, that they may keep them as an eyeball, until an end is made of all wickedness and all sin.'[6]

We have seen how the spiritual elements preponderate in the picture of the Messiah presented in the Psalms of Solomon; and it is only what we should expect when we are told that 'he will not suffer unrighteousness to

---

[1] iii. 573-585.
[2] x. 12, 13; xc. 21, 24; xci. 15.
[3] x. 20.
[4] xci. 17.
[5] xcii. 4, 5.
[6] c. 5.

lodge in the midst of them, and there shall not dwell with them any man who knows wickedness.'[1]

The Assumption of Moses describes the moral results of the manifestation of God's kingdom in few, but significant words:—'Then the devil shall have an end.'[2] From what follows, however, these words seem to refer rather to vengeance on the Gentiles and the exaltation of Israel than to the overthrow of wickedness considered apart from its political bearings.

The Book of Jubilees anticipates a time of everlasting righteousness for the chosen people:—'After this [*i.e.* after a period of sin] will they turn to me in all righteousness, with all their heart and all their soul, and I will circumcise their heart and the heart of their seed, and will make for them a holy spirit, and purify them, that they may no more turn away from me from that day for ever. And their soul shall cleave to me and to all my commandments, and I will be their Father, and they shall be my son, and shall all be named sons of God, and all [sons] of the Spirit. And it shall be known that they are my sons, and I their Father in righteousness and goodness, and that I love them.'[3] But in combination with this more spiritual view it is repeatedly insisted that the ceremonial law is eternally binding. Thus circumcision is declared to be 'an everlasting ordinance;'[4] and the most emphatic language is used in regard to the obligation of eating the tithe of all produce before the Lord[5]:—'It has been established as a law in heaven;' 'For this law there is no end of days; that ordinance is written down for ever.'[6]

Fourth Ezra also predicts that 'the heart of the inha-

---

[1] xvii. 29.
[2] x. 26.
[3] Ch. i., S. 233.
[4] Ch. xv., S. 9.
[5] See Deut. xiv. 22 *sq.*
[6] Ch. xxxii., S. 42.

bitants of the world shall be changed, and turned into another mind. For evil shall be destroyed, and guile extinguished; but faith shall flourish, and corruption be overcome, and truth, which for so long a time was without fruit, shall be displayed.'[1]

We must notice two passages in the Targum of Isaiah, because in both the Law is mentioned in connection with the Messiah, this reference being inserted by the Targumist in explanation of the original text:— 'At that time the Messiah of the Lord shall be for joy and for glory, and the doers of the law for magnificence and for praise;'[2] and again, 'they shall look upon the kingdom of their Messiah, . . . and the doers of the law of the Lord shall prosper in his good pleasure.'[3] The later Targum of the Song of Solomon also represents the study of the reasons for the precepts in the Law as one of the delights of the Messianic time.[4] In opposition to the view which is here expressed Gfrörer cites several passages, chiefly from late authorities, which he thinks declare that the ceremonial law is to be abolished in the time of the Messiah. But most of these passages refer expressly to the future world, and say nothing about the Messiah, and are therefore irrelevant. In two of them, however, the Messiah is spoken of. In Midrash Qoheleth Rabbah[5] it is said, 'Every law [? torah, study] which man learns in this world is vain, compared with the law [torah] of the Messiah.' Here, however, the word rendered 'law' by Gfrörer, refers, not to the Law of Moses, but to the mode of studying the reasons for its precepts, and therefore does not support the desired conclusion. So the Midrash to the Song of Solomon, ii. 12,

---

[1] vi. 26-28.   [2] iv. 2.
[3] liii. 10.   [4] viii. 1.
[5] On Eccles. xi. 8.

says, 'The law will be renewed under the Messiah, and a new one shall be given to the people of Israel.' So Gfrörer translates. I presume that the reference ought to be to verse 13, where it is said that 'the Torah returns to its renewal, and renews itself,'—which, so far from supporting Gfrörer's statement, means that men will engage in the study of the Law even more zealously than before. A much earlier book, Siphra,[1] says, accepting the words of Jeremiah xxxi. 31, 32, that God will make a new covenant with his people; but as the writer does not go at all beyond the Scriptural language, and does not mention the Messiah, we can hardly rest on so literal an interpretation the burden of Gfrörer's inference.[2] The evidence, therefore, reduces itself to a misunderstanding of the Midrashim; and we must conclude that the prevailing view was that not only would there be a great exaltation of the moral and spiritual life, but the Law of Moses would be maintained in its integrity in the time of the Messiah.

[1] Bechuqqothai, i 2.
[2] See the quotations in Gfrörer, *Jahrh. d. H.* ii. S. 341–3.

CHAPTER XVII.

THE CONVERSION OF THE GENTILES.

CLOSELY connected with the moral nature of the Messianic kingdom is the conversion of the Gentiles. Notwithstanding the thirst for vengeance which appears so plainly in some of the Jewish writings, the wider hope of the more noble among the prophets finds no doubtful expression. The Sibyl, with her Alexandrine culture and her evident partiality for the Greeks, looks forward to a time when 'the nation of the great God shall again be strong, who shall be the leaders of life to all mortals,'[1] and believes that in the Messianic period the prosperity of the Israelites will move the Gentiles to repentance :—' And again the sons of the great God shall all live quietly around the temple, rejoicing in those things which the Creator and the just-judging Monarch will give. For he alone would protect them, mightily siding with them, having as it were a wall of burning fire round about. And they shall be without war in the cities and in the country; for the hand of evil war shall not be upon them, but rather the immortal Champion himself will be with them, and the hand of the Holy One. And then all the islands and cities will say, "How greatly the Immortal loves those men; for all things care for them and help them, heaven and the God-sent sun and moon." And the all-producing earth shall shake in those days. And they shall bring

[1] iii. 194-5.

sweet discourse from their mouths in hymns: "Come, all falling on the ground, let us supplicate the Immortal King, the great and most high God. Let us send to the temple, since he alone is ruler; and let us all meditate on the law of the most high God, who is the most just of all on the earth. But we have wandered from the path of the Immortal, and worship with senseless mind handmade work of carved images and deceased men." These things the souls of faithful men shall cry: "Come, falling on our mouths among the people of God, let us in every house delight with hymns our Parent, God."'[1] Greece especially is appealed to, to serve God, and so become partaker in the blessings of the last time.[2]

Even the Book of Enoch expects the Gentiles to be converted, and assembled in the new Jerusalem:—' And I saw all the sheep that remained, and all the beasts on the earth and all the birds of heaven, how they fell down and did homage before those sheep; and they implored, and hearkened to them in every word. . . And all that had been ruined and dispersed, and all the beasts of the field and all the birds of heaven, assembled themselves in that house [the new Jerusalem], and the Lord of the sheep had great joy, because they were all good, and returned to his house. And I saw until they laid down that sword which had been given to the sheep, and brought it back into his house, and they sealed it up before the Lord; and all the sheep were enclosed in that house, and it did not contain them. And the eyes of all of them were opened, that they saw what was good, and there was not one among them that did not see. And I saw that that house was great and broad and very full. And I saw that a white bull was born, with great horns; and all the beasts of the field and all the birds of heaven feared him

---

[1] iii. 702-726.   [2] iii. 732 *sq.*

and intreated him always. And I saw until all their species were changed, and they all became white bulls; and the first among them became a great animal, and had great black horns on his head. And the Lord of the sheep rejoiced over them and over all the bulls.'[1] Again, among the blessings of the last time it is said that 'all the children of men shall become righteous, and all nations shall show me honour and praise me, and all shall adore me.'[2]

The Psalms of Solomon, on the contrary, notwithstanding the spirituality of their Messiah, hold out no hope to the Gentiles. The Messiah 'will bless the people of the Lord;'[3] but he will purify Jerusalem from the Gentiles,[4] and no stranger shall dwell there any more.[5] He will destroy lawless Gentiles with the word of his mouth, and they shall flee before him, while he will gather together the holy people.[6] Gentiles will, indeed, come from the ends of the earth to see his glory, and to bring gifts;[7] but it is evident that they are conceived as doing so only because they are under his yoke,[8] and the circumstance is mentioned merely to enhance the splendour of his dominion.

Philo has some interesting remarks bearing upon this subject in a passage in which he is speaking of the future blessedness of mankind. He says that if there be one virtuous man in a city, he will appear above the city; and a city distinguished by its virtue will be above the country round about it; and a nation with the same excellence will step above all nations, as the head is above the body, so as to be conspicuous on all sides, not for the sake of glory, but in order to benefit the beholders. 'For

---

[1] xc. 30, 33-38.   [2] x. 21.   [3] xvii. 40.   [4] xvii. 25.
[5] xvii. 31. This expression need not exclude the presence of *converted* Gentiles; but their presence is nowhere intimated.
[6] xvii. 27, 28.   [7] xvii. 34.   [8] xvii. 32.

the continual manifestations of excellent examples engrave similar images on souls that are not altogether hardened.'[1]

Fourth Ezra, written amid the deepest distresses of the Jewish nation, breathes only hatred and vengeance against the Gentiles, and in the Apocalypse of Baruch this spirit is only so far softened that the writer has the contemptuous mercy of an expecting conqueror towards those who did not know Israel or tread down the seed of Jacob. While the hostile nations shall be put to the sword, these shall be saved alive by the Messiah, but only that they may be subjects of the chosen people.[2] It is interesting to compare with this the expression of exactly the same view, with its Scriptural proofs, in a work written about a thousand years later, the Yalqut:—'An old man asked a Rabbi, Will the nations of the world also have part in the times of the Messiah? He answered, My son, every nation or kingdom that has oppressed the children of Israel shall see their glory, but then immediately vanish into dust, and live no more for ever, as it is written,[3] "The wicked shall see it, and be grieved, &c." Every kingdom and nation, on the other hand, that has not oppressed and insulted the Israelites, shall come, and shall be our vine-dressers and husbandmen, according to the saying,[4] "Strangers shall stand and feed your flocks, and the sons of the alien shall be your ploughmen and your vine-dressers. But ye shall be named the priests of the Lord."'[5]

In the Talmud different opinions are represented. The more merciful view is contained in the following passage:—'Rabbi Eli'ezer says, All the Gentiles shall become

---

[1] *De Præm. et Pœn.* § 19.　　[2] Ch. lxxii.
[3] Ps. cxii. 10.　　[4] Isai. lxi. 5, 6.
[5] Paragraph 212, on Ex. xii. 48. Referred to by Gfrörer, *Jahrh. d. H.* ii. S. 241.

proselytes in future of their own accord.¹ Rab Yoseph says, What is the verse [to prove it]? "Then will I turn to the people a pure lip, that they may all call upon the name of the Lord."² Then said Abbayé to him, Perhaps this means only that they will turn away from idolatry. Rab Yoseph says to him, It is written, "to serve him with one accord"'³ [*i.e.* in the same way as the Israelites, only without being part of the synagogue]. But elsewhere it is said, 'The Rabbis taught, No proselytes are going to be received in the times of the Messiah. In a similar way they did not receive proselytes either in the days of David or in the days of Solomon. And Rabbi Eli'ezer [Rab El'azar] says, What is the verse for this? "Behold, whoever will dwell with thee besides me:" with thee, that is, when thou art not prosperous: "who will then dwell with thee, he shall fall to thee."'⁴ The meaning is that proselytes will not be received in the time of the Messiah, because their sincerity can be tested only by adverse times. The Gentiles will indeed become proselytes, attracted by the splendour of Judaism; but they will not be received, and they will fall away upon the outbreak of the war with Gog and Magog.⁵

We may conclude this examination with a few words from one of the later Targums: ⁶—'For on account of the miracle and redemption which thou hast wrought for thy Messiah and for the rest of thy people who remain, all peoples, nations, and tongues shall praise and say, There is no God but the Lord, for there is none but thou; and thy people shall say, There is no mighty one save our God.'

---

¹ That is, without being officially received by the Synagogue.
² Zeph. iii. 9.
³ '*Abodah Zarah* 24*a*, referred to by Gfrörer, S. 239–40.
⁴ Isai. liv. 15. *Yebamoth* 24*b*, referred to by Gfrörer, S. 240.
⁵ '*Abodah Zarah* 3*b*, quoted by Gfrörer, S. 240-1.   ⁶ Ps. xviii. 32.

CHAPTER XVIII.

THE RETURN OF THE SCATTERED ISRAELITES.

TURNING from the Gentiles to the Israelites, we find the hope abundantly expressed that they should once more be gathered together in the Holy Land. The writer of the Psalms of Solomon prays in words which must have had an echo in every Jewish heart :—'Turn, O God, thy compassion upon us, and pity us. Assemble the dispersion of Israel with compassion and goodness.'[1] So he predicts that the Messiah 'will assemble the holy people, whom he will lead in righteousness, and will judge the tribes of a people sanctified by the Lord his God,'[2] and he pronounces those blessed who 'arise in those days, to see the good things of Israel in the assembling of the tribes.'[3] The repeated mention of the tribes points to the widest signification for Israel, and indicates an expectation that the lost tribes of the northern kingdom should be at last restored.

We have already noticed a passage in which Philo expresses his belief that the scattered Israelites will return, under a supernatural guidance, to their own land ;[4] but whether he includes the lost tribes is not explicitly stated.

The Book of Jubilees, in a prophecy relating to the whole nation, predicts a universal restoration :—'Afterwards will they turn to me again from the midst of the

---

[1] viii. 33, 34.
[2] xvii. 28.
[3] xvii. 50.
[4] De Exsecrat. §§ 8, 9.

Gentiles with all their heart, and all their soul, and all their strength. And I will assemble them all out of the midst of the Gentiles, ... and I will build up my sanctuary among them, and dwell among them, and will be their God, and they shall be my people in truth and righteousness.'[1]

The fullest account of the return of the ten tribes is contained in Fourth Ezra. In the vision of the man ascending from the sea Ezra saw, after the destruction of the enemies, the man descending from the mountain, and calling to him a peaceful multitude; and many men came to him, some in joy, and some in sorrow.[2] Of this the following explanation is given:—'Whereas thou didst see him collecting to himself another peaceful multitude, these are the ten tribes,[3] which were made captive from their own land in the days of King Josiah,[4] whom Shalmaneser, king of the Assyrians, led away captive; and he removed them beyond the river, and they were removed into another land. But they took this counsel for themselves, that they should leave the multitude of the Gentiles, and set out into a further region, where the human race never dwelt, that they might there observe their laws, which they had not kept in their own region. Now they entered the Euphrates through the narrow entrances of the river; for at that time the Most High worked miracles for them, and stayed the fountains of the river until they passed over. And through that region there was a long journey of a year and a half, and that region is called Arzareth.[5] Then they took up their

---

[1] Ch. i. S. 232.   [2] xiii. 12, 13.
[3] So the Latin has it. Æth. 9. Syr. and Arab. 9½. The Arm. abbreviates the passage so as to lose all reference to the tribes.
[4] This clearly ought to be Hoshea.
[5] Syr. Arzaph; Æth. Azaph; Arab. Acsarâri and Ararawin. This mysterious word Arzareth has been shown by Dr. Schiller-Szinessy to be simply the 'terra alia' of verse 40, formed into a proper name from the אֶרֶץ אַחֶרֶת

abode there until the last time. And when they again begin to come, the Most High will again stay the fountains of the river, so that they can pass over. Therefore thou didst see a multitude assembled in peace.'[1] The same subject is referred to in the Apocalypse of Baruch. Baruch wrote a letter of admonition to the nine-and-a half tribes, who dwelt beyond the Euphrates, and sent it by an eagle. In this he reminded them that their suffering had been brought upon them by their sin, but told them that, if they made a good use of their afflictions, they should receive eternal hope, and God would remember them, for he had promised not to forget them for ever, but to gather together again all who were dispersed.[2]

In the Targum of Jonathan the same hope finds utterance. In Zechariah x. 6 it is said, in reference to the time of the Messiah (introduced in verse 4), 'I will strengthen the house of Judah, and redeem the house of Joseph; and I will assemble their captives, and have pity on them; it shall be as though I had never driven them into banishment, for I, the Lord their God, hearken to their prayer.' So in Lamentations ii. 22 we read:—'Thou shalt proclaim freedom to thy people of the house of Israel by the hand of Messiah, even as thou didst by the hand of Moses and Aaron in the day of the passover, and my young men shall be gathered round about from every place where they were dispersed in the day of the strength of thine anger, O Lord!'[3]

The Talmudists are divided in opinion as to the re-

of Deut. xxix. 27, (28 in the English), 'The Lord rooted them out of their land ... and cast them into another land.' See the *Journal of Philology*, vol. iii. 1870-1, pp. 113-114, referred to by Bensly, *The Missing Fragment*, p. 23, note 1.

[1] xiii. 39-47.   [2] Chs. lxxvii., lxxviii.
[3] See also Jer. xxiii. 5, and Hos. xiv. 8.

storation of the missing tribes. Rabbi Akiba determines that the ten tribes shall not return. Rabbi Eli'ezer is of a different opinion; and Rabbi Yochanan even asks, 'Has Rabbi Akiba forsaken his [ordinary] kindness?' Rabbi Shime'on answers the question in the affirmative, though conditionally.[1]

[1] Mishnah, *Synhed.* x. [xi.] 3. Tal. Bab. *Synhed.* 110*b*. See Gfrörer, *Jahrh. d. H.* ii. S. 237. For the later Targums, which, however, do not specify the lost tribes, but speak generally of a return from captivity, see *Pseudo-Jon.* Deut. xxx. 4; Cant. i. 8; vii. 13, 14; viii. 4.

CHAPTER XIX.

DESTRUCTION OF THE OLD JERUSALEM, AND APPEARANCE OF THE NEW.

For the reception of the returning multitudes a vast and beautiful city must be prepared. The expectation of a new Jerusalem may be sufficiently explained by the desire to ascribe to everything in the Messianic age an ideal magnificence; but it may also have been due in part to the belief that before their final triumph the ancient city of the Jews was to be destroyed by enemies. We have seen how in Daniel the entrance of everlasting righteousness was to be preceded by a hostile destruction of the city and sanctuary.[1] By the writer the destruction had been witnessed, while the approaching blessedness dwelt only in his faith. But the high authority which his work obtained must have brought these two events into an association not easily dissolved, and when the Messianic glory receded into the future, the downfall of Jerusalem must have followed it, and Daniel's words have been converted from history into prophecy.

That the language of Daniel actually received this interpretation we have some evidence in Josephus, though I cannot feel so confident as Gfrörer [2] that the saying which the Jewish historian refers to is the passage in Daniel, and not rather the intimation of some lost apocryphal book. It is probable, however, that, whether directly or indirectly,

[1] ix. 24, 26.   [2] *Jahrb. d. II.* ii. S. 301-2.

the prediction may be traced to Daniel. In his history of the Jewish war,[1] Josephus says:—'Therefore every ordinance of man was trodden down by them [the Zealots], and divine things were laughed at, and they ridiculed the ordinances of the prophets as the idle tale of fortune-tellers. Now these foretold many things about virtue and vice, by transgressing which the Zealots thought fit to fulfil the prophecy against their country. For there was an ancient saying of inspired men, that the city would then be taken, and the most holy place would be burned by law of war, when sedition should fall upon them, and domestic hands should pollute the temple of God.' This is referred to again in rather different words [2]:—'Who does not know the writings of the ancient prophets, and the oracle, now imminent, which falls to the lot of the wretched city? For they foretold its capture, when some one shall begin the slaughter of his own countrymen.' Another prediction is quoted farther on.[3] Josephus says that the Jews had it 'written down in the oracles [4] that the city and the temple would be taken when the sacred enclosure [5] became square,' and he believes that the conditions of this prophecy were clearly fulfilled when the tower of Antonia was destroyed. Gfrörer thinks that in this prediction Daniel ix. 27 is undoubtedly referred to. He grounds this conclusion upon the words וְעַל כְּנַף שִׁקּוּצִים מְשֹׁמֵם, which he translates, 'on the side-wings are the abominations of the destroyer.'[6] The following he supposes was the explanation:—'When the buildings round the temple (particularly the tower) look like (square) side-wings of

---

[1] iv. 6, 3.   [2] vi. 2, 1.   [3] vi. 5, 4.

[4] Ἐν τοῖς λογίοις. It must be admitted that this phrase would best suit accepted Scripture.

[5] Τὸ ἱερόν, the temple with its precincts.

[6] As this seems a strange rendering of the Hebrew, I give the German words:—'und auf den Seitenflügeln sind die Gräuel des Verwüsters.'

the sanctuary, then the destruction comes.' This seems to me quite untenable. There is nothing in Daniel to suggest the idea of squareness, the one only condition which is mentioned in the oracle. And again, Josephus does not suppose the oracle to mean that the tower was to look like a square wing, but that the removal of the tower made the sacred enclosure square; and as the tower was built out from the north-west corner of the temple-precincts, its destruction actually produced this result. It seems, therefore, most probable that the oracles alluded to were contained in some document now unknown, which may, like the Book of Enoch, have obtained a quasi-scriptural authority. It deserves notice that, whether accidentally or not, Josephus connects this oracle with another relating to the Messiah. He proceeds to say, 'What especially incited them to the war was an ambiguous oracle, similarly found in the sacred writings, that at that time one from their country should rule the habitable world.' This he characteristically refers to Vespasian, who was appointed Emperor in Judæa.

We may, with Gfrörer, quote in this connection a passage from Revelation; for though the Christian bias of the writer may have made him more willing to believe in a destruction of Jerusalem, we can hardly doubt that his view represents one phase of Jewish thought :—' There was given me a reed like unto a rod; and the angel stood, saying, Rise, and measure the temple of God, and the altar, and them that worship therein. But the court which is without the temple cast out, and measure it not; for it was given unto the Gentiles; and the holy city shall they tread under foot forty-two months.'[1] The forty-two months, or three and a half years, clearly point to Daniel as the source of the belief which is here expressed.

[1] xi. 1, 2.

This expectation has left its traces in a legend which has been preserved in the Jerusalem Gemara [1] :—' Forty years before the destruction of the sanctuary the western light [2] [of the temple-lamp] went out, and the scarlet thread became even redder,[3] and the lot for the [holy] Name [4] came up in the left hand, and the gates which had been closed at night were found open in the morning. Then spoke Rabban Yochanan ben Zakkai, O temple, why wilt thou throw us into terror? We know that destruction is determined upon thee, for it is written,[5] " Open thy doors, O Lebanon, that the fire may devour thy cedars." '

These quotations sufficiently prove that a destruction of Jerusalem was anticipated by at least a portion of the Jews; and if the passage in Daniel was the principal foundation of this apprehension, the Messianic period must have been expected speedily to follow it.[6] When the city had been actually destroyed by Titus, others besides Josephus must have seen in this catastrophe the fulfilment of the oracles; but, unlike him, they watched for the appearing of the Messiah. We may thus explain the confident hope of Fourth Ezra and the Apocalypse of Baruch.

In the literature, however, of purely Jewish origin, which has been preserved to us from the period before the destruction of Jerusalem, it must be confessed that little

---

[1] *Yoma* vi. 3. Referred to by Gfrörer, *Jahrh. d. H.* ii. S. 304.

[2] From which the priest used to light the other branches of the lamp.

[3] A scarlet thread was tied on the scape-goat, and, if forgiveness was granted, the thread became white (Isai. i. 18).

[4] That is, the goat for God (Lev. xvi. 8). It was a good omen if that goat's lot came up in the right hand of the Priest. In Qabbalah *right* is holiness, success, approval, *left* the opposite.—Dr. Schiller-Szinessy.

[5] Zech. xi. 1.

[6] In confirmation of this I may refer to the close connection in the New Testament between the destruction of Jerusalem and the second coming of Christ.

evidence of the belief in question is to be found. In the Sibylline Oracles, as we have seen, the enemies assemble against Jerusalem, but are baffled in their enterprise. In the Book of Enoch the old Jerusalem is indeed carried away; but this is effected by supernatural agency.[1] In the Assumption of Moses a fierce persecution of the Jews, implying their total discomfiture, is mentioned; but nothing is said about Jerusalem.[2] The just conclusion, therefore, seems to be that while some anticipated the capture of the city by the Gentiles as preliminary to the appearance of the Messiah, others hoped that this last calamity might be averted, and the enemy driven in utter defeat from the walls by the expected king.

We must now turn to the passages in which the new Jerusalem is mentioned. The first is in the Book of Enoch[3]:—'I stood up to see, until he wrapped up that old house; and they carried out all the pillars; and all the beams and decorations of that house were wrapped up along with it, and they carried it out, and laid it in a place in the south of the land. And I saw the Lord of the sheep, until he brought a new house, greater and higher than the first, and erected it on the place of the first, which had been wrapped up. All its pillars were new, and its decorations were new, and greater than those of the first old one which he had carried away.' Agreeably to the peculiar order of events in this book, the new Jerusalem is set up after the judgment, and before the appearance of the Messiah. This order is, however, to some extent altered in the next chapter. It is there said that 'a house shall be built to the praise of the great king for ever and ever' at the end of the world's eighth week.[4] This is to be done, it is true, after a sword has

---

[1] xc. 28.
[2] viii.
[3] xc. 28, 29.
[4] xci. 13.

been given into the hands of the righteous to execute judgment upon sinners; but it is before the final judgment, which is not to take place till the tenth week.

In Fourth Ezra [1] a vision is related by which the fortunes of Jerusalem are typified. Ezra was desired to go into a flowery field, where no house was built; and while he was there, reflecting on the sins of Israel, he saw a woman lamenting, with rent garments, and ashes upon her head. He approached and asked the cause of her grief. She told him that through thirty years of married life she had had no child; but at length a son was born to her, and her husband and fellow-citizens rejoiced. But when her son had grown up, and was on the point of marrying, he fell dead in his chamber; and she had come out into the field to mourn, and meant to stay there in her sorrow until her death. Ezra remonstrated with her for such excessive grief, and reminded her that her affliction was nothing to the affliction of 'Zion, the mother of us all.' But while he dwelt upon the woes of Jerusalem, suddenly her face shone, and lo! he saw no longer a woman, but a city built up from great foundations. This woman was Zion, which had been barren, without an oblation, till Solomon built the temple. The death of her son symbolised the ruin that had fallen upon Jerusalem. And because Ezra had been sorrowing over it, the Most High had shown him 'the brightness of its glory, and the beauty of its adornment;' and all this had taken place in the open field, because no human edifice could be supported in the place where 'the city of the Most High' was displayed. The heavenly Jerusalem is also apparently referred to elsewhere [2] under the title of the 'betrothed and glorious city.'

In the Apocalypse of Baruch we are told that after

[1] ix. 23-x. 55.   [2] vii. 26.

the second destruction of Jerusalem it must be 'renewed in glory, and shall be crowned for ever.'¹ This city of God had existed from the creation of the world. While Baruch mourned over the ruin of Jerusalem, the Lord said to him, 'Dost thou think that this is the city of which I said, "I have graven thee upon the palms of my hands?"² Not that building that is now built in the midst of you is the one which shall be revealed with me, which has been prepared here since I thought of making paradise. And I showed it to Adam before he sinned; but when he cast away my commandment, it was removed from him, as also was paradise. And afterwards I showed it to my servant Abraham by night between the divisions of the victims. And again I also showed it to Moses on Mount Sinai, when I showed him the image of the tabernacle, and all its vessels. And now, behold! it has been kept with me, as also is paradise.'³

We need not dwell on the extravagant fancies of the Rabbinical interpreters. One example from the Talmud, which blends a beautiful idea with its extravagance, may suffice:—'And said Rabbah, who had heard it direct from Rabbi Yochanan, The Holy One (blessed be he!) is going to lift up Jerusalem three parasangs above, because it says,⁴ " It [Jerusalem] shall be lifted up, and yet dwell under it " [*i.e.* still in its own place]. What does this " under it " mean? *As* under it [meaning that the height shall be equal to the original extent of the city]. Whence have you got it that this " under it " was three parasangs? Said Rabbah, Yonder old man [a phrase designating Elijah] told me, "By me was seen the former Jerusalem, and it was three parasangs." And perhaps thou thinkest there

---

¹ Ch. xxxii.   ² Isai. xlix. 16.
³ Ch. iv. Cf. Rev. xxi. 10, where the holy Jerusalem descends out of heaven from God.
⁴ Zech. xiv. 10.

will be trouble in getting up to it. Therefore it says,[1] "Who are these that fly like a cloud, and as doves to their cot?" Said Rab Papa, From this we learn that this cloud must be lifted up three parasangs. Rab Chanina bar Papa said, The Holy One (blessed be he!) wanted [originally] to give [the future] Jerusalem by measure, for it says, Whither art thou going? And he said unto me, To measure Jerusalem, to see what its width, and what its length should be. And the ministering angels before the Holy One (blessed be he!) said, Lord of the universe, many places of the nations of the world didst thou create in thy world, and thou didst not give the measure of their length and of their width; and Jerusalem, in the midst of which is thy name, and in the midst of which is thy temple, and in the midst of which are pious ones, thou art going to give a measure to it? Forthwith he said unto him, Run, speak to yonder lad, saying, Free of walls shall Jerusalem dwell, by reason of the multitude of men and beasts in the midst of it.'[2]

[1] Isai. lx. 8.
[2] *Baba Bathra* 75*b*. It is worthy of notice that this cubical form of the city, enlarged too into the most extravagant dimensions, is found in Rev. xxi. 16, in the beautiful description of the heavenly Jerusalem. See some further citations, which, however, are not very striking, in Wetstein, at Gal. iv. 26; and for a full account of the later view, containing particulars about the temple, the altar, &c., see Schoettgen's 'Dissertatio de Hierosolyma coelesti' in his *Horæ Heb. et Talm.* pp. 1205-1248.

CHAPTER XX.

EARTHLY BLESSEDNESS.

Not only was a new magnificence to descend upon Mount Zion, but the whole earth was to renew its powers, and every sort of outward blessing become the portion of mankind. The Sibyl delineates this side of the Messianic kingdom in language which does not yet transgress the limits of poetry and good taste :—' The all-producing earth shall give to mortals in boundless store the best produce of corn and wine and oil; and from heaven the sweet drink of delicious honey, and trees, and the produce of fruit-trees, and fat flocks, and oxen and lambs and kids; and shall open delicious fountains of white milk. The cities and rich fields shall again be full of good things; nor shall there be a sword upon earth, nor the din of battle; nor any more shall the earth, deeply groaning, be shaken. And there shall be no more war, nor drought upon the earth, nor famine, nor hail, the injurer of fruits. But there shall be profound peace in all the world, and king shall be friendly to king till the end of time, and the Immortal in the starry heaven will make a common law for men through all the world, for as many things as have been done by wretched mortals. For he is God alone, and there is none other, and he would burn with fire the cruel wrath of men. . . And all the paths of the field, and rugged hills, and lofty mountains, and the wild billows of the sea, shall be easy to the foot and pleasant for the ships in those days. For all the peace of good things is coming upon the earth; and the prophets of the great God will take away the sword, for they shall be judges and righteous kings of mortals. And there shall also be righteous wealth among men; for this is the judgment and dominion of the great God. Rejoice, O maiden, and exult; for to thee has he who created heaven and earth given delight for ever. He will dwell in thee, and be to thee an immortal light. And wolves and lambs shall eat grass together on the mountains, and leopards shall feed with kids. Bears shall dwell at pasture with calves; and the carnivorous lion shall eat chaff at the manger like an ox. And quite infant children shall lead them in bonds; for he will tame the wild beast upon the earth. And dragons shall sleep with babes, and not injure them; for the hand of God will be upon them.'[1]

In the Book of Enoch we have at least the germs of the ridiculous hyperbole of a later time:—' And now will all the righteous adore in humility, and they shall remain in life till they beget a thousand children, and they shall finish in peace all the days of their youth and their sabbath [*i.e.* their old age, the time of rest]. In those days shall the whole earth be cultivated in righteousness, and shall be quite planted with trees, and shall be full of blessing. All trees of pleasure shall be planted on it, and vines shall be planted on it. The vine which is planted on it shall bear fruit in abundance; and of every seed that is sown on it shall one measure bear ten thousand, and one measure of olives shall produce ten presses of oil. . . And in those days will I open the storehouses of blessing that are in heaven, to cause them to come down upon the earth, upon the work and the labour of the children of men.'[2]

[1] iii. 743-760 and 776-794.   [2] x. 17-19; xi. 1.

In the treatise of Philo, De Præmiis et Pœnis,[1] there is a remarkable passage in which he describes the outward blessings which he hopes will ultimately be enjoyed by mankind. It is too long for transcription; but I may briefly sketch its contents. To us, who in our island home never trouble ourselves about the assaults of wild beasts, it is at first startling to find that Philo places the taming of fierce animals foremost among the advantages of a happier age. These, he says, are hostile, not to one city or nation, but to the whole human race, and not for a definite, but for an indefinite time. Some of them fear man as a master, and cower before him with spiteful hatred; but the more daring either lie in wait, if they are weak, or if they are strong enough, attack him openly. This is a war without a truce, one which no mortal can terminate. But the Unbegotten will put it down when the wild beasts in the soul have been tamed. Then bears and lions and panthers, and the animals among the Indians, elephants and tigers, and all others that are of unconquerable strength, shall change from their solitary life and become gregarious, and submit to man as their natural ruler; and some, emulating the more manageable creatures, will fawn like lap-dogs. Then scorpions and serpents and the other reptiles shall lose the activity of their poison. The man-devouring animals of the Nile, crocodiles and hippopotamuses, and the innumerable tribes produced by the sea, will hold the virtuous man sacred and inviolate.[2] In consequence of the suppression of this older war the more recent war which prevails between man and man shall come to an end.[3] The second blessing is wealth, which of necessity follows peace and empire. Natural wealth consists of cheap food and shelter. Food is bread and running water, which abound in all parts of

---

[1] § 15–20.   [2] § 15.   [3] § 16, already noticed more at length, pp. 302–3.

the world. Shelter consists of clothing and a house, to guard against the injuries which result from heat and cold; and each of these, if one be willing to dispense with superfluous sumptuousness, is very easily obtained. But those who welcome the gifts of nature, practising temperance and content with little, shall have also in abundance, without having made it an object of pursuit, the wealth of delicate food. 'For those for whom true riches are laid up in heaven, disciplined through wisdom and holiness, have also in abundance the riches of possessions on earth, their storehouses being always filled by the providence and care of God. . . But to those whose lot is not heavenly, on account of impiety or injustice, neither does the possession of the good things on earth find by nature an easy access.'[1] This prosperity will show itself in the towns in the form of magisterial offices and honours and high repute, and in the country in the ample supply of necessaries, corn and wine and oil, and of things that minister to delicate living, namely the various kinds of fruit-trees, and moreover in the multiplicity of cattle and goats and other domestic animals. And as all these things would be useless if one left no heirs, no one will be childless, but every house will be filled with a numerous kindred. Nor shall anyone die before his time; but each shall pass from infancy through the successive stages of life till he reaches his last day, which borders on death, or rather on immortality.[2] A nearer blessing yet remains, health of body. The virtuous man shall have an immunity from disease, or if any infirmity arise, it will not be for the purpose of injuring him, but to remind the mortal that he is mortal, and to improve his character. Health shall be accompanied by keenness of perception and completeness in every part, so that the understanding

[1] § 17.   [2] § 18.

of the wise man, which is really the palace and house of God, may have an unobstructed efficiency.[1]

Length of life is the principal blessing promised by the Book of Jubilees :—'The days shall begin to increase, and the children of men shall become older from generation to generation and from day to day, till their lifetime approaches a thousand years. And there shall be none old or weary of life, but they shall all be like children and boys, and shall finish all their days in peace and gladness, and shall live without a Satan or any other evil destroyer being present; for all their days shall be days of blessing and healing.'[2]

If Fourth Ezra alludes only in the briefest way to the delights of the Messianic time, the Apocalypse of Baruch makes amends by its elaborate descriptions. Here we find what is probably the original form of the absurd passage quoted from Papias by Irenæus[3] as a saying of Christ's. The features of the description are the same, but they are elaborated by the Christian writer into a still wilder extravagance. The following is the passage in Baruch :—[After Messiah is revealed] ' the earth shall yield its fruits, one producing ten thousand, and in one vine shall be a thousand branches, and one branch shall produce a thousand bunches, and one bunch shall produce a thousand grapes, and one grape shall produce a measure of wine. And those who have been hungry shall rejoice; and they shall again see prodigies every day. For spirits shall go forth from my sight to bring every morning the fragrance of spices, and at the end of the day clouds dropping the dew of health. And it shall come to pass at that time, the treasure of manna shall again descend from above, and they shall eat of it in

---

[1] § 20.   [2] Ch. xxiii., S. 24.
[3] Hær. v. 33, 3.

those years.'[1] The picture is completed farther on :—
'It shall come to pass, after he shall have humbled whatever is in the world, and shall have sat down in peace for ever upon the throne of his kingdom, then he shall be revealed in pleasantness, and tranquillity shall appear; and then health shall descend in dew, and infirmity shall retire, and anxiety and distress and groaning shall pass away from men, and joy shall walk in all the earth. Nor again shall one die before his time, nor shall any adversity suddenly befall. And judgments, and accusations, and contentions, and vengeance, and blood, and passions, and envy, and hatred, and whatsoever things are like these, shall go away into condemnation, when they have been removed. For these are the things which have filled this world with evils, and on account of these the life of men has been greatly disturbed. And wild beasts shall come from the forest, and minister to men, and asps and dragons shall come out of their holes to subject themselves to a little child. And women then again shall not have pain when they bring forth, nor shall they be tortured when they give the fruits of the womb. And it shall come to pass in those days, the reapers shall not be weary, nor shall the builders toil; for the works will run spontaneously with those who make them, in great tranquillity.'[2]

One passage may be quoted in illustration of the whimsical views of the Rabbis :—' Rab Chiyya bar Yoseph says, The land of Israel will produce cakes and garments of Millath[3] in the days of the Messiah, as it is written,[4] "There shall be a handful of corn in the earth." Our

---

[1] Ch. xxix.   [2] Chs. lxxiii., lxxiv.
[3] Identified by some as a place in Egypt; but Binyamin Mussaphi thinks it is the old Melita (the present Malta). So I learn from Dr. Schiller-Szinessy.
[4] Ps. lxxii. 16.

Rabbis teach in reference to this saying, there shall be a handful of corn in the earth, upon the top of the mountains, and then the wheat will tower up as a palm-tree, and will rise above the height of mountains. Thou mayest perhaps object that one will find it troublesome to reap it; but it is said [in the words that follow immediately], "the fruit thereof shall shake like Lebanon;" that is, the Holy One (blessed be he!) will bring a wind out of his storehouses, which will blow over it, and furnish the fine flour. And a person goes out into the field, fills his hand, and from that nourishes himself and his household. It is said,[1] "with the fat of kidneys of wheat." They [the Rabbis] say that the time will come when a grain of corn will be as large as two kidneys of the largest ox.'[2] Another passage dwells, like Baruch, on the marvellous productiveness of the vine, assigning it however, to the future world. A single grape will be a load for a waggon or a ship, and then the grape will be put in a corner of the house, and wine be drawn from it, as from a great barrel; and there will be no grape containing less than thirty pails of wine.[3]

[1] Deut. xxxii. 14.
[2] *Kethuboth* 111*b*. Referred to by Gfrörer, *Jahrh. d. II.* ii. S. 242-3.
[3] Ibid., quoted by Gfrörer, S. 243.

CHAPTER XXI.

BEHEMOTH AND LEVIATHAN.

WE have reserved for separate notice one of the strangest fancies connected with the Messianic time. Two huge monsters, Behemoth and Leviathan, were reserved from the creation of the world for the banquet of the saints. Lücke thinks that this notion may have arisen under the influence of the Zoroastrian cosmogony, in which from the primeval bull issue a bull and a cow, which become the parents of all the animals.[1] It is hardly necessary, however, to travel beyond the whimsical system of interpretation of which we have already encountered so many examples. The names, at all events, are drawn from the Scriptures. 'Behold now Behemoth, which I made with thee; he eateth grass as an ox.'[2] Here we have the primitive ox. And it was not difficult to discover his vast size; for was he not called, 'Behemoth [the cattle][3] upon a thousand hills'?[4] Similarly Leviathan is mentioned as though he were an enormous fish:—'Canst thou draw out Leviathan with a hook?'[5] His future destruction also is threatened:— 'In that day the Lord with his sore and great and strong sword shall punish Leviathan the fleeing serpent, even

---

[1] *Einleit. in d. Off. Joh.* S. 168, Anm. 3.   [2] Job xl. 15.
[3] בְּהֵמוֹת; here, no doubt, the genuine plural, in Job the *pluralis excellentiæ*.
[4] Ps. l. 10.   [5] Job xli. 1.

Leviathan the crooked serpent; and he shall slay the dragon that is in the sea.'[1]

It is impossible to say when the absurd belief about these monsters first arose. We cannot trace it with certainty into the pre-Christian period; for though it is found in the Book of Enoch in its present form, it occurs only in a passage which is admitted even by Dillmann to be a later insertion, probably from a book of Noah.[2] The date of this writing is quite unknown; but as a Book of Noah is mentioned in the Book of Jubilees,[3] we may venture to place it provisionally as early as the middle of the first century. The following account, therefore, may be regarded as in all probability the earliest which we possess:—'In that day [probably the time of the deluge] two monsters shall be divided; a female monster named Leviathan, to dwell in the abyss of the sea, above the sources of the waters; but the male is called Behemoth, which occupies with its breast a desolate wilderness named Dêndâin, on the east of the garden where the elect and righteous dwell, where my grandfather [Enoch] was taken up, being the seventh from Adam, the first man whom the Lord of the spirits created. And I asked that other angel to show me the might of these monsters, how they were separated in one day, and one was set in the depth of the sea, the other on the firm land of the wilderness. And he spake to me, "Thou son of man, thou desirest in this to know what has been concealed." And the other angel who went with me, and showed me what is in concealment, spake, . . . "These two monsters are prepared conformably to the greatness of God to be fed, in order that the penal

---

[1] Isai. xxvii. 1, where the prophet probably alludes to Babylon.
[2] *Das Buch Henoch*, S. 181 *sq.*
[3] Ch. x., S. 254, and ch. xxi. S. 18.

judgment of God may not be in vain." [1] I follow in the last sentence the translation of Dillmann, who rejects on good grounds a conjectural emendation of the Æthiopic text, which had been adopted by previous commentators. According to this the monsters were not 'to be fed,' but 'to afford food,' the change being made in order to bring the statement into agreement with the general belief; but as Dillmann points out, the time referred to is not that of the Messiah, but that of the deluge, and the feeding of these monsters, probably with the bodies of the creatures drowned in the flood, is not inconsistent with their future destination as the food of the righteous. The wilderness of Dêndâin, דנדאין, 'the judgment of a judge,' according to the suggestion of Dillmann, is a fictitious place, assigned to the east of the garden of Eden as the region which had been occupied by the descendants of Cain. It is to be observed that the separation of Leviathan and Behemoth is here spoken of as past, agreeably to the later statement that they were separated at the Creation, while their distribution to their respective localities is spoken of in the future tense, and ascribed to the time of the deluge.[2]

The next allusion to these prodigious animals occurs in Fourth Ezra, in a passage where Ezra enumerates the objects produced on the successive days of creation. Speaking of the fifth day Ezra says, 'Then thou didst reserve two animals. The name of one thou didst call Behemoth,[3] and the name of the second thou didst call Leviathan. And thou didst separate them from one another; for the seventh part, where the water was gathered together, was not able to contain them. And

---

[1] lx. 7–11, 24.   [2] See Hilgenfeld, *Jüd. Apok.* S. 178, Anm. 2.
[3] The reading *Enoch* in the Latin, which is an obvious error, is corrected in the Syr. and Æth.

thou didst give to Behemoth one part, which was dried on the third day, to dwell in, where there are a thousand mountains. But to Leviathan thou didst give the seventh wet part; and thou didst keep them to serve for food for those whom thou dost wish, and when thou dost wish.'[1] This passage is omitted in the Arabic and Armenian; but it is sufficiently supported by the authority of the other three versions, and is confirmed by the occurrence of a similar allusion in the Apocalypse of Baruch. It is there said, 'Then Messiah shall begin to be revealed. And Behemoth shall be revealed from his place, and Leviathan shall ascend from the sea, two great monsters which I created in the fifth day of creation, and reserved until that time; and then shall they be for food for all who shall have been left.'[2]

In the Talmud these creatures are multiplied into two pairs of male and female; but lest they should destroy the earth they were made incapable of having any progeny. The female Leviathan was killed and salted for the future enjoyment of the righteous, and the two Behemoths were reserved for the same purpose.[3] In the Targum of Pseudo-Jonathan we find a similar, but less complete representation:—' On the fifth day God created the great monsters of the water, Leviathan and its female, which are prepared for the day of consolation.'[4] In Pireqê de-Rabbi Eli'ezer[5] Behemoth is created on the sixth day, and feeds daily upon a thousand mountains, on which however, the grass grows again every night. The Jordan supplies him with drink, as it is said,[6] 'He trusteth that he can draw up Jordan into his mouth.'

[1] vi. 49–52. [2] Ch. xxix.
[3] *Baba Bathra* 74*b*, quoted by Gfrörer *Jahrh. d. II.* ii. S. 33.
[4] Gen. i. 21.
[5] xi., quoted by Gfrörer, *J. d. II.* ii. S. 32. [6] Job xl. 23.

CHAPTER XXII.

MESSIAH BEN-JOSEPH, AND THE SUFFERINGS OF THE MESSIAH.

BEFORE passing on to the events which mark the close of the Messianic period we must notice two further matters which relate to that period itself. In the later accounts we find, in addition to the son of David, a subordinate Messiah, the son of Joseph or of Ephraim. Even Gfrörer grants that it is most improbable that this doctrine of a second Messiah was pre-Christian.[1] It is first found in the Babylonian Gemara.[2] We there read, 'It is written,[3] "The land shall mourn, every family apart:" ... Wherefore this mourning? On this point Rabbi Dosa and the other teachers are divided. The one party says, On account of Messiah the son of Joseph, who shall have been slain; the others say, On account of evil desire, which shall have been slain.'[4] Again the following occurs in the same treatise:—'The Rabbis have taught: Messiah the son of David who is going to be manifested (Oh! that it may be soon, in our days!)—the Holy One (blessed be he!) says to him, "Ask of me anything, and I will give it thee; for it says, I will refer to what is written in the Law[5] ... I

---

[1] *J. d. H.* ii. S. 264.
[2] That is, if we are right in the dates which we have assigned to the Targums.
[3] Zech. xii. 12.
[4] *Sukkah* 52a. Referred to by Gfrörer, *J. d. H.* ii. S. 258-9.
[5] Ps. ii. 7, rendered 'I will declare the decree' in the *A. V.*

have this day revealed [1] thee; ask of me, and I will give thee nations for an inheritance." [2] And since he [the Messiah] had seen that Messiah the son of Joseph had been slain, he says before him, " Lord of the universe, I ask of thee nothing but life." He [God] says to him, "Life! before thou hadst said this, David thy father had prophesied concerning thee [with respect to this], for it says,[3] Life he asked of thee; thou gavest it unto him, &c." '[4]

The later Targums give a different account, and represent the son of Joseph also as victorious over his enemies. In Pseudo-Jonathan [5] he is the one by whose aid the house of Israel are to vanquish Gog; and in the Targum of Canticles [6] the two Messiahs are placed together as deliverers, like Moses and Aaron.

The absence of the belief in a second Messiah from the earlier Targums and from the Jerusalem Talmud justifies us in assigning to it a late origin. It was probably suggested by the passage quoted from Zechariah, which did not agree with the conception of a triumphant king. When once it arose, however, the idea of the defeat and death of a Messiah was too distasteful to meet with universal acceptance; and yet the second Messiah was not disowned, for it may have seemed only reasonable that the northern tribes should have a Messiah as well as the Jews, and that the future legislator should, like Moses, be provided with a partner in his work.

Our next question relates to the suffering of the Messiah. In the evidence hitherto quoted we have met

---

[1] Generally translated 'begotten.' See Rashi on *Sukkah*.
[2] Ps. ii. 8.   [3] Ps. xxi. 4.
[4] *Sukkah* 52a. Referred to by Gfrörer, S. 259, but not very exactly rendered.
[5] Ex. xl. 11.   [6] iv. 5.

with no anticipation that the Messiah must submit to pain or dishonour. He was indeed to be mortal like other men, but was to die in peace at the end of a triumphant and glorious reign. The impossibility of reconciling the idea of the Messiah with the lowly and suffering life of Jesus was one of the most formidable obstacles which Christianity had to encounter in its controversy with Judaism. We have just seen how the admitted Messianic interpretation of a prophetical passage compelled the Rabbis to invent a secondary Messiah, to whom its mournful words might apply; and the Targum of Jonathan, allowing that Isaiah liii. refers to the Messiah, resorts to the most perverse mistranslations in order to get rid of its obvious meaning.

There are, however, some faint traces of a different view. The earliest is in Justin Martyr. In the Dialogue with Tryphon he says, 'Whatever Scriptures we mention to them which expressly demonstrate that the Christ is both liable to suffering and adorable and a God, they agree with us, being compelled to do so, that these have been said in reference to Christ;'[1] and farther on Tryphon is represented as saying, 'It is evident that the Scriptures proclaim the Christ as liable to suffering,' and as founding his objection only on the crucifixion, which was under the curse of the law.[2] This, however, cannot be relied upon as evidence of the general state of opinion among the Jews even in the second century. Tryphon's admission may describe only his own state of mind, or at most that of his party, and Justin's $\dot{a}\nu a\gamma\kappa a\zeta\acute{o}\mu\epsilon\nu o\iota$ shows that he only extorted a reluctant assent from those who were unable to answer his arguments. It is, nevertheless, quite conceivable that the Christian view may have made some impression, and that the Jews may have begun to

---

[1] Ch. 68. [2] Ch. 89.

find it more convenient to insist on the ignominy of the crucifixion than to deny altogether the possibility of a suffering Messiah. The evidence adduced from the Talmud is of the slenderest character. It is found only in the passages already referred to, in one of which the Messiah is represented as sitting among the sick at the gate of Rome, while in the other it is said, according to a reading adopted by Gfrörer, that his name is 'the pierced' or 'the sick,' on account of the words of Isaiah,[1] 'Surely he hath borne our griefs and carried our sorrows.'[2] The view suggested by this passage of Isaiah is further elaborated in later writings; but we may confidently say that within the period to which our inquiry is directed, although the Jews were not without the general notion that the afflictions of the pious atoned for the sins of the community, they had no expectation of a suffering and atoning Messiah.

[1] liii. 4.
[2] See *Synhed.* 98 *a* and *b*; Gfrörer, *J. d. H.*, ii. S. 266. For 'pierced' the usual reading is 'leper.'

CHAPTER XXIII.

RESURRECTION AND JUDGMENT.

PASSING to the events immediately succeeding the Messianic reign, in accordance with the time usually assigned to it, I think we shall obtain the clearest picture, and best avoid repetition, by treating together the state of the dead, the resurrection, and the final judgment, with its rewards and punishments.

The doctrine of the Book of Daniel receives its fullest expression in chap. xii. 2, 3 :—' Many of them that sleep in the dust of the earth shall awake, some to everlasting life, and some to shame and everlasting contempt. And they that are teachers shall shine as the brightness of the firmament; and they that turn many to righteousness as the stars for ever and ever.' In this passage only a partial resurrection is spoken of ; and if we are to judge from the context, it is confined to the people of Daniel. In an earlier passage, where the judgment was symbolically described, the beast was slain, and his dead body committed to the flames ; and beyond this utter destruction there is no hint of any future punishment of the heathen. The judgment is represented as breaking in upon the course of human history, and redressing upon earth the wrongs which the holy people had suffered :—' I beheld till the thrones were cast down, and the Ancient of days did sit, whose garment was white as snow, and the hair of his head like the pure wool; his throne was like the fiery flame, and his wheels as burning fire. A fiery stream issued and came forth from before him: thousand thousands ministered unto him, and ten thousand times ten thousand stood before him: the judgment was set, and the books were opened. I beheld then because of the voice of the great words which the horn spake: I beheld even till the beast was slain, and his body destroyed, and given to the burning flame. As concerning the rest of the beasts, they had their dominion taken away: yet their lives were prolonged for a season and time.'[1] Then follows the passage about the Son of Man. Here the judgment is obviously passed upon the living, and the conception is quite different from that of the final judgment of the living and the dead, after a general resurrection, which we find in later books. Unfortunately the judgment and the resurrection are not mentioned together in the same description; but apparently the resurrection is expected to take place after the judgment on the Gentiles. For the heathen kingdoms their utter overthrow and subjection seemed a sufficient punishment, and no suffering after death is threatened in their case. But the writer could not believe that those who had nobly perished in endeavouring to establish the kingdom of the saints were to have no fruition of their toil and grief; they must rise from their sleep to witness and enjoy the glory of their people; and especially the teachers of righteousness, those who had faithfully upheld the law, and taught others to observe it, must shine with the splendour of the stars. On the other hand the renegades of Israel, who had favoured the Greeks and abjured the law of their fathers, were worse than the heathen; and it was only just that they should awake to the conscious shame of their apostasy. Such seems to have been the order of thought in the writer's mind.

[1] vii. 9–12.

In the Book of Enoch we find the doctrine of a future life and judgment more fully developed. In contradistinction from other more partial judgments, the final crisis in human affairs is described as 'the great judgment,'[1] 'the great day of judgment,'[2] 'the last judgment,'[3] and 'the judgment for ever.'[4] The most connected description of the judgment is contained in the historical vision, and it will be convenient first to notice this, and then to refer to the fuller details which are scattered through the book. A throne is erected in the 'delightful land,' that is, in Palestine; the Lord of the sheep takes his seat upon it, and then the 'sealed books' are opened before him. The six or seven (the reading is doubtful) principal white ones (that is, the archangels) bring forward the fallen stars—the figure under which the sinning angels are represented in the vision; and then the seventy shepherds are placed bound before the Lord. Sentence is passed first upon the stars, which are found guilty, and cast into a deep place full of fire. Next the shepherds are likewise found guilty, and thrown into the fiery depth. Afterwards a similar depth, full of fire, is opened in the midst of the earth, on the right hand of the house, *i.e.* Jerusalem; the blinded sheep are brought forward, found guilty, and flung into that fiery depth.[5] The new Jerusalem is then introduced, and the time of blessedness already described succeeds. In this representation, though a resurrection is not expressly mentioned, it is implied in regard to the blinded sheep, the apostate Israelites, and also in the assembling into the new Jerusalem of the faithful who had been destroyed. If the seventy shepherds stand, as is generally supposed, for the

---

[1] xvi. 1; xix. 1; xxii. 4; xxv. 4; xciv. 9; xcviii. 10; xcix. 15; c. 4; ciii. 8; civ. 5.
[2] x. 6; xxii. 11.   [3] x. 12.   [4] xci. 15.   [5] xc. 20-27.

heathen powers, they also must be conceived as rising from the dead in order to receive their punishment; and there is then a distinct advance upon the doctrine in Daniel. But the meaning of the shepherds is, as we have seen, by no means certain; for the heathen are represented by the wild animals, and the human form in the vision is otherwise reserved for angelic beings.

These events, however, are described in greater detail in separate portions of the work. We may follow first the fortunes of the fallen angels, who had been the seducers of mankind. Upon their overthrow they were bound under the hills of the earth for seventy generations, until the day of judgment.[1] Meanwhile the place of their final punishment was already in existence, and was shown to Enoch. It was a deep cleft in the earth, with pillars of heavenly fire; and among these, pillars of heavenly fire kept falling down in such abundance, that, looking either up or down, one could not count them. The horror of this abyss was enhanced by a desolate space, cut off alike from heaven and earth, which was situated above it, and where Enoch saw seven stars, like great burning mountains, undergoing their punishment for having transgressed the command of God, and failed to appear at their appointed time.[2] At the day of judgment the fallen angels shall be carried away into the fiery cavern, and shut up in torment for all eternity.[3]

The spirits of departed men also are provided with a dwelling-place, which receives them until the day of judgment. The death of the righteous is in one passage

---

[1] x. 12.

[2] xviii. 11–16; xxi. Although perhaps a later date must be assigned to xvii.-xx., as well as to cvi.-cviii., they may without inconvenience be included in the present survey, as they fill up, without contradicting, the view which is contained in other parts of the book.

[3] x. 6, 13; xix. 1; xxi. 10.

spoken of as 'a long sleep;'[1] but that this sleep does not imply a condition of absolute unconsciousness is evident from the full account of the intermediate state in chapter xxii. According to this the abodes of the dead are situated, not beneath the earth, but in the west. There a great high mountain rears its hard cliffs, and overhangs four suitable places. The purpose of the mountain is not stated; but it may have been intended as a barrier to cut off the realm of death from the living world. In this region all the souls of the children of men were to assemble and take up their abode until their final doom should be determined. Here Enoch saw spirits whose voice of complaint rose up to heaven; and, singling out one of them, he asked the attendant angel whose spirit it was. He was told in reply that it was the spirit which went forth from Abel, and that it complained of Cain until his seed should be destroyed from the face of the earth. Notwithstanding some obscurity in the chapter, we must suppose that this was the first of the four places; for only three subdivisions are afterwards described.[2] We thus obtain two classes of the righteous and two of the wicked. The first class is that just mentioned, the righteous who perished through injustice and persecution. The remaining righteous are in another place, where there is a fountain of water and light. A third division contains those sinners who died and received burial without having suffered judgment in their lifetime. Here their souls are in great pain, until the great day of judgment and punishment and pain shall come upon them for ever. In the last division are the souls of the wicked who complain of their ruin, since they were slain in the days of the sinners; that is to say, they have already in part expiated their offences. Their souls shall not be slain at the

[1] c. 5. [2] See Dillmann *in loco*.

day of judgment, or be taken out of the place in which Enoch saw them—a statement which must mean that they should be exempted, in consideration of their punishment on earth, from the extreme torture to which the rest of the wicked were to be consigned at the judgment, and should be left in that lighter suffering which follows immediately upon death.[1]

Some further light is thrown by a few passages on the mode in which judgment was to be conducted. The names of the righteous are written down in heaven before the glory of the great God.[2] All the evil-doing of sinners is manifest in heaven, and none of their works of violence is concealed; for every sin is daily written down before the Most High.[3] The sun and moon and stars, the clouds, the rain and the dew shall be made witnesses against them;[4] for light and darkness, day and night, see all their sins.[5] All their unrighteous speeches shall be read before the Great and Holy One,[6] and their name shall be blotted out of the books of the saints.[7]

The righteous shall be amply rewarded for their fidelity. All good and joy and honour are prepared for them, and written down for the spirits of those who have died in righteousness. Their toils shall be richly recompensed, and their lot be better than the lot of the living.[8] They shall shine as the lights of heaven, and the portal of heaven shall be opened for them, and they shall have great joy like the angels.[9] The enjoyment of the tree of life is most fully described.[10] Journeying to the south,[1] Enoch saw a magnificent range of seven mountains, composed of precious stones. Three towards the east and

---

[1] The realm of the dead is again referred to in cii. 5 and ciii. 7.
[2] civ. 1.
[3] xcviii. 6-8; civ. 7. Cf. lxxxi. 2, 4.
[4] c. 10, 11.
[5] civ. 8.
[6] xcvii. 6.
[7] cviii. 3.
[8] ciii. 3.
[9] civ. 2-4.
[10] xxiv., xxv.
[11] xviii. 6.

three towards the south rose one above another, and the seventh, towering up in the midst, completed the resemblance to a throne. Around them were fragrant trees; and among these was one tree of unequalled perfume. Its leaves and blossoms and wood never fade, and its fruit is beautiful, like the date of a palm. Michael informed Enoch, in answer to his inquiries, what was meant by these things:—' This high mountain which thou hast seen, whose summit is like the throne of the Lord, is his throne, where the Holy and Great One, the Lord of glory, the eternal King, will sit, when he comes down to visit the earth with good. And this tree of delicious perfume not a single mortal is permitted to touch, until the time of the great judgment: when everything is atoned for and finished for ever, it shall be given over to the righteous and lowly. By its fruit shall life be given to the elect. It shall be transplanted to the north, to the holy place, to the temple of the Lord, the eternal King. Then shall they rejoice, full of joy, and exult in the Holy One; they shall cause its perfume to enter into their bones, and live a long life upon earth, as thy fathers have lived; and in their days no sorrow and no suffering, no toil and trouble shall touch them.'

Enoch's next journey discloses to us the place of punishment. He went into the middle of the earth, and saw a blessed and fruitful region, where was a holy mountain. A description of mountains and valleys is subjoined, which points unmistakeably to Jerusalem. An ' accursed valley,' shown by its position to be the valley of Hinnom, is singled out for especial notice. Uriel informs Enoch that ' this accursed valley is for those who are accursed for ever. Here must all those assemble themselves who utter with their mouth unseemly speeches against God, and speak insolently of his glory. Here are they assembled, and here is the place of their punishment. And in the last time shall the spectacle of a righteous judgment on them be given before the righteous for evermore. For this shall those who found mercy praise the Lord of glory, the eternal King.'[1] This is the earliest passage in which the Valley of Hinnom, or Gehenna, is represented as the place of future punishment. It was selected for this unenviable office on account of the idolatrous abominations which had been committed in it, and for which Jeremiah pronounces a curse against it.[2] Some place, indeed, might have been found at a distance from Jerusalem; but it was thought suitable that the righteous should witness the execution of justice on the wicked, for Isaiah had said, 'They shall go forth, and look upon the carcases of the men that have transgressed against me: for their worm shall not die, neither shall their fire be quenched; and they shall be an abhorring unto all flesh.'[3] According to the Talmud a smoke that indicated subterranean fire ascended from the ground;[4] a deeper cleft, then, might disclose the eternal fires of avenging justice. At all events Enoch regards the region of punishment as a 'fiery furnace,'[5] 'a pool of flames of fire,'[6] but nevertheless a place of darkness,[7] where, in the language of one of the later additions, there shall be 'a sound of lamentation and weeping, and groaning, and dreadful pain.'[8]

It is throughout implied that the judgment introduces the final and unalterable condition of things, and no hope is held out to the wicked when once they have passed from their mortal life.[9]

---

[1] Chs. xxvi., xxvii. [2] vii. 31 sq., xix. 5 sq., xxxii. 35.
[3] lxvi. 24. [4] *'Erubin* 19a. See Dillmann *in loco*.
[5] xcviii. 3. [6] c. 9. See also ciii. 8. [7] ciii. 8. [8] cviii. 5.
[9] For more express statements to this effect I may refer to xxv. 4; xci. 15; ciii. 8.

The doctrine of a bodily resurrection is not taught with any distinctness in this book. A resurrection of some kind is implied, as we have seen, in the historical vision, and is expressly affirmed in the declaration that 'the righteous shall rise up from sleep;'[1] but whether this was supposed to involve a resumption of the old body is nowhere stated. The spirits are regarded as separated from the bodies at death, and going in this incorporeal condition to their abode in the west until the day of judgment; and after the judgment it is still the 'spirits' that suffer reward and punishment.[2] If it be said that in order to eat the fruit of the tree of life they must have material bodies, it must be observed that even in the intermediate state after death the souls are placed amid material surroundings; and water and light[3] are evidently not unimportant sources of pleasure. The probability seems to be that the spirits were not regarded as strictly immaterial, but as composed of matter of the most delicate kind, and as capable therefore of eating and drinking. In this way they might return to the joys of the new Jerusalem without resuming the burden of the flesh, and might be more fittingly spoken of as 'companions of the heavenly hosts.'[4] The tree of life, however, is not promised to those who return to earth from the regions of the dead. The meaning seems rather to be that it shall be assigned to the righteous who are still living on the earth at the time of the judgment; and the result of its enjoyment is not immortal life, but 'a long life upon the earth,' like that of the fathers of mankind. This certainly seems to imply that even these must sooner or later quit the flesh in order to enter on the eternal state.

---

[1] xci. 10; xcii. 3.
[2] For the reward see ciii. 3, 4; for the punishment xcviii. 3, ciii. 8.
[3] xxii. 9.   [4] civ. 6.

But it may be that the author's views upon this point were not very clearly defined even in his own thoughts.

The Wisdom of Solomon teaches the doctrine of immortality no less explicitly:—'God created man for incorruption, and made him an image of his own peculiar nature.'[1] 'The souls of the just are in the hand of God, and torture shall not touch them. They seemed in the eyes of fools to die, and their decease was counted misfortune, and their journey from us ruin; but they are in peace. For even if they be punished in the sight of men, their hope is full of immortality, and having been disciplined a little they shall be greatly benefited; because God tried them, and found them worthy of himself.'[2] This doctrine seems to be associated with a belief in the pre-existence of souls:—'I was a boy of good disposition, and obtained a good soul, or rather being good I came into a pure body.'[3]

The writer of the Second Book of Maccabees is equally confident in his hope. This is most fully expressed in the account of the martyrdom of the seven brothers and their mother.[4] The doctrine of a bodily resurrection is implied where one of the brothers is represented as stretching out his hands, and saying that he hopes to receive these again from God.[5] Apparently, however, the resurrection is confined to the chosen people; for the fourth brother says to Antiochus, 'For thee there shall not be a resurrection into life.' This inference might perhaps be escaped by laying the emphasis on ζωήν; but such a special use of ζωή is hardly suitable to the context.

The Psalms of Solomon contain several allusions to resurrection and judgment, but do not present a fully

[1] ii. 23. [2] iii. 1-5. See also v. 16.
[3] viii. 19, 20. [4] vii. See also xii. 44.
[5] Compare also xiv. 46.

elaborated doctrine on the subject. Their hope is grounded upon moral conceptions :—'God is a righteous Judge, and will not admire the person;'[1] He is 'a righteous Judge over all the peoples of the earth,'[2] 'for the ways of men are known before him continually, and he is aware of what is stored in the heart before it is done.'[3] The righteous are assured of a happy resurrection; but the wicked are threatened with destruction rather than with a penal immortality, though it may be that this destruction was not supposed to involve the loss of consciousness. This antithesis is very frequent, and sometimes reminds us of New Testament phraseology:—The sinner 'fell . . . and shall not rise again; the destruction of the sinner is for ever . . . But those who fear the Lord shall rise into eternal life, and their life shall be in the light of the Lord, and shall fail no more.'[4] 'He who does righteousness treasures up life for himself before the Lord, and he who does unrighteous things is himself the cause of his soul's destruction.'[5] 'Let the sinners perish from before the Lord once for all, and let the holy ones of the Lord inherit the Lord's promises.'[6] 'The Lord will spare his holy ones, and blot out their transgressions in chastisement, for the life of the righteous is for ever; but sinners shall be taken away into destruction, and their memorial shall be found no more.'[7] 'Their inheritance [that of sinners] is Hades and darkness and destruction, and they shall not be found in the day of compassion on the righteous; but the holy ones of the Lord shall inherit life in gladness.'[8] 'Those who do iniquity shall not escape the judgment of the Lord, . . . for the sign of destruction is on their forehead, and the inheritance of sinners is destruction and

---

[1] ii. 19. [2] ix. 4. [3] xiv. 5.
[4] iii. 13, 16. [5] ix. 9. [6] xii. 8.
[7] xiii. 9, 10. [8] xiv. 6, 7.

darkness, and their iniquities shall pursue them down to Hades. . . . The sinners shall perish in the day of the judgment of the Lord for ever, when God will visit the earth in his judgment, to render unto sinners for ever. But those who fear the Lord shall be pitied in that [day], and shall live in the compassion of their God.'[1]

The later Sibyl expects the judgment to be ushered in by a fiery cataract rushing down from heaven:—'When a widow [Cleopatra] shall rule the whole world . . . then all the elements of the world shall be widowed, when God, who dwells in the sky, shall roll up the heaven as a book is rolled up, and the whole multiform firmament shall fall on the divine earth and sea, and a cataract of devouring flame, unwearied, shall flow down, and burn the earth, and burn the sea, and the heavenly firmament, and days, and shall melt into one the creation itself, and pick it out into purity. And there shall be no more the laughing spheres of the heavenly lights, no night, no dawn, nor many days of care, no spring, no summer, no winter, no autumn. And then shall come the judgment of the great God.'[2]

The Assumption of Moses has the following description of God's coming to judgment:—'Then shall appear his kingdom in all his creation ; and then the devil shall have an end, and sorrow shall be led away with him. Then shall be filled the hands of the angel who is stationed on high, who will immediately avenge them of their enemies. For the Heavenly One will arise from the throne of his kingdom, and go forth from his holy habitation with indignation and wrath on account of his sons, and the earth shall tremble and be shaken to its extremities; and high mountains shall be made low and be shaken, and the valleys shall fall. The sun shall not give its light, and

---

[1] xv. 9-15.   [2] iii. 77-91. See also 53-61.

the horns of the moon shall be turned into darkness and broken, and it shall all be turned into blood, and the orb of the stars shall be troubled. And the sea shall sink down to the abyss, and the fountains of waters fail, and the rivers be affrighted. For the supreme God, alone eternal, will arise, and come openly to take vengeance on the Gentiles, and destroy all their idols. Then thou, O Israel, shalt be happy, and ascend above the necks and wings of the eagle, and they shall be filled [or fulfilled], and God will exalt thee, and fix thee in the firmament of the stars, the place of their habitation. And thou shalt look down from on high, and see thy enemies on the earth, and recognise them, and rejoice and give thanks, and confess to thy Creator.'[1] In this passage it is difficult to see how much is to be understood figuratively, and no conclusion can be drawn from it as to the nature of the expected immortality. It is remarkable, however, that the only distinction which is observed is that between Israel and the Gentiles, and the only punishment of the latter which is specified is that their idols shall be destroyed, and they themselves shall be left upon earth while Israel is exalted to the stars.

Fourth Maccabees, in language which reminds us of expressions in the New Testament, teaches the doctrine of a spiritual immortality, unless, indeed, we are to suppose that the passage in which the subject is alluded to refers only to the intermediate state of the dead before the resurrection. In speaking of the martyrdom of the seven brothers the author represents them as saying, 'Let us not fear him who thinks that he kills the body; for there is great danger of eternal torment to the soul, laid up for those who transgress the commandment of God. Let us therefore arm ourselves with the self-control of divine reason; for thus, when we are dead, Abraham and Isaac

[1] x. 26-28.

and Jacob will receive us into their bosoms, and all the fathers will praise us.'[1]

The Book of Jubilees agrees very closely with Enoch in its representations. Here too we find a place for the reception of the spirits of the dead, although there is no laboured description of it. Isaac says to Esau and Jacob, just before his death, 'My sons, I am going upon the way of my fathers into the eternal dwelling, where my fathers are.'[2] 'The realm of the dead' is also referred to in connection with condemnation and punishment, but is apparently placed, not in the west, but in the 'darkness of the depth.'[3] The fallen angels are bound in the depths of the earth till the day of the great judgment; and then the punishment which is written down upon the heavenly tablets shall be inflicted without respect of persons upon small and great, of every nature and every race.[4] We elsewhere hear of 'the day of judgment in which God the Lord will judge them with sword and fire;'[5] but no further details are mentioned. The immortality promised is apparently incorporeal; and the statement in this book reflects some light upon the criticisms which we have already made upon the doctrine of Enoch. Isaac is said to have 'sunk into the eternal sleep,'[6] an expression which, in a writer who believes in the conscious survival of the spirit, is naturally referred to the sleep of the body, a sleep not to be broken even by a resurrection. Another passage seems decisive upon this point. In describing the blessedness which is to come upon Israel after a great penal judgment has fallen upon the earth, the writer, like Enoch, represents human life as once more attaining to

---

[1] Ch. xiii.   [2] Ch. xxxvi.
[3] Ch. v., S. 243; ch. vii., S. 248; ch. xxii., S. 21; ch. xxiv., S. 27.
[4] Ch. v.   [5] Ch. ix., S. 253.
[6] Ch. xxxvi., S. 50.

its pristine length, and enduring for nearly a thousand years; but even then death is the inevitable means of transition to the final beatitude,—'Their bones indeed shall rest in the earth, but their spirit shall have much joy.'[1]

The post-Christian Sibyl, like her predecessor, expects the world to be destroyed by fire before the resurrection and judgment:—'When now all things have become dull ashes, God will lull the unspeakably great fire which he kindled. God himself will shape once more the bones and ashes of men, and set mortals again as they were before. And then shall be a judgment, at which God himself will decide, judging the world again. And as many as impiously sinned, these the piled-up earth shall again cover, and dank Tartarus, recesses and Stygian Gehenna. And as many as are pious shall live again upon earth, God having given them a spirit, and at the same time life and subsistence to them, the pious ones. And all shall then see themselves, looking on the sweet, glad light of the sun. Oh, most blessed the man who shall come unto that time!'[2]

Fourth Ezra is particularly full in relation to this part of our subject; and as the writer's views are contained for the most part in the long passage which has been omitted from the Latin version, and which is therefore not contained in our English Apocrypha, I shall quote them at some length. I shall not confine myself to any single version; but the nature of the subject does not require me to call attention to verbal differences.

Ezra inquires—'If I have found grace in thy sight, O sovereign Lord, inform thy servant about this also, whether after death, when we each render up our soul, we are guarded in peace until those times come in which

---

[1] Ch. xxiii., S. 24.   [2] iv. 178-190. See also 40-46.

thou wilt renew thy creation, or are tormented from that time forward.' After an intimation that he must not reckon himself among the disobedient who are to be tortured, the following answer is given:—'Concerning death this is the account,—when decisive sentence shall have gone forth from the Most High that a man shall die, when the spirit is separated from the body in order to be restored to him who gave it, at first it adores the glory of God. But if it is of the number of scorners, or of those who have not kept the ways of the Most High, or of those who hate men that fear God, those souls do not enter the storehouses,[1] but from this time forward they are in punishment, and groan, and are afflicted in seven ways. The first way is that they resist the law of the Most High. The second way, that they cannot be converted, and do good things whereby they might be saved. The third way, that they see the reward laid up for those who have believed the covenant of the Most High. The fourth way, that they consider the punishment that has been prepared for them in the last time. The fifth way, that they see the storehouses of other souls, which are guarded by angels in much peace. The sixth way, that they see that they shall be carried by them [angels][2] into torture. The seventh way, which is greater than the other ways already mentioned, that they pine away in confusion, and are consumed in shame, and wither in fear, because they see the glory of the Most High, in whose sight they are now sinning while they are alive, and before whom they shall be judged in the last time. But of those souls which have kept the way of the Most High, this is the way, when the day shall have come for them to be liberated

---

[1] In the Arabic, 'bright habitations.' The intermediate abode of good souls is referred to under the name of storehouses in iv. 35, 41; vii. 32; (vi). 54, 60, 68, 74, 76.

[2] See Bensly's note, *The Missing Fragment*, pp. 64-5.

from this corruptible vessel; for at the time in which they dwelt in it they subjected themselves to the Most High in labour, and every hour they endured danger, that they might perfectly keep his law, that law which he laid down for them. Therefore this is the account concerning them. At first they see in great joy the glory of the Most High who receives them; and they rest in seven ways. The first way is, that with much toil they fought to overcome the evil sense that was made in them, lest they should wander from life to death. The second way, that they see the change in which the souls of the wicked are changed and tormented, and the punishment reserved for them. The third way, that they see the testimony which their Maker has borne concerning them, that in their life they kept the law entrusted to them. The fourth way, that they see and understand the rest which now, while they are assembled in their storehouses, they enjoy in great quietness, being guarded by angels, and the glory reserved for them in the last time. The fifth way, that they rejoice at having escaped now from that which is corruptible, and in the fact that they shall inherit that which is to be; and again they see the tribulation and abundance of toil from which they have been liberated, and the refreshment which they are to receive, and the delights which are to be theirs and are immortal. The sixth way, when it shall be shown to them how their faces shall shine as the sun, and how they shall resemble the light of stars, and not again be corrupted. The seventh way, which is greater than the rest that have been already mentioned, is that they glory with trust, and are confident, and are not confounded, and hasten to see the face of him to whom they subjected themselves in their life, even of him by whom they shall be glorified and from whom they shall receive a reward. These are the ways of the souls of the just, which from this time forward are announced. And from this time forward apostates shall receive the afore-mentioned ways of torment.' In answer to a further question Ezra is told that for seven days after their separation from the bodies the souls shall be at liberty, and then they shall be gathered into their storehouses.[1]

From this intermediate condition the souls shall be brought to judgment at the end of the world. After the death of the Messiah, ' the age shall return to its pristine silence for seven days, as it was in the beginning, so that no one shall be left. And it shall come to pass after seven days, the age which now is dormant shall awake, and corruption shall die. And the earth shall give back those who sleep in it, and the dust those who dwell in it in silence, and the storehouses shall give back the souls that have been committed to them.[2] And the Most High shall be revealed upon the throne of judgment, and compassion shall pass away, and long-suffering be contracted. Judgment alone shall remain, and truth shall stand, and faith become strong. And work shall follow, and recompense be shown, and righteous deeds shall waken, and unrighteous deeds shall not sleep. And the abyss[3] of torment shall appear, and opposite to it the place of rest. The furnace of Gehenna shall be revealed, and opposite to it again the paradise of delight. And then the Most High will speak to those peoples that have been raised up: " Behold, and see him whom ye denied, or whom ye did not worship, or whose commandments ye despised. Look, therefore, opposite to you; behold!

---

[1] (vi). 49-70.
[2] From this we may infer that the souls were to be reunited to the bodies prior to the judgment. Compare xiv. 35.
[3] See Bensly's note, *Missing Fragment*, p. 55.

here are joy and rest, and there fire and torment." These things will he say to them in that day of judgment. For that day of judgment is on this wise: there is no sun in it, nor moon, nor stars, nor clouds, nor lightnings, nor thunders, nor winds, nor water, nor air, nor darkness, nor evening, nor morning, nor summer, nor winter, nor spring, nor heat, nor ice, nor cold, nor hail, nor dew, nor rain, nor noon, nor night, nor day, nor light, nor luminary, nor shining, nor splendour, except only the beam of the glory of the Most High, by means of which they shall see what has been appointed. And its duration shall be as it were a hebdomad of years.'[1]

In the time of judgment few shall be saved. 'The Most High made this age on account of many, but the future for the sake of few.'[2] This thought is elaborated in the passage immediately following the description of the judgment. Ezra pronounces those blessed who have kept the commandments of God, but is saddened by the thought that, this being the condition of salvation, the future age must bring joy only to a few, but torment to many; for who among men has not transgressed the divine precept? There is in us an evil heart which has led us to corruption; and this affects by no means a few, but perhaps all that have lived. There is nothing in the answer to relieve this difficulty so far as it relates to the conditions of judgment. It is simply assumed that a few will be found worthy; and it is pointed out that precious stones are few, and that silver is more plenty than gold, and brass than silver, and iron than brass, and lead than iron, and clay than lead, and that, as men rejoice more over that which they possess in small quantity, so God will rejoice over a few who are saved. This does not console Ezra, and he thinks that the cattle are better off

---

[1] vii. 30-(vi). 10.   [2] viii. 1.

than men; for they do not expect judgment or punishment, and no life after death has been promised to them; but we men live only to be tortured, for all are full of iniquity. The reply is that men will have nothing to plead in the day of judgment; for understanding was given to them, and nevertheless they acted unrighteously, and they received commandments, but did not keep them.[1] Ezra recurs to this subject farther on:—'Those who perish are more than those who are saved, as waves are multiplied above a tiny drop.'[2] In the reply which is here given the salvation even of a few is apparently ascribed to arbitrary election. God saw that the world was utterly corrupt; 'and I spared a very little, and saved for myself a cluster of grapes, and a plant from the great forest. Therefore let the multitude perish, because it was made for vanity, and let my cluster and my plant which were made with much labour be saved.'[3]

No intercession will be allowed at the day of judgment. The righteous will not be able to pray for the wicked, nor relatives for relatives, nor friends for friends, for that day is decisive. Intercession is permitted in the present age, because it comes to an end, and the glory of God does not abide constantly in it; but the day of judgment will be the beginning of the immortal age, in which corruption and sin shall pass away, and justice and truth shall increase.[4]

The rewards and punishments which follow the judgment have been alluded to in the above quotations; but there is one other passage in which the blessings of the righteous are summed up:—'For you paradise has been opened, the tree of life planted, the future age prepared, abundance prepared, a city built, rest established, good-

[1] (vi). 18-48.   [2] ix. 15, 16.
[3] ix. 21, 22.   [4] (vi). 77-vii. 45.

ness perfected, wisdom completed. The root of evil has been sealed up from you, infirmity has been destroyed from you, death hidden away, corruption fled into Hades, pains have passed into oblivion, and unto the end the treasure of immortality has been shown.' Ezra is here told not to inquire about the multitude of those who perish; whatever torment may await them, they have brought it on themselves by the abuse of their liberty, 'for the Most High did not wish man to be destroyed.'[1]

The doctrine of the Apocalypse of Baruch, so far as it is unfolded, is substantially the same as that of Fourth Ezra; but it touches lightly the thoughts which are there fully discussed, and dwells at some length on the nature of the resurrection, which in Ezra is so briefly alluded to. In one passage, however, as the text stands, it presents a view peculiar to itself. After a description of the blessings of the Messianic time, the text proceeds thus:—
'And it shall come to pass after these things, when the time of the coming of the Messiah shall be fulfilled, and he shall return in glory, then all who have slept in hope of him shall rise again. And it shall come to pass at that time, the storehouses, in which the number of the souls of the just had been guarded, shall be opened, and they shall go forth, and the multitude of souls shall appear together in one assembly with one mind, and the earlier shall rejoice, and the last shall not be sorrowful. For they know that the time has come concerning which it was said that it was the end of times. But the souls of the impious, when they shall see all these things, shall then pine away the more. For they know that their punishment has come, and their destruction has arrived.'[2] According to this it would seem that the resurrection is to take place in the time of the Messiah. The earlier

[1] viii. 52–62.   [2] Ch. xxx.

part of the passage might suggest the idea of a partial resurrection, leaving the general resurrection for a later period; but the concluding portion shows that this is not intended; it is the end of times, and the impious know that their perdition has arrived. But I cannot help thinking that the opening lines have been tampered with by a Christian hand. Not only is the idea of the Messiah's returning in glory suggestive of Christian belief, but the expression is quite inappropriate where it stands. The blessedness of the Messiah's reign has just been dwelt upon at some length. Nothing has been said about his going away, and therefore to speak of his return merely occasions perplexity; and to refer to his arrival as taking place after he has already arrived is destitute of meaning. According to this book the Messiah is to reign ' until the world of corruption be ended,'[1] so that no time is left for his going away and returning; and his return in glory has no proper contrast, because his first reign was one of glory. For these reasons it seems probable that, just as the corresponding passage in Fourth Ezra has been corrupted by the transcribers, so this also has been altered by a Christian hand, and that the original words referred in some way to the close of the Messianic reign. If this conjecture be correct, the two works agree in their doctrine of a resurrection.

The mode in which the body will be treated at the resurrection is referred to at some length. Baruch asks whether those who rise will resume their present form, or be changed as the world will be. He is told in reply that the earth will restore the dead as it has received them, making no change in their figure. The reason for this is that there may be the power of mutual recognition, and a certainty that it is really the departed who have

[1] Ch. xl.

reappeared. But when this mutual recognition has taken place, and the day of judgment is passed, then their appearance shall be changed. The aspect of the wicked shall become worse than it is now, that they may suffer punishment. But those who have been justified in the divine law, and planted in their hearts the root of wisdom, shall be glorified and made beautiful, that they may be able to receive the world which does not die. The wicked shall see and be grieved at the exaltation of the righteous, and then shall go to be tortured. But the good shall be changed into the splendour of angels, and made equal to the stars, and assume every form they please.[1]

Passing on to the Rabbinical authorities we find the general doctrine of a future life and judgment stated in the words of Rabbi Eli'ezer Haqqappar:[2] 'Those who are born are to die, and the dead to live, and the living to be judged, that one may know, and may cause to know, and may be convinced that he is God, the Former, the Creator, the One possessed of understanding, the Judge, the Witness, the Opponent, and he is going to pronounce judgment. Blessed be he, before him is no injustice, or forgetfulness, or respect of persons, or receiving of a bribe; for everything is his. And know that everything will be according to the reckoning; and let not thy imagination cause thee to trust that Sheol will be a house of refuge for thee; for without thy will thou wast formed, and without thy will thou wast born, and without thy will thou dost live, and without thy will thou shalt die, and without thy will thou art destined to give account and reckoning before the King, the King of kings, the Holy, blessed be he!' Equally universal is the statement in the Targum of Isaiah xxvi. 19. 'Thou art he who revivest the dead, and dost raise up the bones of their corpses.

---

[1] Chs. xlix.-li.   [2] *Aboth* iv. 22 [in some editions 23].

All those who lie in the dust shall live, and give praise before thee; because the dew of light is thy dew to those who do thy will.[1] But as for the impious to whom thou hast given power, and who transgressed thy law, thou wilt surrender them to Gehenna.'

From these passages we should conclude that a universal resurrection and judgment both of the righteous and wicked were expected. Perhaps it is not inconsistent with this view, when presented as above in general terms, that certain special exceptions are pointed out in the Mishnah.[2] It is there said that the following persons 'have no part in the future age; he who says there is no resurrection of the dead according to the Law [*i.e.* taught in the Pentateuch], and the Law is not from heaven, and an Epiqoros.[3] Rabbi Akiba says, Also one who reads foreign books [or books outside the canon, according to some], and who mutters over a wound [as an incantation], and says, "I will put none of these diseases upon thee which I have brought upon Egypt, for I am the Lord that healeth thee."[4] Abba Shaül says, He who pronounces the name [יהוה] by its own letters.'[5] 'Three kings and four ordinary persons have no part in the age to come; three kings, Jeroboam, Ahab, and Manasseh. . . four ordinary persons, Balaam, Doeg, Ahithophel, Gehazi.'[6] The generation of the flood, and of the dispersion [referring to the builders of the tower of Babel], and the men of Sodom are likewise excluded, and of these the first shall not even stand in the judgment. The spies [at the time

---

[1] In the Talmud, *Chagigah* 12b, this dew is represented as the instrument of resurrection. Referred to by Gfrörer, *J. d. H.* ii. S. 284.

[2] *Synhed.* x [xi.] 1–4.

[3] That is, one who despises the Law. It is often rendered *Epicurean*, but it is better to leave the word untranslated.

[4] Ex. xv. 26.

[5] Thus far, Mish 1.   [6] Mish. 2.

of the invasion of Palestine] have no share in the future world, and the generation of the wilderness also shall not stand in the judgment, and the assembly of Korah shall not come forth again.[1] Further, the men of a destroyed city [destroyed on account of having been led into idolatry, in conformity with Deut. xiii. 13–18] have no part in the age to come.[2] So also in the Gemaras certain exceptions are made. In the Jerusalem Gemara[3] we are told that Rabbi Acha asked, in connection with Ecclesiastes ix. 4, 'to him that is joined to all the living there is hope,' whether those who laid hands upon the temple could have hope if they repented? The answer is that they cannot be received, because they stretched out their hand against the temple of the Lord; and they cannot be rejected, because they repented. Therefore the saying shall be fulfilled in them, 'they shall sleep a perpetual sleep, and not wake.'[4] The Rabbis of Cæsarea, it is added, cited this passage to prove that the little ones of the Gentiles and the armies of Nebuchadnezzar [who had not taken a part in the siege of Jerusalem] should come no more to life, and consequently should not be judged. In the Babylonian Gemara[5] we read that Rab El'azar said that the unlearned people [*i.e.* those who have kept themselves away from the Law], should not live again, founding his decision on Isaiah xxvi.14, 'They are dead, they shall not live; they are deceased, they shall not rise.' The reason is that the light of the Law revives everyone who devotes himself to it, but has the

---

[1] Mish. 3, where different opinions are given, on which we need not pause.
[2] Mish. 4.
[3] *Berakhoth* ix. 1 [2 in the old editions].
[4] Jer. li. 57.
[5] *Kethuboth* 111*b*. Referred to by Gfrörer, *J. d. H.* ii. S. 277, where the reference is wrongly given as 101*b*.

contrary effect on everyone who does not so devote himself.

As to the agent by whom the resurrection is to be effected, opinion is divided. In the passage quoted above from the Targum of Isaiah xxvi. 19, God alone is spoken of as bringing it about; and in the Babylonian Gemara it is said that there are three keys which God reserves to himself: the key of a woman on the point of giving birth, of rain, and of the resurrection.[1] On the other hand we have already seen that Rabbi Pinchas ben Yair expected the resurrection to come by the hand of Elijah;[2] and some of the late writers believed that it would be accomplished by the Messiah.[3]

In regard to the manner in which the resurrection should take place some curious questions were asked, and decided with the usual conclusiveness. 'Queen Cleopatra asked Rabbi Meir, and said: I know that the dead live again, for it is said,[4] "They shall flourish out of the city [Jerusalem] like the grass of the earth;" but when they rise up, will they rise naked or clothed? He answered, I will show thee this by a conclusion drawn from the less to the greater, from the grain of wheat. For, behold! the grain of wheat, which is buried naked, springs forth out of the earth with many clothes; how much more the righteous, who were buried with their clothes.'[5] Again, 'Resh Lakish puts these two passages against one another. In one place[6] it is written, "Behold, I will gather them from the coasts of the earth, and with them the blind and the lame, the woman with child, and her that travaileth with child together," and in

---

[1] *Synhed.* 113a.   [2] Mishnah, *Sotah* ix. 15.
[3] See Gfrörer, *J. d. H.* ii. S. 281-2.   [4] Ps. lxxii. 16.
[5] *Synhed.* 90b. See also *Kethuboth* 111b.   [6] Jer. xxxi. 8.

another place[1] it is written, "Then shall the lame man leap as a hart, and the tongue of the dumb sing: for in the wilderness shall waters break out, and streams in the desert." How is this possible? Answer: They shall rise with their defect, but then be healed.'[2] In later times the germ of the resurrection body was supposed to be a bone in the back, named lûz (לוז), and this on the ground that it resisted alike the attacks of fire and water, of hammer and mill.[3]

There is a picturesque description of the judgment in 'Abodah Zarah,[4] which by its resemblances and contrasts cannot fail to remind us of that in Matthew xxv. The passage is rather long, but we may quote a part of it. 'In the future age the blessed God will take the Book of the Law into his bosom, and say, "Whoever has engaged in this Law, let him come here and receive his reward." Immediately all nations will stream up, confusedly mixed together. But God commands them to come singly and in order. First, the Roman empire steps forward. The Lord asks them, "What have ye done in the world?" They answer, "Lord of the world, we have fitted up many market-places, erected baths, collected gold and silver, and all this we have done to favour the children of Israel, so that they could busy themselves with the Law undisturbed." But the Lord answers them, "O ye fools of the world, what ye have done ye have done for yourselves. Ye have fitted up market-places to keep dissolute women in them. Ye have erected baths for the sake of your own voluptuousness. As regards gold and silver, these belong to me, as it is written,[5] The silver is mine, and the gold is mine, saith the Lord of hosts. Is there

---

[1] Isai. xxxv. 6.   [2] *Synhed.* 91b.
[3] See the passages referred to in Gfrörer, *J. d. II.* ii. S. 282-3.
[4] 2a, b. Referred to by Gfrörer, *J. d. II.* ii. S. 287-8.   [5] Hag. ii. 8.

one among you who can say something concerning this [the Law]?" Immediately the Romans go forth with affrighted souls. After them comes the Persian empire. God says again, "What have ye done in the world?" They answer, "Lord of the world, we have built many bridges, subjected many cities, carried on many wars, and all this we have done for the sake of the children of Israel, so that they could busy themselves with the Law undisturbed." But the Lord replies, "What ye have done ye have done for yourselves. Ye have built bridges to levy toll. Ye have subjected cities to impose socage on them. The wars I have carried on myself, as it is written,[1] The Lord is a man of war. Is there one among you who can say anything about this?" Immediately the Persians also shall go forth with affrighted souls. But why did the Persians come before the throne of God, seeing that the Romans got nothing by it? They thought, "They have destroyed the temple of God; by us, on the contrary, it was built."' The other nations likewise present themselves, and receive a similar condemnation.

The judgment is to take place in Jerusalem,[2] and the wicked to be sent into the eternal fire of Gehenna.[3] A second death, to be inflicted on the bodies of the wicked, is mentioned in a few passages.[4] This apparently refers to the destruction of the resurrection-body. We need not dwell on the rewards of the righteous, as no special features are added to the descriptions already given. Their faces shall shine as the sun; they shall have crowns on their heads, and enjoy the light of the Shekhina.[5]

---

[1] Ex. xv. 3.   [2] Targ. Isai. xxxiii. 14.
[3] Ibid. and Targ. Isai. xxvi. 19; lxv. 5.
[4] Targ. Onk. Deut. xxxiii. 6; Jon. Isai. lxv. 5, 15.
[5] See the passages in Gfrörer, *J. d. H.* ii. S. 289–90.

CHAPTER XXIV.

GENERAL VIEW OF THE MESSIANIC IDEA BEFORE THE TIME OF CHRIST.

WE have now concluded our detailed survey of the Messianic Idea. It only remains for us to present in a brief summary the features of that idea which are exhibited in the pre-Christian literature.[1]

Time was divided into two great periods, answering to this 'age' and the 'future' or 'coming age' of the New Testament. These were separated from one another by the occurrence of the judgment, which was to take place 'in the last time' or in the 'end of days.' With a view to ascertaining its ulterior limit the former period was variously subdivided by artificial methods. But this was not sufficient. Mankind should be warned of the approaching consummation by fearful portents. The temple should be desecrated, and unparalleled calamities fall upon the people. Swords should appear in the midnight sky, and blood trickle from the rocks. The whole course of nature should be deranged, and an appalling outbreak of idolatry and wickedness bring to remembrance the days before the flood.

From the eschatology of several pre-Christian books the Messiah is excluded. In the writings in which he

---

[1] In this I include works which are too early to be in any way influenced by Christian teaching, though they may actually fall within the Christian era.

appears he is placed in the first age, except in the Book of Enoch, which seems to place him in the second. His birth-place is not mentioned, but in the Book of Enoch is apparently Jerusalem. His descent from David is distinctly noticed. He is called the Messiah, or Christ, only in the Psalms of Solomon. There also he is styled the 'Son of David;' and he is referred to as the 'Son of God' in a passage in the Book of Enoch, where I have ventured to dispute the genuineness of the words. He is not represented as possessed of a superhuman nature, but simply as a king endowed with high spiritual gifts.

The heathen powers should assemble themselves to wage war against the chosen people, but should be utterly destroyed by the sword, or by the word of the Messiah's mouth. Then the Messiah should reign as a righteous king over Israel, and should hold the Gentiles in servitude beneath his yoke. His kingdom, having its centre in Jerusalem, should extend over all peoples, and endure for ever.

This kingdom is referred to as 'the kingdom of God;' but whether this expression is intended as a distinctive name is very doubtful. The Messianic rule should be adorned by righteousness, and sin and the devil be destroyed. According to some authorities the Gentiles should be converted to the true religion; but the Psalms of Solomon seem opposed to this representation. The scattered tribes of Israel should return; the old Jerusalem be replaced by a new and more glorious city; the earth become marvellously fruitful, the wild animals lose their ferocity, and human life be long and peaceful.

A final and decisive judgment should take place. Till then the souls of the dead should dwell in a region situated, according to varying conceptions, in the west or under the earth. The fallen angels were bound beneath the earth; but at the day of judgment they should be thrown into a fiery abyss. Good men should be richly rewarded, but the wicked be consigned to Gehenna. As to the final condition of the dead opinions were divided, some apparently believing in a spiritual immortality, others in a bodily resurrection. Lastly it must be observed that the Messiah is nowhere represented as the agent through whom the judgment is to be administered; but on this awful occasion, it was conceived, God himself would sit upon the throne of judgment, and pronounce the verdict against which none might appeal.

APPENDIX.

SIBYLLINE ORACLES.—After the present work had gone to the press an elaborate article on 'The Sibylline Books' appeared in the 'Edinburgh Review,' July 1877, pp. 31–67, in which the whole question of this curious literature is treated more at large than our purposes required. The reader who desires general information in a small compass will do well to consult it.

For the benefit of those who may wish to pursue the subject more in detail I may refer to the editions of C. Alexandre. The first edition bears date 1841–1856. The second volume, which appeared in the latter year, consists of seven Excursus, dealing respectively with the Sibyls, the Sibylline verses among the ancient Greeks, the Sibylline books of the Romans, the Sibylline verses among the ancient Christians, the Sibylline books of the present day, the Sibylline doctrine, and the dialect, metre, and poetical art of the Sibyls. The whole comprises 620 pages, and forms an elaborate introduction to the Sibylline literature. The second edition, containing introduction and notes, is more compact, and well suited to the purposes of the student.[1]

FOURTH EZRA.—My attention has been called to an interesting article by Mr. J. S. Wood, on 'The Missing Fragment of the Fourth Book of Esdras,' in the Journal of Philology, vol. vii. No. 14. 1877, pp. 264–278. It contains a copy of the missing fragment of the Latin Version, which was found among the papers of the Rev. John Palmer, formerly 'Professor of Arabick' on Sir T. Adams' Foundation at Cambridge. The

---

[1] ΧΡΗΣΜΟΙ ΣΙΒΥΛΛΙΑΚΟΙ. Oracula Sibyllina. Editio altera ex priore ampliore contracta, integra tamen et passim aucta, multisque locis retractata, curante C. Alexandre. Parisiis MDCCCLXIX.

paper containing the transcript of this fragment states that it was made in 1826, 'from a Latin MS. of the Old and New Testaments which is in the Library "de la Universidad" at Alcalá de Henares.' The MS. is now at Madrid.

An edition of the Arabic codex of Fourth Ezra in the Vatican has just been announced.[1]

APOCALYPSE OF BARUCH.—An article entitled 'L' Apocalypse de Baruch,' from the pen of Ernest Renan, appeared in the Journal des Savants, Avril, 1877, pp. 222–231. Renan places the work later than Fourth Ezra, as bearing decided marks of imitation. He assigns it to the last year of Trajan, when the reverses which attended the Roman arms in the East made it possible to believe that the end of the Roman empire was approaching. This is the first suitable occasion after 97 A.D., the date assigned by Renan to Fourth Ezra; and the work cannot have been later, or it could not have been adopted by the Christians.[2]

THE GREAT SYNAGOGUE.—In his excellent edition of ' Sayings of the Jewish Fathers '[3] Mr. Taylor has a short excursus on the Great Synagogue, in which he accepts the opinion of Jost.[4] He does not, however, notice Kuenen's pamphlet.

[1] Esdrae Liber IV. arabice. E cod. Vaticano nunc primum ed. J. Gildemeister. Bonn.

[2] P. 230.

[3] Sayings of the Jewish Fathers, comprising Pirqe Aboth and Pereq R. Meir in Hebrew and English, with critical and illustrative notes; .. by Charles Taylor, M.A., Fellow and Divinity Lecturer of St. John's College, Cambridge, and Honorary Fellow of King's College, London. Cambridge, 1877.

[4] Pp. 124–5.

INDEX OF MODERN WORKS.[1]

Alexandre, Oracula Sibyllina, 391
Anger, Synopsis Evangeliorum, 117; Vorlesungen über die Gesch. der mess. Idee, 41

Bensly, The Missing Fragment of 4th Ezra, 86
Bertholdt, Christologia Judæorum, 221
Bleek, Ueber die Entsteh. sib. Or., 11
Bretschneider, Das Messiasreich, 84
Buxtorf, Lexicon Chald. Talm. et Rab., 95

Castelli, Il Messia secondo gli Ebrei, 185
Ceriani, Monumenta Sac. et Prof., 74
Colani, Jésus-Christ et les Croy. mess., 41
Cozza : see *Vercellone*.
Credner, Gesch. des neutest. Kanon, 75

Dähne, Gesch. Darstellung der jüd.-alex. Relig.-Phil., 271
Daniel secundum Septuaginta, 259
Davidson, Introduction to O. T., 7
Delitzsch, Daniel, 6
Deutsch, Literary Remains, 148; Talmud, in Quarterly Review, 167; Versions, Targum, in Dict. of Bible, 148
Dillmann, Das Buch der Jubiläen, 143 ; Das Buch Henoch, 19; Henoch, 31 ; Pseudepig. des A. T., 31
Dünner, Halachisch-kritische Forschungen, 176

Edinburgh Review, the Sibylline Books, 391
Eichhorn, Einleit. in das A. T., 149
Ewald, Abh. über des äth. Buches Henokh Entst., 31 ; Das vierte Ezrabuch, 88 ; Die Propheten des Alten Bundes, 192 ; Gesch. des Volkes Israel, 31

[1] This list is given that the reader may be able without difficulty to find the title of any modern work cited in the volume. It indicates the pages where the several works are first referred to, and where their titles are quoted either fully or with sufficient fulness for identification. Though it does not pretend to be exhaustive of the literature, it may perhaps be of some service to the student.

Fabricius, Cod. Apoc. N. T., 90; Cod. Pseud. V. T., 3
Frankel, Zu dem Targum der Proph., 149
Friedlieb, Orac. Sibyl., 12
Fritzsche, Libri Apoc. Vet. Test., 75
Fuller: see *Rose*.

Geiger (*Abraham*), Article in Jüd. Zeitschrift, 152; Urschrift u. Uebersetz. der Bibel, 149
Geiger (*P. E. E.*), Der Psalter Salomo's, 133
Gfrörer, Das Jahrhundert des Heils, 39; Philo u. die al. Theos., 13; Prophetæ Veteres Pseudepigraphi, 19
Gibbon, Decline and Fall, 182
Gieseler, Lehrb. der Kirchengeschichte, 182
Güldemeister, Esdrae Liber IV. arabice, 392
Grabe, LXX., 259
Grätz, Geschichte der Juden, 95
Graf, Daniel, 7
Gutschmid (*von*), Die Apok. des Esra, 86

Hausrath, Neutest. Zeitgeschichte, 41
Hengstenberg, Christology of the Old Test., 227
Hilgenfeld, Die jüd. Apok., 6; Die jüd Apok. u. die neu. Forschungen, 99; Messias Judæorum, 75; Nov. Test. extra Can. recept., 75
Hir (*le*), Du IVe livre d'Esdras, 113
Hitzig, Daniel, in Kurzg. exeg. Handb. zum A. T., 203
Hoffmann, Das Buch Henoch, 19
Hofmann, Article in Zeitsch. der deut. morg. Gesellsch., 29
Holmes, LXX., 259
Holtzmann, Judenthum und Christenthum, 41

Jellinek, Article in Zeitsch. der deut. morg. Gesellsch., 73
Jost, Gesch. der Israeliten, 175; Gesch. des Jud. u. seiner Sekten, 162

Keim, Geschichte Jesu, 41
Köstlin, Ueber die Entsteh. des Buchs Henoch, 35
Kuenen, Over de mannen der groote synagoge, 162; Religion of Israel, 7

Lardner, Works, 11
Laurence, Anabaticon of Isaiah, 4; Book of Enoch, 18; Primi Ezræ Libri Versio Æth., 89
Lightfoot, Horæ Heb. et Talm., 279
Lücke, Einleit. in die Offenb., 6

Macaulay, Hist. of England, 183
Mai, Script. Vet. Nova Col., 11
M. (*R.*), Article on The Book of Daniel, 203
Movers, Apokryphen-Literatur, 135

Nöldeke, Die Alttestament. Literatur, 150

INDEX OF MODERN WORKS. 395

Ockley, Translation of Arab. of 4th Ezra, 88
Oehler, Messias, 41

Palmer: see *Wood*.
Petermann, Trans. of Arm. Version of 4th Ezra, 89
Philippi, Das Buch Henoch, 29
Pressel, Thalmud, 162
Pusey, Daniel the Prophet, 7

Ranke, (*von*), Deutsche Geschichte, 182
Reincccius, LXX., 259
Renan, L'Apocalypse de Baruch, 392; L'Apocalypse de l'an 97, 106
Rönsch, Das Buch der Jubiläen, 71
Rose, Introd. to Book of Daniel, and Com., 7

Sabatier, Bib. Sac. Lat. Vers. ant., 85
Schenkel, Messian. Weissagungen, 73; Messias, 117
Schiller-Szinessy, on the word 'Arzareth,' 334
Schmidt and *Merx*, Assumptio Mosis, 75
Schoettgen, Horæ Heb. et Talm., 322
Schürer, Lehrbuch der neutest. Zeitgesch., 29
Sieffert, Nonnulla ad apoc. lib. Henochi originem &c. pertin., 34
Stanley, Lectures on the Jewish Church, 165
Steiner, Der arab. Auszug des 'Propheten Esra,' 88
Surenhusius, Mischna, 218

Taylor, Sayings of the Jewish Fathers, 392
Tideman, De Apoc. van Henoch, 34
Tischendorf, LXX., 259

Van der Vlis, Disputatio Crit. de Ezræ libro apoc., 101
Vercellone and *Cozza*, Cod. Vat., 259
Volkmar, Beiträge zur Erklär. des Buches Henoch, 43; Das vierte Buch Esra, 16; Eine neutest. Entdeckung, 43; Mose Proph. u. Himmelfahrt, 16

Wechelius, LXX., 259
Westcott, Daniel, The Book of, 6
Wetstein, Nov. Test., 321
Wette (*de*), Einleit. in das A. T., 156
Whiston, Primitive Christianity Revived, 88
Wieseler, Das vierte Buch Esra, 92
Wittichen, Die Idee des Reiches Gottes, 41
Wood, The Missing Fragment of the Fourth Book of Esdras, 391

Young, Christology of the Targums, 278; The Ethics of the Fathers, 170

Zunz, Die gottesdienst. Vorträge der Juden, 149

MARCH 1877

CLASSIFIED LISTS OF BOOKS

(NEW WORKS AND NEW EDITIONS)

IN

MISCELLANEOUS

AND

GENERAL LITERATURE

FOLLOWED BY

AN ALPHABETICAL INDEX UNDER AUTHORS' NAMES

London
Longmans, Green & Co.
Paternoster Row
1877.

ANCIENT HISTORICAL EPO[CHS]

Now in course of publication, uniform with Epochs [of...]
each volume complete in itself,

EPOCHS OF ANCIENT [HISTORY.]

*A Series of Books Narrating the History of Greece an[d ...]
Relations to other Countries at Successive [Epochs.]*

Edited by the Rev. GEORGE W. COX, M.A. late Scholar [of ...]
and jointly by CHARLES SANKEY, M.A. late Scholar of [...]

'The special purpose for which these manuals are intended, they will, we should think, admirably serve. Their clearness as narratives will make them acceptable to the schoolboy as well as to the teacher: and their critical acumen will commend them to the use of the more advanced student who is not only getting up, but trying to understand and appreciate, his HERODOTUS and THUCYDIDES. As for the general plan of the series of which they form part, we must confess, without wishing to draw comparisons for which we should be sorry to [...] have to examine [...] it strikes us as [...] the beginner, at [...] structive, as it i[s ...] natural way of [...] study it by period[s ...] earlier Greek and [...] events, there is no [...] way of his being [...] here period and [...] quasi-technically [...] quently coincide, [...] fairly be called [...] History.'

The **GREEKS and the PERSIANS.** By the Rev. G[...]
Scholar of Trinity College, Oxford; Joint-Editor of the Series [...]
Fcp. 8vo. price 2s. 6d.

The **EARLY ROMAN EMPIRE.** From the Assassina[tion ...]
to the Assassination of Domitian. By the Rev. W. WOLFE CAPE[S ...]
History in the University of Oxford. With 2 Coloured Maps. Fcp [...]

ROME to its CAPTURE by the GAULS. By Wilhe[lm ...]
'History of Rome.' With a Coloured Map. Fcp. 8vo. price 2s. 6d.

The **ATHENIAN EMPIRE from the FLIGHT of XE**[RXES ...]
of ATHENS. By the Rev. G. W. COX, M.A. late Scholar of Trini[ty ...]
Editor of the Series. With 5 Maps. Fcp. 8vo. price 2s. 6d.

The **ROMAN TRIUMVIRATES.** By the Very Rev. C[...]
Dean of Ely; Author of 'History of the Romans under the Empir[e.' ...]
Fcp. 8vo. price 2s. 6d.

The **ROMAN EMPIRE of the SECOND CENTURY,** [or the AGE of the]
ANTONINES. By the Rev. W. WOLFE CAPES, M.A. Reader of Anc[ient History, Univer-]
sity of Oxford. With 2 Coloured Maps. Fcp. 8vo. price 2s. 6d.

The **RISE of the MACEDONIAN EMPIRE.** By Art[hur M. CURTEIS, M.A.]
formerly Fellow of Trinity College, Oxford, and late Assistant-M[aster at Sherborne School.]
With 8 Maps. Fcp. 8vo. price 2s. 6d.

The **GRACCHI, MARIUS, and SULLA.** By A. H. Bee[sly, M.A. Assistant-]
Master, Marlborough College. With 2 Maps. Fcp. 8vo. price 2s. 6[d.]

ROME and CARTHAGE, the PUNIC WARS. By R. B[...]
Assistant-Master, Harrow School.

SPARTAN and THEBAN SUPREMACY. By Charl[es SANKEY, M.A. late]
Scholar of Queen's College, Oxford; Assistant-Master, Marlboroug[h College; Joint-Editor of]
the Series.

London, LONGMANS & CO.

39 Paternoster Row, E.C.
London, *March* 1877.

GENERAL LIST OF WORKS

PUBLISHED BY

Messrs. Longmans, Green, & Co.

	PAGE
Arts, Manufactures, &c.	15
Astronomy & Meteorology	10
Biographical Works	4
Chemistry & Physiology	14
Dictionaries & other Books of Reference	8
Fine Arts & Illustrated Editions	14
History, Politics, Historical Memoirs, &c.	1
Index	25 to 28
Mental & Political Philosophy	5
Miscellaneous & Critical Works	7
Natural History & Physical Science	11
Poetry & the Drama	21
Religious & Moral Works	16
Rural Sports, Horse & Cattle Management, &c.	22
Travels, Voyages, &c.	19
Works of Fiction	20
Works of Utility & General Information	23

HISTORY, POLITICS, HISTORICAL MEMOIRS, &c.

Sketches of Ottoman History. By the Very Rev. R. W. CHURCH, Dean of St. Paul's. 1 vol. crown 8vo. [*Nearly ready.*

The Eastern Question. By the Rev. MALCOLM MACCOLL, M.A. 8vo. [*Nearly ready.*

The History of England from the Accession of James II. By the Right Hon. Lord MACAULAY.

STUDENT'S EDITION, 2 vols. cr. 8vo. 12*s.*
PEOPLE'S EDITION, 4 vols. cr. 8vo. 16*s.*
CABINET EDITION, 8 vols. post 8vo. 48*s.*
LIBRARY EDITION, 5 vols. 8vo. £4.

Critical and Historical Essays contributed to the Edinburgh Review. By the Right Hon. Lord MACAULAY.

CHEAP EDITION, crown 8vo. 3*s.* 6*d.*
STUDENT'S EDITION, crown 8vo. 6*s.*
PEOPLE'S EDITION, 2 vols. crown 8vo. 8*s.*
CABINET EDITION, 4 vols. 24*s.*
LIBRARY EDITION, 3 vols. 8vo. 36*s.*

Lord Macaulay's Works.
Complete and uniform Library Edition. Edited by his Sister, Lady TREVELYAN. 8 vols. 8vo. with Portrait, £5. 5*s.*

A

The History of England
from the Fall of Wolsey to the Defeat of the Spanish Armada. By J. A. FROUDE, M.A.
CABINET EDITION, 12 vols. cr. 8vo. £3. 12s.
LIBRARY EDITION, 12 vols. 8vo. £8. 18s.

The English in Ireland
in the Eighteenth Century. By J. A. FROUDE, M.A. 3 vols. 8vo. £2. 8s.

Journal of the Reigns of
King George IV. and King William IV. By the late C. C. F. GREVILLE, Esq. Edited by H. REEVE, Esq. Fifth Edition. 3 vols. 8vo. price 36s.

The Life of Napoleon III.
derived from State Records, Unpublished Family Correspondence, and Personal Testimony. By BLANCHARD JERROLD. In Four Volumes, 8vo. with numerous Portraits and Facsimiles. VOLS. I. and II. price 18s. each.

** The Third Volume is in the press.

Introductory Lectures on
Modern History delivered in Lent Term 1842; with the Inaugural Lecture delivered in December 1841. By the late Rev. T. ARNOLD, D.D. 8vo. price 7s. 6d.

On Parliamentary Government
in England; its Origin, Development, and Practical Operation. By ALPHEUS TODD. 2 vols. 8vo. price £1. 17s.

The Constitutional History
of England since the Accession of George III. 1760-1870. By Sir THOMAS ERSKINE MAY, K.C.B. D.C.L. Fifth Edition. 3 vols. crown 8vo. 18s.

Democracy in Europe;
a History. By Sir THOMAS ERSKINE MAY, K.C.B. D.C.L. 2 vols. 8vo.
[In the press.

History of Civilisation in
England and France, Spain and Scotland. By HENRY THOMAS BUCKLE. 3 vols. crown 8vo. 24s.

Lectures on the History
of England from the Earliest Times to the Death of King Edward II. By W. LONGMAN, F.S.A. Maps and Illustrations. 8vo. 15s.

History of the Life &
Times of Edward III. By W. LONGMAN, F.S.A. With 9 Maps, 8 Plates, and 16 Woodcuts. 2 vols. 8vo. 28s.

The Life of Simon de
Montfort, Earl of Leicester, with special reference to the Parliamentary History of his time. By GEORGE WALTER PROTHERO, Fellow and Lecturer in History, King's College, Cambridge. Crown 8vo. 9s.

History of England under the Duke of Buckingham and Charles the First, 1624-1628.
By S. R. GARDINER, late Student of Ch. Ch. 2 vols. 8vo. with 2 Maps, 24s.

The Personal Government
of Charles I. from the Death of Buckingham to the Declaration of the Judges in favour of Ship Money, 1628-1637. By S. R. GARDINER, late Student of Ch. Ch. 2 vols. 8vo.
[In the press.

Popular History of
France, from the Earliest Times to the Death of Louis XIV. By ELIZABETH M. SEWELL. With 8 Maps. Crown 8vo. 7s. 6d.

History of Prussia, from
the Earliest Times to the Present Day; tracing the Origin and Development of her Military Organisation. By Capt. W. J. WYATT. VOLS. I. & II. A.D. 700 to A.D. 1525. 8vo. 36s.

A Student's Manual of
the History of India from the Earliest Period to the Present. By Col. MEADOWS TAYLOR, M.R.A.S. Second Thousand. Crown 8vo. Maps, 7s. 6d.

Indian Polity; a View of
the System of Administration in India. By Lieut.-Col. G. CHESNEY. 2nd Edition, revised, with Map. 8vo. 21s.

Essays in Modern Military Biography.
By Col. C. C. CHESNEY, R.E. 8vo. 12s. 6d.

Waterloo Lectures; a Study of the Campaign of 1815. By Col. C. C. CHESNEY, R.E. Third Edition. 8vo. Map, 10s. 6d.

The Oxford Reformers— John Colet, Erasmus, and Thomas More; being a History of their Fellow-Work. By F. SEEBOHM. Second Edition. 8vo. 14s.

The Mythology of the Aryan Nations. By the Rev. G. W. COX, M.A. late Scholar of Trinity College, Oxford. 2 vols. 8vo. 28s.

A History of Greece. By the Rev. G. W. COX, M.A. VOLS. I. & II. 8vo. Maps, 36s.

General Hist. of Greece to the Death of Alexander the Great; with a Sketch of the Subsequent History to the Present Time. By the Rev. G. W. COX, M.A. Crown 8vo. with Maps, 7s. 6d.

General History of Rome from the Foundation of the City to the Fall of Augustulus, B.C. 753–A.D. 476. By Dean MERIVALE, D.D. Crown 8vo. Maps, 7s. 6d.

History of the Romans under the Empire. By Dean MERIVALE, D.D. 8 vols. post 8vo. 48s.

The Fall of the Roman Republic; a Short History of the Last Century of the Commonwealth. By Dean MERIVALE, D.D. 12mo. 7s. 6d.

The History of Rome. By WILHELM IHNE. VOLS. I. & II. 8vo. 30s. VOL. III. is in the press.

The Sixth Oriental Monarchy; or, the Geography, History, and Antiquities of Parthia. By G. RAWLINSON, M.A. With Maps and Illustrations. 8vo. 16s.

The Seventh Great Oriental Monarchy; or, a History of the Sassanians. By G. RAWLINSON, M.A. With Map and 95 Illustrations. 8vo. 28s.

Encyclopædia of Chronology, Historical and Biographical; comprising the Dates of all the Great Events of History, including Treaties, Alliances, Wars, Battles, &c. By B. B. WOODWARD, B.A. and W. L. R. CATES. 8vo. 42s.

The History of European Morals from Augustus to Charlemagne. By W. E. H. LECKY, M.A. 2 vols. crown 8vo. 16s.

History of the Rise and Influence of the Spirit of Rationalism in Europe. By W. E. H. LECKY, M.A. 2 vols. crown 8vo. 16s.

The Native Races of the Pacific States of North America. By H. H. BANCROFT. 5 vols. 8vo. £6. 5s.

History of the Mongols from the Ninth to the Nineteenth Century. By HENRY H. HOWORTH, F.S.A. VOL. I. the Mongols Proper and the Kalmuks; with Two Coloured Maps. Royal 8vo. 28s.

Islam under the Arabs. By ROBERT DURIE OSBORN, Major in the Bengal Staff Corps. 8vo. 12s.

Introduction to the Science of Religion, Four Lectures delivered at the Royal Institution; with Two Essays on False Analogies and the Philosophy of Mythology. By MAX MÜLLER, M.A. Crown 8vo. 10s. 6d.

Zeller's Stoics, Epicureans, and Sceptics. Translated by the Rev. O. J. REICHEL, M.A. Cr. 8vo. 14s.

Zeller's Socrates & the Socratic Schools. Translated by the Rev. O. J. REICHEL, M.A. Crown 8vo. New Edition in the press.

Zeller's Plato & the Older Academy. Translated by S. FRANCES ALLEYNE and ALFRED GOODWIN, B.A. Crown 8vo. 18s.

Sketch of the History of the Church of England to the Revolution of 1688. By T. V. SHORT, D.D. sometime Bishop of St. Asaph. Crown 8vo. 7s. 6d.

The History of Philosophy, from Thales to Comte. By GEORGE HENRY LEWES. Fourth Edition. 2 vols. 8vo. 32*s*.

The Childhood of the English Nation; or, the Beginnings of English History. By ELLA S. ARMITAGE. Fcp. 8vo. 2*s*. 6*d*.

Epochs of Modern History. Edited by E. E. MORRIS, M.A. J. S. PHILLPOTTS, B.C.L. and C. COLBECK, M.A. Eleven volumes now published, each complete in itself, in fcp. 8vo. with Maps & Index:—

Cox's Crusades, 2*s*. 6*d*.

Creighton's Age of Elizabeth, 2*s*. 6*d*.

Gairdner's Houses of Lancaster and York, 2*s*. 6*d*.

Gardiner's Puritan Revolution, 2*s*. 6*d*.

Gardiner's Thirty Years' War, 2*s*. 6*d*.

Hale's Fall of the Stuarts, 2*s*. 6*d*.

Ludlow's War of American Independence, 2*s*. 6*d*.

Morris's Age of Anne, 2*s*. 6*d*.

Seebohm's Protestant Revolution, price 2*s*. 6*d*.

Stubbs's Early Plantagenets, 2*s*. 6*d*.

Warburton's Edward III. 2*s*. 6*d*.

*** Other Epochs in preparation, in continuation of the Series.

The Student's Manual of Modern History; containing the Rise and Progress of the Principal European Nations. By W. COOKE TAYLOR, LL.D. Crown 8vo. 7*s*. 6*d*.

The Student's Manual of Ancient History; containing the Political History, Geographical Position, and Social State of the Principal Nations of Antiquity. By W. COOKE TAYLOR, LL.D. Crown 8vo. 7*s*. 6*d*.

Epochs of Ancient History. Edited by the Rev. G. W. COX, M.A. and by C. SANKEY, M.A. Ten volumes, each complete in itself, in fcp. 8vo. with Maps & Index:—

Beesly's Gracchi, Marius & Sulla, 2*s*.6*d*.

Capes's Age of the Antonines, 2*s*. 6*d*.

Capes's Early Roman Empire, 2*s*. 6*d*.

Cox's Athenian Empire, 2*s*. 6*d*.

Cox's Greeks & Persians, 2*s*. 6*d*.

Curteis's Macedonian Empire, 2*s*. 6*d*.

Ihne's Rome to its Capture by the Gauls, 2*s*. 6*d*.

Merivale's Roman Triumvirates, 2*s*. 6*d*.

Sankey's Spartan & Theban Supremacy. [*In the press*.

Smith's Rome & Carthage, the Punic Wars. [*In the press*.

BIOGRAPHICAL WORKS.

The Life and Letters of Lord Macaulay. By his Nephew, G. OTTO TREVELYAN, M.P. Second Edition, with Additions and Corrections. 2 vols. 8vo. Portrait, 36*s*.

The Life of Sir William Fairbairn, Bart. F.R.S. Partly written by himself; edited and completed by W. POLE, F.R.S. 8vo. Portrait, 18*s*.

Arthur Schopenhauer, his Life and his Philosophy. By HELEN ZIMMERN. Post 8vo. Portrait, 7*s*. 6*d*.

The Life, Works, and Opinions of Heinrich Heine. By WILLIAM STIGAND. 2 vols. 8vo. Portrait, 28*s*.

The Life and Letters of Mozart. Translated from the German Biography of Dr. LUDWIG NOHL by Lady WALLACE. 2 vols. post 8vo. with Two Portraits. [*Nearly ready*.

Felix Mendelssohn's Letters from Italy and Switzerland, and Letters from 1833 to 1847. Translated by Lady WALLACE. With Portrait. 2 vols. crown 8vo. 5*s*. each.

Life of Robert Frampton, D.D. Bishop of Gloucester, deprived as a Non-Juror in 1689. Edited by T. S. EVANS, M.A. Vicar of Shoreditch. Crown 8vo. Portrait, 10s. 6d.

Autobiography. By JOHN STUART MILL. 8vo. 7s. 6d.

Isaac Casaubon, 1559-1614. By MARK PATTISON, Rector of Lincoln College, Oxford. 8vo. 18s.

Biographical and Critical Essays. By A. HAYWARD, Q.C. Second Series, 2 vols. 8vo. 28s. Third Series, 1 vol. 8vo. 14s.

The Memoirs of Sir John Reresby, of Thrybergh, Bart. M.P. 1634-1689. Edited from the Original Manuscript by J. J. CARTWRIGHT, M.A. 8vo. 21s.

Leaders of Public Opinion in Ireland; Swift, Flood, Grattan, O'Connell. By W. E. H. LECKY, M.A. Crown 8vo. 7s. 6d.

Essays in Ecclesiastical Biography. By the Right Hon. Sir J. STEPHEN, LL.D. Crown 8vo. 7s. 6d.

Dictionary of General Biography; containing Concise Memoirs and Notices of the most Eminent Persons of all Ages and Countries. By W. L. R. CATES. 8vo. 25s.

Life of the Duke of Wellington. By the Rev. G. R. GLEIG, M.A. Crown 8vo. Portrait, 5s.

Memoirs of Sir Henry Havelock, K.C.B. By JOHN CLARK MARSHMAN. Crown 8vo. 3s. 6d.

Vicissitudes of Families. By Sir BERNARD BURKE, C.B. Two vols. crown 8vo. 21s.

Maunder's Biographical Treasury. Latest Edition, reconstructed and partly re-written, with above 1,600 additional Memoirs, by W. L. R. CATES. Fcp. 8vo. 6s.

MENTAL and POLITICAL PHILOSOPHY.

Comte's System of Positive Polity, or Treatise upon Sociology. Translated from the Paris Edition of 1851-1854, and furnished with Analytical Tables of Contents :—

VOL. I. **General View of Positivism** and Introductory Principles. Translated by J. H. BRIDGES, M.B., formerly Fellow of Oriel College, Oxford. 8vo. price 21s.

VOL. II. **The Social Statics,** or the Abstract Laws of Human Order. Translated by FREDERIC HARRISON, M.A. 8vo. price 14s.

VOL. III. **The Social Dynamics,** or the General Laws of Human Progress (the Philosophy of History). Translated by Professor BEESLY, M.A. 8vo. 21s.

VOL. IV. **The Synthesis of the Future of Mankind.** Translated by RICHARD CONGREVE, M.D. with an Appendix, containing Comte's Early Essays, translated by H. D. HUTTON, B.A. 8vo.
[*Nearly ready.*

Democracy in America. By ALEXIS DE TOCQUEVILLE. Translated by HENRY REEVE, Esq. Two vols. crown 8vo. 16s.

Essays, Critical and Biographical. By HENRY ROGERS. 2 vols. crown 8vo. 12s.

Essays on some Theological Controversies of the Time. By HENRY ROGERS. Crown 8vo. 6s.

On Representative Government. By JOHN STUART MILL. Crown 8vo. 2s.

On Liberty. By JOHN STUART MILL. Post 8vo. 7s. 6d. crown 8vo. 1s. 4d.

Principles of Political Economy. By JOHN STUART MILL. 2 vols. 8vo. 30s. or 1 vol. crown 8vo. 5s.

Essays on some Unsettled Questions of Political Economy. By JOHN STUART MILL. 8vo. 6s. 6d.

Utilitarianism. By JOHN STUART MILL. 8vo. 5s.

A System of Logic, Ratiocinative and Inductive. By JOHN STUART MILL. 2 vols. 8vo. 25s.

Examination of Sir William Hamilton's Philosophy, and of the principal Philosophical Questions discussed in his Writings. By JOHN STUART MILL. 8vo. 16s.

Dissertations and Discussions. By JOHN STUART MILL. 4 vols. 8vo. price £2. 6s. 6d.

Analysis of the Phenomena of the Human Mind. By JAMES MILL. With Notes, Illustrative and Critical. 2 vols. 8vo. 28s.

The Law of Nations considered as Independent Political Communities; the Rights and Duties of Nations in Time of War. By Sir TRAVERS TWISS, D.C.L. 8vo. 21s.

Church and State; their Relations Historically Developed. By H. GEFFCKEN, Prof. of International Law in the Univ. of Strasburg. Translated, with the Author's assistance, by E. F. TAYLOR. 2 vols. 8vo. 42s.

A Systematic View of the Science of Jurisprudence. By SHELDON AMOS, M.A. 8vo. 18s.

A Primer of the English Constitution and Government. By S. AMOS, M.A. Crown 8vo. 6s.

Outlines of Civil Procedure; a General View of the Supreme Court of Judicature and of the whole Practice in the Common Law and Chancery Divisions. By E. S. ROSCOE, Barrister-at-Law. 12mo. 3s. 6d.

A Sketch of the History of Taxes in England from the Earliest Times to the Present Day. By STEPHEN DOWELL. VOL. I. to the Civil War 1642. 8vo. 10s. 6d.

Principles of Economical Philosophy. By H. D. MACLEOD, M.A. Barrister-at-Law. Second Edition in Two Volumes. VOL. I. 8vo. 15s. VOL. II. PART I. price 12s.

The Institutes of Justinian; with English Introduction, Translation, and Notes. By T. C. SANDARS, M.A. 8vo. 18s.

Lord Bacon's Works, collected & edited by R. L. ELLIS, M.A. J. SPEDDING, M.A. and D. D. HEATH. 7 vols. 8vo. £3. 13s. 6d.

Letters and Life of Francis Bacon, including all his Occasional Works. Collected and edited, with a Commentary, by J. SPEDDING. 7 vols. 8vo. £4. 4s.

The Nicomachean Ethics of Aristotle, newly translated into English by R. WILLIAMS, B.A. Second Edition, thoroughly revised. Crown 8vo. 7s. 6d.

Aristotle's Politics, Books I. III. IV. (VII.) the Greek Text of Bekker, with an English Translation by W. E. BOLLAND, M.A. and Short Introductory Essays by A. LANG, M.A. Crown 8vo. 7s. 6d.

The Politics of Aristotle; Greek Text, with English Notes. By RICHARD CONGREVE, M.A. 8vo. 18s.

The Ethics of Aristotle; with Essays and Notes. By Sir A. GRANT, Bart. M.A. LL.D. 2 vols. 8vo. 32s.

Bacon's Essays, with Annotations. By R. WHATELY, D.D. 8vo. 10s. 6d.

Picture Logic; an Attempt to Popularise the Science of Reasoning. By A. SWINBOURNE, B.A. Fcp. 8vo. price 5s.

Elements of Logic. By R. WHATELY, D.D. 8vo. 10s. 6d. Crown 8vo. 4s. 6d.

Elements of Rhetoric. By R. WHATELY, D.D. 8vo. 10s. 6d. Crown 8vo. 4s. 6d.

An Introduction to Mental Philosophy, on the Inductive Method. By J. D. MORELL, LL.D. 8vo. 12s.

Philosophy without Assumptions. By the Rev. T. P. KIRKMAN, F.R.S. 8vo. 10s. 6d.

The Senses and the Intellect. By A. BAIN, LL.D. 8vo. 15s.

The Emotions and the Will. By A. BAIN, LL.D. 8vo. 15s.

Mental and Moral Science; a Compendium of Psychology and Ethics. By A. BAIN, LL.D. Crown 8vo. 10s. 6d. Or separately, PART I. Mental Science, 6s. 6d. PART II. Moral Science, 4s. 6d.

An Outline of the Necessary Laws of Thought: a Treatise on Pure and Applied Logic. By W. THOMPSON, D.D. Archbishop of York. Crown 8vo. 6s.

On the Influence of Authority in Matters of Opinion. By the late Sir. G. C. LEWIS, Bart. 8vo. 14s.

Hume's Treatise on Human Nature. Edited, with Notes, &c. by T. H. GREEN, M.A. and the Rev. T. H. GROSE, M.A. 2 vols. 8vo. 28s.

Hume's Essays, Moral, Political, and Literary. By the same Editors. 2 vols. 8vo. 28s.

** The above form a complete and uniform Edition of HUME's Philosophical Works.

MISCELLANEOUS & CRITICAL WORKS.

Selections from the Writings of Lord Macaulay. Edited, with Occasional Explanatory Notes, by G. O. TREVELYAN, M.P. Cr. 8vo. 6s.

Lord Macaulay's Miscellaneous Writings.
LIBRARY EDITION, 2 vols. 8vo. 21s.
PEOPLE'S EDITION, 1 vol. cr. 8vo. 4s. 6d.

Lord Macaulay's Miscellaneous Writings and Speeches. Student's Edition. Crown 8vo. 6s.

Speeches of the Right Hon. Lord Macaulay, corrected by Himself. Crown 8vo. 3s. 6d.

The Rev. Sydney Smith's Essays contributed to the Edinburgh Review. Crown 8vo. 2s. 6d. sewed, 3s. 6d. cloth.

The Wit and Wisdom of the Rev. Sydney Smith. Crown 8vo. 3s. 6d.

Miscellaneous and Posthumous Works of the late Henry Thomas Buckle. Edited, with a Biographical Notice, by HELEN TAYLOR. 3 vols. 8vo. £2. 12s. 6d.

Short Studies on Great Subjects. By J. A. FROUDE, M.A.
CABINET EDITION, 2 vols. crown 8vo. 12s.
LIBRARY EDITION, 2 vols. demy 8vo. 24s.
THIRD SERIES, *in the press.*

Manual of English Literature, Historical and Critical. By T. ARNOLD, M.A. Crown 8vo. 7s. 6d.

German Home Life; a Series of Essays on the Domestic Life of Germany. Crown 8vo. 6s.

Miscellaneous Works of Thomas Arnold, D.D. late Head Master of Rugby School. 8vo. 7s. 6d.

Realities of Irish Life. By W. STEUART TRENCH. Crown 8vo. 2s. 6d. sewed, or 3s. 6d. cloth.

Lectures on the Science of Language. By F. MAX MÜLLER, M.A. &c. 2 vols. crown 8vo. 16s.

Chips from a German Workshop; Essays on the Science of Religion, and on Mythology, Traditions & Customs. By F. MAX MÜLLER, M.A. 4 vols. 8vo. £2. 18s.

Chapters on Language. By F. W. FARRAR, D.D. Crown 8vo. price 5s.

Families of Speech. Four Lectures delivered at the Royal Institution. By F. W. FARRAR, D.D. Crown 8vo. 3s. 6d.

Apparitions; a Narrative of Facts. By the Rev. B. W. SAVILE, M.A. Crown 8vo. 4s. 6d.

Miscellaneous Writings of John Conington, M.A. Edited by J. A. SYMONDS, M.A. With a Memoir by H. J. S. SMITH, M.A. 2 vols. 8vo. 28s.

The Essays and Contributions of A. K. H. B. Uniform Cabinet Editions in crown 8vo.

Recreations of a Country Parson, Two Series, 3s. 6d. each.

Landscapes, Churches, and Moralities, price 3s. 6d.

Seaside Musings, 3s. 6d.

Changed Aspects of Unchanged Truths, 3s. 6d.

Counsel and Comfort from a City Pulpit, 3s. 6d.

Lessons of Middle Age, 3s. 6d.

Leisure Hours in Town, 3s. 6d.

Autumn Holidays of a Country Parson, price 3s. 6d.

Sunday Afternoons at the Parish Church of a University City, 3s. 6d.

The Commonplace Philosopher in Town and Country, 3s. 6d.

Present-Day Thoughts, 3s. 6d.

Critical Essays of a Country Parson, price 3s. 6d.

The Graver Thoughts of a Country Parson, Three Series, 3s. 6d. each.

DICTIONARIES and OTHER BOOKS of REFERENCE.

Dictionary of the English Language. By R. G. LATHAM, M.A. M.D. Abridged from Dr. Latham's Edition of Johnson's English Dictionary. Medium 8vo. 24s.

A Dictionary of the English Language. By R. G. LATHAM, M.A. M.D. Founded on the Dictionary of Dr. S. Johnson, as edited by the Rev. H. J. TODD, with numerous Emendations and Additions. 4 vols. 4to. £7.

Thesaurus of English Words and Phrases, classified and arranged so as to facilitate the expression of Ideas, and assist in Literary Composition. By P. M. ROGET, M.D. Crown 8vo. 10s. 6d.

English Synonymes. By E. J. WHATELY. Edited by R. WHATELY, D.D. Fcp. 8vo. 3s.

Handbook of the English Language. For the Use of Students of the Universities and the Higher Classes in Schools. By R. G. LATHAM, M.A. M.D. Crown 8vo. 6s.

A Practical Dictionary of the French and English Languages. By LÉON CONTANSEAU, many years French Examiner for Military and Civil Appointments, &c. Post 8vo. price 7s. 6d.

Contanseau's Pocket Dictionary, French and English, abridged from the Practical Dictionary by the Author. Square 18mo. 3s. 6d.

A New Pocket Dictionary of the German and English Languages. By F. W. LONGMAN, Balliol College, Oxford. Square 18mo. price 5s.

A Practical Dictionary of the German Language; German-English and English-German. By Rev. W. L. BLACKLEY, M.A. and Dr. C. M. FRIEDLÄNDER. Post 8vo. 7s. 6d.

A Dictionary of Roman and Greek Antiquities. With 2,000 Woodcuts illustrative of the Arts and Life of the Greeks and Romans. By A. RICH, B.A. Crown 8vo. 7s. 6d.

A Greek-English Lexicon. By H. G. LIDDELL, D.D. Dean of Christchurch, and R. SCOTT, D.D. Dean of Rochester. Crown 4to. 36s.

A Lexicon, Greek and English, abridged for Schools from Liddell and Scott's Greek-English Lexicon. Square 12mo. 7s. 6d.

An English-Greek Lexicon, containing all the Greek Words used by Writers of good authority. By C. D. YONGE, M.A. 4to. 21s.

Mr. Yonge's Lexicon, English and Greek, abridged from his larger Lexicon. Square 12mo. 8s. 6d.

A Latin-English Dictionary. By JOHN T. WHITE, D.D. Oxon. and J. E. RIDDLE, M.A. Oxon. Sixth Edition, revised. 1 vol. 4to. 28s.

White's College Latin-English Dictionary; abridged from the Parent Work for the use of University Students. Medium 8vo. 15s.

A Latin-English Dictionary adapted for the use of Middle-Class Schools. By JOHN T. WHITE, D.D. Oxon. Square fcp. 8vo. 3s.

White's Junior Student's Complete Latin-English and English-Latin Dictionary. Square 12mo. price 12s.

Separately { ENGLISH-LATIN, 5s. 6d.
{ LATIN-ENGLISH, 7s. 6d.

M'Culloch's Dictionary, Practical, Theoretical, and Historical, of Commerce and Commercial Navigation. Edited and corrected to 1876 by H. G. REID. 8vo. 63s. Second SUPPLEMENT, price 3s. 6d.

A General Dictionary of Geography, Descriptive, Physical, Statistical, and Historical; forming a complete Gazetteer of the World. By A. KEITH JOHNSTON. New Edition (1877), thoroughly revised. Medium 8vo. 42s.

Maunder's Treasury of Knowledge and Library of Reference; comprising an English DICTIONARY and Grammar, Universal Gazetteer, Classical Dictionary, Chronology, Law Dictionary, Synopsis of the Peerage, Useful Tables, &c. Fcp. 8vo. 6s.

The Treasury of Bible Knowledge; being a DICTIONARY of the Books, Persons, Places, Events, and other Matters of which mention is made in Holy Scripture. By the Rev. J. AYRE, M.A. With Maps, Plates, and many Woodcuts. Fcp. 8vo. 6s.

The Public Schools Atlas of Modern Geography, in 31 entirely new Coloured Maps. Edited with an Introduction by Rev. G. BUTLER, M.A. In imperial 8vo. or imperial 4to. price 5s. cloth.

The Public Schools Atlas of Ancient Geography, in 28 entirely new Coloured Maps. Edited with an Introduction by the Rev. G. BUTLER, M.A. In imperial 8vo. or imperial 4to. price 7s. 6d. cloth.

ASTRONOMY and METEOROLOGY.

The Universe and the Coming Transits; Researches into and New Views respecting the Constitution of the Heavens. By R. A. PROCTOR, B.A. With 22 Charts and 22 Diagrams. 8vo. 16s.

Saturn and its System. By R. A. PROCTOR, B.A. 8vo. with 14 Plates, 14s.

The Transits of Venus; A Popular Account of Past and Coming Transits. By R. A. PROCTOR, B.A. 20 Plates (12 Coloured) and 27 Woodcuts. Crown 8vo. 8s. 6d.

Essays on Astronomy. A Series of Papers on Planets and Meteors, the Sun and Sun-surrounding Space, Star and Star Cloudlets. By R. A. PROCTOR, B.A. With 10 Plates and 24 Woodcuts. 8vo. 12s.

The Moon; her Motions, Aspects, Scenery, and Physical Condition. By R. A. PROCTOR, B.A. With Plates, Charts, Woodcuts, and Lunar Photographs. Crown 8vo. 15s.

The Sun; Ruler, Light, Fire, and Life of the Planetary System. By R. A. PROCTOR, B.A. With Plates & Woodcuts. Crown 8vo. 14s.

The Orbs Around Us; a Series of Essays on the Moon & Planets, Meteors & Comets, the Sun & Coloured Pairs of Suns. By R. A. PROCTOR, B.A. With Chart and Diagrams. Crown 8vo. 7s. 6d.

Other Worlds than Ours; The Plurality of Worlds Studied under the Light of Recent Scientific Researches. By R. A. PROCTOR, B.A. With 14 Illustrations. Cr. 8vo. 10s. 6d.

Brinkley's Astronomy. Revised and partly re-written by JOHN W. STUBBS, D.D. and F. BRUNNOW, Ph.D. With 49 Diagrams. Crown 8vo. price 6s.

Outlines of Astronomy. By Sir J. F. W. HERSCHEL, Bart. M.A. Latest Edition, with Plates and Diagrams. Square crown 8vo. 12s.

The Moon, and the Condition and Configurations of its Surface. By E. NEISON, F.R. Ast. Soc. &c. With 26 Maps and 5 Plates. Medium 8vo. 31s. 6d.

Celestial Objects for Common Telescopes. By T. W. WEBB, M.A. With Map of the Moon and Woodcuts. Crown 8vo. 7s. 6d.

A New Star Atlas, for the Library, the School, and the Observatory, in 12 Circular Maps (with 2 Index Plates). By R. A. PROCTOR, B.A. Crown 8vo. 5s.

Larger Star Atlas, for the Library, in Twelve Circular Maps, photolithographed by A. Brothers, F.R.A.S. With 2 Index Plates and a Letterpress Introduction. By R. A. PROCTOR, B.A. Small folio, 25s.

Dove's Law of Storms, considered in connexion with the Ordinary Movements of the Atmosphere. Translated by R. H. SCOTT, M.A. 8vo. 10s. 6d.

Air and Rain; the Beginnings of a Chemical Climatology. By R. A. SMITH, F.R.S. 8vo. 24s.

Air and its Relations to Life, 1774-1874; a Course of Lectures delivered at the Royal Institution of Great Britain. By W. N. HARTLEY, F.C.S. With 66 Woodcuts. Small 8vo. 6s.

Schellen's Spectrum Analysis, in its Application to Terrestrial Substances and the Physical Constitution of the Heavenly Bodies. Translated by JANE and C. LASSELL, with Notes by W. HUGGINS, LL.D. F.R.S. 8vo. Plates and Woodcuts, 28s.

NATURAL HISTORY and PHYSICAL SCIENCE.

Professor Helmholtz' Popular Lectures on Scientific Subjects. Translated by E. ATKINSON, F.C.S. With numerous Wood Engravings. 8vo. 12s. 6d.

On the Sensations of Tone, as a Physiological Basis for the Theory of Music. By H. HELMHOLTZ, Professor of Physiology in the University of Berlin. Translated by A. J. ELLIS, F.R.S. 8vo. 36s.

Ganot's Natural Philosophy for General Readers and Young Persons; a Course of Physics divested of Mathematical Formulæ and expressed in the language of daily life. Translated by E. ATKINSON, F.C.S. Second Edition, with 2 Plates and 429 Woodcuts. Crown 8vo. 7s. 6d.

Ganot's Elementary Treatise on Physics, Experimental and Applied, for the use of Colleges and Schools. Translated and edited by E. ATKINSON, F.C.S. Seventh Edition, with 4 Coloured Plates and 758 Woodcuts. Post 8vo. 15s.

Arnott's Elements of Physics or Natural Philosophy. Seventh Edition, edited by A. BAIN, LL.D. and A. S. TAYLOR, M.D. F.R.S. Crown 8vo. Woodcuts, 12s. 6d.

The Correlation of Physical Forces. By the Hon. Sir W. R. GROVE, F.R.S. &c. Sixth Edition, with other Contributions to Science. 8vo. 15s.

Weinhold's Introduction to Experimental Physics; including Directions for Constructing Physical Apparatus and for Making Experiments. Translated by B. LOEWY, F.R.A.S. With a Preface by G. C. FOSTER, F.R.S. 8vo. Plates & Woodcuts 31s. 6d.

Principles of Animal Mechanics. By the Rev. S. HAUGHTON, F.R.S. Second Edition. 8vo. 21s.

Fragments of Science. By JOHN TYNDALL, F.R.S. Fifth Edition, with a New Introduction. Crown 8vo. 10s. 6d.

Heat a Mode of Motion. By JOHN TYNDALL, F.R.S. Fifth Edition, Plate and Woodcuts. Crown 8vo. 10s. 6d.

Sound. By JOHN TYNDALL, F.R.S. Third Edition, including Recent Researches on Fog-Signalling; Portrait and Woodcuts. Crown 8vo. price 10s. 6d.

Researches on Diamagnetism and Magne-Crystallic Action; including Diamagnetic Polarity. By JOHN TYNDALL, F.R.S. With 6 Plates and many Woodcuts. 8vo. 14s.

Contributions to Molecular Physics in the domain of Radiant Heat. By JOHN TYNDALL, F.R.S. With 2 Plates and 31 Woodcuts. 8vo. 16s.

Six Lectures on Light, delivered in America in 1872 and 1873. By JOHN TYNDALL, F.R.S. Second Edition, with Portrait, Plate, and 59 Diagrams. Crown 8vo. 7s. 6d.

Notes of a Course of Nine Lectures on Light, delivered at the Royal Institution. By JOHN TYNDALL, F.R.S. Crown 8vo. 1s. sewed, or 1s. 6d. cloth.

Notes of a Course of Seven Lectures on Electrical Phenomena and Theories, delivered at the Royal Institution. By JOHN TYNDALL, F.R.S. Crown 8vo. 1s. sewed, or 1s. 6d. cloth.

A Treatise on Magnetism, General and Terrestrial. By H. LLOYD, D.D. D.C.L. 8vo. 10s. 6d.

Elementary Treatise on the Wave-Theory of Light. By H. LLOYD, D.D. D.C.L. 8vo. 10s. 6d.

Text-Books of Science,
Mechanical and Physical, adapted for the use of Artisans and of Students in Public and Science Schools. Small 8vo. with Woodcuts, &c.

Anderson's Strength of Materials, 3s. 6d.
Armstrong's Organic Chemistry, 3s. 6d.
Barry's Railway Appliances, 3s. 6d.
Bloxam's Metals, 3s. 6d.
Goodeve's Mechanics, 3s. 6d.
────── Mechanism, 3s. 6d.
Griffin's Algebra & Trigonometry, 3/6.
Jenkin's Electricity & Magnetism, 3/6.
Maxwell's Theory of Heat, 3s. 6d.
Merrifield's Technical Arithmetic, 3s. 6d.
Miller's Inorganic Chemistry, 3s. 6d.
Preece & Sivewright's Telegraphy, 3/6.
Shelley's Workshop Appliances, 3s. 6d.
Thomé's Structural and Physiological Botany, 6s.
Thorpe's Quantitative Analysis, 4s. 6d.
Thorpe & Muir's Qualitative Analysis, price 3s. 6d.
Tilden's Systematic Chemistry, 3s. 6d.
Unwin's Machine Design, 3s. 6d.
Watson's Plane & Solid Geometry, 3/6.

₄ Other Text-Books, in continuation of this Series, in active preparation.

The Comparative Anatomy and Physiology of the Vertebrate Animals. By RICHARD OWEN, F.R.S. With 1,472 Woodcuts. 3 vols. 8vo. £3. 13s. 6d.

Kirby and Spence's Introduction to Entomology, or Elements of the Natural History of Insects. Crown 8vo. 5s.

Light Science for Leisure Hours; Familiar Essays on Scientific Subjects, Natural Phenomena, &c. By R. A. PROCTOR, B.A. 2 vols. crown 8vo. 7s. 6d. each.

Homes without Hands; a Description of the Habitations of Animals, classed according to their Principle of Construction. By the Rev. J. G. WOOD, M.A. With about 140 Vignettes on Wood. 8vo. 14s.

Strange Dwellings; a Description of the Habitations of Animals, abridged from 'Homes without Hands.' By the Rev. J. G. WOOD, M.A. With Frontispiece and 60 Woodcuts. Crown 8vo. 7s. 6d

Insects at Home; a Popular Account of British Insects, their Structure, Habits, and Transformations. By the Rev. J. G. WOOD, M.A. With upwards of 700 Woodcuts. 8vo. price 14s.

Insects Abroad; being a Popular Account of Foreign Insects, their Structure, Habits, and Transformations. By the Rev. J. G. WOOD, M.A. With upwards of 700 Woodcuts. 8vo. 14s.

Out of Doors; a Selection of Original Articles on Practical Natural History. By the Rev. J. G. WOOD, M.A. With 6 Illustrations. Crown 8vo. 7s. 6d.

Bible Animals; a Description of every Living Creature mentioned in the Scriptures, from the Ape to the Coral. By the Rev. J. G. WOOD, M.A. With 112 Vignettes. 8vo. 14s.

The Polar World: a Popular Description of Man and Nature in the Arctic and Antarctic Regions of the Globe. By Dr. G. HARTWIG. With Chromoxylographs, Maps, and Woodcuts. 8vo. 10s. 6d.

The Sea and its Living Wonders. By Dr. G. HARTWIG. Fourth Edition, enlarged. 8vo. with numerous Illustrations, 10s. 6d.

The Tropical World. By Dr. G. HARTWIG. With about 200 Illustrations. 8vo. 10s. 6d.

The Subterranean World. By Dr. G. HARTWIG. With Maps and Woodcuts. 8vo. 10s. 6d.

The Aerial World; a Popular Account of the Phenomena and Life of the Atmosphere. By Dr. G. HARTWIG. With Map, 8 Chromoxylographs & 60 Woodcuts. 8vo. 21s.

Maunder's Treasury of
Natural History, or Popular Dictionary of Animated Nature; in which the Zoological Characteristics that distinguish the different Classes, Genera and Species, are combined with a variety of interesting Information illustrative of the Habits, Instincts, and General Economy of the Animal Kingdom. Fcp. 8vo. with 900 Woodcuts, 6s.

A Familiar History of
Birds. By E. STANLEY, D.D. late Bishop of Norwich. Fcp. 8vo. with Woodcuts, 3s. 6d.

Rocks Classified and Described.
By B. VON COTTA. English Edition by P. H. LAWRENCE (with English, German, and French Synonymes), revised by the Author. Post 8vo. 14s.

The Geology of England
and Wales; a Concise Account of the Lithological Characters, Leading Fossils, and Economic Products of the Rocks. By H. B. WOODWARD, F.G.S. Crown 8vo. Map & Woodcuts, 14s.

The Primæval World of
Switzerland. By Professor OSWAL HEER, of the University of Zurich. Edited by JAMES HEYWOOD, M.A. F.R.S. President of the Statistical Society. With Map, 19 Plates, & 372 Woodcuts. 2 vols. 8vo. 28s.

The Puzzle of Life and
How it Has Been Put Together: a Short History of Vegetable and Animal Life upon the Earth from the Earliest Times; including an Account of Pre-Historic Man, his Weapons, Tools, and Works. By A. NICOLS, F.R.G.S. With 12 Illustrations. Crown 8vo. 5s.

The Origin of Civilisation, and the Primitive Condition of Man;
Mental and Social Condition of Savages. By Sir J. LUBBOCK, Bart. M.P. F.R.S. Third Edition, with 25 Woodcuts. 8vo. 18s.

The Ancient Stone Implements, Weapons, and Ornaments of Great Britain.
By JOHN EVANS, F.R.S. With 2 Plates and 476 Woodcuts. 8vo. 28s.

The Elements of Botany
for Families and Schools. Eleventh Edition, revised by THOMAS MOORE, F.L.S. Fcp. 8vo. Woodcuts, 2s. 6d.

The Rose Amateur's Guide.
By THOMAS RIVERS. Latest Edition. Fcp. 8vo. 4s.

A Dictionary of Science, Literature, and Art.
Re-edited by the late W. T. BRANDE (the Author) and the Rev. G. W. COX, M.A. 3 vols. medium 8vo. 63s.

The History of Modern Music,
a Course of Lectures delivered at the Royal Institution of Great Britain. By JOHN HULLAH. Second Edition. Demy 8vo. 8s. 6d.

Mr. Hullah's 2nd Course
of Lectures on the Transition Period of Musical History, from the Beginning of the Seventeenth to the Middle of the Eighteenth Century. Second Edition. Demy 8vo. 10s. 6d.

Structural and Physiological Botany.
By OTTO W. THOMÉ, Professor of Botany at the School of Science and Art, Cologne. Translated and edited by A. W. BENNETT, M.A. B.Sc. F.L.S. Lecturer on Botany at St. Thomas's Hospital. With about 600 Woodcuts and a Coloured Map. Small 8vo. 6s.

The Treasury of Botany,
or Popular Dictionary of the Vegetable Kingdom; with which is incorporated a Glossary of Botanical Terms. Edited by J. LINDLEY, F.R.S. and T. MOORE, F.L.S. With 274 Woodcuts and 20 Steel Plates. Two Parts, fcp. 8vo. 12s.

Loudon's Encyclopædia
of Plants; comprising the Specific Character, Description, Culture, History, &c. of all the Plants found in Great Britain. With upwards of 12,000 Woodcuts. 8vo. 42s.

De Caisne & Le Maout's System of Descriptive and Analytical Botany. Translated by Mrs. HOOKER; edited and arranged according to the English Botanical System, by J. D. HOOKER, M.D. With 5,500 Woodcuts. Imperial 8vo. 31s. 6d.

Hand-Book of Hardy Trees, Shrubs, and Herbaceous Plants; containing Descriptions &c. of the Best Species in Cultivation. With 720 Original Woodcut Illustrations. By W. B. HEMSLEY. Medium 8vo. 12s.

CHEMISTRY and PHYSIOLOGY.

Miller's Elements of Chemistry, Theoretical and Practical. Re-edited, with Additions, by H. MACLEOD, F.C.S. 3 vols. 8vo.
PART I. CHEMICAL PHYSICS, New Edition in the press.
PART II. INORGANIC CHEMISTRY, 21s.
PART III. ORGANIC CHEMISTRY, New Edition in the press.

Health in the House: Twenty-five Lectures on Elementary Physiology in its Application to the Daily Wants of Man and Animals. By Mrs. C. M. BUCKTON. Crown 8vo. Woodcuts, 2s.

Outlines of Physiology, Human and Comparative. By J. MARSHALL, F.R.C.S. Surgeon to the University College Hospital. 2 vols. crown 8vo. with 122 Woodcuts, 32s.

An Introduction to the Study of Chemical Philosophy; or, the Principles of Theoretical and Systematic Chemistry. By W. A. TILDEN, F.C.S. Small 8vo. 3s. 6d.

Select Methods in Chemical Analysis, chiefly Inorganic. By WM. CROOKES, F.R.S. With 22 Woodcuts. Crown 8vo. 12s. 6d.

A Dictionary of Chemistry and the Allied Branches of other Sciences. By HENRY WATTS, F.C.S. assisted by eminent Scientific and Practical Chemists. 7 vols. medium 8vo. £10. 16s. 6d.

Supplementary Volume, completing the Record of Chemical Discovery to the year 1876.
[*In preparation.*

The FINE ARTS and ILLUSTRATED EDITIONS.

Poems. By W. B. SCOTT. Illustrated by Seventeen Etchings by L. A. TADEMA and W. B. SCOTT. Crown 8vo. 15s.

Half-hour Lectures on the History and Practice of the Fine and Ornamental Arts. By W. B. SCOTT. Cr. 8vo. Woodcuts, 8s. 6d.

A Dictionary of Artists of the English School: Painters, Sculptors, Architects, Engravers, and Ornamentists. By S. REDGRAVE. 8vo. 16s.

In Fairyland; Pictures from the Elf-World. By RICHARD DOYLE. With a Poem by W. ALLINGHAM. With 16 coloured Plates, containing 36 Designs. Folio, 15s.

Lord Macaulay's Lays of Ancient Rome. With 90 Illustrations on Wood from Drawings by G. SCHARF. Fcp. 4to. 21s.

Miniature Edition, with G. Scharf's 90 Illustrations reduced in Lithography. Imp. 16mo. 10s. 6d.

Moore's Lalla Rookh, TENNIEL'S Edition, with 68 Wood Engravings from Original Drawings. Fcp. 4to. 21s.

Moore's Irish Melodies, MACLISE'S Edition, with 161 Steel Plates. Super royal 8vo. 21s.

The New Testament, Illustrated with Wood Engravings after the Early Masters, chiefly of the Italian School. Crown 4to. 63s.

Sacred and Legendary Art. By Mrs. JAMESON. 6 vols. square crown 8vo. price £5. 15s. 6d.

Legends of the Saints and Martyrs. With 19 Etchings and 187 Woodcuts. 2 vols. 31s. 6d.

Legends of the Monastic Orders. With 11 Etchings and 88 Woodcuts. 1 vol. 21s.

Legends of the Madonna. With 27 Etchings and 165 Woodcuts. 1 vol. 21s.

The History of our Lord, with that of his Types and Precursors. Completed by Lady EASTLAKE. With 13 Etchings and 281 Woodcuts. 2 vols. 42s.

The Three Cathedrals dedicated to St. Paul in London; their History from the Foundation of the First Building in the Sixth Century to the Proposals for the Adornment of the Present Cathedral. By W. LONGMAN, F.S.A. With numerous Illustrations. Square crown 8vo. 21s.

The USEFUL ARTS, MANUFACTURES, &c.

The Amateur Mechanics' Practical Handbook; describing the different Tools required in the Workshop, the uses of them, and how to use them. By A. H. G. HOBSON. With 33 Woodcuts. Crown 8vo. 2s. 6d.

The Engineer's Valuing Assistant. By H. D. HOSKOLD, Civil and Mining Engineer, 16 years Mining Engineer to the Dean Forest Iron Company. 8vo. [*In the press*.

The Whitworth Measuring Machine; including Descriptions of the Surface Plates, Gauges, and other Measuring Instruments made by Sir J. WHITWORTH, Bart. By T. M. GOODEVE, M.A. and C. P. B. SHELLEY, C.E. Fcp. 4to. with 4 Plates and 44 Woodcuts. [*Nearly ready*.

Industrial Chemistry; a Manual for Manufacturers and for Colleges or Technical Schools; a Translation of Stohmann and Engler's German Edition of PAYEN'S 'Précis de Chimie Industrielle,' by Dr. J. D. BARRY. With Chapters on the Chemistry of the Metals, by B. H. PAUL, Ph.D. 8vo. Plates & Woodcuts. [*In the press*.

Gwilt's Encyclopædia of Architecture, with above 1,600 Woodcuts. Revised and extended by W. PAPWORTH. 8vo. 52s. 6d.

Lathes and Turning, Simple, Mechanical, and Ornamental. By W. H. NORTHCOTT. Second Edition, with 338 Illustrations. 8vo. 18s.

Hints on Household Taste in Furniture, Upholstery, and other Details. By C. L. EASTLAKE. With about 90 Illustrations. Square crown 8vo. 14s.

Handbook of Practical Telegraphy. By R. S. CULLEY, Memb. Inst. C.E. Engineer-in-Chief of Telegraphs to the Post-Office. 8vo. Plates & Woodcuts, 16s.

A Treatise on the Steam Engine, in its various applications to Mines, Mills, Steam Navigation, Railways and Agriculture. By J. BOURNE, C.E. With Portrait, 37 Plates, and 546 Woodcuts. 4to. 42s.

Recent Improvements in the Steam Engine. By J. BOURNE, C.E. Fcp. 8vo. Woodcuts, 6s.

C

Catechism of the Steam
Engine, in its various Applications. By JOHN BOURNE, C.E. Fcp. 8vo. Woodcuts, 6s.

Handbook of the Steam
Engine By J. BOURNE, C.E. forming a Key to the Author's Catechism of the Steam Engine. Fcp. 8vo. Woodcuts, 9s.

Encyclopædia of Civil
Engineering, Historical, Theoretical, and Practical. By E. CRESY, C.E. With above 3,000 Woodcuts. 8vo. 42s.

Ure's Dictionary of Arts,
Manufactures, and Mines. Seventh Edition, re-written and enlarged by R. HUNT, F.R.S. assisted by numerous contributors. With 2,100 Woodcuts. 3 vols. medium 8vo. £5. 5s.

VOL. IV. Supplementary, completing all the Departments of the Dictionary to the beginning of the year 1877, is preparing for publication.

Practical Treatise on Metallurgy.
Adapted from the last German Edition of Professor KERL'S Metallurgy by W. CROOKES, F.R.S. &c. and E. RÖHRIG, Ph.D. 3 vols. 8vo. with 625 Woodcuts. £4. 19s.

The Theory of Strains in
Girders and similar Structures, with Observations on the application of Theory to Practice, and Tables of the Strength and other Properties of Materials. By B. B. STONEY, M.A. M. Inst. C.E. Royal 8vo. with 5 Plates and 123 Woodcuts, 36s.

Treatise on Mills and
Millwork. By Sir W. FAIRBAIRN, Bt. With 18 Plates and 322 Woodcuts. 2 vols. 8vo. 32s.

Useful Information for
Engineers. By Sir W. FAIRBAIRN, Bt. With many Plates and Woodcuts. 3 vols. crown 8vo. 31s. 6d.

The Application of Cast
and Wrought Iron to Building Purposes. By Sir W. FAIRBAIRN, Bt. With 6 Plates and 118 Woodcuts. 8vo. 16s.

Practical Handbook of
Dyeing and Calico-Printing. By W. CROOKES, F.R.S. &c. With numerous Illustrations and specimens of Dyed Textile Fabrics. 8vo. 42s.

Anthracen; its Constitution,
Properties, Manufacture, and Derivatives, including Artificial Alizarin, Anthrapurpurin, &c. with their Applications in Dyeing and Printing. By G. AUERBACH. Translated by W. CROOKES, F.R.S. 8vo. 12s.

Mitchell's Manual of
Practical Assaying. Fourth Edition, revised, with the Recent Discoveries incorporated, by W. CROOKES, F.R.S. Crown 8vo. Woodcuts, 31s. 6d.

Loudon's Encyclopædia
of Gardening; comprising the Theory and Practice of Horticulture, Floriculture, Arboriculture, and Landscape Gardening. With 1,000 Woodcuts. 8vo. 21s.

Loudon's Encyclopædia
of Agriculture; comprising the Laying-out, Improvement, and Management of Landed Property, and the Cultivation and Economy of the Productions of Agriculture. With 1,100 Woodcuts. 8vo. 21s.

RELIGIOUS and MORAL WORKS.

An Exposition of the 39
Articles, Historical and Doctrinal. By E. H. BROWNE, D.D. Bishop of Winchester. Latest Edition. 8vo. 16s.

An Introduction to the
Theology of the Church of England, in an Exposition of the 39 Articles. By T. P. BOULTBEE, LL.D. Fcp. 8vo. 6s.

Historical Lectures on the Life of Our Lord Jesus Christ. By C. J. Ellicott, D.D. 8vo. 12s.

Sermons Chiefly on the Interpretation of Scripture. By the late Rev. Thomas Arnold, D.D. 8vo. 7s. 6d.

Sermons preached in the Chapel of Rugby School; with an Address before Confirmation. By Thomas Arnold, D.D. Fcp. 8vo. price 3s. 6d.

Christian Life, its Course, its Hindrances, and its Helps; Sermons preached mostly in the Chapel of Rugby School. By Thomas Arnold, D.D. 8vo. 7s. 6d.

Christian Life, its Hopes, its Fears, and its Close; Sermons preached mostly in the Chapel of Rugby School. By Thomas Arnold, D.D. 8vo. 7s. 6d.

Synonyms of the Old Testament, their Bearing on Christian Faith and Practice. By the Rev. R. B. Girdlestone. 8vo. 15s.

The Primitive and Catholic Faith in Relation to the Church of England. By the Rev. B. W. Savile, M.A. 8vo. 7s.

The Eclipse of Faith; or a Visit to a Religious Sceptic. By Henry Rogers. Latest Edition. Fcp. 8vo. 5s.

Defence of the Eclipse of Faith. By Henry Rogers. Latest Edition. Fcp. 8vo. 3s. 6d.

Three Essays on Religion: Nature; the Utility of Religion; Theism. By John Stuart Mill. 8vo. 10s. 6d.

A Critical and Grammatical Commentary on St. Paul's Epistles. By C. J. Ellicott, D.D. 8vo. Galatians, 8s. 6d. Ephesians, 8s. 6d. Pastoral Epistles, 10s. 6d. Philippians, Colossians, & Philemon, 10s. 6d. Thessalonians, 7s. 6d.

The Life and Epistles of St. Paul. By Rev. W. J. Conybeare, M.A. and Very Rev. John Saul Howson, D.D. Dean of Chester. Three Editions, copiously illustrated.

Library Edition, with all the Original Illustrations, Maps, Landscapes on Steel, Woodcuts, &c. 2 vols. 4to. 42s.

Intermediate Edition, with a Selection of Maps, Plates, and Woodcuts. 2 vols. square crown 8vo. 21s.

Student's Edition, revised and condensed, with 46 Illustrations and Maps. 1 vol. crown 8vo. 9s.

Evidence of the Truth of the Christian Religion derived from the Literal Fulfilment of Prophecy. By Alexander Keith, D.D. 40th Edition, with numerous Plates. Square 8vo. 12s. 6d. or in post 8vo. with 5 Plates, 6s.

The Prophets and Prophecy in Israel; an Historical and Critical Inquiry. By Dr. A. Kuenen, Prof. of Theol. in the Univ. of Leyden. Translated from the Dutch by the Rev. A. Milroy, M.A. with an Introduction by J. Muir, D.C.L. 8vo. 21s.

Mythology among the Hebrews and its Historical Development. By Ignaz Goldziher, Ph.D. Translated by Russell Martineau, M.A. 8vo. 16s.

Historical and Critical Commentary on the Old Testament; with a New Translation. By M. M. Kalisch, Ph.D. Vol. I. Genesis, 8vo. 18s. or adapted for the General Reader, 12s. Vol. II. Exodus, 15s. or adapted for the General Reader, 12s. Vol. III. Leviticus, Part I. 15s. or adapted for the General Reader, 8s. Vol. IV. Leviticus, Part II. 15s. or adapted for the General Reader, 8s.

The History and Literature of the Israelites, according to the Old Testament and the Apocrypha. By C. DE ROTHSCHILD & A. DE ROTHSCHILD. 2 vols. crown 8vo. 12s. 6d. Abridged Edition, 1 vol. fcp. 8vo. 3s. 6d.

Ewald's History of Israel. Translated from the German by J. E. CARPENTER, M.A. with Preface by R. MARTINEAU, M.A. 5 vols. 8vo. 63s.

Ewald's Antiquities of Israel. Translated from the German by H. S. SOLLY, M.A. 8vo. 12s. 6d.

Behind the Veil; an Outline of Bible Metaphysics compared with Ancient and Modern Thought. By the Rev. T. GRIFFITH, M.A. Prebendary of St. Paul's. 8vo. 10s. 6d.

The Trident, the Crescent & the Cross; a View of the Religious History of India during the Hindu, Buddhist, Mohammedan, and Christian Periods. By the Rev. J. VAUGHAN, Nineteen Years Missionary in India. 8vo. 9s. 6d.

The Types of Genesis, briefly considered as revealing the Development of Human Nature. By ANDREW JUKES. Crown 8vo. 7s. 6d.

The Second Death and the Restitution of all Things; with some Preliminary Remarks on the Nature and Inspiration of Holy Scripture. By A. JUKES. Crown 8vo. 3s. 6d.

History of the Reformation in Europe in the time of Calvin. By the Rev. J. H. MERLE D'AUBIGNÉ, D.D. Translated by W. L. R. CATES. 7 vols. 8vo. price £5. 11s.

VOL. VIII. translated by W. L. R. CATES, and completing the English Edition of Dr. D'AUBIGNÉ's Work, is in the press.

Supernatural Religion; an Inquiry into the Reality of Divine Revelation. 2 vols. 8vo. 24s.

Commentaries, by the Rev. W. A. O'CONOR, B.A. Rector of St. Simon and St. Jude, Manchester.

Epistle to the Romans, crown 8vo. 3s. 6d.
Epistle to the Hebrews, 4s. 6d.
St. John's Gospel, 10s. 6d.

An Introduction to the Study of the New Testament, Exegetical, and Theological. By the Rev. S. DAVIDSON, D.D. L.L.D. 2 vols. 8vo. 30s.

Passing Thoughts on Religion. By ELIZABETH M. SEWELL. Fcp. 8vo. 3s. 6d.

Thoughts for the Age. by ELIZABETH M. SEWELL. New Edition. Fcp. 8vo. 3s. 6d.

Some Questions of the Day. By ELIZABETH M. SEWELL. Crown 8vo. 2s. 6d.

Self-examination before Confirmation. By ELIZABETH M. SEWELL. 32mo. 1s. 6d.

Preparation for the Holy Communion; the Devotions chiefly from the works of Jeremy Taylor. By ELIZABETH M. SEWELL. 32mo. 3s.

Bishop Jeremy Taylor's Entire Works; with Life by Bishop Heber. Revised and corrected by the Rev. C. P. EDEN. 10 vols. £5. 5s.

Hymns of Praise and Prayer. Corrected and edited by Rev. JOHN MARTINEAU, LL.D. Crown 8vo. 4s. 6d. 32mo. 1s. 6d.

Spiritual Songs for the Sundays and Holidays throughout the Year. By J. S. B. MONSELL, LL.D. Fcp. 8vo. 5s. 18mo. 2s.

Lyra Germanica; Hymns translated from the German by Miss C. WINKWORTH. Fcp. 8vo. 5s.

Hours of Thought on Sacred Things; a Volume of Sermons. By JAMES MARTINEAU, D.D. LL.D. Crown 8vo. Price 7s. 6d.

Endeavours after the Christian Life; Discourses. By JAMES MARTINEAU, D.D. LL.D. Fifth Edition. Crown 8vo. 7s. 6d.

The Pentateuch & Book of Joshua Critically Examined. By J. W. COLENSO, D.D. Bishop of Natal. Crown 8vo. 6s.

Lectures on the Pentateuch and the Moabite Stone; with Appendices. By J. W. COLENSO, D.D. Bishop of Natal. 8vo. 12s.

TRAVELS, VOYAGES, &c.

A Year in Western France. By M. BETHAM-EDWARDS. Crown 8vo. Frontispiece, 10s. 6d.

Journal of a Residence in Vienna and Berlin during the eventful Winter 1805-6. By the late HENRY REEVE, M.D. Published by his SON. Crown 8vo. 8s. 6d.

One Thousand Miles up the Nile; a Journey through Egypt and Nubia to the Second Cataract. By AMELIA B. EDWARDS. With Facsimiles of Inscriptions, Ground Plans, Two Coloured Maps, and 80 Illustrations engraved on Wood from Drawings by the Author. Imperial 8vo. 42s.

The Indian Alps, and How we Crossed them: a Narrative of Two Years' Residence in the Eastern Himalayas, and Two Months' Tour into the Interior. By a Lady Pioneer. With Illustrations from Original Drawings by the Author. Imperial 8vo. 42s.

Discoveries at Ephesus, Including the Site and Remains of the Great Temple of Diana. By J. T. WOOD, F.S.A. With 27 Lithographic Plates and 42 Wood Engravings. Medium 8vo. 63s.

Through Bosnia and the Herzegovina on Foot during the Insurrection, August and September 1875. By ARTHUR J. EVANS, B.A. F.S.A. Second Edition. Map & Illustrations. 8vo. 18s.

Italian Alps; Sketches in the Mountains of Ticino, Lombardy, the Trentino, and Venetia. By DOUGLAS W. FRESHFIELD. Square crown 8vo. Illustrations, 15s.

Over the Sea and Far Away; a Narrative of a Ramble round the World. By T. W. HINCHLIFF, M.A. F.R.G.S. President of the Alpine Club. With 14 full-page Illustrations engraved on Wood. Medium 8vo. 21s.

The Frosty Caucasus; an Account of a Walk through Part of the Range, and of an Ascent of Elbruz in the Summer of 1874. By F. C. GROVE. With Eight Illustrations and a Map. Crown 8vo. price 15s.

Tyrol and the Tyrolese; an Account of the People and the Land, in their Social, Sporting, and Mountaineering Aspects. By W. A. BAILLIE GROHMAN. Crown 8vo. with Illustrations, 14s.

Two Years in Fiji, a Descriptive Narrative of a Residence in the Fijian Group of Islands. By LITTON FORBES, M.D. Crown 8vo. 8s. 6d.

Memorials of the Discovery and Early Settlement of the Bermudas or Somers Islands, from 1615 to 1685. By Major-General J. H. LEFROY, R.A. C.B. F.R.S. &c. Governor of the Bermudas. 8vo. with Map. [*In the press.*

Eight Years in Ceylon. By Sir SAMUEL W. BAKER, M.A. Crown 8vo. Woodcuts, 7s. 6d.

The Rifle and the Hound in Ceylon. By Sir SAMUEL W. BAKER, M.A. Crown 8vo. Woodcuts, 7s. 6d.

NEW WORKS published by LONGMANS & CO.

The Dolomite Mountains. Excursions through Tyrol, Carinthia, Carniola, and Friuli. By J. GILBERT and G. C. CHURCHILL, F.R.G.S. Square crown 8vo. Illustrations, 21s.

The Alpine Club Map of the Chain of Mont Blanc, from an actual Survey in 1863-1864. By A. ADAMS-REILLY, F.R.G.S. In Chromolithography, on extra stout drawing paper 10s. or mounted on canvas in a folding case 12s. 6d.

The Alpine Club Map of the Valpelline, the Val Tournanche, and the Southern Valleys of the Chain of Monte Rosa, from actual Survey. By A. ADAMS-REILLY, F.R.G.S. Price 6s. on extra stout drawing paper, or 7s. 6d. mounted in a folding case.

Untrodden Peaks and Unfrequented Valleys; a Midsummer Ramble among the Dolomites. By AMELIA B. EDWARDS. With numerous Illustrations. 8vo. 21s.

Guide to the Pyrenees, for the use of Mountaineers. By CHARLES PACKE. Crown 8vo. 7s. 6d.

The Alpine Club Map of Switzerland, with parts of the Neighbouring Countries, on the scale of Four Miles to an Inch. Edited by R. C. NICHOLS, F.R.G.S. In Four Sheets in Portfolio, price 42s. coloured, or 34s. uncoloured.

The Alpine Guide. By JOHN BALL, M.R.I.A. late President of the Alpine Club. Post 8vo. with Maps and other Illustrations.

The Eastern Alps, 10s. 6d.

Central Alps, including all the Oberland District, 7s. 6d.

Western Alps, including Mont Blanc, Monte Rosa, Zermatt, &c. Price 6s. 6d.

Introduction on Alpine Travelling in general, and on the Geology of the Alps. Price 1s. Either of the Three Volumes or Parts of the 'Alpine Guide' may be had with this Introduction prefixed, 1s. extra. The 'Alpine Guide' may also be had in Ten separate Parts, or districts, price 2s. 6d. each.

How to see Norway. By J. R. CAMPBELL. Fcp. 8vo. Map & Woodcuts, 5s.

WORKS of FICTION.

The Atelier du Lys; or an Art-Student in the Reign of Terror. By the author of 'Mademoiselle Mori.' Third Edition. Crown 8vo. 6s.

Novels and Tales. By the Right Hon. the EARL of BEACONSFIELD. Cabinet Editions, complete in Ten Volumes, crown 8vo. 6s. each.

Lothair, 6s.	Venetia, 6s.
Coningsby, 6s.	Alroy, Ixion, &c. 6s.
Sybil, 6s.	Young Duke &c. 6s.
Tancred, 6s.	Vivian Grey, 6s.

Henrietta Temple, 6s.
Contarini Fleming, &c. 6s.

Whispers from Fairyland. By the Right Hon. E. H. KNATCHBULL-HUGESSEN, M.P. With 9 Illustrations. Crown 8vo. 6s.

Higgledy-Piggledy; or, Stories for Everybody and Everybody's Children. By the Right Hon. E. H. KNATCHBULL-HUGESSEN, M.P. With 9 Illustrations. Crown 8vo. 6s.

Becker's Gallus; or Roman Scenes of the Time of Augustus. Post 8vo. 7s. 6d.

Becker's Charicles: Illustrative of Private Life of the Ancient Greeks. Post 8vo. 7s. 6d.

The Modern Novelist's Library.

Lothair. By the Rt. Hon. the EARL of BEACONSFIELD. Price 2s. boards; or 2s. 6d. cloth.
Atherstone Priory, 2s. boards; 2s. 6d. cloth.
Mlle. Mori, 2s. boards; 2s. 6d. cloth.
The Burgomaster's Family, 2s. & 2s. 6d.
MELVILLE'S Digby Grand, 2s. and 2s. 6d.
——— General Bounce, 2s. & 2s. 6d.
——— Gladiators, 2s. and 2s. 6d.
——— Good for Nothing, 2s. & 2s. 6d.
——— Holmby House, 2s. & 2s. 6d.
——— Interpreter, 2s. and 2s. 6d.
——— Kate Coventry, 2s. and 2s. 6d.
——— Queen's Maries, 2s. & 2s. 6d.
TROLLOPE'S Warden, 2s. and 2s. 6d.
——— Barchester Towers, 2s. & 2s. 6d.
BRAMLEY-MOORE'S Six Sisters of the Valleys, 2s. boards; 2s. 6d. cloth.
Elsa, a Tale of the Tyrolean Alps. Price 2s. boards; 2s. 6d. cloth.
Unawares, a Story of an old French Town. Price 2s. boards; 2s. 6d. cloth.

Stories and Tales.

By ELIZABETH M. SEWELL. Cabinet Edition, in Ten Volumes, each containing a complete Tale or Story:—

Amy Herbert, 2s. 6d.
Gertrude, 2s. 6d.
The Earl's Daughter, 2s. 6d.
Experience of Life, 2s. 6d.
Cleve Hall, 2s. 6d.
Ivors, 2s. 6d.
Katharine Ashton, 2s. 6d.
Margaret Percival, 3s. 6d.
Laneton Parsonage, 3s. 6d.
Ursula, 3s. 6d.

Tales of Ancient Greece.

By the Rev. G. W. COX, M.A. late Scholar of Trinity College, Oxford. Crown 8vo. 6s. 6d.

POETRY and THE DRAMA.

Milton's Lycidas. Edited, with Notes and Introduction, by C. S. JERRAM, M.A. Crown 8vo. 2s. 6d.

Lays of Ancient Rome; with Ivry and the Armada. By LORD MACAULAY. 16mo. 3s. 6d.

Lord Macaulay's Lays of Ancient Rome. With 90 Illustrations on Wood from Drawings by G. SCHARF. Fcp. 4to. 21s.

Miniature Edition of Lord Macaulay's Lays of Ancient Rome. with G. Scharf's 90 Illustrations reduced in Lithography. Imp. 16mo. 10s. 6d.

Horatii Opera. Library Edition, with English Notes, Marginal References & various Readings. Edited by the Rev. J. E. YONGE, M.A. 8vo. price 21s.

Southey's Poetical Works, with the Author's last Corrections and Additions. Medium 8vo. with Portrait, 14s.

Beowulf, a Heroic Poem of the Eighth Century (Anglo-Saxon Text and English Translation), with Introduction, Notes, and Appendix. By THOMAS ARNOLD, M.A. 8vo. 12s.

Poems by Jean Ingelow. 2 vols. fcp. 8vo. 10s.

FIRST SERIES, containing 'Divided,' 'The Star's Monument,' &c. Fcp. 8vo. 5s.
SECOND SERIES, 'A Story of Doom,' 'Gladys and her Island,' &c. 5s.

Poems by Jean Ingelow. First Series, with nearly 100 Woodcut Illustrations. Fcp. 4to. 21s.

The Iliad of Homer, Homometrically translated by C. B. CAYLEY, Translator of Dante's Comedy, &c. 8vo. 12s. 6d.

The Æneid of Virgil. Translated into English Verse. By J. CONINGTON, M.A. Crown 8vo. 9s.

Bowdler's Family Shakspeare. Cheaper Genuine Edition, complete in 1 vol. medium 8vo. large type, with 36 Woodcut Illustrations, 14s. or in 6 vols. fcp. 8vo. 21s.

RURAL SPORTS, HORSE and CATTLE MANAGEMENT, &c.

Annals of the Road; or, Notes on Mail and Stage-Coaching in Great Britain. By Captain MALET, 18th Hussars. To which are added Essays on the Road, by NIMROD. With 3 Woodcuts and 10 Coloured Illustrations. Medium 8vo. 21s.

Down the Road; or, Reminiscences of a Gentleman Coachman. By C. T. S. BIRCH REYNARDSON. Second Edition, with 12 Coloured Illustrations. Medium 8vo. 21s.

Blaine's Encyclopædia of Rural Sports; Complete Accounts, Historical, Practical, and Descriptive, of Hunting, Shooting, Fishing, Racing, &c. With above 600 Woodcuts (20 from Designs by J. LEECH). 8vo. 21s.

A Book on Angling; or, Treatise on the Art of Fishing in every branch; including full Illustrated Lists of Salmon Flies. By FRANCIS FRANCIS. Post 8vo. Portrait and Plates. 15s.

Wilcocks's Sea-Fishermen: comprising the Chief Methods of Hook and Line Fishing, a glance at Nets, and remarks on Boats and Boating. Post 8vo. Woodcuts, 12s. 6d.

The Fly-Fisher's Entomology. By ALFRED RONALDS. With 20 Coloured Plates. 8vo. 14s.

Horses and Stables. By Colonel F. FITZWYGRAM, XV. the King's Hussars. With 24 Plates of Illustrations. 8vo. 10s. 6d.

Youatt on the Horse. Revised and enlarged by W. WATSON, M.R.C.V.S. 8vo. Woodcuts, 12s. 6d.

Youatt's Work on the Dog. Revised and enlarged. 8vo. Woodcuts, 6s.

The Dog in Health and Disease. By STONEHENGE. With 73 Wood Engravings. Square crown 8vo. 7s. 6d.

The Greyhound. By STONEHENGE. Revised Edition, with 25 Portraits of Greyhounds, &c. Square crown 8vo. 15s.

Stables and Stable Fittings. By W. MILES. Imp. 8vo. with 13 Plates, 15s.

The Horse's Foot, and How to keep it Sound. By W. MILES. Imp. 8vo. Woodcuts, 12s. 6d.

A Plain Treatise on Horse-shoeing. By W. MILES. Post 8vo. Woodcuts, 2s. 6d.

Remarks on Horses' Teeth, addressed to Purchasers. By W. MILES. Post 8vo. 1s. 6d.

The Ox, his Diseases and their Treatment; with an Essay on Parturition in the Cow. By J. R. DOBSON, M.R.C.V.S. Crown 8vo. Illustrations, 7s. 6d.

WORKS of UTILITY and GENERAL INFORMATION.

Maunder's Treasury of Knowledge and Library of Reference; comprising an English Dictionary and Grammar, Universal Gazetteer, Classical Dictionary, Chronology, Law Dictionary, Synopsis of the Peerage, Useful Tables, &c. Fcp. 8vo. 6s.

Maunder's Biographical Treasury. Latest Edition, reconstructed and partly re-written, with above 1,600 additional Memoirs, by W. L. R. CATES. Fcp. 8vo. 6s.

Maunder's Scientific and Literary Treasury; a Popular Encyclopædia of Science, Literature, and Art. Latest Edition, in part re-written, with above 1,000 new articles, by J. Y. JOHNSON. Fcp. 8vo. 6s.

Maunder's Treasury of Geography, Physical, Historical, Descriptive, and Political. Edited by W. HUGHES, F.R.G.S. With 7 Maps and 16 Plates. Fcp. 8vo. 6s.

Maunder's Historical Treasury; General Introductory Outlines of Universal History, and a Series of Separate Histories. Revised by the Rev. G. W. COX, M.A. Fcp. 8vo. 6s.

Maunder's Treasury of Natural History; or, Popular Dictionary of Zoology. Revised and corrected Edition. Fcp. 8vo. with 900 Woodcuts, 6s.

The Treasury of Bible Knowledge; being a Dictionary of the Books, Persons, Places, Events, and other Matters of which mention is made in Holy Scripture. By the Rev. J. AYRE, M.A. With Maps, Plates, and many Woodcuts. Fcp. 8vo. 6s.

A Practical Treatise on Brewing; with Formulæ for Public Brewers & Instructions for Private Families. By W. BLACK. 8vo. 10s. 6d.

Chess Openings. By F. W. LONGMAN, Balliol College, Oxford. Second Edition. Fcp. 8vo. 2s. 6d.

English Chess Problems. Edited by J. PIERCE, M.A. and W. T. PIERCE. With 608 Diagrams. Crown 8vo. 12s. 6d.

The Theory of the Modern Scientific Game of Whist. By W. POLE, F.R.S. Eighth Edition. Fcp. 8vo. 2s. 6d.

The Correct Card; or, How to Play at Whist; a Whist Catechism. By Captain A. CAMPBELL-WALKER, F.R.G.S. New Edition. Fcp. 8vo. 2s. 6d.

The Cabinet Lawyer; a Popular Digest of the Laws of England, Civil, Criminal, and Constitutional. Twenty-Fourth Edition, corrected and extended. Fcp. 8vo. 9s.

Pewtner's Comprehensive Specifier; a Guide to the Practical Specification of every kind of Building-Artificer's Work. Edited by W. YOUNG. Crown 8vo. 6s.

Hints to Mothers on the Management of their Health during the Period of Pregnancy and in the Lying-in Room. By THOMAS BULL, M.D. Fcp. 8vo. 2s. 6d.

The Maternal Management of Children in Health and Disease. By THOMAS BULL, M.D. Fcp. 8vo. 2s. 6d.

The Treasury of Botany, or Popular Dictionary of the Vegetable Kingdom; with which is incorporated a Glossary of Botanical Terms. Edited by J. LINDLEY, F.R.S. and T. MOORE, F.L.S. With 274 Woodcuts and 20 Steel Plates. Two Parts, fcp. 8vo. 12s.

D

Modern Cookery for Private Families, reduced to a System of Easy Practice in a Series of carefully-tested Receipts. By ELIZA ACTON. With 8 Plates and 150 Woodcuts. Fcp. 8vo. 6s.

The Elements of Banking. By H. D. MACLEOD, M.A. Second Edition. Crown 8vo. 7s. 6d.

The Theory and Practice of Banking. By H. D. MACLEOD, M.A. 2 vols. 8vo. 26s.

Our New Judicial System and Civil Procedure as Reconstructed under the Judicature Acts, including the Act of 1876; with Comments on their Effect and Operation. By W. F. FINLASON, Barrister-at-Law. Crown 8vo. 10s. 6d.

Willich's Popular Tables for ascertaining, according to the Carlisle Table of Mortality, the value of Lifehold, Leasehold, and Church Property, Renewal Fines, Reversions, &c. Also Interest, Legacy, Succession Duty, and various other useful tables. Eighth Edition. Post 8vo. 10s.

INDEX.

	PAGE
Acton's Modern Cookery	24
Alpine Club Map of Switzerland	20
Alpine Guide (The)	20
Amos's Jurisprudence	6
—— Primer of the Constitution	6
Anderson's Strength of Materials	12
Armitage's Childhood of the English Nation	4
Armstrong's Organic Chemistry	12
Arnold's (Dr.) Christian Life	17
—— Lectures on Modern History	2
—— Miscellaneous Works	7
—— School Sermons	17
—— Sermons	17
—— (T.) Manual of English Literature	7
—— Beowulf	21
Arnott's Elements of Physics	11
Atelier (The) du Lys	20
Atherstone Priory	21
Autumn Holidays of a Country Parson	8
Ayre's Treasury of Bible Knowledge	9, 23
Bacon's Essays, by *Whately*	6
—— Life and Letters, by *Spedding*	6
—— Works	6
Bain's Mental and Moral Science	7
—— on the Senses and Intellect	7
—— Emotions and Will	7
Baker's Two Works on Ceylon	19
Ball's Guide to the Central Alps	20
—— Guide to the Western Alps	20
—— Guide to the Eastern Alps	20
Bancroft's Native Races of the Pacific	3
Barry on Railway Appliances	12
Beaconsfield's (Lord) Novels and Tales	20
Becker's Charicles and Gallus	20
Beesly's Gracchi, Marius, and Sulla	4
Black's Treatise on Brewing	23
Blackley's German-English Dictionary	9
Blaine's Rural Sports	22
Bloxam's Metals	12
Bolland and *Lang's* Aristotle's Politics	6
Boultbee on 39 Articles	16
Bourne's Catechism of the Steam Engine	16
—— Handbook of Steam Engine	16
—— Treatise on the Steam Engine	15
—— Improvements in the same	15
Bowdler's Family *Shakespeare*	21
Bramley-Moore's Six Sisters of the Valleys	21
Brande's Dictionary of Science, Literature, and Art	13
Brinkley's Astronomy	10
Browne's Exposition of the 39 Articles	16

	PAGE
Buckle's History of Civilisation	2
—— Posthumous Remains	7
Buckton's Health in the House	14
Bull's Hints to Mothers	23
—— Maternal Management of Children	23
Burgomaster's Family (The)	21
Burke's Vicissitudes of Families	5
Cabinet Lawyer	23
Campbell's Norway	20
Capes's Age of the Antonines	4
—— Early Roman Empire	4
Cates's Biographical Dictionary	5
—— and *Woodward's* Encyclopædia	3
Cayley's Iliad of Homer	21
Changed Aspects of Unchanged Truths	8
Chesney's Indian Polity	2
—— Modern Military Biography	2
—— Waterloo Campaign	3
Church's Sketches of Ottoman History	1
Colenso on Moabite Stone &c.	19
——'s Pentateuch and Book of Joshua	19
Commonplace Philosopher in Town and Country	8
Comte's Positive Polity	5
Congreve's Politics of Aristotle	6
Conington's Translation of Virgil's Æneid	21
—— Miscellaneous Writings	8
Contanseau's Two French Dictionaries	8
Conybeare and *Howson's* Life and Epistles of St. Paul	17
Counsel and Comfort from a City Pulpit	8
Cox's (G. W.) Aryan Mythology	3
—— Athenian Empire	4
—— Crusades	4
—— General History of Greece	3
—— Greeks and Persians	4
—— History of Greece	3
—— Tales of Ancient Greece	21
Creighton's Age of Elizabeth	4
Cresy's Encyclopædia of Civil Engineering	16
Critical Essays of a Country Parson	8
Crookes's Anthracen	16
—— Chemical Analyses	14
—— Dyeing and Calico-printing	16
Culley's Handbook of Telegraphy	15
Curteis's Macedonian Empire	4
Davidson's Introduction to the New Testament	18
D'Aubigné's Reformation	18
De Caisne and *Le Maout's* Botany	14

	PAGE
De Tocqueville's Democracy in America...	5
Dobson on the Ox	22
Dove's Law of Storms	10
Dowell's History of Taxes	6
Doyle's (R.) Fairyland	14
Eastlake's Hints on Household Taste	15
Edwards's Rambles among the Dolomites	20
———— Nile	19
———— Year in Western France	19
Elements of Botany	13
Ellicott's Commentary on Ephesians	17
————————— Galatians	17
————————— Pastoral Epist.	17
————————— Philippians, &c.	17
————————— Thessalonians	17
———— Lectures on Life of Christ	17
Elsa, a Tale of the Tyrolean Alps	21
Epochs of Ancient History	4
———— Modern History	4
Evans' (J.) Ancient Stone Implements	13
———— (A. J.) Bosnia	19
Ewald's History of Israel	18
———— Antiquities of Israel	18
Fairbairn's Application of Cast and Wrought Iron to Building	16
———— Information for Engineers	16
———— Life	4
———— Treatise on Mills and Millwork	16
Farrar's Chapters on Language	8
———— Families of Speech	8
Finlason's Judicial System	24
Fitzwygram on Horses and Stables	22
Forbes's Two Years in Fiji	19
Frampton's (Bishop) Life	5
Francis's Fishing Book	22
Freshfield's Italian Alps	19
Froude's English in Ireland	2
———— History of England	2
———— Short Studies	7
Gairdner's Houses of Lancaster and York	4
Ganot's Elementary Physics	11
———— Natural Philosophy	11
Gardiner's Buckingham and Charles	2
———— Personal Government of Charles I.	2
———— First Two Stuarts	4
———— Thirty Years' War	4
Geffcken's Church and State	6
German Home Life	7
Gilbert & Churchill's Dolomites	20
Girdlestone's Bible Synonyms	17
Goldziher's Hebrew Mythology	17
Goodeve's Mechanics	12
———— Mechanism	12
Grant's Ethics of Aristotle	6
Graver Thoughts of a Country Parson	8
Greville's Journal	2
Griffin's Algebra and Trigonometry	12
Griffith's Behind the Veil	18
Grohman's Tyrol and the Tyrolese	19
Grove (Sir W. R.) on Correlation of Physical Forces	11
———— (F. C.) The Frosty Caucasus	19
Gwilt's Encyclopædia of Architecture	15

	PAGE
Hale's Fall of the Stuarts	4
Hartley on the Air	10
Hartwig's Aerial World	12
———— Polar World	12
———— Sea and its Living Wonders	12
———— Subterranean World	13
———— Tropical World	12
Haughton's Animal Mechanics	11
Hayward's Biographical and Critical Essays	5
Heer's Primeval World of Switzerland	13
Heine's Life and Works, by Stigand	4
Helmholtz on Tone	11
Helmholtz's Scientific Lectures	11
Hemsley's Trees and Shrubs	14
Herschel's Outlines of Astronomy	10
Hinchliff's Over the Sea and Far Away	19
Hobson's Amateur Mechanic	15
Hoskold's Engineer's Valuing Assistant	15
Howorth's Mongols	3
Hullah's History of Modern Music	13
———— Transition Period	13
Hume's Essays	7
———— Treatise on Human Nature	7
Ihne's Rome to its Capture	4
———— History of Rome	3
Indian Alps	19
Ingelow's Poems	21
Jameson's Legends of the Saints & Martyrs	15
———— Legends of the Madonna	15
———— Legends of the Monastic Orders	15
———— Legends of the Saviour	15
Jenkin's Electricity and Magnetism	12
Jerram's Lycidas of Milton	21
Jerrold's Life of Napoleon	2
Johnston's Geographical Dictionary	9
Jukes's Types of Genesis	18
———— on Second Death	18
Kalisch's Commentary on the Bible	17
Keith's Evidence of Prophecy	17
Kerl's Metallurgy, by *Crookes* and *Röhrig*.	16
Kirby and *Spence's* Entomology	12
Kirkman's Philosophy	7
Knatchbull-Hugessen's Whispers from Fairy-Land	20
———— Higgledy-Piggledy	20
Kuenen's Prophets and Prophecy in Israel	17
Landscapes, Churches, &c.	8
Latham's English Dictionaries	8
———— Handbook of English Language	8
Lawrence on Rocks	13
Lecky's History of European Morals	3
———— Rationalism	3
———— Leaders of Public Opinion	5
Lefroy's Bermudas	19
Leisure Hours in Town	8
Lessons of Middle Age	8
Lewes's Biographical History of Philosophy	4
Lewis on Authority	7

NEW WORKS published by LONGMANS & CO.

	PAGE
Liddell and *Scott's* Greek-English Lexicons	9
Lindley and *Moore's* Treasury of Botany..13,	22
Lloyd's Magnetism	11
———— Wave-Theory of Light	11
Longman's (F. W.) Chess Openings	23
———— German Dictionary	9
———— (W.) Edward the Third	2
———— Lectures on History of England	2
———— Old and New St. Paul's	15
Loudon's Encyclopædia of Agriculture	16
———— Gardening	16
———— Plants	13
Lubbock's Origin of Civilisation	13
Ludlow's American War	4
Lyra Germanica	18
Macaulay's (Lord) Essays	1
———— History of England	1
———— Lays of Ancient Rome 14,	21
———— Life and Letters	4
———— Miscellaneous Writings	7
———— Speeches	7
———— Works	1
———— Writings, Selections from	7
MacColl's Eastern Question	1
McCulloch's Dictionary of Commerce	9
Macleod's Economical Philosophy	6
———— Theory and Practice of Banking	24
———— Elements of Banking	24
Mademoiselle Mori	21
Malet's Annals of the Road	22
Marshall's Physiology	14
Marshman's Life of Havelock	5
Martineau's Christian Life	19
———— Hours of Thought	19
———— Hymns	18
Maunder's Biographical Treasury 5,	23
———— Geographical Treasury	23
———— Historical Treasury	23
———— Scientific and Literary Treasury	23
———— Treasury of Knowledge 9,	23
———— Treasury of Natural History..13,	23
Maxwell's Theory of Heat	12
May's History of Democracy	2
———— History of England	2
Melville's Digby Grand	21
———— General Bounce	21
———— Gladiators	21
———— Good for Nothing	21
———— Holmby House	21
———— Interpreter	21
———— Kate Coventry	21
———— Queen's Maries	21
Mendelssohn's Letters	4
Merivale's Fall of the Roman Republic	3
———— General History of Rome	3
———— Roman Triumvirates	4
———— Romans under the Empire	3
Merrifield's Arithmetic and Mensuration	12
Miles on Horse's Foot and Horse Shoeing	22
———— on Horse's Teeth and Stables	22
Mill (J.) on the Mind	6
———— Dissertations & Discussions	6
———— Essays on Religion	17
———— Hamilton's Philosophy	6
———— (J. S.) Liberty	5
———— Political Economy	5

	PAGE
Mill (J. S.) Representative Government	5
———— System of Logic	6
———— Unsettled Questions	5
———— Utilitarianism	5
———— Autobiography	5
Miller's Elements of Chemistry	14
———— Inorganic Chemistry	12
Mitchell's Manual of Assaying	16
Modern Novelist's Library	21
Monsell's Spiritual Songs	18
Moore's Irish Melodies, Illustrated Edition	15
———— Lalla Rookh, Illustrated Edition	15
Morell's Mental Philosophy	7
Mozart's Life and Letters	4
Müller's Chips from a German Workshop	8
———— Science of Language	8
———— Science of Religion	3
Neison on the Moon	10
New Testament, Illustrated Edition	15
Nicols's Puzzle of Life	13
Northcott's Lathes & Turning	15
O'Conor's Commentary on Hebrews	18
———— Romans	18
———— St. John	18
Osborn's Islam	3
Owen's Comparative Anatomy and Physiology of Vertebrate Animals	12
Packe's Guide to the Pyrenees	20
Pattison's Casaubon	5
Payen's Industrial Chemistry	15
Pewtner's Comprehensive Specifier	23
Pierce's Chess Problems	23
Pole's Game of Whist	23
Preece & *Sivewright's* Telegraphy	12
Present-Day Thoughts	8
Proctor's Astronomical Essays	10
———— Moon	10
———— Orbs around Us	10
———— Other Worlds than Ours	10
———— Saturn	10
———— Scientific Essays (Two Series)	12
———— Sun	10
———— Transits of Venus	10
———— Two Star Atlases	10
———— Universe	10
Prothero's De Montfort	2
Public Schools Atlas of Ancient Geography	9
———— Atlas of Modern Geography	9
Rawlinson's Parthia	3
———— Sassanians	3
Recreations of a Country Parson	8
Redgrave's Dictionary of Artists	14
Reeve's Residence in Vienna and Berlin	19
Reilly's Map of Mont Blanc	20
———— Monte Rosa	20
Reresby's Memoirs	5
Reynardson's Down the Road	22

NEW WORKS published by LONGMANS & CO.

	PAGE
Rich's Dictionary of Antiquities	9
Rivers's Rose Amateur's Guide	13
Rogers's Eclipse of Faith	17
—— Defence of Eclipse of Faith	17
—— Essays	5
Roget's Thesaurus of English Words and Phrases	8
Ronald's Fly-Fisher's Entomology	22
Roscoe's Outlines of Civil Procedure	6
Rothschild's Israelites	18
Sandars's Justinian's Institutes	6
Sankey's Sparta and Thebes	4
Savile on Apparitions	8
—— on Primitive Faith	17
Schellen's Spectrum Analysis	10
Scott's Lectures on the Fine Arts	14
—— Poems	14
Seaside Musing	8
Seebohm's Oxford Reformers of 1498	3
—— Protestant Revolution	4
Sewell's History of France	2
—— Passing Thoughts on Religion	18
—— Preparation for Communion	18
—— Questions of the Day	18
—— Self-Examination for Confirmation	18
—— Stories and Tales	21
—— Thoughts for the Age	18
Shelley's Workshop Appliances	12
Short's Church History	3
Smith's (*Sydney*) Essays	7
—— Wit and Wisdom	7
—— (Dr. R. A.) Air and Rain	10
—— (R. B.) Rome and Carthage	4
Southey's Poetical Works	21
Stanley's History of British Birds	13
Stephen's Ecclesiastical Biography	5
Stonehenge on the Dog	22
—— on the Greyhound	22
Stoney on Strains	16
Stubbs's Early Plantagenets	4
Sunday Afternoons at the Parish Church of a University City	8
Supernatural Religion	18
Swinbourne's Picture Logic	6
Taylor's History of India	2
—— Manual of Ancient History	4
—— Manual of Modern History	4
—— (*Jeremy*) Works, edited by *Eden*	18
Text-Books of Science	12
Thomé's Structural and Physiological Botany	12, 13
Thomson's Laws of Thought	7
Thorpe's Quantitative Analysis	12
Thorpe and *Muir's* Qualitative Analysis	12
Tilden's Chemical Philosophy	12, 14

	PAGE
Todd on Parliamentary Government	2
Trench's Realities of Irish Life	7
Trollope's Barchester Towers	21
—— Warden	21
Twiss's Law of Nations	6
Tyndall's American Lectures on Light	11
—— Diamagnetism	11
—— Fragments of Science	11
—— Heat a Mode of Motion	11
—— Lectures on Electricity	11
—— Lectures on Light	11
—— Lectures on Sound	11
—— Molecular Physics	11
Unawares	21
Unwin's Machine Design	12
Ure's Dictionary of Arts, Manufactures, and Mines	16
Vaughan's Trident, Crescent, and Cross	18
Walker on Whist	23
Warburton's Edward the Third	4
Watson's Geometry	12
Watts's Dictionary of Chemistry	14
Webb's Objects for Common Telescopes	10
Weinhold's Experimental Physics	11
Wellington's Life, by *Gleig*	5
Whately's English Synonymes	8
—— Logic	6
—— Rhetoric	6
White and *Riddle's* Latin Dictionaries	9
Whitworth's Measuring Machine	15
Wilcocks's Sea-Fisherman	22
Williams's Aristotle's Ethics	6
Willich's Popular Tables	24
Wood's (J. G.) Bible Animals	19
—— Homes without Hands	12
—— Insects at Home	12
—— Insects Abroad	12
—— Out of Doors	12
—— Strange Dwellings	12
—— (J. T.) Ephesus	19
Woodward's Geology	13
Wyatt's History of Prussia	2
Yonge's English-Greek Lexicons	9
—— Horace	21
Youatt on the Dog	22
—— on the Horse	22
Zeller's Plato	3
—— Socrates	3
—— Stoics, Epicureans, and Sceptics	3
Zimmern's Life of Schopenhauer	4

MODERN HISTORICAL EPOCHS.

In course of publication, each volume in fcp. 8vo. complete in itself,

EPOCHS OF MODERN HISTORY:

A SERIES OF BOOKS NARRATING THE

HISTORY of ENGLAND and EUROPE

At SUCCESSIVE EPOCHS SUBSEQUENT to the CHRISTIAN ERA.

EDITED BY

E. E. MORRIS, M.A. Lincoln Coll. Oxford;
J. S. PHILLPOTTS, B.C.L. New Coll. Oxford; and
C. COLBECK, M.A. Fellow of Trin. Coll. Oxford.

'This striking collection of little volumes is a valuable contribution to the literature of the day, whether for youthful or more mature readers. As an abridgment of several important phases of modern history it has great merit, and some of its parts display powers and qualities of a high order. Such writers, indeed, as Professor STUBBS, Messrs. WARBURTON, GAIRDNER, CREIGHTON, and others, could not fail to give us excellent work. . . . The style of the series is, as a general rule, correct and pure; in the case of Mr. STUBBS it more than once rises into genuine, simple, and manly eloquence; and the composition of some of the volumes displays no ordinary historical skill. . . . The Series is and deserves to be popular.'

THE TIMES, Jan. 2, 1877.

Eleven Volumes Now Published:—

The ERA of the PROTESTANT REVOLUTION. By F. SEEBOHM, Author of 'The Oxford Reformers—Colet, Erasmus, More.' With 4 Coloured Maps and 12 Diagrams on Wood. Price 2s. 6d.

'Mr. SEEBOHM's Era of the Protestant Revolution shews an admirable mastery of a complex subject; it abounds in sound and philosophic thought, and as a composition it is very well ordered. . . . This volume, in short, is of the greatest merit.'
THE TIMES, Jan. 2.

The CRUSADES. By the Rev. G. W. Cox, M.A. late Scholar of Trinity College, Oxford; Author of the 'Aryan Mythology' &c. With a Coloured Map. Price 2s. 6d.

'The earliest period, in point of time, is that of the Crusades, of which we have a summary from the accomplished pen of the well-known Author of one of the best and latest histories of Greece. Mr. Cox's narrative is flowing and easy, and parts of his work are extremely good.'
THE TIMES, Jan. 2.

The THIRTY YEARS' WAR, 1618–1648. By SAMUEL RAWSON GARDINER, late Student of Ch. Ch.; Author of 'History of England from the Accession of James I. to the Disgrace of Chief Justice Coke' &c. With a Coloured Map. Price 2s. 6d.

'The narrative—a singularly perplexing task—is on the whole remarkably clear, and the Author gives us a well-written summary of the causes that led to the great contest, and of the most striking incidents that marked its progress. Mr. GARDINER's judgments, too, are usually just....The Author, we should add, is very skilful in his delineation of historical characters.'
THE TIMES, Jan. 2.

The HOUSES of LANCASTER and YORK; with the CONQUEST and LOSS of FRANCE. By JAMES GAIRDNER, of the Public Record Office; Editor of 'The Paston Letters' &c. With 5 Coloured Maps. Price 2s. 6d.

'Mr. GAIRDNER's Epoch, 'Lancaster and York, is usually correct and sensible, and the conclusions of the Author are just and accurate.'
THE TIMES, Jan. 2.

London, LONGMANS & CO.   [*Continued.*

EPOCHS OF MODERN HISTORY—*continued*.

EDWARD THE THIRD. By the Rev. W. WARBURTON, M.A. late Fellow of All Souls College, Oxford; Her Majesty's Senior Inspector of Schools. With 3 Coloured Maps and 3 Genealogical Tables. Price 2s. 6d.

'This Epoch is a very good one, and is well worth a studious reader's attention. Mr. WARBURTON has reproduced extremely well the spirit and genius of that chivalric age.' THE TIMES, Jan. 2.

The AGE of ELIZABETH. By the Rev. M. CREIGHTON, M.A. late Fellow and Tutor of Merton College, Oxford. With 5 Maps and 4 Genealogical Tables. 2s. 6d.

'Mr. CREIGHTON has thoroughly mastered the intricate mysteries of the foreign politics of the whole period; and he has described extremely ably the relations between this country and the other States of Europe, and the character of the policy of the Queen and her counsellors.' THE TIMES, Jan. 2.

The FALL of the STUARTS; and WESTERN EUROPE from 1678 to 1697. By the Rev. EDWARD HALE, M.A. Assistant-Master at Eton. With Eleven Maps and Plans. Price 2s. 6d.

'Mr. HALE has thoroughly grasped the great facts of the time, and has placed them in a very effective light.' THE TIMES, Jan. 2.

The FIRST TWO STUARTS and the PURITAN REVOLUTION, 1603–1660. By SAMUEL RAWSON GARDINER, Author of 'The Thirty Years' War, 1618–1648.' With 4 Coloured Maps. Price 2s. 6d.

'Mr. GARDINER's "First Two Stuarts and the Puritan Revolution" deserves more notice than we can bestow upon it. This is in some respects a very striking work. Mr. GARDINER's sketch of the time of James I. brings out much that had hitherto been little known.' THE TIMES, Jan. 2.

The WAR of AMERICAN INDEPENDENCE, 1775–1783. By JOHN MALCOLM LUDLOW, Barrister-at-Law. With 4 Coloured Maps. Price 2s. 6d.

'Mr. LUDLOW's account of the obscure annals of what afterwards became the Thirteen Colonies is learned, judicious, and full of interest, and his description of the Red Indian communities is admirable for its good feeling and insight. . . . The volume is characterised by impartiality and good sense.' THE TIMES, Jan. 2.

The EARLY PLANTAGENETS. By the Rev. W. STUBBS, M.A. Regius Professor of Modern History in the University of Oxford. With 2 coloured Maps. Price 2s. 6d.

'As a whole, his book is one of rare excellence. As a comprehensive sketch of the period it is worthy of very high commendation. . . . As an analyst of institutions and laws Mr. STUBBS is certainly not inferior to HALLAM. His narrative, moreover, is, as a rule, excellent, clear, well put together, and often picturesque; his language is always forcible and sometimes eloquent; his power of condensation is very remarkable, and his chapter on the contemporaneous state of Europe is admirable for its breadth and conciseness.' THE TIMES, Jan. 2.

The AGE of ANNE. By E. E. MORRIS, M.A. of Lincoln College, Oxford; Head Master of the Melbourne Grammar School, Australia; Original Editor of the Series. With 7 Maps and Plans. Price 2s. 6d.

Volumes in preparation, in continuation of the Series:—

The NORMANS in EUROPE. By Rev. A. H. JOHNSON, M.A., Fellow of All Souls College, Oxford. [*Nearly ready.*

The BEGINNING of the MIDDLE AGES; Charles the Great and Alfred; the History of England in connexion with that of Europe in the Ninth Century. By the Very Rev. R. W. CHURCH, M.A. Dean of St. Paul's. [*In the press.*

The EARLY HANOVERIANS. By the Rev. T. J. LAWRENCE, B.A. Warden of Cavendish College, late Fellow and Tutor of Downing College, Cambridge.

The FRENCH REVOLUTION to the BATTLE of WATERLOO, 1789–1815. By BERTHA M. CORDERY, Author of 'The Struggle Against Absolute Monarchy.'

FREDERICK the GREAT and the SEVEN YEARS' WAR. By F. W. LONGMAN, of Balliol College, Oxford.

London, LONGMANS & CO.

www.ingramcontent.com/pod-product-compliance
Lightning Source LLC
Chambersburg PA
CBHW022145300426
44115CB00006B/348